Lecture Notes in Computer Science 3592

Commenced Publication in 1973
Founding and Former Series Editors:
Gerhard Goos, Juris Hartmanis, and Jan van Leeuwen

Sokratis Katsikas   Javier López
Günther Pernul (Eds.)

Trust, Privacy, and Security in Digital Business

Second International Conference, TrustBus 2005
Copenhagen, Denmark, August 22-26, 2005
Proceedings

 Springer

Volume Editors

Sokratis Katsikas
University of the Aegean
Department of Information and Communication Systems Engineering
Karlovassi, 83200 Samos, Greece
E-mail: ska@aegean.gr

Javier López
University of Málaga
Departamento de Lenguajes y Ciencias de la Computación
Complejo Tecnológico, Campus de Teatinos, 29071 Málaga, Spain
E-mail: jlm@lcc.uma.es

Günther Pernul
University of Regensburg
Department of Information Systems
Universitätsstr. 31, 93053 Regensburg, Germany
E-mail: guenther.pernul@wiwi.uni-regensburg.de

Library of Congress Control Number: 2005930335

CR Subject Classification (1998): K.4.4, K.4, K.6, E.3, C.2, D.4.6, J.1

ISSN   0302-9743
ISBN-10   3-540-28224-6 Springer Berlin Heidelberg New York
ISBN-13   978-3-540-28224-2 Springer Berlin Heidelberg New York

Springer is a part of Springer Science+Business Media

springeronline.com

© Springer-Verlag Berlin Heidelberg 2005
Printed in Germany

Typesetting: Camera-ready by author, data conversion by Scientific Publishing Services, Chennai, India
Printed on acid-free paper   SPIN: 11537878   06/3142   5 4 3 2 1 0

Preface

Sincerely welcome to the proceedings of the 2nd International Conference on Trust, Privacy, would be and Security in Digital Business, held in Copenhagen, Denmark, from August 22nd till 26th, 2005. This conference was the successor to the successful TrustBus 2004 conference, held in 2004 in conjunction with the DEXA conferences in Zaragoza. It was our goal that this event would be a forum to bring together researchers from academia and commercial developers from industry to discuss the state of the art of technology for establishing trust, privacy, and security in digital business. We thank the attendees for coming to Copenhagen to participate and debate the new emerging advances in this area.

The workshop program consisted of one invited talk and 11 regular technical paper sessions. The invited talk and keynote speech was delivered by Hannes Federrath from the Chair for Management of Information Security at the University of Regensburg, Germany, on "Privacy Enhanced Technology, Methods – Markets – Misuse". A paper covering his talk is also contained in this book.

The regular paper sessions covered a broad range of topics, from access control issues to electronic auctioning, from trust and protocols to smart cards. The conference attracted over 100 submissions of which the Program Committee accepted 32 papers for presentation and inclusion in the conference proceedings. The authors of the accepted papers come from 16 different countries. The proceedings contain the revised versions of all accepted papers.

We would like to express our thanks to the people who helped put together the program: the Program Committee members and external reviewers for their timely and rigorous reviews of the papers; the DEXA Organizing Committee members in particular Mrs. Gabriela Wagner, for their help in administrative work; and, last but not least, Mr. Christian Schläger who was the main organizational force behind most of the involved tasks in making the conference possible.

Finally we would like to thank all authors who submitted papers, authors who presented papers, and the attendees who made this event an intellectually stimulating one. We hope they enjoyed the conference.

Athens, Màlaga, Regensburg   Sokratis Katsikas
August 2005   Javier López
                                                                Günther Pernul

Program Committee

General Chairperson
Sokratis Katsikas, University of the Aegean, Greece

Conference Program Chairpersons
Javier Lopez, University of Malaga, Spain
Guenther Pernul, University of Regensburg, Germany

Program Committee Members
Mike Burmester, Florida State University, USA
Marco Cassasa Mont, HP Labs, Bristol, UK
David W. Chadwick, University of Kent, UK
Elizabeth Chang, Curtin University of Technology, Australia
Frederic Cuppens, ENST Bretagne, France
Ernesto Damiani, University of Milan, Italy
Ed Dawson, Queensland University of Technology, Australia
Gurpreet Dhillon, VCU School of Business Richmond, USA
Tharam Dillon, University of Technology Sydney, Australia
Claudia Eckert, Technical University, Darmstadt, Germany
Hannes Federrath, University of Regensburg, Germany
Eduardo B. Fernandez, Florida Atlantic University, USA
Elena Ferrari, University of Insubria at Como, Italy
Simone Fischer-Huebner, Karlstad University, Sweden
Steven Furnell, University of Plymouth, UK
Juan M. González Nieto, Queensland University of Technology, Australia
Rüdiger Grimm, University of Technology Ilmenau, Germany
Dimitrios Gritzalis, Athens Univ. of Economics and Business, Greece
Stefanos Gritzalis, University of the Aegean, Greece
Ehud Gudes, Ben-Gurion University, Israel
Sigrid Gürgens, Fraunhofer SIT, Germany
Dipak Khakhar, Lund University, Sweden
Hiroaki Kikuchi, Tokai University, Japan
Klaus Kursawe, Katholieke Universiteit Leuven, Belgium
Costas Lambrinoudakis, University of the Aegean, Greece
Antonio Lioy, Politecnico di Torino, Italy
Diego Lopez, RedIRIS, Spain
Peter Lory, University of Regensburg, Germany
Olivier Markowitch, Université Libre de Bruxelles, Belgium
Fabio Martinelli, National Research Council - C.N.R. Pisa, Italy
Fabio Massacci, Università Degli Studi di Trento, Italy
Jose A. Montenegro, University of Malaga, Spain
Eiji Okamoto, University of Tsukuba, Japan
Martin Olivier, University of Pretoria, South Africa
Rolf Oppliger, eSECURITY Technologies, Switzerland

Ahmed Patel, University College, Dublin, Ireland
Andreas Pfitzmann, University of Technology, Dresden, Germany
Hartmut Pohl, University of Applied Sciences, Bonn-Rhein-Sieg, Germany
Karl Posch, University of Technology, Graz, Austria
Torsten Priebe, University of Regensburg, Germany
Gerald Quirchmayr, University of Vienna, Austria
Kai Rannenberg, Goethe University Frankfurt, Germany
Arnon Rosenthal, MITRE Corporation, USA
Christoph Ruland, University of Siegen, Germany
Germán Sáez, Universitat Politècnica de Catalunya, Spain
Pierangela Samarati, University of Milan, Italy
Matthias Schunter, IBM Zurich Research Lab, Switzerland
Jose M. Sierra, Univ. Carlos III, Spain
Mikko T. Siponen, University of Oulu, Finland
Adrian Spalka, University of Bonn, Germany
Leon Strous, De Nederlandsche Bank, Netherlands
Stephanie Teufel, University of Fribourg, Switzerland
Marianne Winslett, University of Illinois, USA
Jianying Zhou, I2R, Singapore

External Reviewers

Andersson, Christer
Balopoulos, Thodoris
Bergmann, Mike
Böhme, Rainer
Borcea, Katrin
Boyd, Colin
Carminati, Barbara
Clauß, Sebastian
De Capitani di
  Vimercati, Sabrina
Dobmeier, Wolfgang
Dresp, Wiebke
Dritsas, Stelios
Erat, Andreas
Franz, Elke
Fritsch, Lothar
Geneiatakis, Dimitris
Gilberg, Jörg
González-Deleito,
  Nicolás
Herranz, Javier

Iliadis, John
Kalloniatis, Christos
Kambourakis, George
Kantzavelou, Ioanna
Kim, Jintae
Kokolakis, Spyros
Köpsell, Stefan
Kriegelstein, Thomas
Lee, Adam
Lekkas, Dimitris
Martucci, Leonardo
McManus, Leonie
Merten, Patrick
Mitrou, Evangelia
Mori, Paolo
Moussas, Vassilios
Munoz, Antonio
Muschall, Björn
Nowey, Thomas
Olson, Lars
Petrocchi, Marinella

Pisko, Evgenia
Platis, Agapios
Plössl, Klaus
Radmacher, Mike
Rossnagel, Heiko
Royer, Denis
Schläger, Christian
Schlienger, Thomas
Soriano, Miquel
Squicciarini, Anna
  Cinzia
Steinbrecher, Sandra
Steinert, Martin
Svensson, Anders
van Le, Tri
Wendolsky, Rolf
Westfeld, Andreas
Wölfl, Thomas
Zhang, Charles

Table of Contents

Certificate Revocation/Index Search

Trust

Digital Signature

Privacy Enhanced Technologies:
Methods – Markets – Misuse

Hannes Federrath

University of Regensburg
hannes.federrath@wiwi.uni-regensburg.de

Abstract. Research in Privacy Enhancing Technologies has a tradition
of about 25 years. The basic technologies and ideas were found until 1995
while the last decade was dominated by the utilisation of such technologies. The question arises if there is a market for Privacy Enhanced Technology. The answer is yes, however Privacy Enhancing Technology may
not have been broadly known yet in order to make it profitable. The governments or non-profit organisations must therefore run such systems or
at least promote their further development and deployment. Especially
governments have however conflicting interests: While governments of
democratic nations are responsible to keep the freedom of citizens (and
privacy as a part of it), governments also need instruments to prose-
cute criminal activities. Subsequently, Privacy Enhancing Technologies
have to consider law enforcement functionality in order to balance these
different targets.

1   Introduction

Privacy Enhancing Technology (PET) enables the user of communication systems to protect himself or herself from being traced his or her activities and
behaviour. PET addresses **confidentiality** aspects:

- Anonymity of a sender or recipient (hiding the identity of a user),
- Unobservability of communication relations (hiding who is communicating
  with whom) or
- generally the unlinkability of actions (events).

The terminology and attacker models mostly used in PET are described in [1].
John Borking can be considered as the creator of the term "Privacy Enhancing
Technology (PET)" when he invented the Identity Protector [2].

Encryption (or cryptography in general and public-key encryption in particular) can be understood as a basic building block for PET systems. Other
building blocks are dummy traffic and broadcasting:

- Sending random bits at every time interval hides when a meaningful encrypted message is sent.
- Sending every encrypted message to everybody hides which message a receiver is interested in and who is the intended recipient.

S. Katsikas, J. López, G. Pernul (Eds.): TrustBus 2005, LNCS 3592, pp. 1–9, 2005.

Table 1. Timeline of the development of modern PET

Year	Idea / PET system
1978	Public-key encryption [3]
1981	MIX, Pseudonyms [4]
1983	Blind signature schemes [5]
1985	Credentials [6]
1988	DC network [7]
1990	Privacy preserving value exchange [8]
1991	ISDN-Mixes [9]
1995	Blind message service [10]
1995	Mixmaster [11]
1996	MIXes in mobile communications [12]
1996	Onion Routing [13]
1997	Crowds Anonymizer [14]
1998	Stop-and-Go (SG) Mixes introduced [15]
1999	Zeroknowledge Freedom Anonymizer (service meanwhile closed)
2000	AN.ON/JAP Anonymizer [16]
2004	TOR [17]

The timeline of development of modern PET systems has its beginning in 1981 when Chaum published his paper "Untraceable Electronic Mail, Return Addresses and Digital Pseudonyms" [4]. From this time Chaum published further striking ideas (see Table 1) every two or three years for about a decade. Based on Chaum's new building blocks (MIX, blind signatures, credentials, DC network) the field has become broader and moved towards research in applications of Privacy Enhancing Technologies.

2 Methods

Since 2000 the research community on PET systems has its own Workshop on Privacy Enhancing Technology (PET 20xx). Another related conference is the Workshop on Information Hiding (IH). Technical descriptions of new ideas in PET can mostly be found in the PET- and IH-Workshop-Proceedings.

2.1 Building Blocks

As usual in the development of security systems a lot in PET systems is about trust. Most privacy enhanced systems should fulfil strong requirements, such as:

- no trust into the network operator, *and*
- no trust into one centralised station.

When reading "new" ideas on PET systems many young researchers in the field firstly think of a trusted third party to protect the privacy (or more general the security) of someone. However, almost everything can be protected by a trustworthy third station. For example, hiding communication relations is easy if an intermediate station (proxy) is used. However, the communication parties must trust this proxy. The idea of strong PET systems is to avoid this kind of trust: Users should not feel compelled to trust the network operator, nor one single station.

The most important methods and building blocks for PET systems are

- for privacy preserving communication systems (e.g. anonymous communication):
  - Chaumian MIXes [4] and their descendants Mixmaster [11] and SG-Mixes [15],
  - DC networks [7], and
  - Blind-message service [10],
- for privacy preserving transactions (e.g. anonymous payment, identity management):
  - Blind signatures [5], and
  - Credentials [6].

2.2   Example: MIXes

From a practical point of view the MIX concept is the best-known and mostly used. MIXes [4] realise the unlinkability of the sender and recipient of a message. A MIX works as an intermediate station (similar to a proxy). However, by sending a message through more than one MIX the users need not trust one station. It is clear that the attacker is not allowed to control all MIXes of a chain: At least one MIX operator must be trustworthy – *no matter who*.

A MIX collects a number of messages of equal lengths from many distinct senders, discards repeats, changes their encoding, and forwards the messages to a successor-MIX in a different order. The last MIX in the chain sends the message to the recipient. Change of encoding of a message can be implemented using public-key encryption. Since decryption is a deterministic operation, repeats of messages have to be discarded. Otherwise, the change of encoding does not prevent tracing messages by traffic analysis.

For a further description and comparison of MIX-types and their attacker models we suggest reading [18]. A comprehensive bibliography of PET can be found at [19]. The MIX concept is used for example in Mixmaster [11], JAP [20], and TOR [21].

3   Market

Is there a market for such systems? First of all we consider privacy as a natural need of people. Therefore over the last 15 years so-called privacy activists have been running lots of systems free of charge to the users, e.g. anonymous remailer systems (anon.penet.fi, Cypherpunk-Remailers, Mixmaster) and World Wide Web anonymisers (Anonymizer.com, JAP [20], TOR [21]). Some of these systems are still hard to use: They come just as command line tools, without graphical user interfaces, with very limited availability and reliability.

In order to make privacy tools useable for a broad mass, developers have to concentrate on the improvement of user interfaces. Pretty Good Privacy (PGP) can be seen as a very good example in terms of dramatically increased usability from its first versions until now.

Besides availability and reliability issues, the **usability** of PET systems may decide whether a system is ready for the market and for commercial use. Therefore, the well-known MIX-based anonymiser JAP could be a good basis for market research because JAP has been designed to fulfil both requirements: security *and* usability. See Figure 1 for a screenshot of JAP. [22] gives a short description of the JAP system architecture.

Fig. 1. Screenshot of JAP

3.1   Willingness to Pay for Anonymity

The following results are based on the JAP anonymity system and its usage. In her survey [23] Spiekermann found out that about 3/4 of the users are power users, and 1/4 are normal or sporadic users (see Table 2): If someone is using an anonymity system he or she will probably use it heavily.

In [24] similar results are shown – differentiated by European and US users. Because these numbers represent the users of a system free of charge, people were asked for their willingness to pay for anonymity services. 60 % of the users are willing to pay, 40 % are not (see Table 3).

An interesting point is that the willingness to pay for anonymity is independent of the heaviness of usage [23].

Table 2. Heaviness of usage of anonymity systems

	Type of user
73 %	heavy users (use an anonymity system at least daily)
10 %	protect their privacy at least twice a week
17 %	use such systems sporadic (less than twice the week)

Table 3. Willingness to pay for anonymity services

	Charge for anonymity service
40 %	not willing to pay
50 %	would pay between 2,50 EUR and 5 EUR monthly
10 %	willing to pay a monthly charge above 5 EUR

3.2 Anonymised Content

Another interesting question is which content or requests people want to anonymise. The following analysis has been done with 150 requests randomly picked from URLs anonymised by the JAP system in June 2005.

About 44 % of the anonymised requests can be categorised as entertainment (see Table 4). About 18 % of the JAP users stay anonymously when using Web-based services (search engines, route planners, etc.). E-shops are surprisingly not approached anonymously. Nearly the same applies for health-portals.

Table 4. Requested content via an anonymity service

	Category of content
44 %	Entertainment:
	33 % erotic, pornography
	8 % private homepages, cinema, amusement, ...
	3 % games
18 %	Services: search engines, route planners, stock quotes, ...
8 %	Companies, institutions, universities, ...
8 %	Web-based E-mail services (e.g. Hotmail, GMX, ...)
3 %	News, newspapers, magazines, sports news
1 %	Health information
0 %	Shops, markets, ebay, e-commerce, ...
18 %	Misc: not reachable, not categorisable

3.3 Regions

Although anonymity services hide the connection between clients (users) and servers (e.g. web-sites) such systems do not hide who is using an anonymity service (but of course what the user is looking for). From May–June 2005 the JAP project has classified the incoming IP addresses according to countries

Table 5. Regions of JAP usage

	Region
60 %	Europe
27 %	Asia
12 %	America
1 %	Rest of the world

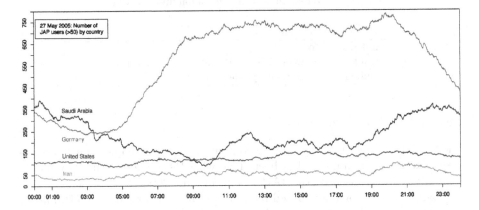

Fig. 2. Usage of JAP (day-line)

and regions in order to find out from where the JAP anonymity system is used. Table 5 shows that JAP is used mainly in Europe and Asia. In America the TOR system [21] as a comparable system funded by the Electronic Frontier Foundation (EFF) will probably attract Americans more than JAP (as a European project). Another problem for American users could be that the main part of the JAP servers (MIXes) is currently installed in Europe. Therefore, the connection to JAP servers might be too slow for Americans.

Because JAP is a German project it was clear that a significant proportion of the users would come from Germany. We furthermore suspected that the project is sufficiently known in the US to attract users. An analysis of the data brought to light that a remarkable portion of the users came from the Arab part of the world. See for example the day-line of 27 May 2005 (Figure 2): During the night-hours (Central European Time) the largest number of users came from Saudi Arabia.

4   Misuse

Staying anonymous on the Internet may attract criminals.

The JAP project is currently approached 4-5 times per month on average by law enforcement agencies and private complaints. See Figure 3 for the development of inquiries between July 2001 and December 2004. We are pleased that

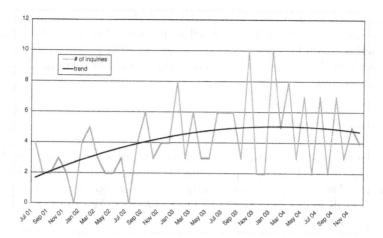

Fig. 3. Number of inquiries by law enforcement agencies and private complaints

there is relatively few abuse compared to the 3-4 terabytes of anonymised data every month by the JAP project.

A typical inquiry by law enforcement agencies contains the date and time of the incident and the IP address of the anonymity service (usually the IP address of the last MIX), and asks for the IP address assigned to the related user at the entry point (usually the first MIX) of the anonymity service. Because anonymity services should provide unlinkability of incoming and outgoing messages no data exists to answer the inquiry. An observation will only be possible if all MIXes in the chain log connections. MIXes will however usually not log anything since logging is equivalent to "self-mutilation".

Although the number of JAP users grew over the time, the number of inquiries did not. We think that this has the following reasons:

- More and more honest people are using JAP. At the beginning of the service probably criminals were highly attracted. However, the vast majority is using anonymity services for legal purposes.
- Law enforcement agencies are meanwhile used to the fact that anonymity services like JAP do not collect any data. As soon as the police is recognising that JAP has been used, an inquiry would not provide new evidences. The anonymity service therefore won't learn about the real dimension of misuse.

German operators of telecommunication systems are obliged by German law to intercept transmissions if a court is ordering it. This court order can be issued if and only if the crime is listed in a catalogue of very grave crime types. In June 2003 the JAP project received such an order.[1] Since then the open-source software of the JAP-MIX servers contains a function for tracking users.

---

[1] Details of the so-called "BKA case" (BKA is the German Federal Bureau of Criminal Investigation) are reported at http://anon.inf.tu-dresden.de/strafverfolgung/index_en.html.

This function has to be activated in all MIXes of a chain if a certain outgoing (anonymised) message has to be linked to its originator, i.e. sender. To make this function useful for criminal investigations all MIXes have to receive such a court order. If the MIXes are spread over the whole world international law is necessary to oblige the MIX operators.

Acknowledgements

I'd like to thank Patrizia Buckel, Stefan Köpsell, Henry Krasemann and Wolfgang Pöppl for their help in providing and analysing the empirical data on JAP usage, Thomas Nowey for critically reading through the paper, and finally Christian Schläger for his patience. Furthermore the JAP project is grateful for funding by the German government.

References

1. Pfitzmann, A., Köhntopp, M.:   Anonymity, unobservability, pseudonymity, and identity management – A proposal for terminology (2000-2004) http://dud.inf.tu-dresden.de/Literatur_V1.shtml.
2. Hes, R., Borking, J.J., eds.:   Privacy Enhancing Technologies: The path to anonymity. revised edition, A&V 10, The Hague (1998)
3. Rivest, R.L., Shamir, A., Adleman, L.: A Method for Obtaining Digital Signatures and Public-Key Cryptosystems. CACM **21** (1978) 120–126 reprinted: 26/1 (1983) 96-99.
4. Chaum, D.:   Untraceable Electronic Mail, Return Addresses and Digital Pseudonyms. Communications of the ACM **24** (1981) 84–88
5. Chaum, D.: Blind Signatures for Untraceable Payments. In Rivest, R.L., Sherman, A., Chaum, D., eds.: Proc. CRYPTO '82, New York, Plenum Press (1983) 199–203
6. Chaum, D.:   Security without Identification: Transaction Systems to Make Big Brother Obsolete. Communications of the ACM **28** (1985)
7. Chaum, D.: The Dining Cryptographers Problem: Unconditional Sender and Recipient Untraceability. Journal of Cryptology **1** (1988) 65–75
8. Bürk, H., Pfitzmann, A.: Value exchange systems enabling security and unobservability. Computers & Security **9** (1990) 715–721
9. Pfitzmann, A., Pfitzmann, B., Waidner, M.: ISDN-Mixes: Untraceable Communication with Very Small Bandwidth Overhead. In: Proc. Kommunikation in verteilten Systemen (KiVS). IFB 267, Springer-Verlag, Berlin (1991) 451–463
10. Cooper, D.A., Birman, K.P.: Preserving privacy in a network of mobile computers. In: 1995 IEEE Symposium on Research in Security and Privacy, IEEE Computer Society Press, Los Alamitos (1995) 26–38 http://cs-tr.cs.cornell.edu:80/Dienst/UI/1.0/Display/ncstrl.cornell/TR85-1490.
11. Cottrell, L.:   Mixmaster & Remailer Attacks (1995) http://www.obscura.com/~loki/remailer-essay.html.
12. Federrath, H., Jerichow, A., Pfitzmann, A.: Mixes in Mobile Communication Systems: Location Management with Privacy. In Anderson, R.J., ed.: Proc. 1st Workshop on Information Hiding. Volume 1174 of Lecture Notes in Computer Science., Springer-Verlag, Berlin (1996) 121–135

13. Goldschlag, D.M., Reed, M.G., Syverson, P.F.: Hiding routing information. In Anderson, R.J., ed.: Proc. 1st Workshop on Information Hiding. Volume 1174 of Lecture Notes in Computer Science., Springer-Verlag, Berlin (1996) 137–150
14. Reiter, M.K., Rubin, A.D.: Crowds: Anonymity for Web Transactions. DIMACS Technical Report **97** (1997)
15. Kesdogan, D., Egner, J., Büschkes, R.: Stop-and-Go-MIXes Providing Probabilistic Security in an Open System. In Aucsmith, D., ed.: Proc. 2nd Workshop on Information Hiding. Volume 1525 of Lecture Notes in Computer Science., Springer-Verlag, Berlin (1998) 83–98 http://www.cl.cam.ac.uk/~fapp2/ihw98/ihw98-sgmix.pdf.
16. Berthold, O., Federrath, H., Köhntopp, M.: Project "Anonymity and Unobservability in the Internet". In: Proc. Workshop on Freedom and Privacy by Design / Conference on Freedom and Privacy 2000, Toronto/Canada, April 4–7, 2000, Association for Computing Machinery, ACM, ISBN 1-58113-256-5 (2000) 57–65
17. Dingledine, R., Mathewson, N., Syverson, P.: Tor: The second-generation onion router. In: Proceedings of the 13th USENIX Security Symposium. (2004)
18. Raymond, J.F.: Traffic Analysis: Protocols, Attacks, Design Issues, and Open Problems. In Federrath, H., ed.: Designing Privacy Enhancing Technologies. Proc. Workshop on Design Issues in Anonymity and Unobservability. Volume 2009 of Lecture Notes in Computer Science., Springer-Verlag, Berlin (2001) 10–29
19. The Free Haven Project: Anonymity bibliography (2005) http://www.freehaven.net/anonbib/.
20. JAP: The JAP Anonymity & Privacy Homepage (2000-2005) http://www.anon-online.de.
21. TOR: An anonymous Internet communication system (2004) http://tor.eff.org/.
22. Golembiewski, C., Hansen, M., Steinbrecher, S.: Experiences running a web anonymising service. In: Proc. 14th Intl. Workshop on Database and Expert Systems Applications (DEXA'03), Prague, Czech Republic, IEEE Computer Society (2003) 482–486
23. Spiekermann, S.: Die Konsumenten der Anonymität – Wer nutzt Anonymisierungsdienste? Datenschutz und Datensicherheit DuD **27** (2003) 150–154
24. Spiekermann, S.: The desire for privacy: Insights into the views and nature of the early adopters of privacy services. International Journal of Technology and Human Interaction **1** (2004)

Sec-Shield: Security Preserved Distributed Knowledge Management Between Autonomous Domains

Petros Belsis[1], Stefanos Gritzalis[1], Apostolos Malatras[2], Christos Skourlas[3], and Ioannis Chalaris[3]

[1] Department of Information and Communication Systems Engineering,
University of the Aegean, Karlovasi, Samos, Greece
{pbelsis, sgritz}@aegean.gr
[2] Department of Electronic Engineering, Centre for Communications Systems Research,
University of Surrey, UK
a.malatras@surrey.ac.uk
[3] Department of Informatics, Technological Education Institute, Athens, Greece
{cskourlas, ixalaris}@teiath.gr

Abstract. Knowledge Management (KM) comprises of a variety of distinct technologies and techniques, relative to the uniform treatment of tangible and intangible resources. Attempts to extend the traditional single organizational resource-sharing scheme, confront various challenges, relative to the management of security and heterogeneity issues. In this paper we discuss the various security models, presenting potential limitations - as well as the advantages - relative to their support to extend the single-domain security management framework, to a resilient and robust distributed multi-domain Knowledge Management scheme. We present the architecture of a security enhanced prototype that supports decentralization, while it maintains the autonomic character of the participating domains. We also argue about the implementation dependent choices relative to the alleviation of the multifaceted problems that a collaborative Inter-organizational knowledge asset exchange framework arises.

1 Introduction

Knowledge Management (KM) systems emerged during the last decade and rapidly transformed into a basic business function for many organizations; still though, their flexibility is limited within the borders of a single organization. Among others, a serious challenge is the expansion of the capabilities of such a system to utilize knowledge assets from other organizations according to Nonaka's spiral model [1], with the basic prerequisite that this management of knowledge assets will happen efficiently and through automated, transparent procedures from the user's perspective.

Ordinary KM systems attempt to provide the user with the necessary knowledge to efficiently fulfill her tasks and by doing so, to raise her productivity as well as the overall organization's response to new emerging challenges that demand accurate, constantly updated and on time-fetched knowledge. Still, when it comes to attempt to utilize knowledge from distinct organizations through engagement in a cooperative framework, serious obstacles are posed that retard knowledge exchange and diffusion.

S. Katsikas, J. López, G. Pernul (Eds.): TrustBus 2005, LNCS 3592, pp. 10–19, 2005.
© Springer-Verlag Berlin Heidelberg 2005

The establishment of the necessary pre-coalition procedures and the exact definition of the level of mutual sharing of vital knowledge sources is a long-term and time consuming procedure that poses an important overhead on the overall process. Our system focuses on providing with sufficient solutions towards the alleviation of this problem: first by introducing a scalable and robust solution for correlating roles between different organizations, and second by treating heterogeneity problems which are a commodity between different information systems.

Our goals are: a) to enable the realization of cooperation between autonomous, policy-managed Information Systems and b) to identify the distributed knowledge assets transparently, using agent and ontology technology.

The rest of the paper is organized as follows: after a brief introduction in section 1, section 2 presents the basic concepts and requirements related with distributed KM as well as a review of related work on the area; section 3 presents security architectures supporting the necessary collaborative frameworks; section 4 presents authorization schemes able to support the demands of similar architectures, together with our choices which ensure scalability among other characteristics; section 5 presents the architecture of our developed prototype, while section 6 concludes the paper and provides the directions of our future work.

2   Distributed KM – Related Work

The advent of emerging technologies such as portable devices, which enhance decentralization of resources, directs traditional KM techniques in failure to meet their initial expectations. Users often create knowledge ad-hoc and use their own individual IT infrastructure [2]. Although the need for decentralized KM solutions is obvious, the amplitude of the field of solutions is still very narrow. A number of both technological as well as socio-technical aspects of the problem pose interesting research challenges [3]:

- Heterogeneity (semantic, syntactic).
- Security.
- Network efficiency [4].

In [5], a conceptual architecture is presented for a system based on the notion of trust for distributed KM. This system (ADAM), utilizes agent-technique to perform knowledge discovery and authorization. ADAM architecture is based on a pair of agents one responsible for querying for knowledge and the other handling the authorization issues. This system though, manages mainly knowledge about its users and bases the authorization process on grounds of reputation collected for a user from other nodes. Even though it handles scalability issues very efficiently, this system gives the chance to somebody to create a new identity or retain multiple identities concurrently and attempt to enter into relations with the system. The application of these principles on systems such as Internet transactions (e-commerce) where a security failure could direct to financial is not doubted for its validity. ADAM authorizes transactions and not users. Furthermore, it functions on total absence of explicitly stated organizational policy.

XAROP [4], is a peer-to-peer system which utilizes ontologies for handling heterogeneity issues arising from the different conceptualizations among different domains. The notion of security is rather simplistic and cannot be applied to critical environments, comprising of rules manually posed by the user which has to classify for each document separately authorized users or groups. Authentication is based on PKI infrastructure, where root and subordinate certificate authorities are denoted within the XAROP infrastructure.

3 Security Architectures for Collaborative Environments

Security policies emerged in the last decades and have attracted considerable attention in distributed computing, due to their ability to simplify security management and access control enforcement for a large number of heterogeneous components which often span across organizational boundaries [6]. A more complicated situation is related with the attempt to create a policy-managed collaboration scheme between different organizations. In most of the cases, establishing a collaboration access scheme involves negotiation off-line, by extra technological means, and includes complex procedures, such as identification of the negotiating parties, and common agreement every time upon the conditions of sharing a resource, after a new claim has been posed.

Two kinds of systems can be considered under this (collaborating) framework: peer-to-peer networks, and autonomous domains. Peer to peer networks resemble communities with common interests, the terms of bounding though are more loosely coupled than autonomous domains. The second category of systems can be met in many real-life systems, such as e-government environments, or healthcare systems which consist of several cooperating hospitals. In the latter case, sensitivity of the data poses more security restrictions and establishing a common state for knowledge exchange requires both that organizational roles are well defined in terms of access rights and obligations based on the grounds of a well-stated security policy, while a common access state between different organizations is unambiguously allocated.

We can classify these systems according to the access models they adopt, to the following two categories:

1. Trust based systems. The notion of trust is introduced mainly in complex, non-hierarchical or inter-related systems such as the Internet, where unknown totally roles might be interested to enter into relations between them, or to cooperate on basis of financial terms. This situation is often on Internet transaction systems, such as e-commerce etc. The authorization of a transaction is based on the basis of estimating the cost and the substantial loss for a specific role, considering a prerequisite the potential risk, according to the degree of trust that can be associated to his role, for example by questioning his previous activity or users associated with him.
2. Autonomous systems, with well formed security policy and well defined organizational structure.

We will restrict our scenario to the second category of systems, which are characterized by well defined organizational policy and cooperate and on the grounds of a commonly agreed target, such as improvement of efficiency of the governing infrastructure or the reducing of response times for health treatment of patients within the national healthcare system.

Our approach supports the formation of coalitions, based on the idea of establishing mappings between the policies recorded in XML (Extensible Markup Language [14]) type format and by utilizing XML transformation to database techniques and accordingly converting the policy mapping problem to a database mapping problem, gaining on the same time by obtaining policy non-disclosure (due to the easier manipulation of privacy issues based on database technology than through XML files where the policy is recorded).

4 Authorization Schemes

4.1 Trust Based Versus Policy-Managed Autonomous Systems

We can distinguish two approaches [9] concerning authorization schemes: The first can be applied on distributed environments which cooperate on the grounds of a non-formal negotiation scheme. The second applies to more restricted organizational schemes, which cooperate under a formal framework, where most of the access rules are posed by a strict organizational policy and cooperation is substitute to tight rein.

Loosely coupled authorization scheme

Under this framework, we can distinguish two access-control approaches. The first uses predefined set of role mappings. It requires from the constituent systems to indicate the level of sharing they want to allow and to establish a consistent set of mediation rules for inter-domain access. The second relies on bringing together unknown individuals by examining their credentials and mapping assigning a level of trust which corresponds to a specific level of trust.

Federal environments

In this case, criticality can arise as a key concept. Federal environments have a role common security policy organizational scheme and local roles correspond to a generic

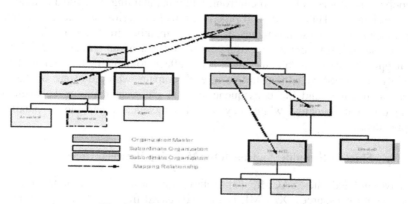

Fig. 1. Role mapping across different domains

representation scheme. These systems can be e-government environments, for example ministries that participate in the federal government infrastructure and share a common policy interpretation model. Typically the roles of a designated system have to map to the generic role representation scheme. In Figure 1 a typical representation of organizational structure and relative roles from federal environments, are mapped through mapping relations (arrows) to a global organizational schema. We utilize security clearance levels which are frequently used for critical environments and reflect typical situations within military or governmental systems. This organizational structure and the interrelated role correlation and security attributes can be – together with other organizational assets – represented in XML files (policy files), something that facilitates -in terms of interoperability- the effective and automated management of resources and simplifies administration tasks as already mentioned.

4.2 Automating the Authorization Process

Mapping between roles has been proposed as a potential solution for multi-domain environments [9] [8]; many issues still remain to be resolved. Recording roles and their attributes needs an appropriate, both human and machine interpretable format, which can be easily integrated in the security policy requirements and codified in means of duties, obligations and permissions as security policy languages demand. For interoperability issues, the usage of languages that export their rules in XML format is highly required.

The mapping process between roles needs additive handling on grounds of interrelating similar documents that record each organization's structure (policy files). In order to automate the authorization process, we apply a direct mapping between security levels (clearances) of different organizations. More specifically, the global role scheme to which all the subordinate organizations have to comply, establishes several security levels. Mapping of domain roles and their security levels to the global role scheme and to the corresponding global level of security clearance is handled by the administrator of the global domain. This is a typical necessity in order to reduce complexity. In our approach we have adopted a general mapping scheme, to which the cooperating domains have to confront, while maintaining their local autonomy in policy declaration. This is a typical practice in real scenarios, such as e-government environments, where establishment of rules is mainly directed centrally, without affecting the establishment of procedures in the interior of subordinate organizations. The mapping process which at the lower level reflects to mapping between XML files is mainly performed by administrators in each domain, who are aware of the legal, ethical implications and the consequences of an incorrect mapping between roles among different domains, while they are also technically capable to handle the mapping details.

4.3 Sec – Shield's Scalable Approach for Mapping Between Roles

We have utilized the XACML [7] policy framework for enabling distributed management of resources. XACML is an XML based framework for specifying and applying access control for Web-based resources. XACML specification supports both identical and role based access control and incorporates contextual information such as location and time and under several extensions XACML can be applied also to secure Web-services environments [10].

The administrator for each domain is editing the local policy and classifies the access rights to the resources for each role within the organizational borders. For each domain an XML file is retained, determining the access rights and the security clearance level for each person. A mapping between the general role scheme and the role schemes for the local domains is an administrator's task. An appropriate ontology which is an essential part of the system can maintain information about the security clearance level of certain roles or individuals within an organization.

5   Sec-shield's System Architecture

We will refer to the key concepts of our implemented prototype, the functionality of which continuously arises; namely the design of agents in our framework, the role of ontology and techniques utilized, and we will describe the overall architecture of the platform.

5.1   The Role of Agent and Ontology Technologies

The presence of agents was decided in order to enable transparent identification of assets and to provide automated authorization for users. For each domain an agent performing the knowledge assets identification, while another one carries the user credentials and according to the security policy and the role the user is assigned to, provides her with access to the resource or in the opposite case denies access to the resource. The agents in our system were implemented with the aid of the JADE platform [11]. The agents exchange communication messages based on the agent specific FIPA-ACL language [15].

In order to handle semantic heterogeneity issues between the different domains [3], the Resource Description Framework (RDF) [13] technology is being utilized. The RDF ontology enables upon querying, provision of semantically enhanced answers.

For example, a user upon providing a query for an expert who is specialized on certain field, the system will look only to return experts who are specialized in the specific area and will regard other knowledge sources that are related to the specific subject. In order to enable performance optimization and in order to avoid information disclosure to the agents such as the security clearance level for a specific role, a transformation of the RDF file to relational database is performed.

This enables better optimization in terms of avoiding network congestion when performing queries on the central ontology. For the transformation process of RDF to relational schema, the hybrid inlining algorithm [12] has been utilized. Conceptually, we consider a Document Type Definition (DTD) of an XML (or alternatively an RDF) file as similar to a schema in relational databases. Having this in mind, the process of storing and querying RDF files to a relational database, consists of transforming basically the DTD to relational tables. A sample of DTD used for our purposes is represented in Table 1.

<?xml version="1.0" encoding="UTF-8"?>		
<! ELEMENT	SecurityFileXL	(Security*)>
<!ELEMENT	Security	(Field+,ComplexField+,Field+,Researchers+, Field+)>
<!ELEMENT	Field	(title, Resource+)>
<!ELEMENT	Title	(#PCDATA)>
<!ELEMENT	Resource	(title, url, description)>
<!ELEMENT	url	(#PCDATA)>
<!ELEMENT	description	(#PCDATA)>
<!ELEMENT	ComplexField	(title, Field+)>
<!ELEMENT	Researchers	(Researcher+)>
<!ELEMENT	Researcher	(Name,Email,PersonalPage,ClearanceLevel>
<!ELEMENT	Name	(#PCDATA)>
<!ELEMENT	Email	(#PCDATA)>
<!ELEMENT	PersonalPage	(#PCDATA)>
<!ELEMENT	ClearanceLevel	(#PCDATA)>

Now the basic idea is to transform first the DTD to a graph, and accordingly for the major concepts to create relational tables. The graph of the DTD of Table 1 is presented on Fig 2.

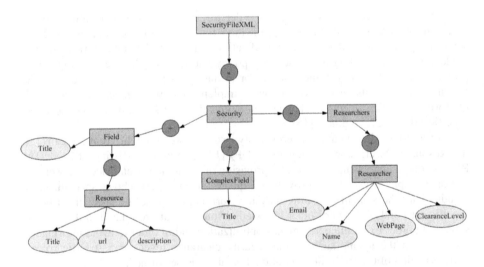

Fig. 2. DTD to relational schema transformation

Accordingly, for concepts like the researcher (domain expert), which represents a role within one domain, a relational table can be defined. One of the major attributes defined for our scenario, is the clearance level. The value stored in this attribute can be easily hidden for non-disclosure purposes to all non authorized users, with the facilities most DBMS's provide and can be easily retrieved for authorized purposes with easy to form SQL queries. Therefore, we edit security policies in XML format, accordingly this XML-type policy transformed and stored in relational schema, which can be further queried for policy mappings and can be efficiently protected against non-authorized disclosure.

5.2 Overall *Sec-shield* Architecture

Our prototype implementation consists of an organizational memory, consisting of the organization's past experience codified in semi-structured documents, while at the same time we correlate the document-based information with each domain's human network of experts. Support is provided also for multimedia files (images, videos) through a special purpose repository implemented in Java and Oracle 9i. For multimedia file retrieval purposes, a set of meta-data is stored in the organizational memory module. This architecture is deployed in different domains, each one maintaining its own autonomy. For each domain there is a policy decision point (PDP) which directs the policy enforcement point (PEP) to provide -or not- access to distributed resources of the system upon a user's request.

Upon a user query for a topic of his/her interest, initially the local document management module is utilized and accordingly, the knowledge discovery agent queries the other domains for similar knowledge sources. The messages exchanged between the domain specific agents are based on FIPA protocols [15], and the content embodied is based on the RDF ontology, which plays also a key role relative to the facilitation of heterogeneous assets knowledge discovery. After resources identification is performed, the next step is related with the authorization process activation. For transparency reasons, the authorization process will be treated through the authorization agent (Auth-agent, fig3). The authorization agent provides the user

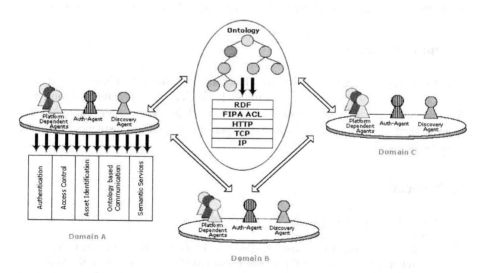

Fig. 3. Overall system architecture

credentials, and the security clearance associated with the user's role on the local domain, is exalted to the global security role mapping-scheme, as mentioned in section 4.1. Accordingly, a role on the remote domain is assigned to the user and on the basis of the remote security policy, the PDP authorizes or not the user upon the requested resources. Therefore, the user is provided with the chance to utilize knowledge from multiple domains transparently, where all the asset discovery procedures and authorization between the domains, are treated by the system, through the use of the pair of Auth-Agent and Discovery-Agent, assigned to each domain.

6 Conclusions

Contemporary KM approaches suffice to utilize knowledge residing in different organizational domains, limiting the resource sharing potential of the developed KM systems. *Sec-shield* pays special emphasis on covering this aspect. *Sec-shield* is characterized by its extended functionalities relative to multi-domain knowledge utilization, such as heterogeneous files management (images, text), transparency relative to knowledge asset identification, user authorization and access control enforcement. Our solution while it maintains its scalability potential, it is characterized by its robustness and supports well defined policy frameworks in comparison with other approaches [4] that put more emphasis on knowledge sharing rather than on access control enforcement. Based on its policy dependent security management, it can support large scale infrastructures with frequent changes in the policy specification or the number of participating users. In the future, we plan to expand our framework to integrate the identification and authorization of knowledge assets through the creation of Web-services running independently for each domain.

Acknowledgments

This work was co-funded by 75% from E.E. and 25% from the Greek Government under the framework of the Education and Initial Vocational Training Program – Archimedes. The authors would like to thank John Varnas for aiding at the improvement of the aesthetics of the paper, by providing assistance with the drawings.

References

1. Nonaka I., Takeuchi H. (1995). "The knowledge Creating Company", Oxford University Press.
2. Bonifacio M., Bouquet P., Danieli A., Dona A., Mameli G., Nori M.: "Keex: A peer-to-peer solution for distributed Knowledge Management". In Tochtermann K., Maurer H. eds.: Proceedings on the 4th International Conference on Knowledge Management Graz Austria, 2004

3. Belsis P., Gritzalis S.: "Distributed autonomous Knowledge Acquisition and Dissemination ontology based framework", in Proceedings of PAKM 04 5th International Conference on Practical Aspects of Knowledge Management – Workshop on Enterprise Modeling and Ontology: Ingredients for Interoperability H. Kuhn (ed.) Dec. 2004 Vienna Austria, Univ. of Vienna.

4. Tempich C., Ehrig M., Fluit C., Haase P., Marti E.L., Plechawski M., Staab S. "XAROP: A Midterm Report on Introducing a Decentralized Semantics based Application, Proceedings of Practical Aspects of Knowledge Management (PAKM) 2004, Vienna Austria, LNAI 3336 Kluwer Academic publishers, pp. 259-270.

5. Seleznyov A., Mohamed A., Hailes S. "ADAM: An agent-based Middleware Architecture for Distributed Access Control" Twenty-Second International Multi-Conference on Applied Informatics: Artificial Intelligence and Applications, 2004.

6. Damianou, N., N. Dulay, E. Lupu and M. Sloman . Managing Security in Object-based Distributed Systems using Ponder. In Proceedings of the 6th Open European Summer School (Eunice 2000), Enchede, The Netherlands, 13-15 September 2000.

7. Organization for the Advancement of Structured Information Standards (OASIS), "XACML Extensible access control markup language specification 2.0", OASIS Standard, (available at http://www.oasis-open.org

8. Belokosztolski A., "Role based access control for policy administration", available at http://www.cl.cam.ac.uk/ as technical report No 586, university of Cambridge, UK.

9. Joshi J.B.D., Bhatti R., Bertino E., Ghafoor A., "Access Control Language for Multi-Domain Environments", IEEE Internet Computing, Nov. 2004

10. Bhatti R., Bertino E., Ghafoor A., Joshi J.B.D., XML-based Specification for Web services Document Security. IEEE Computer, April 2004, pp. 41-50.

11. The JADE agent development kit. Available at http://jade.tilab.com/

12. Lee Dongwon, Chu Wesley, (2001) CPI: Constraints- Preserving Inlining algorithm for mapping XML DTD to relational schema, Data and Knowledge Engineering, 39, pp. 3-25.

13. S. Decker, S. Melnik, F. van Harmelen, D. Fensel, M. Klein, J. Broekstra, M. Erdmann, I. Horrocks, The semantic web: the roles of XML and RDF, IEEE Internet Comput. 4 (5) (2000) 63–74.

14. Extensible Markup Language Specification (XML), http://www.w3.org/XML/.

15. FIPA standard status specifications www.fipa.org/repository/standardspecs.html

Protection Mechanisms Against Phishing Attacks

Klaus Plössl, Hannes Federrath, and Thomas Nowey

Universität Regensburg
{klaus.ploessl, hannes.federrath, thomas.nowey}@wiwi.uni-regensburg.de

Abstract. Approaches against Phishing can be classified into modifications of the traditional PIN/TAN-authentication on the one hand and approaches that try to reduce the probability of a scammer being successful without changing the existing PIN/TAN-method on the other hand. We present a new approach, based on challenge-response-authentication. Since our proposal does not require any new hardware on the client side, it can be implemented with little additional cost by financial institutions or other web retailers and therefore is a good compromise compared to the other approaches. A big drawback is that it doesn't protect against man-in-the-middle attacks but most of the other approaches don't either.

1 Introduction

Phishing – "the hottest, and most troubling, new scam on the Internet" [1] – is a relatively new fraud technique, utilizing methods of Social Engineering. The "victim", an online customer, is tricked into divulging personal data (e.g. passwords, credit card number or online banking account) to an attacker. In 1996 the term Phishing – a combination of "password" and "fishing" – was first mentioned on the internet in the alt.2600 hacker newsgroup. See [2] for further information.

The Anti-Phishing Working Group (APWG), an association of financial institutions, internet service providers, online-retailers, and other it-companies, is collecting information on Phishing incidents. The collected data is published in the monthly Phishing Activity Trends Report, which clearly shows the dramatical increase in Phishing attacks during the last few months (see Fig. 1). Another study conducted by Gartner showed that 57 million US citizens have already been victims of a Phishing attack. 1.4 million or 2.5 % of them passed sensitive data unknowingly to third parties which cost banks and credit card companies $ 1.2 billion in 2003 [4]. According to the APWG-data even 5 % of the attacked are supposed to become victims.

Timeline of a Phishing Attack. According to [5] there is a characteristic procedure:

1. In most cases the attack begins with an email that pretends to come from a reputable service provider like a bank. At the first glance the fraudulent

S. Katsikas, J. López, G. Pernul (Eds.): TrustBus 2005, LNCS 3592, pp. 20–29, 2005.
© Springer-Verlag Berlin Heidelberg 2005

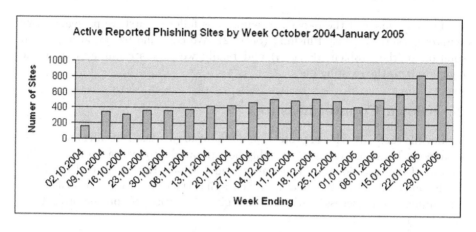

Fig. 1. Active Reported Phishing Sites by Week October 2004-January 2005 [3]

email looks reliable regarding its sender, form, and content and is thus almost indistinguishable from a real one. Frequently a necessary update, a loss of data or even a security problem is the pretended reason for the mail.

2. With the email the victim is tricked in following a hyperlink to a counterfeited website. Like the initial email this website is hardly to identify as an imitation, because its look and feel is adapted to that of the original one. The target of the hyperlink within the email can easily be counterfeited using html-mails. There are several methods to disguise the address in the address-field of the browser, like:
   - Using a similar domain-name (e.g. https://www.postbank-deutschland. com instead of https://www.postbank.de)
   - Exploiting bugs in the browser software (e.g. using long addresses containing the @ character)
   - Using sophisticated methods like "Floating Windows" – small Java Script programs that overlap the original address-field of the browser (containing the address of the scammer's website) with another window containing the pretended address.
3. The faked website asks for personal data or access information from the user that is then used for fraudulent transactions.

The tricks and methods of the Phisher become technically more and more sophisticated what makes them also more dangerous for the victims. A recent example is a Phishing email containing scripting code that is used to manipulate the hosts-file of windows-machines [6]. Since this file is used for the resolution of domain-names the user is automatically redirected towards the attackers page when he enters the original URL of the service. It is noteworthy that with this type of attack the content of the fraudulent email does not necessarily have to have any relation to the later target, what makes the user even more careless. This type of attack is also known as "Pharming".

The remainder of the paper is organized as follows. First we present known countermeasures against Phishing (Sect. 2). We continue by proposing a new solution to the problem (Sect. 3) and finally we evaluate our approach and compare it to the existing ones.

2   Known Countermeasures

Meanwhile there are a lot of protection mechanisms against Phishing and online-scammers. These proposals can roughly be separated into two categories: modifications of the traditional authentication and authorisation-method (PIN/TAN) on the one hand (Sect. 2.2) and approaches that try to reduce the probability of a scammer being successful without changing the procedure on the other hand (Sect. 2.1).

2.1   Minimizing the Risks

This group can be divided into user-dependent and user-independent approaches.

User-Dependent Approaches. Most user-dependent approaches are based on a kind of guideline that is given to the users and contains information about the correct usage of the service. The complexity of those guidelines is varying heavily. Some examples are [5], [7], and [1]. The problem with these guidelines is that the average Internet user is likely not to put into practice all of those recommendations – either because he is not capable of doing so or for convenience reasons. Tools can support the user in terms of security.

Spam-Filters and Filters for Outgoing Data. Manufacturers of anti-virus software try to hamper Phishing by the use of filters. Already known Phishing mails and faked hyperlinks can be identified and the corresponding email can be classified as spam. Filtering Software is also capable of scanning the outgoing traffic for sensitive data, blocking it and immediately sending a notification to the user.

Browser Plug-Ins. Browser plug-ins like SpoofStick make it easy to verify the URL of the currently visited website. The plug-in-software shows the name of the currently displayed website in a user-configurable color and size (e.g. "You're on ebay.com"). This is an effective countermeasure against attacks aiming to confuse the user by modifying the address-bar.

The plug-ins ScamBlocker, TrustWatch and Phish Net all use blacklists with well-known Phishing-sites. Everytime the user wants to visit a website it is compared to the list and in case of a match a warning is displayed to the user. Additionally Phish Net prevents any kind of navigation through the elements of that site. The software also stores sensitive user data and issues a notification to the user every time such data should be transmitted via the Internet.

SpoofGuard visualizes its classification of a website by a traffic light (see Fig. 2) and if necessary a pop-up-window with a warning. The classification depends on various indicators that can be invidually assessed by the user. For further information see [8].

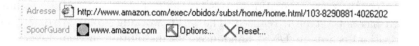

Fig. 2. SpoofGuard

Another tool from the developers of SpoofGuard is PwdHash, an Internet Explorer plug-in, that computes a hash value from the domain-name of the currently visited website and the password entered in the password field of the site. Instead of the password chosen by the user the hash value is transmitted to the website. Thus the "passwords" (read hashes) transmitted are different for all domains and a scammer will not get the right password for another domain by luring the user to a faked domain.

User-Independent Approaches. All tools mentioned above have to be installed manually by the user. The service provider has no influence on the (correct) usage of these security measures. In contrast the methods illustrated in the following can be implemented solely by the service provider.

Spam-Trap and Domain-Watch. Spam-Trap and Domain-Watch are two different approaches that aim on informing the service provider at an early stage of an attack. Then he is able to give a warning to his customers early enough to protect them.

- For Spam-Trap email-addresses are dropped in numerous newsgroups, guestbooks and websites with the goal to get as many spam-mails as possible to that addresses. The incoming emails are subsequently analyzed and if a new Phishing attack is identified the affected service provider is notified.
- Domain-Watch monitors the registration of new domain-names. Every time a domain with a name similar to that of an existing service provider is registered a notification is sent. By this means the service provider can prepare the suspension of that domain in case of an attack. According to [3], the time domains used for Phishing attacks were reachable and working, averages 5.8 days. By identifying the owner of that domain before the attack begins, the service provider is able to considerably shorten that time-period and may even be able to prevent the attack.

Meanwhile there are a couple of firms that monitor spam and domain-registrations for other firms (see [9]). They even offer countermeasures for the case of emergency that can go as far as denial-of-service attacks on identified Phishing sites.

Validation of Sender Information. Sender-validation-techniques are designed to identify spam and Phishing emails respectively to determine their real originator. According to [10] all currently available techniques are based on an extension of the mailserver-entries in the DNS.

Although there are several proposals for the technical realisation a common standard has not yet been realized. The IETF working group MARID (MTA AuthorizationRecords in DNS) announced its dissolution in September 2004, after a controversy over patent claims of Microsoft Corp. concerning the "Sender ID" method, which was the favoured method of the working group up to that point [11]. Now the different proposals are supposed to be submitted as individual RFC-drafts to the IETF.

Fraud Detection. Major enterprises normally have the ability to analyze all data for irregularities in real time. Such irregularities can usually be observed when a scammer tries to use information obtained by a phishing attack for a transaction. The Internet Payment Service PayPal uses a 24/7 fraud and spoof detection system, that is capable of identifying anomalous transactions within one hour. Each transaction is checked for plausibility (amount, frequency of usage, etc.) and can be revoked if necessary [9].

2.2 Variations of the Authorization and Authentication Procedure

The approaches described so far are either user-dependent, not yet available (validation of sender information) or merely supporting measures (Fraud Detection, Spam Trap and Domain Watch). For reasons like carelessness and ignorance of the users a solution to the problem cannot solely rely on user behaviour. Furthermore a solution should be available soon. The supporting measures alone cannot prevent Phishing, they are just a possibility to quickly react on attacks. Thus the only way to effectively solve the problem is to use methods that change the existing PIN/TAN procedure for authentication and authorization. Therefore we focus on that kind of approach for the remainder of the paper.

Hardware Tokens. The PIN/TAN-procedure is replaced by a small piece of hardware (hardware token) that is given to all users and that can be used to generate one-time-passwords.

- According to [12] AOL uses RSA Security's SecurID hardware token. In order to log in, users have to type in a 6-digit-Code displayed by the token and changed every minute, in addition to their regular password.
- A one-time-password token provided by Kobil Systems does not change the passwords periodically but on user request. Every time the user needs a password he has to push a button on the token [13].
- A third method is used by the Swedish SEB-bank. It uses a token-based challenge-response-system [14]. When logging into the bank website with his ID the user activates his hardware token by entering a PIN. He is shown a challenge that he has to enter in his token. The response (that is only valid for 30 seconds) is then computed by the token and has to be transmitted to the website by the user.

PKI and Digital Signature. When using a Public-Key-Infrastructure (PKI) the user usually gets a key pair and a certificate guaranteeing the authenticity of his public key. A time stamp and a digital signature is then added to every request sent to the service provider. The service provider can subsequently verify the request by using the users public key. Thus this approach can guarantee authenticity and integrity of the transmitted data if the private keys are kept absolutely confidential and the mapping between a party and its public key is correct. Usually the private key is stored on a smartcard that is protected from unauthorized access by a PIN. For the effectiveness of the time-stamp the clocks of the participating parties should be synchronized.

3   New Proposal

The mechanisms against Phishing shown in the previous sections either need proper behaviour of the user or additional soft- or hardware. But equipping all users with additional soft- and/or hardware can be very costly and there are additional costs associated with installation and user support. Therefore we propose a new procedure that avoids additional hardware.

3.1   How it Works

The new proposal is mainly the combination of the known PIN/TAN-approach with a paper-based challenge-response-technique. It differs from PIN/TAN in the way that the user gets a list with challenge-response-pairs instead of a list with TANs. Before completing a transaction a challenge is presented to the user who must enter the corresponding response. If the response is incorrect the transaction is not carried out.

If the new technique should (also) be used for access control the user has to enter his ID and then sees a challenge from his list (see Fig. 3). If he enters the correct response he is granted access. If he finally wants to carry out a transaction he has to complete the challenge-response procedure again.

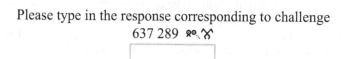

Please type in the response corresponding to challenge
637 289

Fig. 3. Challenge-Response Input-Screen

Any challenge is sent to the user only once regardless of the fact if the response was correct or not. If nearly all challenges of the list are used the user gets a new list. After a predefined number of failed attempts to enter the correct response (e.g. three) the user should be notified and his account should be locked (at least temporary). To complicate man-in-the-middle attacks it is reasonable to limit the validity of the challenge to a short period of time so that the attacker only has little time available to act.

The usability is increased if challenge and response are clearly distinguishable. This could be achieved by using a sequence of numbers as challenge and a

Challenge	Response
037 490 ✆☆⚓	ZSJUFS
193 887 ⚙☷	HAGTUH
~~283 749 ☁⚒~~	~~BSUNBI~~
~~345 938 ⚕⚔~~	~~XNAJSK~~
473 648 ⚬⚕	OKALSZ
637 289 ♞☓	WQNNIV
~~836 445 ⚚⚛⚘~~	~~HEUCNP~~
837 465 ⚓⚒	AFSOPN
...	...

Never give a challenge away!

Fig. 4. Challenge-Response-List

sequence of letters as response. Additionally such a challenge is very easy to find in an ordered list. To prevent attacks that ask the user to give away a challenge with the corresponding response the challenge should include some symbols that simply can't be keyed in (see Fig. 4, symbols taken from the Ewok language). If challenge and response are constructed like shown in Fig. 4 the probability for an attacker to guess the corresponding response to a given challenge is approximately 1 to 308 millions. Crossing out used pairs is not necessary but it can be done to keep the look and feel of the traditional TAN lists.

[15] states that it is a major problem that TAN-lists can easily be copied without the kowledge of the user. He solves this problem by adding a physical layer that has to be scratched away before the user can see the TAN. This approach has two drawbacks:

1. The user always has to carry along the list to be able to conduct a transaction what may result in destroying the physical layer accidentially.
2. In some cases the user may actually want to copy the list, e.g. if he has two residences and doesn't want to sway the list between these.

We propose to employ visual cryptography to solve this problem. The user then gets a sheet of paper and a transparency that he has to keep on two different places. When carrying out a transaction he has to combine these two things to be able to see the challenge-response-pairs. Thus on the one hand the legitimate user can still copy the two things easily, but on the other hand for an adversary it is much more difficult to get the two duplicates unnoticed than just copying one list. In short: employing visual cryptography doesn't protect against copying the list but complicates this process for an attacker.

3.2 Evaluation

The new proposal is evaluated according to the criteria in [16]. Thus it's easily possible to compare it with the PIN/TAN-alternatives evaluated there. [16]

uses a long list of criteria that is limited to the one's relevant for Phishing in this paper. These are the main criterions security, user acceptance and costs. Additionally this paper introduces the criterion "Protection against Phishing". The token based approaches have also been included in the evaluation. Table 1 summarizes the results. Following [16] ++ stands for very good, + for good, ∼ for average, − for substandard and −− for not good.

The currently used passwords and TANs provide no protection against Phishing at all. In contrast using PKI and digital signatures has the potential to protect against Phishing completely because the digitally signed (order-)data cannot be modified unnoticed provided that the user really signs his data (e.g. by using an external tamper-proof signing hardware with data visualisation).

As for hardware tokens there are slight differences in the protection against Phishing depending on the option used: If the one-time-password is changed periodically the scammer has to carry out a man-in-the-middle attack to be able to (mis-)use a grifted password. If the token computes a time independent password on demand of the user he can usually use the password(s) till the victim logs on to the real website again.

The new proposal protects better against Phishing than a method based on the latter type of tokens because the scammer needs the correct response to a specific challenge. And since any challenge is sent to the user only once the scammer cannot get a pool of challenges to trick the user. It is only possible to implement a man-in-the-middle attack. Thus the new proposal proctects against Phishing in nearly the same manner as tokens that generate one-time-passwords periodically.

Paper based lists like the ones used in the new proposal are very reliable but they could be misplaced, stolen or copied. By employing visual cryptography unnoticed copying can be made very difficult. Hardware tokens may − besides of being stolen or misplaced − stop working because of power breakdown or external forces.

There is no installation effort for the user neither with hardware tokens nor with paper based challenge-response-lists. Both alternatives are easy to use but the new proposal seems more applicable than the use of hardware tokens because it works more like the well known PIN/TAN-authentication.

Regarding the criterion wide user spectrum the approaches are similar to passwords. For any new service the user needs a new token or a new list and any method can be used for other applications like authentication at an ATM. The transparency of the methods is very high because the user always knows what he has to do and why. He can completely control what he wants to enter.

The software costs for the two alternatives are low. The new proposal just requires an extension of the PIN/TAN-authentication module that can easily be implemented in most cases. If tokens are used a new authentication module must be implemented or integrated into the system.

There are no additional hardware costs for the new proposal. Just the lists have to be printed but this is similar to the PIN/TAN-method. Due to the similarity to the well known PIN/TAN-approach the training costs are low. The

Table 1. Evaluation of PIN/TAN alternatives from [16], own evaluations *in italic*

Mechanism	Security		User Acceptance				Costs			
	Protection against Phishing	Reliability	Installation Effort	Applicability	Wide User Spectrum	Transparency of Method	Software Costs	Hardware Costs	Training Costs	Administration Costs
Password	--	~	+	+	+	+	+	+	+	-
New proposal	+	++	++	++	+	++	+	+	+	+
Token: Password periodical	+	+	++	+	+	++	+	-	~	+
Token: Password on demand	~	+	++	+	+	++	+	-	~	+
PKI with smart card support	++	+	+	++	++	++	-	-	~	~

administration costs are likely to be lower than for traditional passwords because the users can't forget their passwords any more.

In contrast the token based methods are quite expensive because every user has to get his own token. Also the costs for training and administration are higher than for password based methods because the users have to be taught how to use the tokens.

4 Summary

Reliable protection against Phishing can not be achieved with the existing password and PIN/TAN-mechanism. Thus this method has to be changed to some degree. Using digital signatures is the best solution in terms of security. Unfortunately there are a lot of additional costs for necessary hardware, user training, support, PKI, and so on. Another drawback is that the user is no longer highly mobile because most solutions require a card reader plugged into the PC and the necessary drivers. But in many cases plugging hardware into a PC and installing drivers is nearly impossible e.g. on a journey in an Internet Cafe.

Using hardware tokens with periodically changing one-time-passwords is also a reliable protection against Phishing. But this alternative causes a lot of additional costs for hardware, user training, and support, too. These are lower than the costs associated with using digital signatures but not neglectable. In addition the users won't be willing to take a unique hardware token with them for every service they use.

The new paper-based challenge-response-approach suggested in this paper seems to be a good compromise between security and costs because it protects nearly as reliable against Phishing as hardware tokens while causing considerably lower costs. The major drawback is that it doesn't protect against man-in-the-middle attacks but this is also true for the alternatives that employ the mentioned hardware tokens. Due to the similarity to the well known PIN/TAN-authentication the additional costs for user training and support are very low. The user's mobility is nearly the same as before, he just needs a single sheet (and probably a transparency) with the challenge-response-pairs for every service he wants to use.

The paper shows that there are many reasonable mechanisms to protect against Phishing. They just have to be implemented by financial institutions, web retailers and other service providers.

References

1. FBI National Press Office: FBI Says Web "Spoofing" Scams are a Growing Problem, Washington D.C. (2003) http://www.fbi.gov/pressrel/pressrel03/ spoofing072103.htm.
2. Anti-Phishing Working Group: Proposed Solutions to Address the Threat of Email Spoofing Scams. (2003)
3. Anti-Phishing Working Group: Phishing Activity Trends Report. (2005) http://www.antiphishing.org/APWG_Phishing_Activity_Report-January2005.pdf.
4. Litan, A.: Phishing Victims Likely Will Suffer Identity Theft Fraud. (2004)
5. Nassauische Sparkasse: Tipps zur Sicherheit gegen Phishing-Attacken. (2004) http://www.naspa .de/05_ebanking/05_6_7_tipps_phishing.php.
6. heise news: Phishing-Tricks werden immer ausgefeilter. (2004) http://www.heise. de/newsticker/meldung/52935.
7. Bundesverband deutscher Banken: Online-Banking-Sicherheit. Informationen für Online-Banking-Nutzer, Berlin. (2004) http://www.bdb.de/index.asp?channel= 901010.
8. Chou, N., Ledesma, R., Teraguchi, Y., Boneh, D., Mitchell, J.C.: Client-side defense against web-based identity theft. (2004) http://crypto.stanford.edu/Spoof Guard/webspoof.pdf.
9. Dragoon, A.: Fighting Phish, Fakes and Frauds. (2004) http://www.cio.com/ archive/090104/phish.html.
10. Böhm, H.: Phishing-Betrüger bevorzugen den Finanzsektor, Wien. (2004) http:// www.zt-prentner.at/phishing/Pressemitteilung%20Phishing%20Long.pdf.
11. heise news: Anti-Spam-Arbeitsgruppe MARID der IETF streicht die Segel. (2004) http://www.heise.de/newsticker/meldung/51379.
12. Financial Times Deutschland: AOL bringt neues Sicherheitskonzept gegen Phishing-Mails. (2004) http://www.ftd.de/tm/me/1095597904304.html?nv=wn.
13. KOBIL Systems GmbH: Whitepaper KOBIL SecOVID. (2003) http://www.kobil. de/d/support/download/documents/Whitepaper_SecOVID_ver31_20030519.pdf.
14. Schmidt, N.: Tokens statt PIN/TAN: Sicheres Online-Banking ohne Kartenleser. (2004) http://www.zdnet.de/itmanager/tech/0,39023442,39125970,00.htm.
15. Oppliger, R.: Sichere streichlisten. digma. Zeitschrift für Datenrecht und Informationssicherheit 1 (2005) 34–35
16. Essmayr, W., Leonhardsberger, H., Probst, S., Stockner, W., Weippl, E.: Qualitative evaluation of authentication approaches for ebanking. Technical Report SCCH-TR-0215, Software Competence Center Hagenberg, Hagenberg (2001)

Dropout-Tolerant TTP-Free Mental Poker

Jordi Castellà-Roca, Francesc Sebé, and Josep Domingo-Ferrer

Rovira i Virgili University of Tarragona,
Dept. of Computer Engineering and Maths,
Av. Països Catalans 26, E-43007 Tarragona, Catalonia, Spain
{jordi.castella, francesc.sebe, josep.domingo}@urv.net

Abstract. There is a broad literature on distributed card games over communications networks, collectively known as *mental poker*. Like in any distributed protocol, avoiding the need for a Trusted Third Party (TTP) in mental poker is highly desirable, because really trusted TTPs are not always available and seldom free. This paper deals with the player dropout problem in mental poker without a TTP. A solution based on zero-knowledge proofs is proposed. While staying TTP-free, our proposal allows the game to continue after player dropout.

Keywords: Mental poker, player dropout.

1 Introduction

According to Merryll Lynch, the online gambling business is expected to grow to $48 billion by 2010 and $177 billion by 2015. This booming turnover must be accompanied by enough security guarantees for online players; unfortunately, this is not always the case, especially as far as e-poker (mental poker) is concerned. Mental poker is played like a conventional card game with the difference that players communicate over a network and do not need to be in the same physical place. In this situation, cheating becomes especially tempting and must be prevented. A mental poker solution must offer all protocols needed to complete a game. These are: shuffling, drawing, discarding and opening.

The above protocols should offer the same security properties as conventional physical poker, plus some security properties specific to electronic gaming. Such properties were identified and enumerated by Crépeau in [4].

Dropout tolerance was not listed in [4] as a requirement, but it is nonetheless a major challenge in remote gaming. In electronic gaming, no one can prevent a player from quitting a game. Two kinds of dropout can be distinguished:

- **Intentional:** A player decides to quit the game. This may be attractive for a player to whom the game is not being favorable.
- **Accidental:** A player cannot go on playing, for example due to a network problem.

Whatever the reason for player dropout, the remaining players should be able to continue the game. If a Trusted Third Party (TTP) is controlling the game,

S. Katsikas, J. López, G. Pernul (Eds.): TrustBus 2005, LNCS 3592, pp. 30–40, 2005.
© Springer-Verlag Berlin Heidelberg 2005

handling player dropout is greatly simplified. However, a TTP is not always available or desirable: it may not be trusted by everybody, it may charge some fee, etc. When no TTP is assumed, dropout becomes a nontrivial problem.

1.1   Contribution and Plan of This Paper

This paper proposes a solution for player dropout in mental poker without a TTP. The solution is based on zero-knowledge proofs and allows the game to continue after the dropout.

Section 2 reviews literature on TTP-free mental poker offering player confidentiality. Our proposed protocol is described in Section 3. Security is examined in Section 4. Finally, Section 5 is a conclusion. The Appendix contains the security proofs.

2   Background on TTP-Free Mental Poker Offering Player Confidentiality

All schemes mentioned in this section fulfill all security requirements identified in [4], including the confidentiality of player strategy. We next review them by focusing on their ability to handle player dropout.

Schemes [5,9] do not consider player dropout. In both proposals, each player has some secret information needed to draw cards from the deck. Without this information, the game cannot proceed.

In [1] it is proposed that players who quit the the game should disclose their secret information. However, this solution is only applicable if dropout is intentional *and* the player leaving the game is willing to collaborate. In case of accidental dropout (*e.g.* due to a network problem) or malicious intentional dropout, there is no guarantee that the remaining players can go on playing.

The schemes [7,10] represent each card in the deck by a different numerical value. During card shuffling, those values are encrypted and permuted by each player. The effect of encryption is analogous to reversing cards in a physical deck. A secret-sharing scheme is used, so that at least t players are needed to decrypt values. The goal is that the game can proceed if at least t players remain, which allows for some dropouts. In [7] the secret sharing scheme is applied to cards. Each value representing a card is divided into as many shares as there are players. Then each share is encrypted under the public key of a different player. A card cannot be decrypted unless at least t players co-operate. In [10], players create a key pair using the procedure proposed in [8]. Players generate a public key so that each player gets a share of the private key; thus, the private key cannot be used unless at least t players co-operate. Even if those schemes based on secret sharing do offer some dropout tolerance, the bad news is that secret sharing makes it possible for a sufficiently large collusion of players to obtain all deck information. Thus, dropout tolerance is traded off against collusion tolerance. This is frustrating because collusion tolerance is a basic security property already identified as relevant in [4].

3   Our Proposal

There is a first round where cards are dealt as in the poker game, and each player obtains five cards. If a player discards some cards from her hand, a new dealing round is started so that the player can obtain as many cards as she has discarded.

We use Protocol 1 to obtain a new deck of cards in each dealing round, in a similar way as proposed in [12]. In the second and successive dealing rounds each player *vetoes* (*i.e.* marks as unavailable) those cards that she has previously drawn. Protocol 2 is used to veto drawn cards. If a player obtains a vetoed card, she cannot use it and she does not know either the value of the vetoed card or who vetoed it; what the player can do is to show that she obtained a vetoed card and then draw a new card.

If a player leaves the game, the rest of players generate a new deck and use it in the game. The new deck includes the cards that were drawn by the player who left the game, because the latter is no longer there to veto her cards when the new deck is generated.

We shall use the following notation in the subsequent protocols.

n : number of players (we assume some ordering among the n players);
$\mathcal{P}_i$: the i-th player in the ordered set of n players;
λ_i : set of cards in $\mathcal{P}_i$'s hand;
Λ : set of all cards in the hands of all players, *i.e.* $\Lambda = \cup_{i=1}^{n} \lambda_i$;
δ_i : set of cards discarded by $\mathcal{P}_i$.

3.1   System Set-Up

Before a game starts, players $\mathcal{P}_1, \ldots, \mathcal{P}_n$ must set some parameters. They choose a large prime p so that $p = 2q+1$ and q is also prime; they also pick one element $g \in \mathbb{Z}_p^*$ of order q.

Using the key generation protocol described in [6], players jointly generate a public key $y = \prod_{i=1}^{n} y_i$. Each player $\mathcal{P}_i$ keeps her corresponding share α_i of the private key and publishes $y_i = g^{\alpha_i}$.

3.2   Deck Generation

Each card is represented by a value jointly computed by all players in Protocol 1. We first explain what Protocol 1 does and then describe the protocol in detail.

Let us assume that we are in the k-th dealing round. We can see in Step 1 of Procotol 1 below that every player uses Procedure 1 to compute 52 new values. These values are sent to the rest of players in Step 2 of Protocol 1. Once every player gets the new values from the rest of players, the new deck D_k is computed by all players at Step 3. We use the term face-up deck of cards because every player can see the value of each card; the j-th value $d_{k,j}$ in D_k represents the j-th card in the deck.

If $d_{k,j}$ is a face-up card, then we denote by $e_{k,j}$ the corresponding face-down card. $e_{k,j}$ contains the encrypted version of the exponents that have been used to compute $d_{k,j} \in D_k$ from $d_{k-1,j} \in D_{k-1}$. To prove ownership of a card $d_{k,j}$, a player must prove knowledge of those exponents, *i.e.* prove knowledge of the discrete logarithm $\log_{d_{k-1,j}}(d_{k,j})$.

In the first round, all cards are available and $E_1 = C_{1,0}$ is the face-down deck of cards without shuffling (see Step 4 of Protocol 1). In subsequent rounds, each player vetoes the cards in her hand using Protocol 2 (called at Step 5a of Protocol 1); the goal is that cards already drawn should become unavailable. After using Protocol 2, a player gets one re-masking factor for each card in the deck; a vetoed card is re-masked with a factor which does not allow decryption, whereas a non-vetoed card is re-masked with a factor allowing decryption.

In Step 5b players re-mask the encrypted exponents with these factors, and obtain the face-down deck of cards without shuffling, $C_{k,0}$.

We denote by D_l the deck of cards of the l-th round; we denote by $\mathbf{D}$ the set of all decks that have been generated in all rounds, *i.e.* $\mathbf{D} = \{D_1, \ldots, D_k\}$. In order to run our protocol, we define $D_0 = \{d_{0,1}, \ldots, d_{0,52}\}$, where $d_{0,j} = g$, $\forall j \in \{1, \ldots, 52\}$.

Protocol 1 $(k \geq 1, D_{k-1})$

1. *Each player $\mathcal{P}_i$ uses Procedure 1 on D_{k-1} and obtains $D_{k,i} = \{d_{k,i,1}, \ldots, d_{k,i,52}\}$ and $E_{k,i} = \{e_{k,i,1}, \ldots, e_{k,i,52}\}$, where $d_{k,i,j} = d_{k-1,j}^{m_{k,i,j}}$ and $e_{k,i,j} = E_y(m_{k,i,j})$;*
2. *Each $\mathcal{P}_i$ publishes $D_{k,i}$ and $E_{k,i}$;*
3. *All players compute the face-up deck of cards $D_k = \{d_{k,1}, \ldots, d_{k,52}\}$ and $E_k = \{e_{k,1}, \ldots, e_{k,52}\}$, where $d_{k,j} = \prod_{i=1}^{n} d_{k,i,j} = d_{k-1,j}^{m_{k,1,j}+\ldots+m_{k,n,j}}$ and $e_{k,j} = \{e_{k,1,j}, \ldots, e_{k,n,j}\}$;*
4. *If $k = 1$, players compute the face-down deck of cards $C_{1,0} = \{c_{1,0,1}, \ldots, c_{1,0,52}\}$, where $c_{1,0,j} = e_{1,j} \in E_1$;*
5. *If $k > 1$ then players do the following*

   (a) *Run the vetoing protocol (Protocol 2) and obtain $G_k = \{g_{k,1}, \ldots, g_{k,52}\}$, where $g_{k,j} = \{g_{k,1,j}, \ldots, g_{k,n,j}\}$;*
   (b) *Compute the face-down deck of cards $C_{k,0} = \{c_{k,0,1}, \ldots, c_{k,0,52}\}$, where $c_{k,0,j} = e_{k,j} \cdot g_{k,j} = \{e_{k,1,j} \cdot g_{k,1,j}, \ldots, e_{k,n,j} \cdot g_{k,n,j}\}$. Drawn cards in this face-down deck have been vetoed.*

In the k-th dealing round, each player $\mathcal{P}_i$ computes a new value $d_{k,i,j}$ for each card j. This new value is obtained from $d_{k-1,j}$ (the value used in round $k-1$ to represent card j) raised to a random value $m_{k,i,j}$. The exponent $m_{k,i,j}$ is encrypted into $E_y(m_{k,i,j})$ and sent along with the new value. Players use Procedure 1 to compute these new values for each card.

Procedure 1 (y, p, D)

1. *For each d_j in $D = \{d_1, \ldots, d_{52}\}$ do:*
   (a) *generate a random value m_j, where $2 < m_j < q$;*
   (b) *compute $d_j^{m_j}$;*

(c) *encrypt m_j into $E_y(m_j)$ under public key y;*

(d) *prove in zero-knowledge to the rest of players that $E_y(m_j)$ is the encryption of $\log_{d_j}(d_j^{m_j})$ using [11];*

2. *Return the sets $D' = \{d_1^{m_1}, \ldots, d_{52}^{m_{52}}\}$ and $E = \{E_y(m_1), \ldots, E_y(m_{52})\}$.*

Prior to describing Protocol 2 we define $\xi_{l,i}$ as the number of cards that P_i has drawn in the l-th dealing round; we also define ξ_i as the sum of all cards drawn by P_i in all previous dealing rounds, that is, $\xi_i = \sum_{l=1}^{k-1} \xi_{i,l}$.

In Step 1a of Protocol 2 each player in turn computes a re-masking factor for each card $d_{k,j} \in D_k$. Using the construction of [3], P_i proves in Step 1b of Protocol 2 that $52 - \xi_i$ factors have been properly computed (as many factors as the number of cards P_i has not drawn); in this proof, P_i does not reveal which subset of factors was properly computed. In Step 1c, P_i again uses the construction of [3] to prove that she has computed ξ_i re-masking factors which veto the cards P_i has drawn (see in Section 4 the lemma that a player vetoes the cards she has drawn). The re-masking factors that veto all drawn cards by any player are pooled together in Step 2.

Protocol 2 (D_k)

1. *For each P_i ($i = 1, \ldots, n$):*
   (a) *P_i uses Procedure 2 with $(D_k, \lambda_i, \delta_i, \mathbf{D})$ and obtains $G_i = \{(u_{i,1}, v_{i,1}), \ldots, (u_{i,52}, v_{i,52})\}$.*
   (b) *P_i proves in zero-knowledge that at least $52 - \xi_i$ values $(u_{i,j}, v_{i,j})$ properly re-mask a card, i.e. they do not veto the card. This is done using the construction of [3] in order to show that P_i can correctly perform at least $52 - \xi_i$ executions of the set of zero-knowledge proofs $\{CP_{i,1}, \ldots, CP_{i,52}\}$, where $CP_{i,j} = CP(g, y, u_{i,j}, v_{i,j})$[1].*
   (c) *For $l = 1$ to k, P_i proves in zero-knowledge that she has vetoed as many cards as the number $\xi_{l,i}$ of cards she obtained in the l-th dealing round. This is done using the construction of [3] in order to prove that she can perform at least $\xi_{l,i}$ executions among the following set of zero-knowledge proofs $\{CP_{l,i,1}, \ldots, CP_{l,i,52}\}$, where $CP_{l,i,j} = CP(d_{l-1}, u_{i,j}, d_{l,j}, d_j)$;*

2. *Compute $G = \{g_1, \ldots, g_{52}\}$, where $g_j = (u_j, v_j)$, and $u_j = \prod_{i=1}^{n} u_{i,j}$ and $v_j = \prod_{i=1}^{n} v_{i,j}$, with $(u_{i,j}, v_{i,j}) \in G_i$.*

3. *Let $G_0 = \{(g_{0,1,1}, \ldots, g_{0,n,1}), \ldots, (g_{0,1,52}, \ldots, g_{0,n,52})\} := G$, that is, $g_{0,\varsigma,j} = g_j \; \forall \varsigma \in \{1, \ldots, n\}$ and $\forall j \in \{1, \ldots, 52\}$, and $g_j = (u_j, v_j) \in G$;*

4. *For each P_i ($i = 1, \ldots, n$):*
   (a) *receive $G_{i-1} = \{(g_{i-1,1,1}, \ldots, g_{i-1,n,1}), \ldots, (g_{i-1,1,52}, \ldots, g_{i-1,n,52})\}$ from P_{i-1};*
   (b) *compute $G_i = \{(g_{i,1,1}, \ldots, g_{i,n,1}), \ldots, (g_{i,1,52}, \ldots, g_{i,n,52})\}$, where $g_{i,\varsigma,j} = g_{i-1,\varsigma,j}^{r_{i,\varsigma,j}} = (u_{i-1,\varsigma,j}^{r_{i,\varsigma,j}}, v_{i-1,\varsigma,j}^{r_{i,\varsigma,j}})$ and $1 < r_{i,\varsigma,j} < q$ is a value obtained at random;*

---

[1] We will denote by $CP(g, y, u, v)$ the Chaum-Pedersen [2] zero-knowledge proof, *i.e.* the proof that $\log_g u = \log_y v$.

(c) for each $g_{i,\varsigma,j}$ = $(u_{i,\varsigma,j}, v_{i,\varsigma,j})$ in G_i run
$CP(u_{i-1,\varsigma,j}, v_{i-1,\varsigma,j}, u_{i,\varsigma,j}, v_{i,\varsigma,j})$;
(d) send G_i to the next player;
5. *Return G_n.*

Procedure 2 is used by every player to compute the values used in re-masking. If card j is not vetoed then a pair (u_j, v_j) is computed such that $\log_g u_j = \log_y v_j$. However, if card j must be vetoed, a pair (u_j, v_j) such that $\log_g u \neq \log_y v$ is computed, in order to prevent a correct decryption.

As will be described in Section 3.4, when $\mathcal{P}_i$ obtains a card j at round k, $\mathcal{P}_i$ obtains the discrete logarithm $\tau_{k,j} = \log_{d_{k-1,j}} d_{k,j}$. In subsequent rounds $\mathcal{P}_i$ uses that logarithm to veto this card.

Procedure 2 $(D, \lambda, \delta, \mathbf{D})$

1. *For each d_j in $D = \{d_1, \ldots, d_{52}\}$ do:*
   (a) if the card represented by d_j is in $\lambda \cup \delta$ do:
      i. generate a random value R_j, where $1 < R_j < p$;
      ii. let us assume that the card represented by d_j has been obtained in round l. In this case $\tau_{l,j} = \log_{d_{l-1,j}}(d_{l,j})$ is known (where $d_{l-1,j}$ and $d_{l,j}$ are in $\mathbf{D}$), so $g_j = (u_j, v_j)$ is computed, where $u_j = d_j^{\tau_{l,j}^{-1}}$ and $v_j = R_j$;
   (b) if the card represented by d_j is not in $\lambda \cup \delta$ do:
      i. generate a random r_j, where $1 < r_j < q$;
      ii. compute $g_j = (u_j, v_j)$, where $u_j = g^{r_j}$ and $v_j = y^{r_j}$;
2. *Return $G = \{g_1, \ldots, g_{52}\} = \{(u_1, v_1), \ldots, (u_{52}, v_{52})\}$.*

3.3 Card Shuffling

This is done using the procedure described in [1]. The different players in turn shuffle and re-mask the face-down deck C_0 obtained with Protocol 1.

Protocol 3 (C_0)

1. *For each player $\mathcal{P}_i$ $(i = 1, \ldots, n)$ do:*
   (a) Generate a permutation σ_i of 52 elements;
   (b) Permute the elements $c_{i-1,j}$ of the face-down deck C_{i-1} with σ_i to obtain C_i^*;
   (c) Re-mask the encrypted messages contained in each card of C_i^* without modifying their content to obtain C_i; this is done by re-masking all ciphertexts contained in each face-down card $C_i^* = \{c_{i,1}^*, \ldots, c_{i,52}^*\}$, where $c_{i,j}^* = \{e_{i,j,1}^*, \ldots, e_{i,j,n}^*\}$; specifically, $\mathcal{P}_i$ computes $C_i = \{c_{i,1}, \ldots, c_{i,52}\}$, where $c_{i,j} = \{e_{i,j,1}^* \cdot E_y(1, r_{i,j,1}), \ldots, e_{i,j,n}^* \cdot E_y(1, r_{i,j,n})\}$; values $\{r_{i,j,1}, \ldots, r_{i,j,n}\}$ are obtained at random;
   (d) Use the proof in [1] to prove in zero-knowledge that C_i is a permuted and re-masked version of C_{i-1}.

After running the shuffling protocol, players get the set C_n, that is, the shuffled face-down deck of cards.

3.4 Card Drawing

The card extraction procedure is as follows. Let us assume that extraction is performed by player $\mathcal{P}_i$:

Protocol 4

1. $\mathcal{P}_i$ randomly selects an element from C_n, namely, $c_j = (e_{j,1}, \ldots, e_{j,n})$;
2. $\mathcal{P}_i$ asks the rest of players to verifiably send her information to decrypt the messages $e_{j,\zeta}$ contained in c_j using [6];
3. After decrypting these messages, $\mathcal{P}_i$ obtains $\{m_1, \ldots, m_n\}$, where $m_\zeta = D(e_{j,\zeta})$;
4. $\mathcal{P}_i$ searches for an element $d_{k,t} \in D_k$ (the k-th dealing round deck) such that $d_{k-1,t}^{m_1 + \ldots + m_n} \equiv d_{k,t}$;
5. If $d_{k,t} \in D_k$ then $\mathcal{P}_i$ stores $\tau_t = (m_1 + \ldots + m_n)$;
6. If $d_{k,t} \notin D_k$ then $\mathcal{P}_i$ has obtained a vetoed card. In this case, she shows that the card was vetoed and requests a new one.

3.5 Card Opening

A player must prove to the rest of players that she is the owner of her cards. The card opening protocol is used to that end.

Let us assume that a player $\mathcal{P}_i$ has drawn a card $c_j \in C_n$. $\mathcal{P}_i$ has received the partial decryption from the rest of players, and she has verified that each partial decryption is correct.

$\mathcal{P}_i$ opens a card when she publishes the remaining part of the decryption of c_j. With this information, all players can know the value of c_j, that is, the decrypted card exponents $D(e_{j,1}), \cdots, D(e_{j,n})$. The decryption is verifiably performed as detailed in [6].

3.6 Card Discarding

A player discards a card when she commits herself to not using it. Let us assume that player $\mathcal{P}_i$ has drawn a card $c_j \in C_n$ using Protocol 4.

$\mathcal{P}_i$ discards c_j by sending a message *discard* with c_j to the rest of players. c_j is added to the set λ_i. If $\mathcal{P}_i$ wants to open a discarded card, the rest of players can detect the cheating because the card is in λ_i.

3.7 Player Dropout

In case one of the players leaves the game, the rest of players can go on playing. Assuming that player $\mathcal{P}_i$ with public key y_i leaves the game, the game public key is updated as $y := y/y_i$. Next, the rest of players continue as if player $\mathcal{P}_i$ had never joined the game. This implies that cards once extracted by $\mathcal{P}_i$ will be back in the deck.

4   Security

Security results in this section basically state that: i) vetoed cards cannot be opened; and ii) the set of vetoed cards is the set of drawn cards. Proofs are given in the Appendix.

Lemma 1. *If $\mathcal{P}_i$ succeeds in performing $CP_{i,j} = CP(g, y, u_{i,j}, v_{i,j})$ at Step 1b of Protocol 2, then $(u_{i,j}, v_{i,j})$ will not veto the face-down card $c_{k,0,j}$ at Step 5b of Protocol 1.*

The Corollary below follows from the above lemma and from Step 1b of Protocol 2.

Corollary 1. *Let 52 be the total number of cards. Let ξ_i be the cards drawn by a player $\mathcal{P}_i$. Then the number of cards x_i not vetoed by $\mathcal{P}_i$ is such that $x_i \geq 52 - \xi_i$.*

Lemma 2. *If, at round k, $\mathcal{P}_i$ succeeds in performing $CP_{l,i,j} = CP(d_{l-1}, u_{i,j}, d_{l,j}, d_j)$, $l < k$, at Step 1c of Protocol 2, then $(u_{i,j}, v_{i,j})$ vetoes the face-down card $c_{k,0,j}$ at Step 5b of Protocol 1.*

Lemma 3. *A player can only veto a card she has drawn.*

Lemma 4. *The number of cards vetoed by a player is at least the number of cards drawn by the player.*

Theorem 1. *The set of cards vetoed by a player is the same as the set of cards drawn by the player.*

Theorem 2. *A vetoed card cannot be opened.*

5   Conclusions

We have presented a mental poker protocol which, to our best knowledge, is the first TTP-free proposal tolerating both intentional and accidental player dropout. Future research will explore applications of the protocol in this paper to secure multi-party computation problems other than mental poker.

References

1. A. Barnett and N. Smart, "Mental poker revisited", in *Proc. Cryptography and Coding*, LNCS 2898, pp. 370–383, December, 2003.
2. D. Chaum and T. Pedersen, "Wallet databases with observers" in *Advances in Cryptology – CRYPTO'92* , LNCS 740, pp. 89–105, 1992.
3. R.Cramer, I.Damgård and B.Schoenmakers, "Proofs of partial knowledge and simplified design of witness hiding protocols", in *Advances in Cryptology – CRYPTO'94* , LNCS 839, pp. 174–187, 1994.
4. C. Crépeau, "A secure poker protocol that minimizes the effect of player coalitions", in *Advances in Cryptology - CRYPTO'85*, LNCS 218, pp. 73-86, 1986.

5. C. Crépeau, "A zero-knowledge poker protocol that achieves confidentiality of the players' strategy or how to achieve an electronic poker face", in *Advances in Cryptology - CRYPTO'86*, LNCS 263, pp. 239-250, 1986.
6. Y. Desmedt and Y. Frankel, "Threshold cryptosystems", in *Advances in Cryptology – CRYPTO'89*, LNCS 335, pp. 307–315, 1990.
7. K. Kurosawa, Y. Katayama and W. Ogata, "Reshufflable and laziness tolerant mental card game protocol", *TIEICE: IEICE Transactions on Communications/Electronics/Information and Systems*, vol. E00-A, 1997.
8. T. P. Pedersen, "A Threshold cryptosystem without a trusted party", in *Advances in Cryptology - EUROCRYPT'91*, LNCS 547, pp. 522-526, 1992.
9. C. Schindelhauer, "A toolbox for mental card games", Medizinische Universität Lübeck, 1998. `http://citeseer.nj.nec.com/schindelhauer98toolbox.html`
10. W. H. Soo, A. Samsudin and A. Goh, "Efficient mental card shuffling via optimised arbitrary-sized based permutation network", in *Information Security*, LNCS 2433, pp. 446-458, 2002.
11. M. Stadler, "Public verifiable secret sharing", in *Advances in Cryptology - EUROCRYPT'96*, LNCS 1070, pp 190-199, 1996.
12. M. Yung, "Cryptoprotocols: subscription to a public key, the secret blocking and the multi-player mental poker game", in *Advances in Cryptology- CRYPTO'84*, LNCS 196, pp 439-453, 1985.

Appendix

Proof (Lemma 1). A face-down card $c_{k,0,j}$ is formed by a set of ciphertexts $(e_{k,1,j}, \cdots, e_{k,n,j})$. When a card is *not* vetoed in Protocol 2, a re-masking factor $(u_{i,j}, v_{i,j})$ is used which still allows recovery of the cleartexts from the card ciphertexts. To allow correct decryption, the re-masking factor must satisfy $\log_g u_{i,j} = \log_y v_{i,j}$. This is exactly the property proven by $CP(g, y, u_{i,j}, v_{i,j})$. $\square$

Proof (Lemma 2). Let us assume a card drawn in a dealing round l previous to the current round k (*i.e.* $l < k$). Let the face-up value of that card be $d_{k,j}$. $CP(d_{l-1}, u_{i,j}, d_{l,j}, d_{k,j})$ proves that:

$$\tau = \log_{d_{l-1,j}}(d_{l,j}) = \log_{u_{i,j}} d_{k,j} \tag{1}$$

From Equation 1 we have

$$u_{i,j} = (d_{k,j})^{\tau^{-1}} \tag{2}$$

Now if $(u_{i,j}, v_{i,j})$ does not actually veto $d_{k,j}$, the following holds:

$$\log_g(u_{i,j}) = \log_y(v_{i,j}) = \log_{g^\alpha}(v_{i,j}) = \frac{1}{\alpha} \log_g(v_{i,j})$$

The above is equivalent to

$$\alpha \cdot \log_g(u_{i,j}) = \log_g(v_{i,j}) \tag{3}$$

Combining Equations (2) and (3) yields

$$\log_g((d_{k,j})^{\tau^{-1}})^\alpha = \log_g v_{i,j} \tag{4}$$

If logarithms are removed, we get $v_{i,j} = ((d_{k,j})^{\tau^{-1}})^\alpha$. Thus, re-masking factor $(u_{i,j}, v_{i,j})$ will pass $CP(d_{l-1}, u_{i,j}, d_{l,j}, d_{k,j})$ without actually vetoing $d_{k,j}$ only if it has the form

$$(u_{i,j}, v_{i,j}) = (d_{k,j}^{\tau^{-1}}, ((d_{k,j})^{\tau^{-1}})^\alpha) \tag{5}$$

However, computing $v_{i,j}$ in Expression (5) without knowledge of α nor $(d_{k,j})^\alpha$ is as hard as the Diffie-Hellman problem. Obtaining α from the public key y is as hard as the discrete logarithm problem. Thus, passing the verification at Step 1c of Protocol 2 implies that card $d_{k,j}$ is actually vetoed.   □

Proof (Lemma 3). Assume that the current dealing round is round k; let $\{d_{1,j}, \cdots, d_{l,j}, \cdots, d_{k,j}\}$ be the expressions for the j-th card at each dealing round l, where $\tau_{l,j} = \log_{d_{l-1,j}} d_{l,j}$ for $1 \le l < k$. Assume now that $\mathcal{P}_i$ wants to construct a proof of veto for $d_{t,j}$, for some $t < k$. Then $\mathcal{P}_i$ needs to construct $(u_{i,j}, v_{i,j})$ so that she can perform $CP_{t,i,j} = CP(d_{t-1}, u_{i,j}, d_{t,j}, d_{k,j})$. This means $\log_{d_{t-1,j}} d_{t,j} = \log_{u_{i,j}} d_{k,j}$, which requires $u_{i,j} = d_{k,j}^{\tau_{t,j}^{-1}}$ so that $\mathcal{P}_i$ needs to know $\tau_{t,j} = \log_{d_{t-1,j}}(d_{t,j})$ But this logarithm is only known to $\mathcal{P}_i$ if she drew the card at round t (see Protocol 4).   □

Proof (Lemma 4). Let us assume that $\mathcal{P}_i$ has extracted ξ_i cards in previous dealing rounds. At Step 1c of Protocol 2 $\mathcal{P}_i$ uses the proof by Cramer et al. [3] for the ξ_i re-masking factors corresponding to the ξ_i drawn cards. According to Lemma 2, this guarantees that the ξ_i drawn cards are vetoed.   □

Proof (Theorem 1). If a re-masking factor $(u_{i,j}, v_{i,j})$ passes the proof that it is a vetoing factor for card j, then by Lemma 2 it vetoes card j. On the other hand, if a re-masking factor $(u_{i,j}, v_{i,j})$ passes the proof that it is a non-vetoing factor for card j, then by Lemma 1, it does not veto card j. Now, a re-masking factor $(u_{i,j}, v_{i,j})$ cannot at the same time veto and not veto card j. Thus, $(u_{i,j}, v_{i,j})$ cannot pass both the proof that it is a vetoing factor and the proof that it is a non-vetoing factor.

Let us assume that player $\mathcal{P}_i$ has drawn ξ_i cards. By Lemma 1, the number of cards not vetoed by $\mathcal{P}_i$ is at least $52 - \xi_i$. By Lemma 4, the number of cards vetoed by $\mathcal{P}_i$ is at least ξ_i. Therefore, $\mathcal{P}_i$ vetoes *exactly* ξ_i cards. Finally, by Lemma 3, a player can only veto cards she has drawn. Therefore the set of drawn cards is the same as the set of vetoed cards.   □

Proof (Theorem 2). Without loss of generality we assume $n = 2$ players $\mathcal{P}_1$ and $\mathcal{P}_2$. Assume that a round k card $d_{k,j}$ is computed from $d_{k-1,j}$ by raising a round $k - 1$ card $d_{k-1,j}$ to exponents m_1 and m_2, i.e. $d_{k,j} = d_{k-1,j}^{m_1+m_2}$. Note that m_i is secret and only known to $\mathcal{P}_i$, for $i = 1, 2$, whereas $d_{k,j}$ is public and obtained at Step 3 of Protocol 1.

At Step 5a of Protocol 1 the vetoing protocol is called to compute re-masking factors $g_{k,1,j} = (u_1, v_1)$ and $g_{k,2,j} = (u_2, v_2)$; at Step 5b these factors are applied to the encrypted card exponents $e_{k,j} = (e_{k,1,j}, e_{k,2,j})$ to veto card $d_{k,j}$. Now, (u_1, v_1) and (u_2, v_2) have been computed by the vetoing protocol (Protocol 2), so they satisfy

$$\log_g u_i \neq \log_y v_i \text{ for } i = 1, 2 \tag{6}$$

The computations for vetoing $d_{k,j}$ at Step 5b of Protocol 1 are:

$$e_{k,j} \cdot g_{k,j} = \{e_{k,1,j} \cdot g_{k,1,j}, e_{k,2,j} \cdot g_{k,2,j}\} = \{E_y(m_1) \cdot (u_1, v_1), E_y(m_2) \cdot (u_2, v_2)\}$$

$$= \{(g^{r_1} \cdot u_1, m_1 \cdot y^{r_1} \cdot v_1), (g^{r_2} \cdot u_2, m_2 \cdot y^{r_2} \cdot v_2)\} \tag{7}$$

Opening card $d_{k,j}$ means extracting the secret exponents m_1 and m_2 from the face-down card expression $e_{k,j} \cdot g_{k,j}$. From Expression (7), we have that

$$m_1 = \frac{m_1 \cdot y^{r_1} \cdot v_1}{(g^{r_1} \cdot u_1)^\alpha} \quad , \quad m_2 = \frac{m_2 \cdot y^{r_2} \cdot v_2}{(g^{r_2} \cdot u_2)^\alpha} \tag{8}$$

Some algebraic manipulation of Equations (8) leads to

$$\log_g u_1 = \log_y v_1 \quad , \quad \log_g u_2 = \log_y v_2 \tag{9}$$

Equations (9) contradict Equations (6). Thus, the card cannot be opened.   □

A Self-healing Mechanism for an Intrusion Tolerance System

Bumjoo Park[1], Kiejin Park[2], and Sungsoo Kim[3]

[1] Samsung Electronics, Suwon, Korea
bumjoo@samsung.com
[2] Division of Industrial & Information Systems Engineering,
Ajou University, Suwon, Korea
kiejin@ajou.ac.kr
[3] Graduate School of Information and Communication,
Ajou University, Suwon, Korea
sungsoo@ajou.ac.kr

Abstract. The dependability analysis of an ITS (Intrusion Tolerance System - a system that performs continuously minimal essential services even when the computer system is partially compromised because of intrusions) is essential for the design of the ITS. In this paper, we applied self-healing mechanism, the core technology of autonomic computing to analyze the dependability of the ITS. In other words, we described the state transition of the ITS composed of a primary server and a backup server utilizing two factors of self-healing mechanism (fault model and system response) and analyzed it using M/G/1 queuing technique. We also evaluated the availability of the ITS through simulation experiments.

1 Introduction

With the intrusion tolerance method, the network-based computer systems continuously provides minimal essential services even when the system is partially compromised because of the internal and/or external intrusions such as DoS (Denial of Service) [1]. Application of the ITS (Intrusion Tolerance System) method has been arousing a lot of interest recently. This phenomenon results from a limitation of the well-known security technologies such as firewall, vaccine and intrusion detection that have individual weaknesses causing them to be vulnerable to accidental or intentional attacks and faults that are not known to them. Additionally, when we summarize the characteristics of attacking tools recently discovered, they have characteristics such as being stealthy, distributed, automated and performing as an

[1] This work is supported by an Ajou University grant.
[2] This work is supported in part by the 21st Century Frontier Research and Development (R&D) Program "National Center of Excellence in Ubiquitous Computing and Network" from the Ministry of Information and Communication of Korea.
[3] This work is supported in part by the Ministry of Education & Human Resources Development of Korea (Brain Korea 21 Project supervised by Korea Research Foundation).

S. Katsikas, J. López, G. Pernul (Eds.): TrustBus 2005, LNCS 3592, pp. 41–49, 2005.

agent. Therefore, the problems are bigger than ever. The intrusion tolerance method is being actively studied as prevention and countermeasure against various malicious attacks to network-based computer systems.

Intrusion tolerance is different from intrusion detection. It does not guarantee that it will beat all the malicious attacks but it guarantees that it will provide services continuously by the ITS with dependability (reliability, availability, maintainability, safety, survivability etc.) even when some parts of the system are damaged because of the successful malicious attacks. In Europe, IST(Information Society Technologies) performed studies through the MAFTIA(Malicious-and Accidental-Fault Tolerance for Internet Applications) project to develop an ITS [2], and the USA is performing intrusion tolerance related projects such as HACQIT(Hierarchical Adaptive Control of Quality of service for Intrusion Tolerance), SITAR(Scalable Intrusion Tolerant Architecture), and ITUA(Intrusion Tolerance by Unpredictable Adaptation) through OASIS(Organically Assured and Survivable Information System) program of DARPA(Defense Advanced Research Projects Agency) [3,4,5].

On the other hand, a new approach using a self-healing mechanism is being proposed [6] where one of the four core technologies of autonomic computing is utilized to implement an ITS with dependability. Although the self-healing method includes various factors related to the dependability of the system just like fault tolerant methods, self-healing provides broader protection than the existing fault tolerant method, in that it can provide appropriate responses to the unexpected internal and external attacks together self-optimization, self-configuration, and self-protection [7].

2 Related Works

In [3], they adopted design diversity to enforce fault tolerant functions of the ITS and configured that the primary server and the backup server would have different OS and web server applications. However, as both servers were interoperating using the Hot-standby method (e.g., dynamic redundancy), both of them can be damaged from external attacks. Study [8] shows the state transition diagram to describe the dynamic abnormal behaviors of intrusion tolerance against external attacks. In this study, they performed the study on intrusion tolerance framework regarding how to model the vulnerabilities and risk factors of the system. In [9], they attempted quantitative performance analysis of several attacks such as DoS based on state transition diagrams. ITS frameworks can be divided into two, which is a layer based one and a replication based one. The layer-based structure may be applied to a single host. In this model, data integrity will be emphasized. The replication-based structure is to increase availability of the distributed computing environments. However, because of the increase of replications, secrecy would be threatened [10]. On the other hand, [11] shows examples applying self-healing technology to enhance the dependability of the distributed embedded system.

As the ITS is to respond to dynamic abnormal behaviors that are made by attackers according to system vulnerabilities or risk factors, it should be able to describe their state changes. In other words, we need to identify the attack type and present state of the ITS and express it into the state transition model in order to make a quantitative performance analysis of the transition process from the damaged to normal state. In this paper, we described the state transition of an ITS composed of a primary server and a backup server utilizing the two factors of the self-healing mechanism (fault model and system response) and analyzed it using M/G/1 queuing technique. We also evaluated the availability of the ITS through simulation experiments.

3 Intrusion Tolerance System Utilizing Self-healing Mechanism

Self-healing is the core technology of autonomic computing to enhance dependability of the system by minimizing malfunctions of the system through the detection, diagnosis and repair of the faults or errors arising from external attacks or internal system problems [12]. To implement self-healing technology as a system, there should be definitions of four factors such as fault model, system response, system completeness and design context [6].

The fault model defines the characteristics of faults that the system should tolerate and system response is a detailed definition regarding the fault detection, response to the fault and recovery strategy against external attacks. For example, DoS such as SYN Flood and Smurfing may cause the performance degradation of system resource by sending malicious requests to a certain server such as DNS(Domain Name Server). However, even in this situation, the 'Gracefully Degradation' concept that guarantees the essential services of the system should be included in elements in system response. On the other hand, system completeness is regarding the element should be implemented to overcome the structural imperfection of the system implementation in the real world. Design context shows self-healing element to secure homogeneity and linearity of the system to be implemented. To let the ITS have self-healing functions, a system state transition diagram was drawn with the detailed items related to fault model and system response among the four self-healing components described above.

Figure 1 shows the state transition of the Cold-standby ITS reflecting self-healing components. It also shows the detailed factors of the fault model responding to DoS, and elements corresponding to those factors such as fault detection, degradation, fault response and fault recovery. The followings are the assumptions that are applied for the intrusion tolerance system modeling.

- The switchover mechanism between the primary server and the backup server of ITS would follow the Cold-standby method.
- The sojourn time in each state of ITS would follow a general distribution.
- The system is properly working in the initial state and intrusion would be only possible in this state.
- After the switchover between the primary server and the backup server, the works will be transferred to the primary server when the backup server is only in normal state (0,1).

When vulnerability is exposed in the state of normal operation of both servers (1,1), the ITS will be transferred to (V,1). If the intrusion tolerance module defends all the vulnerability attacks through network traffic and IP address analysis, it will be recovered after a specified time to the initial state. However, if it does not happen, the primary server will be attacked (A,1) with the probability of $P_{(V,1)}$. When the attack state of the primary server continues for a certain time, the system damage will be

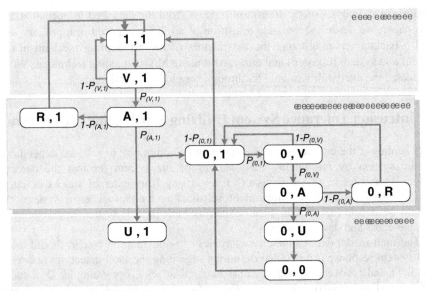

※ State (Primary server, Backup server)
※ V : Vurnerable state, A : Attack state, R : Rejuvenation state, U : Undetected state

Fig. 1. State transition diagram of intrusion tolerance system

accumulated. If the intrusion diagnosis module analyzes system CPU load and memory state and the meaningful performance degradation is detected at the probability of 1- $P_{(A,1)}$, it will transfer primary server into rejuvenation(restoration, reconfiguration or recovery) state (R,1). If it cannot diagnose the performance degradation, it is transferred to (U, 1), which means Undetected. Finally, the switchover takes place and the backup server will do the job on behalf of the primary server (0,1). To prevent the simultaneous down of both servers by external attacks, Cold-standby configuration was adopted. In this case, the time needed for switchover will be prolonged. The process from the state that the backup server plays the role of the primary server (0,1) to the state that the backup server is down (0,0) is same as the job transition from the primary server to the backup server in the initial state.

Generally, in Figure 1, the normal stage is the one where system degradation does not happen at all. The intrusion tolerance stage is the one where there is a certain level of damage but the system performs its essential services. Failure stage is the one where the primary server is not recovered and at the same time, the backup server cannot provide services regardless of the operation of the ITS.

To calculate the availability of the steady-state of the proposed ITS, the stochastic process of equation 1 was defined. Through SMP (Semi-Markov Process) analysis applying M/G/1 whose service time is general distribution, we calculated the steady-state probability in each state.

$$X(t) : t > 0$$

$$X_S = \{(1,1),(V,1),(A,1),(R,1),(U,1),(0,1),(0,V),(0,A),(0,R),(0,U),(0,0)\} \qquad (1)$$

As all the states shown in Figure 1 are attainable to each other, they are irreducible. Additionally, as they do not have a cycle and can return to a certain state they satisfy the ergodicity (aperiodic, recurrent, and nonnull) characteristics. Therefore, there is a probability in the steady-state of SMP for each state of ITS and each corresponding SMP can be induced by embedded DTMC (Discrete-time Markov Chain) using transition probability in each state [13].

If we define the mean sojourn times in each state of SMP as h_i's and define DTMC steady-state probability as d_i's, the steady-state probability in each state of SMP (π_i) can be calculated like equation 2 [14].

$$\pi_i = \frac{d_i h_i}{\sum_j d_j h_j}, \qquad i, j \in X_S \tag{2}$$

Whereas, steady-state probability of DTMC d_i's will have the following relationship as shown in equation 3 and equation 4.

$$\vec{d} = \vec{d} \cdot P \tag{3}$$

$$\sum_i d_i = 1 \quad i \in X_S \tag{4}$$

where, $\vec{d} = [d_{(1,1)}\ d_{(V,1)}\ d_{(A,1)}\ d_{(R,1)}\ d_{(U,1)}\ d_{(0,1)}\ d_{(0,V)}\ d_{(0,A)}\ d_{(0,R)}\ d_{(0,U)}\ d_{(0,0)}]$ and P is transition probability matrix of DTMC expressed by the transition probability in each state of X_S in Figure 1 ($p_{(i,j)}$). If we calculate the steady-state probability of DTMC from them, the following equation is made.

$$d_{(1,1)} = \frac{1 - P_{(0,1)}}{2(1 + P_{(V,1)})(1 - P_{(0,1)}) + P_{(V,1)}P_{(A,1)}(1 + P_{(0,1)} + 2P_{(0,1)}P_{(0,V)} + P_{(0,1)}P_{(0,V)}P_{(0,A)})}$$

$$d_{(V,1)} = d_{(1,1)}$$

$$d_{(A,1)} = d_{(V,1)}P_{(V,1)}$$

$$d_{(R,1)} = d_{(A,1)}(1 - P_{(0,1)})$$

$$d_{(U,1)} = d_{(A,1)}P_{(A,1)}$$

$$d_{(0,1)} = d_{(U,1)} + d_{(0,V)}(1 - P_{(0,V)}) + d_{(0,R)} + d_{(0,0)} \tag{5}$$

$$d_{(0,V)} = d_{(0,1)}P_{(0,1)}$$

$$d_{(0,A)} = d_{(0,V)}P_{(0,V)}$$

$$d_{(0,R)} = d_{(0,A)}(1 - P_{(0,A)})$$

$$d_{(0,U)} = d_{(0,A)}P_{(0,A)}$$

$$d_{(0,0)} = d_{(0,U)}$$

On the other hand, if we put the DTMC steady-state probability calculated in equation 5 into equation 2, we can have the steady-state probability of each state of SMP (π_i). The system availability in the steady-state is defined as equation 6, which is same as the exclusion of the probability of being in (U,1), (0,U) and (0,0) in each state of X_S in the state transition diagram.

$$Availability = 1 - (\pi_{(U,1)} + \pi_{(0,U)} + \pi_{(0,0)}) \tag{6}$$

4 Simulation Analysis and Availability Enhancement Methods

To analysis the SMP model for ITS, we need to set parameters for the transition probability and the mean sojourn time in each state. In this paper, simulations were

Table 1. Simulation Parameter

Input Variables	Set Value
Mean Sojourn Time	$h_{(1,1)} = 0.5,\ h_{(V,1)} = 1/3,\ h_{(A,1)} = 0.25,\ h_{(U,1)} = 0.5,\ h_{(R,1)} = 0.2,\ h_{(0,1)} = 0.5$ $h_{(0,V)} = 1/3,\ h_{(0,A)} = 0.25,\ h_{(0,R)} = 0.2,\ h_{(0,U)} = 0.5,\ h_{(0,0)} = 0.5$
Transition Probability	Among 5 transition probabilities ($p_{(V,1)},\ p_{(A,1)},\ p_{(0,1)},\ p_{(0,V)},\ p_{(0,A)}$), we fixed 3 values and changed 2 values (from 0 to 1) (eg . : $P_{(A,1)} = P_{(0,V)} = P_{(0,A)} = 0.5,\ \ 0 < p_{(V,1)}, p_{(0,1)} < 1$)

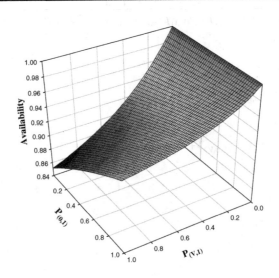

Fig. 2. *Availability analysis according to the changes in $P_{(V,1)}$ and $P_{(0,1)}$*

made based on the values shown in Table 1 [15,16]. As the mean sojourn time in each state does not follow a specific distribution, the values are only meaningful as relative difference. To analyze the independent influences of each transition probability at the 5 points shown in the state transition diagram, we set the initial transition probabilities with the same value, which is 0.5.

Figure 2 shows the system availability fluctuation trend according to the changes in probability that the primary server is attacked because of non-detection of vulnerability ($P_{(V,1)}$) and the probability that the backup server is exposed to the vulnerability ($P_{(0,1)}$), in order to identify the influences of initial state responding competencies of the ITS on the availability in the environments with external malicious attacks.

When the Cold-standby ITS proposed in Figure 1 is configured, the availability is increased when the primary and backup server can detect abnormal behaviors of the system in the initial state before they are exposed to the attacks or vulnerable environments. When $P_{(V,1)}$ and $P_{(0,1)}$ are getting bigger (In other words, detection capabilities in initial state are degraded), the availability of the system is reduced dramatically. However, if $P_{(V,1)}$ is greater than 0.5 and $P_{(0,1)}$ gets bigger, the availability will be increased. It is because the bigger $P_{(V,1)}$ is, the bigger the probability that the primary server fails (U,1) will be. Therefore, even when the switchover is made from the primary server to the backup server, the continued service by the backup server through intrusion tolerance in the state of (0,V) and (0,A) rather than the service through the immediate recovery of the primary server will be better, because it will reduce the probability to make the system be in the state of (U,1).

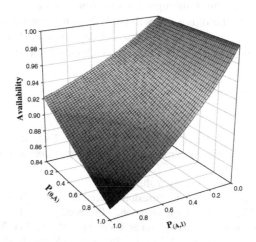

Fig. 3. *Availability analysis according to the changes in $P_{(A,1)}$ and $P_{(0,A)}$*

Figure 3 shows the changes in availability according to the changes of the attack success probability to the primary server, $P_{(A,1)}$ and to the backup server, $P_{(0,A)}$ in order to judge the system response capabilities in the situations exposed to attacks. In case of $P_{(A,1)}$ is zero regardless of the transition probability related to detection capabilities of abnormal behavior in the initial state($P_{(V,1)}$ and $P_{(0,1)}$), we can see from the graph that the availability is ideal (1.0). In other words, if we can detect meaningful performance degradation immediately in initial state through diagnosis functions of the ITS in (A,1) and (0,A) where primary-backup servers are exposed to attacks, we can guarantee availability by returning the system to the initial state through the switchover to rejuvenation state. However, if $P_{(A,1)}$ and $P_{(0,A)}$ approach 1, the probabilities that the system will be put into no service state which are (U,1),(0,U) and (0,0) and the availability will be reduced.

On the other hand, in Figure 2 and Figure 3, when $P_{(A,1)}$ and $P_{(0,A)}$ are 1, the availability is nearly the same as that in the state where $P_{(V,1)}$ and $P_{(0,1)}$ have the worst values in the system. It is because even though the system does not detect abnormal behavior in the initial state, the structure of the Cold-standby ITS reduces the probability of no service or system down thanks to switchover, recovery and rejuvenation in the environments with external malicious attacks and thereby the availability will not be reduced any more.

5   Conclusion

In this paper, it was proposed to graft the self-healing mechanism, the core technology of autonomic computing in order to analyze the dependability of the ITS. We defined 11 states of a Cold-standby ITS composed of a primary server and a backup server and analyzed system availability by calculating DTMC steady-state probability and SMP steady-state probability through the transition probability and the mean sojourn time of each state. In the future, we will study how to improve system dependability through considering system completeness and design context in addition to the two factors of the self-healing mechanism that have already been considered in this paper.

References

[1] F. Wang, R. Uppalli, and C. Killian, "Analysis of   Techniques for Building Intrusion Tolerant Server Systems," Proceedings of Military Communications Conference, pp. 729-734, Oct. 2003.

[2] http://www.laas.research.ec.org/maftia/

[3] J. Reynolds, et. al., "On-line Intrusion Detection Attack Prevention Using Diversity Generate-and-Test, and   Generalization," Proceedings of the 36th Annual Hawaii International Conferences on System Sciences, pp. 335-342, Jan. 2003.

[4] F. Wang, et. al., "SITAR : A Scalable Intrusion-Tolerant Architecture for Distributed Services," Proceedings of the Foundations of Intrusion Tolerant Systems, pp. 359-367, 2003.

[5] T. Courtney, et. al., "Providing Intrusion Tolerance with ITUA," Proceedings of the International Conference on Dependable Systems & Networks, pp. C-5-1 - C-5-3, June 2002.

[6] P. Koopman, "Elements of the Self-Healing System Problem Space," Workshop on Architecting Dependable Systems, pp. 31-36, May 2003.

[7] D. Chess, C. Palmer, and S. White, "Security in an Autonomic Computing Environment," IBM Systems Journal, Vol. 42, No.1, pp. 107-118, 2003.

[8] K. Goseva-Popstojanova, et. al., "Characterizing Intrusion Tolerant Systems using a State Transition Model," DARPA Information Survivability Conference and exhibition, Vol 2, pp. 211-221, June 2001.

[9] D. Wang, B. Madan, and K. Trivedi, "Security Analysis of SITAR Intrusion Tolerance System," Proceedings of the ACM Workshop on Survivable and Self-Regenerative Systems, pp. 23-32, Oct. 2003.

[10] G. Kim, M. Choi, and K. Lee, "Classification of the Intrusion Tolerant Systems and Integrated Framework for Survivability Enhancement," The Korea Information Processing Society Transactions, Vol. 10C, No. 3, pp.295-304, 2003.

[11] C. Shelton, P. Koopman, and W. Nace, "A Framework for Scalable Analysis and Design of System-Wide Graceful degradation in distributed Embedded Systems, " Eighth IEEE International Workshop on Object-oriented Real-time Dependable Systems, pp.156-163, Jan. 2003.

[12] J. Kephart, and D. Chess, "The Vision of Autonomic Computing," IEEE Computer, Vol. 36, No. 2, pp. 41-50, 2003.

[13] L. Kleinrock, Queueing Systems: Volume 1 Theory, John Wiley & Sons, pp. 417, 1975.

[14] K. Trivedi, Probability and Statistics with Reliability Queueing and Computer Science Applications, John Wiley & Sons, Inc., pp. 472, 2002.

[15] B. Madan, et. al., "Modeling and Quantification of Security Attributes of Software Systems," International Conference on Dependable Systems and Networks, pp. 505-514, June 2002.

[16] B. Madan, et. al., "A method for modeling and quantifying the security attributes of intrusion tolerant systems," Performance Evaluation, Vol. 56, Issues 1-4, pp. 167-186, 2004.

Protecting Online Rating Systems from Unfair Ratings

Jianshu Weng, Chunyan Miao, and Angela Goh

School of Computer Engineering, NTU
{weng0004, ASCYMiao, ASESGoh}@ntu.edu.sg

Abstract. Online rating systems have been widely adopted by online trading communities to ban "bad" service providers and prompt them to provide "good" services. However, the performance of the online rating systems is easily compromised by various unfair ratings, e.g. balloting, badmouthing, and complementary unfair ratings. How to mitigate the influence of the unfair ratings remains an important issue in online rating systems. In this paper, we propose a novel entropy-based method to measure the rating quality as well as to screen the unfair ratings. Experimental results show that the proposed method is both effective and practical in alleviating the influence of different types of unfair ratings.

1 Introduction

With the development of Internet, a large number of people carry out transactions through online trading communities such as eBay. Nevertheless, people still regard online trading as a risk since it is hard to determine whether to trust various online sellers before the transactions [1]. Therefore, reputation mechanisms have been introduced into online trading communities to establish trust between sellers and buyers [2]. One way to establish such mechanism is the online rating systems [2]. The main idea of online rating systems is to allow each buyer give a rating for the seller after each transaction. The existing ratings of a particular seller will then be used by the potential buyers to derive the seller's reputation score, which serves as an indicator whether the seller will provide "good" service or not in future transactions.

Online rating systems have already been adopted by many online trading communities, e.g. eBay [1], and have been credited to their success. Despite the wide adoption of online rating systems, there are still some open issues, especially the issue of *unfair ratings*. That is, buyers might give ratings which are different from their real experiences, e.g. although seller provides "good" service in one transaction, buyer gives rating as "bad", and vice verse. The performance of online rating systems would easily be compromised by unfair ratings [2].

Finding effective ways to guard against unfair ratings has attracted many research efforts in recent years, e.g. [3,4,5]. Most of the existing methods depend on assumptions that sellers' behaviors (as well as buyers' ratings) follow a particular distribution, which hinders their general application to other settings,

S. Katsikas, J. López, G. Pernul (Eds.): TrustBus 2005, LNCS 3592, pp. 50–59, 2005.

e.g. Beta distribution [4,5]. In this paper, we propose an entropy-based method to tackle the issue of unfair ratings in online rating systems. An entropy-based metric is designed to measure the rating quality based on which unfair ratings can be further screened. Unlike existing methods, the proposed entropy-based method is distribution-free. It does not make any assumption regarding the distribution of the ratings. In our current research, the proposed method is explored in context of *Bayesian* rating system. Nevertheless, the proposed method is not limited to *Bayesian* rating system. It can be easily extended to other types of rating systems due to its distribution-independent nature.

The remainder of this paper is organized as follows. A review of related work is given in Section 2. Section 3 gives a brief review of the *Bayesian* rating system. Section 4 presents the proposed method to screen unfair ratings in the context of *Bayesian* rating system. The effectiveness of the proposed method has been shown through experimental results in Section 5. Finally, Section 6 concludes the paper with an overview of future work.

2   Related Work

Online rating systems have played an important role in many online trading communities, e.g. eBay [1]. The presence of unfair ratings is a threat to online rating systems [2]. Some methods have been proposed to address this issue.

Whitby et al. [4] propose to screen ratings reported by others (i.e. testimonies) in Bayesian rating system by determining whether a testimony is outside the $q\%$ quantile and $(1 - q)\%$ quantile of the majority opinion. If it is, the testimony is considered as an unfair rating and will be excluded. Then the majority opinion will be calculated again with the remaining testimonies. This process is carried out iteratively until no other testimony can be excluded. One major limitation of this method is that it does not scale well with the increase in the number of testimonies due to its iterative nature. Moreover, this work depends on an assumption that the ratings follow a Beta distribution. However, it is not easy to justify this assumption especially in the scenarios where few observations are available in the ratings (either local rating or testimonies).

Buchegger and Boudec [5] propose a method to address the issue of unfair ratings in the context of mobile ad-hoc network. This method has two main limitations. First, this method does not consider the majority opinions when screening testimonies. Instead, testimonies that are different from a node's own experience (i.e. local rating) are rejected. This may not be true in general, since one single node's experience might not reflect the target node's behavior. Secondly, it is also based on an assumption that nodes' behavior follows a Beta distribution.

Garg et al. [6] developed a reputation system in context of structured P2P network. After one peer interacts with the target peer, it rates the target peer and sends the rating to all the M score managers who are responsible for calculating and answering other peers' query of the target node's reputation score. The M score managers then aggregate ratings from all peers who have report testimonies on the target peer and calculate the target peer's reputation score. When calculating the reputation score, each testimony is given a weight based on the credibility of the peer who reports the rating. The credibility is determined based on the difference between this peer's testimony and score managers' aggregated rating (i.e. majority opinion). The limitation of this work is that it also assumes that peers' behaviors in the reputation system follow a normal distribution.

In contrast, the proposed method in this paper applies an entropy-based metric to screen the testimonies. It does not make any assumption regarding the distribution of ratings. The proposed method also takes the majority opinion into account to make the screening more accurate. And more desirable, it scales linearly with the increase in the number of available testimonies.

3   *Bayesian* Rating System

In our current research, we explore an entropy-based method for filtering unfair ratings in the context of Bayesian rating systems. Before presenting the proposed method, this section reviews Bayesian rating systems. We reiterate that the proposed method is not limited to Bayesian rating system. It can be easily extended to other types of rating systems due to its distribution-independent nature.

There are primarily two components in *Bayesian* rating system [7]: one for collecting seller's behaviors in the past transactions, another for predicting seller's behaviors in the future transactions.

3.1   Collecting Seller's Past Behaviors

With Bayesian rating systems, buyers give feedbacks of the seller's behavior after a transaction is cleared. Buyer assigns a positive rating of "1" to the seller if he thinks that the seller provided a "good" service; otherwise it assigns a negative rating of "0". Buyer B's rating for seller S in transaction T can be presented in vector notion as:

$$r_{BS}^T = \begin{bmatrix} p \\ n \end{bmatrix}, \quad \text{where } \begin{bmatrix} p \\ n \end{bmatrix} = \begin{bmatrix} 1 \\ 0 \end{bmatrix} \text{ or } \begin{bmatrix} 0 \\ 1 \end{bmatrix} \quad (1)$$

Instead of maintaining ratings of all the past transactions, a buyer usually only maintains a summary of ratings for the past transactions within a window of size W. This is reasonable since a seller's behavior is usually changing from one transaction to another. Moreover, buyers generally choose to "care" more about a seller's recent behavior and "forget" its past behavior. By introducing a forgetting factor (λ), which controls the rate that the seller's old behaviors are forgotten, the summary of ratings within the window can be represented in vector notion as:

$$r_{BS} = \begin{bmatrix} pf \\ nf \end{bmatrix} = \sum_{T=T_c-W+1}^{T_c} \lambda^{T_c-T} \begin{bmatrix} p \\ n \end{bmatrix}, \quad (T_c - T) \leq W \quad (2)$$

where W is the window size, T_c is the latest transaction, and T is the transaction after which rating was collected, and r_{BS} is termed as the B's *local rating* of S.

3.2   Predicting Seller's Behaviors

In *Bayesian* rating system, it is assumed that seller's behavior (and buyer's rating as well) follows a Beta distribution. The probability density function (PDF) of Beta distribution is given by:

$$ beta(Pr|\alpha, \beta) = \frac{1}{B(\alpha, \beta)} Pr^{\alpha-1}(1 - Pr)^{\beta-1}; \quad 0 < Pr < 1, \alpha \geq 1, \beta \geq 1 \quad (3) $$

where $B(\alpha, \beta)$ is the beta function. This PDF expresses the probability (Pr) that a seller will provide "good" services in future transactions. Then buyers predict the probability that the seller will provide "good" service in the next transaction as the expectation value of the Beta distribution, which is given by:

$$ E(Pr) = \frac{\alpha}{\alpha + \beta}, \quad \alpha = pf + 1, \quad \beta = nf + 1 \quad (4) $$

When a buyer has not transacted with a particular seller before, $pf = nf = 0$, α and β are set to be 1 correspondingly, which causes $E(Pr) = 0.5$. It is interpreted that the seller has equal probabilities of providing "good" or "bad" service. Then with the update of pf and nf after each transaction, the buyer also updates its prediction of the seller's behavior.

3.3   Problems Caused by Unfair Ratings

When making prediction of a seller's behavior, a buyer will request and aggregate ratings from other buyers who have transacted with the same seller before [7,4]. The initiating buyer B, who is predicting the seller's behavior, will send out a requesting message first. Upon receiving the requesting message from the initiating buyer, the answering buyers will simply reply as testimonies their local ratings of the target seller (if any)[1]. The initiating buyer then updates α and β by aggregating all the returned testimonies with its local rating (if any). That is:

$$ \alpha = 1 + pf_B + \sum_{X \in C} pf_X, \quad \beta = 1 + nf_B + \sum_{X \in C} nf_X \quad (5) $$

where pf_B and nf_B denote the number of positive and negative ratings in B's local rating respectively, C denotes the set of the answering buyers, and pf_X, nf_X refer to the numbers of positive and negative ratings in the testimony returned by a particular buyer X in the set C. Then the initiating buyer updates its prediction of the seller's behavior using Eq. (4).

---

[1] A good testimony propagation algorithm is expected to scale with the size of the community [2]. Although it is also a very important issue, it is not the focus of this paper. Instead, we assume in this paper that the initiating buyer can always receive the testimonies they need.

However, if the initiating buyer aggregates all returned testimonies blindly, the answering buyers can easily diverge the initiating buyer's predictions by reporting unfair ratings that are different from their real experiences. For example, buyer B is now evaluating whether to buy from a potential seller S. B requests testimonies from other buyers who have interacted with S before. S colludes with some buyers, who report unfairly higher ratings than the real quality of services that S delivered. Those unfair positive ratings will increase the value of α and decrease the value of β in Eq. (5), which immediately leads to an increase in B's predicted probability that S will provide "good" service. As this simple example shows, the performance of online rating systems would easily be compromised by the presence of *unfair ratings* [4,8]. Making the rating systems robust to avoid or mitigate the influence of unfair ratings is a fundamental issue in building online rating systems [4,8].

4   Entropy-Based Ratings Screening

Motivated by the problems caused by unfair ratings in current online rating system, in this paper, we propose an entropy-based metric to measure the quality of the ratings (both local rating and testimonies), based on which to screen ratings and to mitigate the influence of unfair ratings. The basic idea of the proposed method is that: if, compared with the quality of the already-aggregated testimonies (i.e. majority opinion), there is a significant quality improvement or downgrade in the testimony from a particular buyer, the testimony is away from the majority opinion. Thus it can be considered as a possible unfair rating.

Entropy, a measure of *uncertainty* contained in information [9], is employed as the basis of the rating quality metric. The entropy of a variable V can be calculated as: $H(V) = -\sum Pr(v)\log(Pr(v))$, where v is a possible value of variable V, and $Pr(v)$ is the corresponding probability of V taking the value v.

Since rating in *Bayesian* rating system is basically binary, it can be seen as a discrete variable taking two possible values. Consequently, uncertainty (of seller's behavior in future transactions) observed in buyer B's rating can be measured as: $H(r_B) = -Pr_p\log(Pr_p) - Pr_n\log(Pr_n)$. Here Pr_p and Pr_n denote the probabilities of positive ratings and negative ratings observed in the window of past W transactions, which are given by:

$$Pr_p = \frac{\alpha}{\alpha + \beta}, \quad Pr_n = \frac{\beta}{\alpha + \beta}. \tag{6}$$

Here α and β share the same meanings as in Eq. (4).

The maximum uncertainty $H_{max}(r_B)$ occurs when there are identical probabilities of positive and negative rating in the past W transactions [9]. In this case $H_{max}(r_B) = 1$. Minimum uncertainty $H_{min}(r_B)$ appears when only positive (or negative) ratings are observed in all the past W transactions.

Now, we can measure the **Quality** of the rating as:

$$Q(r_B) = 1 - \frac{H(r_B) - H_{min}(r_B)}{H_{max}(r_B) - H_{min}(r_B)} = \frac{H_{max}(r_B) - H(r_B)}{H_{max}(r_B) - H_{min}(r_B)} \tag{7}$$

Quality of testimonies from other buyers can be measured likewise. Then buyer B aggregates testimony from X if:

$$|Q(r_X) - Q(r)| <= \varepsilon$$

where $Q(r_X)$ is the quality of the testimony reported by X, $Q(r)$ is the quality of buyer B's current aggregated rating $(Q(r) = Q(r_B)$ initially). ε is a screening threshold (usually $\varepsilon \in [0,1]$), which controls the sensitivity to the presence of unfair ratings. With a larger ε, the screening is less sensitive to unfair testimonies, whereas with a smaller ε, the screening is more sensitive. Both cases may lead to divergent prediction. A balanced selection of ε is necessary to make the screening work effectively. Experimental results show that $\varepsilon \in [0.35, 0.45]$ generally shows a good balance (See Section 5.4).

The proposed screening method can be outlined as Algorithm 1:

Algorithm 1. Entropy-based rating screening algorithm

B denotes the buyer initiating the testimony aggregation
C denotes the set of buyers whose testimonies are requested
X denotes a particular buyer in the set C
1: measure *Quality* of buyer B's local rating $Q(r_B)$ using Eq. (7)
2: $Q(r) = Q(r_B)$
3: **for all** X in C **do**
4:    measure the *Quality* of the testimony $Q(r_X)$ reported by X using Eq. (7)
5:    **if** $|Q(r_X) - Q(r)| <= \varepsilon$ **then**
6:       aggregate X's testimony by updating α and β using Eq. (5) accordingly, and then update the quality of the aggregated rating $Q(r)$
7:    **else**
8:       discard X's testimony
9:    **end if**
10: **end for**

---

5   Experimental Results

5.1   Setup

We simulate a trading community, in which there is one seller[2] and 100 buyers. There are a total of 1000 transactions in each round of simulation. The seller's behavior is mainly controlled by its loyalty, which denotes its willingness to provide "good" services. The seller may change its loyalty from one transaction to another due to many reasons, e.g. the fluctuation of the profit by providing services. In each round of simulation, seller's initial loyalty is set to be 0.9. We simulate three styles of changes of the seller's loyalty in the course of each simulation: increases and decreases from the one in previous transaction, and remains same as the one in previous transaction. The ratios of different styles of changes are chosen to be 1/3 respectively. The window size of the past transactions is set

---

[2] The goal of the experiment is to investigate whether *Bayesian* rating system can predict seller's behaviors truly even with presence of unfair ratings. *Bayesian* rating system is a distributed rating system [2], in which each seller (and buyer) is treated equally. One seller is sufficient to meet our goal.

to 50 (i.e. W=50 in Eq. (2)). And the forgetting factor is set to 0.9 (i.e. $\lambda = 0.9$ in Eq. (2)). P_{unfair} is set to 70%.

Before each transaction, buyer will predict the probability that the seller will provide "good" service based on other buyers' testimonies and its local rating (if any). As the unfair ratings usually lead to divergent prediction of the seller's behaviors, we can measure the effectiveness of the proposed method by measuring how close it is between the predicted probability and the seller's loyalty for each transaction. We can measure the "closeness" as the *Mean Squared Error* (MSE) between the predicted probabilities and seller's loyalties averaged over all the 1000 transactions. Ideally $MSE = 0$, which means the predicted probabilities are always equal to the seller's loyalties in all transactions.

5.2   Types of Unfair Ratings

There are three types of unfair ratings studied in the experiments [8,10]:

- **Ballot-stuffing**. A buyer, with a probability P_{unfair}, reports that seller provides "good" service regardless of its real experience.
- **Badmouthing**. A buyer, with a probability P_{unfair}, reports that seller provides "bad" service regardless of its real experience.
- **Complementary**. A more general type of unfair rating is the Complementary unfair rating. That is, a buyer, with a probability P_{unfair}, reports a rating opposite to the real experience.

Before proceeding, we demonstrate the influence of unfair ratings first. Fig. 1(a) shows the seller's loyalties and predicted probabilities by one buyer[3] over 1000 transactions. It can be seen that *Bayesian* rating system predicts the seller's behaviors quite close to the seller's loyalties without the presence of unfair ratings. Fig. 1(b) shows seller's loyalties and predicted probabilities over the 1000 transactions with presence of *badmouthing* unfair rating. It can be observed that the predicted probabilities now deviate from seller's loyalties.

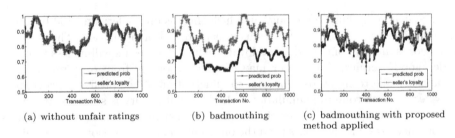

(a) without unfair ratings   (b) badmouthing   (c) badmouthing with proposed method applied

Fig. 1. Influence of unfair ratings and effectiveness of ratings screening

---

[3] Since *Bayesian* rating system is a distributed rating system, each buyer maintains a local view of the seller's behaviors, one buyer's prediction is enough for studying the effectiveness of the proposed method.

Table 1. Comparison of MSEs

Types of unfair rating	proposed method not applied	proposed method applied
ballot-stuffing	$1.7883 * 10^{-3}$	$1.7816 * 10^{-3}$
badmouthing	$22.4487 * 10^{-3}$	$4.6240 * 10^{-3}$
complementary	$4.9041 * 10^{-3}$	$1.3683 * 10^{-3}$

5.3 Effectiveness of the Proposed Method

Fig. 1(c) shows the seller's loyalties and the predicted probabilities in the presence of *badmouthing* with the proposed screening method applied. Compared with Fig. 1(b), the predicted probabilities follow seller's loyalties more closely. MSEs in scenarios with and without the proposed screening method applied are listed in Table 1.

Compared with corresponding scenarios without proposed method applied, the proposed method manages to reduce the MSEs by 0.4%, 79.4%, and 72.1% in scenarios with the presence of ballot-stuffing, badmouthing, complementary unfair ratings respectively. The relatively lower effectiveness in the presence of ballot-stuffing is due to the reason that unfair ratings (i.e. 1 in this case) are already quite close to the seller's loyalties (around 0.9 in the simulation). The proposed method's effectiveness in mitigating the influence of the unfair ratings is thus justified.

Experiments are also conducted to study the proposed screening method's effectiveness in the presence of various ratios of unfair ratings. MSEs in different scenarios are plotted in Fig. 2(a)-2(c). With the increase of unfair rating ratio, the predicted probabilities deviate from seller's loyalties more significantly in scenarios both *with* and *without* the proposed method applied. However, with the proposed method applied, improvement over the scenarios without the pro-

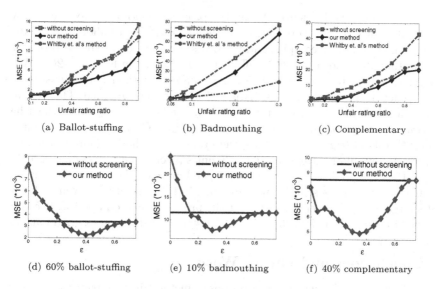

(a) Ballot-stuffing   (b) Badmouthing   (c) Complementary

(d) 60% ballot-stuffing   (e) 10% badmouthing   (f) 40% complementary

Fig. 2. Change of MSE w.r.t. different unfair rating ratios and ε

posed method applied is still observable. It can be observed from Fig. 2(a)-2(c) that the proposed method mitigates the influence of the unfair ratings most effectively in scenarios with less than 60% ballot-stuffing, 10% badmouthing, and 40% complementary respectively.

We also compare the performance of the proposed screening method against the one proposed by Whitby et al. in [4]. We implement their method with q value instantiated as 0.01 since $q = 0.01$ is a good balance as reported in [4]. MSEs by applying their method are also plotted in Fig. 2(a)-2(c). It can be observed that our method outperforms Whitby et al.'s method in the presence of both ballot-stuffing and complementary unfair ratings. However, our method is not as effective as Whitby et al.'s method in the presence of badmouthing unfair ratings. This is because in our experiments, the seller's loyalties are around 0.9, which means seller would provide "good" service 90% of all the transactions. However high ratio of badmouthing might make the Pr_p and Pr_n in Eq. (6) swap their values, which makes the quality of the unfair ratings same as the honest ones. For example, the majority opinion reports that the seller provides "good" service in 8 out of 10 transactions, while an unfair rating reports the seller provides "bad" service in 8 out of 10 transactions. Qualities of both the majority opinion and the unfair rating are $-0.8\log(0.8) - 0.2\log(0.2)$. In this case, our method becomes ineffective in screening unfair ratings. However, the proposed method is much faster than Whitby et al.'s method. It takes about 0.0217 second to screen 100 testimonies for one transaction by average. In contrast, Whitby et al.'s method takes about 1.4577 seconds. Moreover, their method does not scale well with the increase in the number of testimonies due to its iterative nature, whereas the proposed method scales linearly with the increase in the number of available testimonies.

5.4 Effectiveness with Different Screening Threshold ε

In order to study the influence of ε on the proposed method's effectiveness, we choose different screening thresholds ε in scenarios with 60% ballot-stuffing, 10% badmouthing, and 40% complementary. MSEs between the predicted probabilities and the seller's loyalties with different ε are plotted in Fig. 2(d)-2(f). With a larger threshold (e.g. $\varepsilon = 0.6, 0.65$), the proposed method is less sensitive to the presence of the unfair ratings. Larger MSEs are thus observed. The extreme of this case is that all testimonies are not discarded (e.g. $\varepsilon \geq 0.7$), which has the same effect as without proposed method applied. On the other hand, with a smaller threshold (e.g. $\varepsilon = 0.25, 0.3$), the proposed method is more sensitive to the presence of unfair ratings, more testimonies (even some honest ones) are discarded, thus the predicted probabilities depend more on the buyer's local rating and may not reflect the seller's loyalties truly. In this case, it may even make the MSEs larger than the scenarios without the proposed method applied. It can be observed from Fig. 2(d)-2(f) that $\varepsilon \in [0.35, 0.45]$ generally shows a good balance.

6 Conclusions and Future Work

To the best of our knowledge, the proposed method in this paper is the first one to tackle the issue of unfair ratings from a perspective of entropy. It is distribution-independent, and it scales linearly with the increase in the number of testimonies. Our experimental results showed that it manages to mitigate the influence of different types of unfair ratings. However, as there is no unified platform and benchmark available, a comprehensive comparison of the proposed method between other existing methods is not practical for the time being. With the planned release of "Trust Competition Testbed[4]" in July 2005, a more detailed comparison is planned as future work.

The proposed method is not effective enough in some scenarios, e.g. high loyalty with large ratios of badmouthing unfair ratings as shown by the experimental results. We plan to improve the proposed method's performance in those scenarios in our future work. The rationale of the proposed method is that sellers provide indiscriminate services to all buyers. However, there are also cases that sellers provide "good" service to everyone except a few specific buyers that they do not "like". In those cases, even the majority opinion might not reflect the seller's real behavior, and the proposed method would become ineffective. Effectiveness of the proposed method in those cases is to be further investigated.

References

1. Resnick, P., Zeckhauser, R.: Trust among strangers in internet transactions: Empirical analysis of ebay's reputation system. In Baye, M.R., ed.: The Economics of the Internet and E-commerce. Volume 11 of Advances in Applied Microeconomics. Elsevier (2002) 127–157
2. Jøsang, A., Ismail, R., Boyd, C.: A survey of trust and reputation systems for online service provision. Decision Support System **To appear** (2005)
3. Ekström, M.A., Björnsson, H.C.: A rating system for AEC e-bidding that accounts for rater credibility. In: Proceedings of 10th Joint W055 - W065 International Symposium on Construction Innovation and Global Competitiveness (CIB W055, W065). (2000)
4. Whitby, A., Jøsang, A., Indulska, J.: Filtering out unfair ratings in bayesian reputation systems. In: Proceedings of the Workshop on Trust in Agent Societies, at the 3rd International Joint Conference on Autonomous Agents and Multi Agent Systems (AAMAS2004). (2004)
5. Buchegger, S., Boudec, J.Y.L.: A robust reputation system for mobile ad-hoc networks. Technical Report IC/2003/50, EPFL-IC-LCA (2003)
6. Garg, A., Battiti, R., Costanzi, G.: Dynamic self-management of autonomic systems: The reputation, quality and credibility (RQC) scheme. (2004)
7. Jøsang, A., Ismail, R.: The beta reputation system. In: Proceedings of the 15th Bled Conference on Electronic Commerce. (2002)
8. Dellarocas, C.: Immunizing online reputation reporting systems against unfair ratings and discriminatory behavior. In: Proceedings of the 2nd ACM conference on Electronic commerce, ACM Press (2000) 150–157
9. Cover, T.M., Thomas, J.A.: Elements of Information Theory. Wisley (1991)
10. Yu, B., Singh, M.P., Sycara, K.: Developing trust in large-scale peer-to-peer systems. In: Proceedings of 1st IEEE Symposium on Multi-Agent Security and Survivability. (2004)

---

[4] http://www.lips.utexas.edu/ kfullam/competition/

Anonymous Payment in a Fair E-commerce Protocol with Verifiable TTP

M. Magdalena Payeras-Capellà, Josep Lluís Ferrer-Gomila,
and Llorenç Huguet-Rotger

Universitat de les Illes Balears, C. Valldemossa, Km. 7.5, 07122,
Palma de Mallorca, Spain
mpayeras@uib.es

Abstract. An electronic purchase represents an exchange between money and a digital product or the receipt of a physical product. Atomicity is a desired feature for electronic payment systems because it allows fair purchases. We present a fair payment protocol useful in electronic purchases involving electronic coins. The protocol is fair, asynchronous and efficient, and can be used with existing payment systems. Moreover we have evaluated the role of the TTP in the fair exchange protocol, showing that the incorrect behavior of the TTP can be demonstrated in all cases, so the TTP is verifiable.

Keywords: Atomicity, Verifiability, Fair exchange, Electronic coins, Anonymity.

1 Introduction

Some electronic services require the atomic exchange of elements between two or more users. The fair exchange of values always provides a fair deal to all users. Thanks to fairness, at the end of the execution of an exchange, all parties have the element they wanted to obtain. Instead, if the execution has not been successful, no party has the desired element.

Among the electronic applications that require a fair exchange of information we can find electronic contract signing, certified electronic mail and payment in exchange for a receipt (or in the event of purchase of a digital product, the exchange for a product).

An electronic purchase represents the exchange of a payment for a receipt or for a product in which the payment can be carried out by means of different types of systems. One of them is electronic cash.

In the purchase of a tangible product, a receipt can be used as a proof of the payment to demonstrate, without possible repudiation on the part of the merchant, that the user has carried out the payment. When the payment is carried out in the purchase of a digital product, the exchange of the money for the product can be carried out directly, but the need of fairness remains in the exchange, since the buyer doesn't want to take a risk paying without the security that he will receive the product, while the merchant doesn't want to send the product before receiving the payment, neither (digital goods can be copied and therefore demanding the refund of the product doesn't make sense).

S. Katsikas, J. López, G. Pernul (Eds.): TrustBus 2005, LNCS 3592, pp. 60–69, 2005.

The classification of fair exchange protocols is based in the presence or absence of trusted third parties (TTP) during the execution of the protocol, and in this case, the dependence degree.

- **Protocols for fair exchange that don't require a TTP.** These protocols, by themselves, guarantee the security of the exchange and therefore they don't require the intervention of any TTP. This independence of a third party is a desirable feature, but some of these protocols require great number of interactions between the parties as good as high calculation complexity.
- **Protocols for fair exchange of values with intervention of a TTP.** Among them, the protocols that require the intervention of the TTP in each execution of the protocol can be distinguished from those where the TTP only intervenes in case the exchange doesn't conclude with success (optimistic protocols). The constant presence of the TTP has some inconveniences: the cost that the service represents for users, the possible congestion in the communication with the TTP and the additional delay caused by the communications between the user and the TTP in each execution of the protocol. In optimistic protocols the participation of the TTP is limited to some cases. They have an exchange subprotocol in which the TTP doesn't intervene. If the exchange subprotocol concludes correctly, then it is not necessary to involve the TTP in the execution. If not, another subprotocol will be executed, involving the TTP. In function of the presented proofs, the TTP will be able to send messages or to make decisions to guarantee the fairness of the exchange.

From the previous classification it is deduced that for efficiency reasons it is desirable that a TTP exists, but that it only intervenes to solve disputes when the execution of the protocol leads to an unfair situation. In consequence, the desirable properties are formulated for optimistic exchanges [1]. These features are:

- **Fairness.** When the execution of the protocol concludes, either both parties have the wanted objects, or none of the parties has them.
- **Timeliness.** A protocol provides timeliness if all of the parties can, at any moment, conclude the exchange preserving the fairness.
- **Non repudiation.** After the exchange, each participant can prove the origin of the object that he or she has received, that is to say, a party cannot refuse the emission of the own object.
- **Verifiability of the TTP.** If the TTP intervenes in the execution of the exchange and acts incorrectly, then the fraudulent behavior should be demonstrable.
- **Efficiency.** An efficient protocol will use the smallest possible number of interactions among the users.
- **Privacy.** A protocol is confidential if it allows hiding the content of the exchange, even to the TTP if it is the case.

2 Payment per Receipt Protocols

In a payment using a credit card, the purchase order that includes the number of the card (and the signature) is exchanged for the receipt of the payment or for the product.

The exchange of a signed purchase order in exchange for a receipt of the payment can be considered an application of the contract signing protocols. On the other hand, in payments with electronic cash, the coin becomes the element to exchange on the part of the buyer, and the exchange cannot be considered solved with contract signing protocols, since there are specific situations that origin the interruption of the exchange and could cause the loss of the coin for the two parties or the loss of anonymity to some of them. For example, when in an off-line electronic cash system an error causes that a payer doesn't know if the receiver has received or not the coin, the payer cannot take the risk to use the coin again since if the payment had been concluded, the payer not only would be identified but also he or she would be accused of reutilization.

Besides providing fairness, it is desirable that the exchange protocols allow demonstrating which object the other party has received, and therefore, in the event of later dispute, they can present proofs of the exchange. Purchase protocols can provide atomic exchange, certified delivery for some or all the parties involved in the exchange, or both.

In [9], atomicity of the money is defined as the feature that avoids the creation or destruction of money during its transfer. Therefore, these protocols don't provide fair exchange. Atomicity of goods is defined also in [9] and is applied to the protocols that not only present atomicity of the money but also allow the fair exchange between the product and the coin.

Certified delivery [9] provides coin and goods atomicity, and also provides evidences to both parties of what they have sent and of what the other party has received. This certified delivery can be unilateral or bilateral [4], in function of how many parties possess reception proofs. Certified and atomic delivery [7] provides atomicity of both the good and the coin and the parties have come to an agreement in the initial negotiation and the exchange provides proofs that the goods and the coin have been received. It has, at the same time, atomicity of the good and certified delivery. Finally, distributed atomic purchase [7] provides atomicity of the money and of the good when more than one merchant is involved in the purchase.

The solution adopted in [9] is useful in the event of shortcomings of the system, but it is not useful in case of fraud intent. The system uses a coordinator that knows the identity of all the parts, so the system doesn't allow anonymous payments. The protocols described in [4, 6, 9, 10] carry out the exchange with an on-line TTP. In [6], the active TTP is a blackboard where all users can read and write. [4] provides unilateral certified delivery, and the bank that acts as a TTP is involved in the payment. [9] presents an on-line payment where the bank also acts as a TTP and it guarantees the fair exchange during the payment. Similar solutions are [7] and [8] where a coordinator of on-line payment is used.

Other solutions, as [5], don't need a TTP. In this case the authors opted to divide the coin in two parts that will be sent before and after the reception of the good. The merchant is not protected; he can't contact a TTP if he doesn't receive the second part of the coin. Coins can have an ambiguous state if the buyer doesn't take the risk of being identified in case of reutilization. As a conclusion, it doesn't provide atomicity, and it only provides little protection to the payer. [12] doesn't satisfy the ideal features, if the exchange doesn't finish in a satisfactory way, the client won't be able to get the good, he will only be able to recover the money, that is to say, the exchange can be cancelled, but not finished. [11] doesn't include the analysis of the payment system that would be used in the exchange. The purchase is not certified; the merchant cannot demonstrate that the client has received the good.

According to the ideal features, the objective is a certified and atomic purchase in a protocol that provides anonymity, at least to the payer, maintaining the anonymity that provides the payment system.

3 Features of the Proposed Protocol

The proposed protocol presents the following features:

- **Bilateral certified delivery:** The merchant can demonstrate that the buyer has received the product or receipt. On the other hand the buyer can demonstrate that the merchant has received the payment, as well as which element he has received.
- **Anonymity:** The buyer will be anonymous if the payment system used in the exchange is an anonymous one, and will remain anonymous although he contacts the TTP. If the exchange concludes with the participation of the TTP and the client uses the coin again, the reutilization is detected as usual and the buyer is identified.
- **Exchange:** The payment is carried out in **two stages.** In the first one, a part of the coin is sent to the merchant while in the second stage a secret proof related with the coin, only known by the payer, is revealed. The payee cannot deposit the coin if he doesn't receive the second part of the payment. However, with the first part of the coin the payee can contact the TTP to finish the exchange.
- **Security of the payment:** The exchange protocol keeps the security of the payment system used in the exchange: it can detect double spending, identify double spenders and prevent overspending.
- **Off-line TTP:** The TTP is involved only to solve conflicts when the exchange has not been completed or some party has acted maliciously.
- **Efficient and functional with habitual payment systems:** The exchange protocol is appropriate for the use with various electronic cash systems. The features that these systems must satisfy are:

  - Coin created by the bank (debit system).
  - The bank cannot relate the coins with the payer's identity: anonymous coins.
  - The merchant can verify the coin when he receives it. He cannot prevent double spending.
  - The payment has a challenge-response stage.
  - Double spenders are identified a posteriori.
  - The payer remains anonymous if he behaves correctly.

  These features are given in numerous electronic cash protocols, like [2] and [3] that have been adapted and used to prove the applicability of the exchange protocol.
- **Exchange finalization:** once the purchase commitment is established (2 steps), the protocol allows to finish the exchange, not only to cancel it.

4 Description of the Fair E-commerce Protocol

Three parties are involved in the protocol: the buyer (or payer), the merchant (or payee) and the TTP. The buyer wants to buy a product identified as *Product_code*. The notation used in the description of the protocol is included in table 1.

Table 1. Notation

C	Anonymous buyer	PR_x	x's private key
M	Merchant	PU_x	x's public key
T	TTP	Sign[x,y]	Signature on x that proves the knowledge of a secret element, y
H[]	Hash Function	a	First part of the coin
E_k[]	Ciphering with secret key k	b	Secret element, second part of the coin
D_k[]	Deciphering with secret key k	CANCELLED FINISHED	Boolean variables, false by default.
Id	Exchange identifier	Product_code	H[Product_description]

The protocol is formed by three subprotocols: exchange, cancellation and finalization. The exchange subprotocol, described in table 2, is formed by the following steps:

- **Step 0. Product selection and purchase order.** C sends the purchase order referencing *Product_code* and the first part of the coin that will be involved in the payment to M.
- **Step 1. First part of the purchase commitment: challenge.** M generates a challenge for the payment (*pc*). This will be the challenge used in the electronic payment system. M encrypts the requested product or receipt using the session secret key k, then the secret session key using T's public key. Finally, M signs the relationship between both elements and sends them to C.
- **Step 2. Second part of the purchase commitment: response to the challenge.** C responds to the payment challenge and signs the relationship between a (first part of the coin) and the ciphered product or receipt (c), proving that he knows the second part of the coin (secret element b). The response to the payment challenge, *rpc*, can be used to identify the client in case of double spending. Once this message is received, both parties can request the finalization of the exchange.
- **Step 3. M sends the session key.** After the reception of the message sent in step 2, M verifies the answers received from C: *Sign(d, b)* and *rpc* and sends the key k for the deciphering of the product or receipt.
- **Step 4. C sends the secret proof.** C sends the secret proof that will allow the deposit of the coin.

Steps 1 and 2 of the exchange subprotocol form the purchase commitment. After step 2, T can finish the exchange at C or M request executing the finalization subprotocol. If the exchange is stopped before the reception of step 2, the commitment is not established, and T cannot conclude it. In order to invalidate the elements sent in step 1, M can request the cancellation of the exchange using the cancellation subprotocol. A protocol without the fourth step would be vulnerable; without the fourth step the receiver of the coin, after step 2, could lie and begin the cancellation subprotocol claiming that he hadn't received the coin. Then, if C uses the coin again he would lose privacy because his identity would be revealed.

Table 2. Exchange subprotocol

EXCHANGE SUBPROTOCOL	
0. $C \rightarrow M$:	Product_code, a
1. $M \rightarrow C$:	pc, c = E_k(product), $K_t = PU_T(k)$, $H_M = PR_M\{H[H(c), Kt], Id\}$
2. $C \rightarrow M$:	rpc, d = $H[a, c, Id]$, Sign(d, b)
3. $M \rightarrow C$:	$K_M = PR_M$ (k, Id)
4. $C \rightarrow M$:	b

The cancellation and finalization subprotocols are executed between C or M and T, whenever the exchange subprotocol doesn't conclude successfully. T can choose between concluding and canceling the exchange in function of the presented proofs, the purchase order and previous decisions.

Table 3. Cancellation subprotocol

CANCELLATION SUBPROTOCOL		
	$M \rightarrow T$:	a, c, k_T, h_M, $h_{MTI} = PR_M(c, k_t, h_M, a)$
IF (FINISHED = TRUE)	$T \rightarrow M$:	rpc, d, Sign(d, b), $P_{TM} = PR_T(b)$
ELSE	$T \rightarrow M$:	Cancellation proof = PR_T("cancelled", h_M)
	T:	CANCELLED = TRUE

Table 4. C's finalization subprotocol

C's FINALIZATION SUBPROTOCOL		
	$C \rightarrow T$:	a, pc, c, k_T, h_M, rpc, d, Sign(d, b), b
IF (CANCELLED = TRUE)	$T \rightarrow C$:	Cancellation proof = PR_T("canc.", Sign (d, b))
ELSE	$T \rightarrow C$:	$PR_T(k)$
	T:	FINISH = TRUE

The cancellation subprotocol can only be executed by M in case the purchase commitment doesn't conclude (M doesn't receive the message of the second step of the exchange subprotocol). The finalization subprotocol can be executed by both parties once the purchase commitment has concluded, that is, if C doesn't receive the key k (step 3) or the merchant doesn't receive the proof of the coin, b (step 4). The subprotocols are described in tables 3 and 4.

Table 5. M's finalization subprotocol

M's FINALIZATION SUBPROTOCOL		
	$M \rightarrow T$:	a, pc, c, k_T, h_M, rpc, d, Sign(d, b), $h_{MT2} = PR_M(c, k_t, h_m, a, rrp, Sign (d, b))$
IF (FINISHED = TRUE)	$T \rightarrow M$:	$P_{TM} = PR_T(b)$
ELSE	$T \rightarrow M$: T:	Deposit authorization without b FINISHED = TRUE CANCELLED = FALSE

4.1 Fairness

In order to evaluate the fairness of the protocol, we will analyze all possible situations derived from the execution of the protocol, involving or not involving the TTP.

- **Concluded Exchange.** If the exchange has been carried out without problems, C has the product or the receipt ($D_k(c)$) and he or she can demonstrate that it is the received product or receipt ($H_M=PR_M\{H[H(c), Kt], Id\}$). Moreover, C can demonstrate that he carried out the payment, since he can provide the key: $K_M=PR_M(k, Id)$. M has both parts of the payment: a, rpc, $Sign(d, b)$ and the secret proof of the coin: b. With the last element he can demonstrate that C has received the product or receipt.
- **Unfinished exchange.** If the exchange doesn't conclude successfully, both parties can contact T and begin the execution of the finalization or cancellation subprotocols. The exchange can be broken up in different stages:
  - **M doesn't receive the message of step 2.** If either step 1 or step 2 are not executed, the purchase commitment is not settled down. M can request the cancellation of the exchange while C can request its finalization. M cannot request the finalization of the exchange since he or she doesn't have the element $Sign(d, b)$. In function or the request order, the following situations are possible:
    - C finishes, M cancels: T sends the key k to C and b to M.
    - M cancels, C finishes: T sends a cancellation proof to M. C won't receive the key, k.
  - **C doesn't receive the message of step 3 or M doesn't receive the message of step 4.** M can finish or cancel the exchange while C can only finish the exchange, so in this case there are four possible situations:
    - M finishes, C finishes: M will obtain an authorization to deposit without b. When C tries to finish, T sends him the key, k.

- **M cancels, C finishes**: M and C will obtain a cancellation proof.
- **C finishes, M cancels or C finishes, M finishes**: C will obtain the key k and M will obtain b.

In any case, the execution of the subprotocols leads to a fair situation.

5 Verifiability of the Trusted Third Party

During the execution of the cancellation or the finalization subprotocol, T decides the final state of the exchange checking the values of the boolean variables and the information received in the request. If T doesn't follow the subprotocol and sends inadequate elements to the parties, it is acting unfairly. The parties or an external verifier have to be able to detect and prove the fraudulent behavior of T. If the fraud can be detected and demonstrated the protocol is verifiable.

All possible fraudulent behaviors are listed and explained below.

- If M doesn't receive the message of step 2, the parties can act as follow:
  - **M cancels, C finishes**. In this case T must send a cancellation proof to M and then the same element to C. However, T can act incorrectly, giving a cancellation proof to M, and revealing the key k to C. This fraudulent behavior will be called **FB1**. Another incorrect action would be to provide b to M, but T cannot do it since T ignores its value.
  - **C finishes, M cancels**. In this case T has to send $P_{RT}(k, id)$ to C and P_{TM} to M. If T doesn't give the key k to C (instead T sends a cancellation proof to C), saying that the exchange has already been canceled, and gives b to M, is again acting fraudulently. This situation will be called **FB2**. In this same situation, T can give the key k to C even though he doesn't give b to M, saying that the exchange has not concluded. This is the behavior called **FB1**, as above.
- If C **doesn't receive the message of step 3 or M doesn't receive the message of step 4** the following situations are possible:
  - **M finishes, C finishes**. T must send a deposit authorization to M and the key to C. If T doesn't give k to C, and authorizes M to deposit the coin without the knowledge of the secret proof, second part of the coin, b is acting fraudulently. This behavior will be called **FB3**.
  - **C finishes, M finishes**. T must send the secret proof to M and the key to C. **FB3** is again possible. Moreover, T can give the key k to C and authorize M to deposit the coin without the knowledge of b. This behavior will be called **FB4**.

Four different fraudulent behaviors have been described. Now we will explain how they can be detected:

- **FB1**: M has a cancellation proof and C has the key, k. This situation can be the result of two kinds of execution. In the first one, C obtains the key from M. Later, M requests the cancellation of the exchange and obtains a cancellation proof. T has acted correctly; M is the one that has acted fraudulently, since he could have requested the finalization of the exchange. C can reveal the identity of the fraudulent party, showing the received signature on the pair k, id, that is, C can demonstrate M's fraud showing M's signature on k, id sent in step 3 of the exchange subprotocol, while T has h_{MTI}. The second kind of execution is the cancellation of the exchange at M's request followed by the transfer of k from T to C. To demonstrate the fraudulent behavior of T, M can request C to show the signature on k, id. Now C can't provide the element K_M. If C cannot provide it, but instead C shows $PR_T(k)$ the fraudulent behavior of T can be demonstrated.

- **FB2**: Once C has obtained a cancellation proof, he can contact with the bank to deposit the coin or to request its change for a coin not used in any purchase attempt, without any risk. But now the bank detects that the coin has been deposited previously by M, and therefore, the bank suspects that when providing a cancellation proof to C, T acted incorrectly. However, T can defend itself providing H_{MTI} if T has it, since in this case T demonstrates that it was M who acted incorrectly when he requested the cancellation of the exchange.
- **FB3**: This case can be demonstrated as FB2.
- **FB4**: M can deposit the coin, but he can also prove that, although without damages, T has acted incorrectly giving k to C if C didn't have K_M and on the other hand C has $PR_T(k)$, since the TTP should have sent b to M, instead of giving him an authorization to deposit the coin.

Anyway, the incorrect behavior of T can be demonstrated, and therefore the TTP is verifiable.

6 Conclusions

The electronic purchase of a product requires a fair exchange. One of the values to exchange is an electronic coin and the other is the product or its receipt, depending on the kind of product (digital or physical). This paper presents a fair exchange protocol that can be used with existing payment systems. The buyer and the merchant can exchange their elements in only 4 steps without the intervention of the TTP. In this protocol, however, a TTP can be invoked for dispute resolution. For this reason, a fraudulent behavior of the third party would lead to an unfair exchange. We explain how the protocol allows the detection of fraud attempts. As a conclusion the TTP is verifiable and the exchange is always fair.

References

1. Asokan, N., Shoup, V., Waidner, M.: "Asynchronous protocols for optimistic fair exchange", IEEE Symposium on Research in Security and Privacy, pages 86-99, 1998.
2. Brands, S.: "Untraceable off-line cash in wallet with observers", Crypto'93, LNCS 773, pages 302-318, Springer Verlag, 1994.
3. Chaum, D., Fiat, A., Naor, M.: "Untraceable electronic cash", Crypto'88, LNCS 403, pages 319-327. Springer Verlag, 1988.
4. Camp, J., Harkavy, M., Tygar, J.D., Yee, B.: "Anonymous atomic transactions", 2nd USENIX workshop on electronic commerce, pages 123-133, 1996.

5. Jakobsson, M.: "Ripping coins for a fair exchange", Eurocrypt'95, LNCS 921, pages 220-230, Springer Verlag, 1995.
6. Pagnia, H., Jansen, R.: "Towards multiple payment schemes for digital money", Financial Cryptography' 97, LNCS 1318, pages 203-216, Springer Verlag, 1997.
7. Schuldt, H., Popovivi, A., Schek, H.: "Execution guarantees in electronic commerce payments", 8th international workshop on foundations of models and languages for data and objects (TDD'99), LNCS 1773, Springer Verlag, 1999.
8. Su, J., Tygar, J.D.: "Building blocs for atomicity in electronic commerce", 6th USENIX security symposium, 1996.
9. Tang, L.: "Verifiable transaction atomicity for electronic payment protocols", IEEE ICDCS'96, pages 261-269, 1996.
10. Tygar, J.D.: "Atomicity in electronic commerce", 15th ACM symposium on distributed computing", pages 8-26, 1996.
11. Vogt, H., Pagnia, H., Gärtner, F.C.: "Modular fair exchange protocols for electronic commerce", 15th Annual Computer Security Applications Conference'99, pages 3-11, 1999.
12. Xu, S., Yung, M., Zhang, G., Zhu, H. "Money conservation via atomicity in fair off-line e-cash", International security workshop ISW'99, LNCS 1729, pages 14-31, Springer Verlag, 1999.

Designing Secure E-Tendering Systems[*]

Rong Du, Ernest Foo, Juan González Nieto, and Colin Boyd

Information Security Institute (ISI)
{r.du, e.foo, j.gonzaleznieto, c.boyd}@qut.edu.au

Abstract. Security requirements for e-tendering systems have not been closely scrutinised in the literature. This paper identifies key issues to be addressed in the design of secure e-tendering systems. In particular, the issues of secure timing and record keeping are raised. This paper also classifies existing e-tendering system designs by presenting common e-tendering architectures. A new e-tendering architecture, using distributed trusted third parties is proposed which may be suitable for secure large scale operations.

1 Introduction

Tendering has been seen as the fairest means of awarding government contracts and the method most likely to secure a favourable outcome for a government in its spending of public money. The basic principles of the tendering process have been applied to many business areas, such as purchasing goods, seeking service providers, business consulting, or the selection of main contractors for construction work. The demand of the electronic environment for business processes has generated many e-tendering systems around the world with untested legal and security compliance.

The main parties in an e-tendering system are the principal and the tenderers. For this paper we consider that the e-tendering process to be conducted as following. Various tenderers will be pre-qualified and registered by a principal. The principal then advertises or issues a public invitation to qualified tenderers. Qualified tenderers make offers or tender submissions to the principal before a specfied tender closing time. Some time after the tender closing time, the tender submissions are opened and non-conforming tenders are rejected. The principal then performs tender evaluation and selects the winner of the tender. The parties can then form a contract and archive documents that are related to this tender process.

An investigation of e-tendering systems is important as the process is inherently linked to legal proceedures. A legally binding contract is the product of the e-tendering process. The amount of money and resources involved in many tendered projects may tempt insiders to collude. Ensuring the security of the e-tendering process is paramount.

---

[*] This research was supported by the Construction Innovation Cooperative Research Centre project CRC2002-067-A.

Few papers concerning the security of e-tendering systems have been published, although international organisations have been standardizing e-tendering business processes and message formats through ebXML standards. The United Nations is developing an E-Tendering ebXML Standard. The Business Requirement Specification of E-Tendering [1]. eLEGAL [2] was another research project within the European Information Society Technologies program. eLEGAL targeted the contractual process in the construction industry; and attempted to develop some ebXML standards for legal elements.

More recently, Du et. al [3], have defined security services for electronic tendering with consideration for its legal nature. Du et. al [4] have also developed a protocol to preserve e-tendering communication integrity and to protecting contractual evidence. However, only limited e-tendering security issues have been addressed by them.

The contribution of this paper is to identify key issues to be addressed in the design of secure e-tendering systems. This paper also classifies existing e-tendering system designs by presenting common e-tendering architectures. A new e-tendering architecture is proposed.

The next section of this paper will identify e-tendering security requirements. Next e-tendering systems are studied and classified into system architectures. A short discussion then follows analysing the e-tendering architectures.

2   E-Tendering Security Requirements

Some e-tendering security requirements are similar to other electronic commerce systems. There is a need to address the integrity, confidentiality, authentication and non-repudiation in e-tendering communications.

E-tendering needs to provide secure access to critical systems, particularly in the case of the tender box which temporarily stores tender submissions after the tender closing time. Submitted tenders are highly confidential documents, which are always the target for business collusion.

System availability is crucial, particularly during the tender submission stage before the close of tender time.

However, we believe the most important security requirements that are relevant to e-tendering are those that are dependent on legal requirements. These requirements provide mechanisms that may be called on to provide evidence in the case of litigation. Specifically, these e-tendering requirements are non-repudiation and authentication, secure time, and record keeping. These will be discussed in detail in the following subsections.

2.1   Non-repudiation and Authentication

Non-repudiation property, in a technical sense, is proof or evidence that a particular action has taken place. The algorithm for non-repudiation can also be an extension of the authentication process. It provides a defence against denial of their actions by a participating party.

Non-repudiation is critical in most electronic commerce applications. In the e-tendering process, non-repudiation is required to provide reliable evidence to prove that the principal has advertised the tender specification documents or awarded the winning tender. Non-repudiation should also be used to prove that an authorised pre-qualified tenderer has submitted a particular tender offer document.

Non-repudiation property is usually implemented through the use of a digitally signed message. Digitally signed messages are often as legally binding as traditional signatures. Public key cryptography enables the use of digital signatures. In an e-tendering system, the digital signature mechanism [5,6,7], can provide authentication and non-repudiation. E-Tendering system design should include a public key infrastructure to support a digital signature mechanism.

2.2   Secure Time

The security of an e-tendering system relies crucially on the recording of the date and time at which events occur within the system, as well as on the compliance to agreed timelines. This is particularly important at the close of tender as late tenders may be deemed to be nonconforming. There are three main areas of concern relating to secure time: Time integrity, the closing and opening of the e-tender box and the time of receipt of electronic communications.

Time Integrity. In e-tendering, it is important for litigation to estabish when key events occur. The integrity of timestamps for the e-tendering process can be provided by a time stamping mechanism [8,9], which associates a date and time to a system event. An example of this event is the receipt of an electronic document or the opening of the e-tender box. The evidentiary value of recorded temporal information depends on the technical assurance that derives from both the particular choice of time stamping mechanism and from their correct deployment and maintenance.

The first option for time stamping an event is to generate a log record that includes a description of the event and the time of occurrence as measured by the clock of the local host computer. A second option involves using a digital time stamping service that associates date and time information to electronic documents in a cryptographic manner. Digital time stamping services are usually provided by third parties. The third party digital time-stamping provides a high level of assurance with respect to the authenticity and integrity of time stamped documents. However they incur high overhead costs of running or contracting the service. They also presuppose the existence of a public key infrastructure. There already exist standards for digital time stamping [10,11] as well as commercial digital time stamping service providers [1].

Closing/Opening Time of E-Tender Box. The closing time for e-tender submission and the opening time of the e-tender box are critical from both a

---

[1] http://www.digistamp.co and www.e-timestamp.com.au

legal and security point of view. No tender submissions should be allowed after the stipulated closing time. In order to mitigate the threat of insider collusions, submitted tenders should not be opened before the established opening time, which must be set to be after submission closing time. There may be situations when deadlines need to be extended in response to extraordinary circumstances, such as when due to technical failure of the e-tendering system tenderers have been unable to submit tenders for a prolonged period. The e-tendering system should ensure that the functionality for extending submission deadlines is only available to authorised parties.

A submission closing time and a reasonable transmission time frame need to be clearly stated in tender specification. A tender submission should be initiated before the closing time and completed within this reasonable time frame. A time synchronisation mechanism needs to be in place. Sometimes there are multiple tender boxes, both electronic or physical. Synchronisation of electronic boxes can be achieved using time synchronisation protocols, such as NTP [12], which afford high accuracy and cryptographic authentication.

For the control of e-tender box opening time, there are a variety of technical mechanisms that can be considered in order to protect the confidentiality of submitted tenders until the pre-accorded opening time. There are two types relevant mechanisms, ordinary access control mechanisms and encryption-based access control mechanisms.

Ordinary access control mechanisms rely on the access control policies enforced by the operating system that stores the documents. Such a mechanism would typically allow the e-tendering application to limit access to tender submissions to specific users (e.g. users with the role of evaluator for a given tender). Unfortunately, it does not prevent authorised users from accessing tenders before submission closing time; it merely aims to detect and record such access.

Encryption-based access control mechanisms protect against the main security threat posed by inside attackers to the e-tender box. The use of encryption appears to be a more suitable mechanism for protecting submitted tenders. The tender/offer will be encrypted and stored as encrypted before opening time. Even if an insider manages to get access to the submitted tender files, no information will be revealed. The control of decryption key releasing time can be achieved by many technologies such as time vault service [13] using pairing based encryption.

Time of Receipt of Electronic Communications. From a legal point of view, in case of litigation, it is important to know when a communication was recieved by the system. A clear definition of time-of-receipt for communications that occur as part an e-tendering process is required. For email based communication clarification of time of receipt is required as there may be a delay between when the message is sent and when the receiver reads the message. When using slow communication links there needs to be clarification as to whether time of receipt should be recorded at the beginning of the file transfer or whether the time of receipt should be recorded when the file transfer is complete.

2.3   Secure Record-Keeping

E-tendering systems generate and process electronic documents that are part of business activities and hence need to be preserved as records within a record keeping system in order to comply with relevant legislation and standards. A key legal requirement for recordkeeping is the preservation of the evidentiary integrity of records, both documents and contextual data; this poses a major technical challenge in an electronic environment.

To maximise the evidentiary weight of electronic records, the e-tendering system needs to ensure that evidentially significant electronic records are identified, are available and are usable; identify the author of electronic records; establish the time and date of creation or alteration; establish the authenticity of electronic records; and establish the reliability of computer programs.

A detailed assessment of the electronic information within an e-tendering system that has evidentiary value needs to be performed. Such assessment should employ a risk management approach, taking into account the likelihood of a record being used for evidentiary purposes together with the severity of the consequence of the record not being accepted as evidence. The following e-tendering documents are important evidential material: tenderer document submissions; tender specification and addenda produced by the principal; tender revocation notices submitted by tenderers; negotiation communications post tender close time; request for explanation communications pre-tender close time; award of tender announcement; and any receipt of message acknowledgments.

When determining the evidentiary weight of a record, it may be necessary to demonstrate that the software that generated the record was operating correctly. Assuring high levels of reliability of complex information systems is a difficult and expensive engineering task. It requires methodological design and deployment, as well as detailed evaluation. A number of strategies can be taken to enhance the demonstrable reliability of the software in relation to the evidential value of records. The first strategy involves identifying and isolating the functionality within the e-tendering system on which the evidential value of the record relies upon. Another strategy involves using certified products which are assessed by an accredited body according to the existing security evaluation standards [14,15]. Finally , the use of trusted operating systems, such as Sun Trusted Solaris of Sun Microsystems Inc. [2], that provide strong assurance of the operating system's access control mechanisms.

3   E-Tendering System Architectures

This section introduces and classifies e-tendering system architecture. These architectures have been the result of interviews, system demonstrations and discussions with four government bodies and two international level private companies. E-tendering web sites were also studied for systems in Australia, China

---

[2] http://www.sun.com/software/security/blueprints/

HongKong , Japan , UK and the US . This paper describes three possible system architectures for e-tendering; principal based, trusted third party (TTP) based and distributed TTP architecture. The principal and TTP based architectures have been implemented by many organisations. The distributed TTP architecture is our new proposal.

Each of the e-tendering architectures has the ability to address the issues raised in the previous section. It is assumed that trusted operating systems apply suitable mechanisms for access control to simulate the electronic tender box and that suitable measures have been taken to ensure system availability, and record keeping. Secure communication, including authentication and non-repudiation is assumed to be achieved using public key cryptography and a public key infrastructure. Secure time is provided through a time-stamping secure time server. It is the interaction of participating parties, certificate authorities and time servers that provides the unique advantages and disadvantages in each system.

3.1 Principal Based Architecture

The principal based architecture is mostly used by government e-tendering organisations. This architecture only requires two types of parties: the principal and the tenderer.

The principal is the main administrator of the tendering process and communicates directly with the tenderers. The principal is responsible for ensuring the authentication of the tenderers. Tenderers usually verify the identity of the principal and all correspondence coming from the principal, including tender specification documents and addenda, using a certificate distributed by the principal. Tenderers submit tender documents directly to the principal. The principal maintains the tender box application and must store all submitted tender documents securely, and ensure that no tender documents are submitted after, or viewed before the designated tender close time. The principal is also responsible for the secure storage and archiving of documents after the tender has been awarded.

This architecture places a great deal of trust in the principal. Tenderers place their trust in the access control system employed by the principal to ensure that collusion or internal malfeasance by the principal's users is difficult. The principal must also develop a scheme for verifying the identity and authenticating documents from the tenderers. To achieve this, it is likely that the principal would run a certificate authority, issue certificates and conduct a cryptographic key generation process with tenderers when they complete the pre-qualification process. The principal is responsible for providing a standard time for the e-tendering process.

In summary the principal based architecture depends on the principal to enforce and maintain the essential e-tendering requirements of non-repudiation and authentication, secure time and secure record keeping.

3.2 Trusted Third Party Based Architecture

The TTP based architecture is commonly used by private industry, or independent government bodies. Unlike the principal based architecture, the TTP architecture passes all communications between the principal and tenderers through a TTP. The TTP is the main administrator in this architecture. The TTP is responsible for ensuring the authentication of the tenderers and the principal. All tender documents including tender specification documents, addenda and negotiation messages are stored by the TTP. The system is usually implemented using the HTTP protocol with tenderers uploading offer documents to a web site. The principal also uploads tender specifications and addenda to the web site. The TTP maintains the tender box application by controlling who views or downloads the documents. Thus the TTP will only allow the principal to view tender offers from the tenderer after the tender close time. The TTP can also act as a messenger so no separate communication between th e! principal and the tenderer needs to be sent via email. All messages can be verified and authenticated or kept confidential if necessary by the TTP.

Because the TTP holds all documents during the tender process, it is also the TTP's responsibility to secure the storage and archiving of documents after the tender has been awarded.

Like the principal in the principal based architecture, the TTP is responsible for authentication of all parties in the architecture. To enable this, the TTP should act as a certificate authority issuing certificates and cryptographic keys to the principal and tenderers. The TTP should also act as a secure time server. The principal and tenderers should synchronise their clocks with the time published by the TTP.

Thus in the TTP based architecture the TTP entity is responsible for enforcing and maintaining the e-tendering requirements of non-repudiation, authentication, secure time and record keeping.

3.3 Distributed Trusted Third Party Architecture

The distributed TTP uses multiple TTPs to provide security services such as the secure time server (STS) and the certificate authority (CA). The STS performs two functions, time synchronisation and time controlled key release for accessing submitted tenders. The CA has the function of key registration and key verification. These are separate TTPs although both these services may be provided by the same entity. Because of the separation of these roles this architecture lends itself to a large scale e-tendering implementation.

Unlike the TTP based architecture, the distributed TTP does not host the e-tender box, but only provide security services to protect e-tendering process integrity. The interaction of parties involved in the distributed TTP architecture can be described in the following steps.

Pre-qualification and Registration stage of the e-tendering process requires potential tenderers to submit a registration form to the principal for qualification assessment. The principal will assess each registration and issue pre-qualification status for each qualified potential tenderer to access the e-tendering system. This status is usually based on the ability of the potential tenderer. The CA will distribute user identities, cryptographic keys and credentials to successful tenderers.

Public Invitation stage of the e-tendering process, the principal creates a public invitation to tender for a particular project. Tender specification documents are digitally signed and distributed by the principal. Tenderers can use the CA to verify the principal's signature and origin of the message.

During this period, tender document clarification may be required by tenderers. The principal will send addenda and distribute to all tenderers who are participating in tendering for the project. On receiving the addenda, each tenderer will connect to a CA to verify the signature on the addenda to confirm its origin and integrity.

During **Tender Submission** stage the tenderers prepare and submit encrypted tender offer documents to the electronic tender box. The principal should not be able to view the tender offer documents before the close of tender. Tender submissions should be digitally signed by the tenderer and verified with the CA. The principal must ensure that its clock is synchronised with the STS and that the correct submission time is recorded.

Close of Tender stage covers the close of the tender box at a time specified by the principal. Documents submitted by tenderers are then released to the principal for evaluation. The principal will request a key to decrypt the offers from the STS. The STS will only release the key when the tender box is to be opened at or after the tender close time. After the submission deadline, the principal can reject any late or non conforming tenders according to the time-stamping information and tender specification.

During the **Tender Evaluation**, the principal may need to request more information from the tenderer. These messages should be signed and the receiver should verify the message using a CA.

In **Award of Tender** stage, the principal will accept a tender and send notification to the winning tenderer. It also involves the public announcement of the result. A formal contract can then be signed between the principal and the winning tenderer if it is required. Both the principal and the tenderers will use a CA to verify each other's signatures.

For **Archiving**, both tenderers and the principal need to find a secure way to store their documents. The document retention will consider the file format, access, viewing software and integrity verification.

In terms of e-tendering requirements, the distributed TTP architecture differs from the principal based architecture and TTP based architecture. Different entities are responsible for each security requirement. Non-repudiation and authentication are provided by the CA. Secure time is maintained by the STS. The principal is responsible for secure record keeping.

4 Architecture Analysis and Discussion

In a principal based system, tenderers must put their full trust in the principal, therefore the principal has the potential to manipulate the system. For a TTP based system, both tenderers and principals must put their full trust in the TTP, which is the service provider. For example, both principal and tenderers have to trust the third party to store their confidential documents, such as biding strategy. This is an uncomfortable situation for many companies. However, the TTP architecture may reduce the principal's capacity for collusion or internal malfeasance of the system.

A key question is how impartial can the TTP be. The principal is in a position to choose which third party's system to use, and tenderers are forced to go along with the decision. It is obvious that principals will have more favourable relationship with the TTP than any tenderers in the process.

The trust in the distributed TTP architecture is shared and inter-controlled by separate TTPs. It minimises the reliance on one party thus reducing the chance of collusion and single point failure problems. Also the documents for each tendering project are not stored on a third party system.

CA and STS are specialized security services in controlling of key registration, certificate verification and opening time of submitted tender document. These security functions address security issues discussed in section 2, improve process integrity and increase evidential weight in e-tendering process. In the distributed TTP architecture, the privilege of controlling these security services has been separated from the parties who host the e-tendering business process, principal or single TTP. Tenderers could have the opportunity to choose the service provider without affecting their ability to tender for a project. The CA and STS in the distributed TTP architecture are more impartial than the TTP in existing systems.

The use of an impartial TTP as a certificate authority (CA) allows for a more trustworthy authentication and identification system. The implementation of public key infrastructure allows for the user of digital signatures to provide non-repudiation of documents, although this solution is available for all architectures. An impartial STS allows parties to be sure that the time cannot be changed to suit the principal or a malicious tenderer.

The distributed TTP architecture can be easily integrated into current systems for both principal and TTP based architectures. Other security mechanisms can be added on in the future by using more TTPs. Each party can focus on its speciality. The e-tendering business process system can be standardised and developed as universal software for commercial sale. The security services can be developed and modifed to suite local legal and security requirements.

5   Conclusion

This paper identifies security requirements and classfies security archtectures for e-tendering. It also proposes a high level overview of a distributed TTP architecture for e-tendering sytems which may be suitable for large scale operations. The distributed TTP architecture needs to be investigated in more detail. Specific cryptographic protocols and mechanisms need to be developed to ensure security, particularly secure time issues. In addition, the legal aspect of the e-tendering process needs to be addressed. Contract terms and conditions for e-tendering need to be developed that will support security mechanisms.

References

1. UN/CEFACT-tbg6: Electronic Tendering International Standardization - Business Requirement Specification. Technical Report ETP020 6.0, UN/CEFACT, http://www.etendering-tbg6.net/doc_specification_01.html (2005)
2. Carter, C., Hassan, T., Mangini, M., Valikangas, P., Ott, E.: User Requirements for Legal Support. Technical Report IST-1999-20570, Information Society Technology-European Community, http://cic.vtt.fi/projects/elegal/public.html (2001)
3. Du, R., Foo, E., Boyd, C., Fitzgerald, B.: Defining security services for electronic tendering. In: The Australasian Information Security Workshop (AISW2004). Volume 32., Australian Computer Society Inc and ACM (2004) 43–52
4. Du, R., Foo, E., Boyd, C., Fitzgerald, B.: Secure communication protocol for preserving e-tendering integrity. In: Fifth Asia-Pacific Industrial Engineering and Management Systems Conference (APIEMS'2004). Volume 14., Asian Pacific Industrial Engineering and Management Society (2004) 16.1–16.15
5. Diffie, W., Hellman, M.E.: New directions in cryptography. IEEE Transactions on Information Theory IT-22 (1976) 644–654
6. ElGamal, T.: A public key cryptosystem and a signature scheme based on discrete logarithms. IEEE Transactions on Information Theory 31(4) (1985) 469–472
7. Rivest, R., Shamir, A., Adleman, L.: A method for obtaining digital signatures and public-key cryptosystems. Communications of the ACM 21 (1978) 120–126
8. Haber, S., Stornetta, W.S.: How to time-stamp a digital document. Journal of Cryptology 3(2) (1991) 99–111
9. Buldas, A., Laud, P., Lipmaa, H., Villemson, J.: Time-stamping with Binary Linking Schemes. In Krawczyk, H., ed.: Advances on Cryptology — CRYPTO '98. Volume 1462 of Lecture Notes in Computer Science., Santa Barbara, USA, Springer-Verlag (1998) 486–501
10. The Internet Engineering Task Force: Internet x.509 public key infrastructure time stamp protocols (tsp) (rfc 3161). http://www.ietf.org/rfc/rfc3161.txt (2001)
11. The Internet Engineering Task Force: Electronic signature formats for long term electronic signatures (rfc 3126). http://www.ietf.org/rfc/rfc3126.txt (2001)
12. The Internet Engineering Task Force: Network time protocol (version 3) (rfc 1305). http://www.ietf.org/rfc/rfc1305.txt (1992)
13. Casassa, M., Harrison, K., Sadler, M.: The HP time vault service: exploiting IBE for timed release of confidential information. In: Proceedings of the twelfth international conference on World Wide Web, May 2004, Budapest, Hungary, ACM (2003) 160–169
14. Commission of the European Communities, ITSEC,: Information technology security evaluation criteria version 1.2. http://www.ssi.gouv.fr/en/confidence/methodology.html (1991)
15. International Standards Organisation, International Electrotechnical Commission: Standard iso/iec 15408: Evaluation criteria for information technology. http://www.iso-standards-international.com/iso-5725-kit70.htm (1999)

A Multilateral Secure Payment System for Wireless LAN Hotspots

Stephan Groß, Sabine Lein, and Sandra Steinbrecher

Technische Universitt Dresden,
Department of Computer Science,
Institute for System Architecture,
D-01062 Dresden, Germany
{st.gross, sl15, steinbrecher}@inf.tu-dresden.de

Abstract. Beginning with the adoption of the de-facto standard for wireless LAN communications IEEE 802.11 in 1999 we can observe a continuous growth of public wireless LAN hotspots that provide access to the Internet for modern road warriors. Unfortunately, current hotspots still suffer from several security drawbacks. In this paper we analyse how payment schemes used in current hotspot architectures consider the security requirements of both hotspot providers and subscribers. We identify a conflict between subscribers' wish for privacy and hotspot providers' interest in prohibiting unlicensed (and thus unpaid) usage of the hotspot as the most challenging security objectives a future payment system has to fulfill. As a solution solving this conflict we propose a multilateral secure payment system for wireless LAN hotspots based on electronic coins invented by David Chaum. As a side effect our approach also supersedes the sophisticated authentication techniques used in current hotspot implementations, thus, simplifying the roaming between different providers' hotspots.

1 Introduction

The last years have seen the vision of mobile computing becoming more and more true. Today, in many public places like airports, railway stations, restaurants or hotels so-called wireless LAN hotspots offer immediate access to the Internet using any IEEE 802.11 enabled device like a notebook or a PDA. Recent developments even go further and utilize wireless LAN technology to build Voice-over-IP enabled mobile phones as an alternative to common DECT or even GSM and UMTS based phones [1].

Wireless hotspot providers want their service to succeed now and in the future and to receive an economical benefit for their investments. This means providers necessarily have to assure that potential subscribers trust in their service and thus have to consider their requirements. Providers either are financed by external partners e.g., by advertising shown to the subscribers [2], or might charge a fee for the usage to the subscribers. In the latter case correct and non-repudiable charging of the used services is necessary. Thus, current hotspot systems put great effort in the accounting of generated traffic [3]. This is typically realized by utilizing common AAA (Authentication, Authorizing and Accounting) systems [4]. Unfortunately, this leads to a decrease of usability. Before one

S. Katsikas, J. López, G. Pernul (Eds.): TrustBus 2005, LNCS 3592, pp. 80–89, 2005.

can actually use a hotspot he has first to register with the hotspot provider. During registration the subscriber has to choose a payment method (e.g. credit card). Depending on the method chosen he has to provide detailed information about himself, e.g. his name and his credit card number. In return he receives some token from the hotspot provider (for instance a login name and a password) to legitimate himself at the hotspot. The services used by him are then taken into account by the provider and charged to him. Beside from the already mentioned usability aspects this procedure also suffers from a significant security drawback: combining the user data acquired during the registration phase with the data gathered at the hotspots facilitates the generation of detailed user profiles. Consequently, the lack of security is still seen as an obstacle of current hotspot systems by the majority of possible subscribers [5,6]. Wireless LAN Hotspots will only become successful if further efforts are taken to increase security, usability, interoperability and easy accounting of the service provided.

The integration of techniques and methods from other network standards like GSM, GPRS and UMTS [7,8,9] will help as well as the usage of Single-Sign-On authentication methods [10]. Multilateral security in GSM networks has been studied in detail (e.g., [11]), but so far no similar study exists for wireless LAN.

In this paper we propose a multilateral secure payment system for wireless LAN hotspots based on electronic coins that allows its anonymous but non-repudiable use. In addition it supports a better usability as it needs no complicated authentication mechanisms, therefore allowing easy roaming between different hotspot providers. In section 2 we start with a collection of the requirements the participants in a hotspot scenario have and come to the conclusion that the only potential conflict lies in the hotspot subscriber's wish of privacy and the hotspot provider's strong interest in accountability of usage, i.e. preventing unpaid use. Going on we classify the available payment methods and examine how far they fulfill the security requirements. In section 3 we describe the design of our multilateral secure payment scheme. Section 4 is dedicated to the prototype implementation in Java and section 5 to some concluding remarks.

2   Requirements Analysis

The parties involved in a wireless LAN payment system can be divided into two groups: the service providers and the subscribers. Speaking of the service provider we further distinguish [3] between:

Hotspot Property Owner: entity which provides the locality for a wireless LAN hotspot, e.g. the owner of a hotel or a restaurant.

Hotspot Operator: entity which provides a wireless network for public Internet access at hotspots, i.e. technical equipment, maintenance support and backbone connection.

Clearinghouse: entity which provides the measures needed to invoice the subscriber for the services he used.

In the following we ignore the hotspot property owner as far as he is not involved in the operation of the hotspot (e.g. by combination of both hotspot property owner and hotspot operator in one person) and not paid on a pro-rata basis depending on the profit realised. In the latter case he must be treated like a hotspot operator.

Accounting systems used in present hotspot architectures adopt the browser-based Universal Access Method (UAM) defined by the Wi-Fi Organization [3]. Thus, the subscriber can access a hotspot with only a Wi-Fi network interface and an Internet browser on his device. The functional part of such a hotspot consists of four phases:

Registration: Before a subscriber can access a hotspot he has to declare some static data (e.g., name, address, bank account) to a clearing house associated with the hotspot operator. The clearinghouse in return provides him with valid access data.

Login: To initiate a wireless Internet access at a hotspot one has to authenticate himself using the access data received during the registration. This leads to dynamic connection data collected by the hotspot operator for each session.

Accounting: So-called accounting events [12] trigger the hotspot to ascertain the accounting data from the connection data.

Billing: The hotspot operator transmits the accounting data to the clearing house which associates them with static data from the respecting subscribers, subsumes all accumulated accounting data and issues an invoice for the customer.

Figure 1 depicts the interaction of the involved parties with the accounting system and the corresponding data flows.

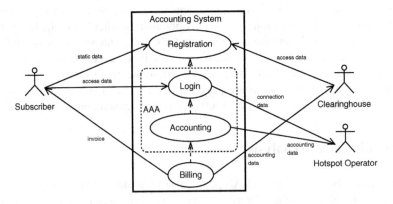

Fig. 1. Basic Functions of an Accounting System for Wireless LAN Hotspots

2.1   Security Requirements

Most of the involved parties' security interests are about the handling and separation of the data processed within the system. Due to the lack of space we only summarize their major issues briefly in table 1.

The most central conflict in the sense of multilateral security occurs between the subscriber's wish to minimize the amount of data transmitted and stored and all participants' interest to reach integrity and accountability of network usage that needs data to be stored as proofs. This conflict is already known from telephone accounts.

Table 1. Summary of all Participant's Security Interests

	Subscriber	Service Provider	
		Hotspot Operator	Clearinghouse
Authenticity of communicating partners	+ +	+	+ +
Confidentiality of transmission			
→ Access data	+ +	+ +	+ +
→ Accounting data	+ +	+ +	+ +
→ Connection data	+ +	○	○
Confidentiality of subscriber identity	+ +	− −	− −
Confidentiality of location data	+ +	−	−
Integrity of transmission			
→ Access data	+	+	+
→ Accounting data	+ +	+ +	+ +
→ Connection data	+	○	○
Accountability	+ +	+	+ +
Availability	+ +	+ +	+ +

+ +... great interest, + ... normal interest, ○ ... no special interest, − ... dislike, − −... great dislike

2.2 Roaming

Beneath the security requirements roaming is one of the most essential features to make a business model for hotspots successful. Roaming means that the subscriber is a client of only one provider who makes agreements with other providers that the subscribers might use their infrastructure and the client's provider collects the money for this from his client. The usage of mobile phones has already shown that people travelling much have to use different providers to guarantee permanent reachability. When travelling through Europe by train permanent changes of providers occur but subscribers usually do not notice it in their reachability because of the roaming agreements between the different providers. In a similar easy way subscribers like to use wireless LAN hotspots. Independent of their current whereabouts and the provider of the access point at this place they like to use the respective existing network in an easy way. Requirements on and specification of possible roaming business models have been studied in [13].

2.3 Payment Methods

Prepaid. Prepaid payment needs no personal data to be gathered as static data, because the customer pays the provider in advance. Following multilateral security this fulfills both requirements of subscribers and providers: Unlinkability and anonymity of data can be realized easily as well as the risk of accountability can be transferred to the subscriber. The amount to pay will be booked to the subscriber's prepaid account with his begin of usage (and then in certain time or data units). If the credit balance the subscriber pays in advance is stored centrally at the provider the subscriber only holds the access data which he uses to identify himself within the login, e.g. by username-password-combination or a remote access card. If the credit balance is stored locally at the user's device or smart card it needs to be protected additionally against misuse by the user with physical measures. The payment needs signals from the provider to the user side. To control the other party the one not holding the credit balance must also log the usage of the service. Altough prepaid payments might be recharged they should only be used once to prevent the building of at least pseudonymous user profiles.

A special kind of local storage are anonymous digital coins [14] which try to implement the typical features hard cash has. They are issued by a bank and can be used independently from concrete merchants. The coins allow unlinkability of payments as well as anonymity of the subscriber using them as long as he only uses a coin once. This is realized by the usage of blind signatures. Unfortunately, there exists no practical system that implements all the above features, not to speak of efficiency of communication if taking this classical approach of anonymous digital coins.

For hotspot usage it is imaginable to save the communication with a bank if the service provider takes the role of the bank and issues coins that are usable at his hotspots and all other hotspots that allow roaming. The usage of coins in the login process supersedes other identification methods. While digital coins did not succeed in payment for non-digital items or services for the payment of digital services they can be a good solution because no change of medium occurs.

Postpaid. Postpaid payment necessarily needs the collection of connection data and the creation of accounting data as well as the storage of corresponding static data. Connection data can be deleted some time after the invoice and should be stored separately from the static data. Postpaid payment can also be combined with pseudonymous usage of the service if identity management systems guarantee the necessary accountability of subscribers to the service providers. But this solution would require an appropriate infrastructure to exist.

Individual Accounting. A fair solution for accounting is that every subscriber only has to pay the amount of data or time he used an access point. Technically the individual accounting will be realized by small time slices or data amounts that will be charged for fixed prices. This kind of accounting is applicable to both post- and prepaid payment. Especially the concept of anonymous coins exactly meets the necessary requirements.

Flat Rate. A popular model for internet usage are flat rates where subscribers get a certain amount of time or traffic he can consume for a fixed price. This business model is both applicable to pre- and postpaid payment. But only the unlimited amount of traffic makes the creation of connection and accounting data obsolete.

3   Design of a Multilateral Secure Payment System

Based on the security requirements and possible payment methods we present our design for a multilateral secure payment system. It is divided into a class model and several basic interaction protocols describing the static system architecture and the dynamic system behaviour respectively. We conclude this section with some remarks on the limitations of our approach.

3.1   System Architecture

The central requirements for a multilateral secure payment system identified in the previous section were the confidentiality and integrity of the transmitted access data as

well as the concurrent confidentitality of the subscriber's identity and the accountability of the used/provided services. These requirements will be considered in the system
architecture. Of course, availability aspects are of great importance as well, but due to
the lack of space we have to postpone a detailed consideration for future work.

As we have stated in section 2.3 postpaid payments make the anonymous use of a
hotspot more difficult. Thus, we base our system on prepaid vouchers that are used to
transfer real money into electronic coins. In our prototype this transaction is performed
by the subscriber and the clearinghouse. However, it can be easily extended with a third
party acting as a bank to introduce universal usable coins instead of distinct currencies
for each clearinghouse. Apart from the anonymity aspects our solution offers a second
major advantage over current implementations: there is no longer a need for a complicated authentication phase at the hotspot. Hence, the roaming between different hotspot
operators becomes more easy as you only have to check the validity of the coins spent.

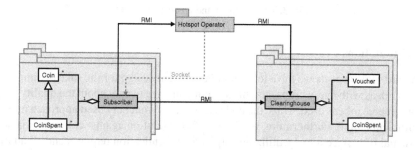

Fig. 2. Basic Architecture of our Payment System

Figure 2 gives an overview of our system architecture. It is basically divided into
three subsystems, one for the subscriber, one for the hotspot operator, and one for the
clearinghouse respectively. The directed connections indicate the interaction between
the three parties. E.g. the subscriber has to cooperate with the hotspot to initiate a new
session who again falls back on services provided by the clearinghouse to perform
this task. The subscriber's main task is to manage the subscriber's purse whereas the
clearinghouse cares about issuing and cashing coins. The hotspot operator's only task
is to provide an Internet connection for the time paid by the subscriber.

3.2   System Interaction

Our system's interaction is defined by two central protocols: The *Withdrawal Protocol*
to generate new coins, and the *Payment and Deposit Protocol* to initiate a new hotspot
session. The entities in both protocols (*Subscriber, Clearinghouse, Hotspot Operator*)
correspond to the partners described in Chaum's scheme [14]. Whereas the Withdrawal
Protocol is more or less a direct adaption of the general model our Payment and Deposit
Protocol is summarized in figure 3.

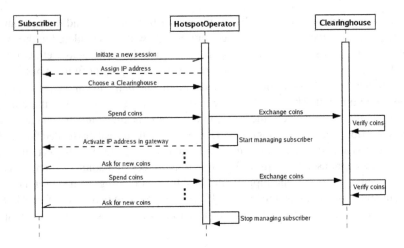

Fig. 3. The Payment and Deposit Protocol

3.3 Limitations

There are some aspects we have left out in our current design for the sake of simplicity. First of all, as with every cryptographic system you have to care about the quality of the cryptographic tokens used. Thus, the codes used in our voucher based approach must be of sufficient length. Furthermore, we do not offer a solution against common hijacking and denial of service attacks utilizing forged deauthentication requests and IP address spoofing. The transfer of electronic coins between different devices of a subscriber as well as their protection against loss by theft or system failure is left for future work, too. The most important limitation of our design is probably its lack of formality. We deliberately tackled the problem stated in a more pragmatic way to show how easy one can build a system that respects the interests of all parties involved. Nevertheless, this approach does not consider some important aspects like the atomicity of the multi-party protocols used. For example, the coin generation and the payment protocol must be fair, i.e. no party taking part at these protocols should be cheated if the transaction fails because of system failure or fraud. Having said this, we still believe that our approach presents an important step-forward compared to the hotspot systems currently in use.

4   Prototype Implementation

Our prototype implementation is based on Java. The functionality is capsuled in four fundamental blocks as specified in the following subsections. For the concrete implementation of anonymous digital money we currently revert to the Lucre project [15], a Java-based implementation of a Diffie-Hellman variant on Chaumian blinding. Due to the modular structure of our implementation this can be easily replaced by another implementation. The purse is currently stored in an XML file on the subscriber's device. The subscriber's access to the Internet is regulated at the hotspot by reconfigurating the firewall settings of the underlying Linux system.

In addition to the functional part we have also implemented a simple graphical user interface for better usability. Figure 4 gives an impression of the subscriber's part of this interface. The main window represents the subscriber's purse. It is divided into two tabs, one for the coins already spent and one for those not. At a hotspot the subscriber chooses between the available clearinghouses and then spends the required amount of coins (see small window on the bottom right). The small window on the bottom left shows the process of cashing a voucher for new coins. Comparable interfaces exist for the clearinghouse and the hotspot operator.

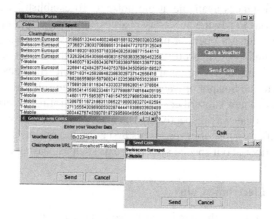

Fig. 4. The Subscriber's GUI

4.1   Implementation of the Clearinghouse

The clearinghouse's interface declares several remotely accessible methods. The most interesting ones are *getNumberOfCoins*, *getAmount* and *processCoinRequest*. Whereas *getNumberofCoins* calculates the number of coins to be generated for a given valid voucher code and a fixed coin value, *processCoinRequest* is used to sign several raw coins as requested by a subscriber. Last but not least *getAmount* is called by the hotspot operator to transfer the signed coins given by the subscriber. The coin is checked for correctness and for resubmission. If both tests pass correctly the coin is marked as spent by storing its serial number and the available credit is returned to the hotspot operator.

4.2   Implementation of the Subscriber

The abstract class *Subscriber* represents the subscriber's device. Its main function is the administration of the electronic purse. The purse is filled by passing a valid voucher code and a corresponding clearinghouse address to the method *generateCoins*. The communication under the hood is realised with Java RMI. Later, the method *spendCoin* is used to initiate an Internet connection at the hotspot. First, it checks which clearing-houses are available (method *getClearinghouseList*). Then the so-called *SocketListener* is started. This class keeps the running connection under surveillance by opening a socket communication for signaling messages about the status of the connection, e.g. to inform the subscriber if he runs out of credit. Finally, the hotspot operator's method *dischargeCoin* is called to actually spend the coin and enable the Internet connection.

4.3 Implementation of the Hotspot Operator

The most interesting functions of the Hotspot Operator party are those initiated by the subscriber via RMI calls. This interface is defined in the class *HotspotOperator*. As already mentioned in section 4.2 the method *getClearinghouseList* delivers a list of all clearinghouse instances available at the hotspot. To establish an Internet connection the subscriber has to pay the necessary charge using the hotspot operator's method *dischargeCoin*. The hotspot operator processes this request (*processCoin*) by sending the handed over coins to the appropriate clearinghouse where the coin is checked for correctness and resubmission. If none of the tests fails the clearinghouse returns the corresponding credit to the hotspot operator who increases the subscriber's *SessionTimer* accordingly or opens a new subscriber session by reconfigurating the firewall settings on the hotspot's Internet gateway respectively. The class *SessionTimer* represents a thread initiated directly after a subscriber spends his first coin. It manages a socket connection to notify the subscriber about special system events such as ceasing credits.

4.4 Handling of Electronic Coins

For the sake of modularity the handling of electronic coins is capsuled in a separate package. This package provides all the functionality used by the subscriber and the clearinghouse during the generation of new coins. It basically contains three classes: *PublicCoinRequest* represents the blended and encrypted serial number of a coin to be signed. It is accompanied by its counterpart *SignedCoinRequest* that contains the matching signature. Last but not least, *CoinRequest* contains all encryption and decryption parameters known to a *Subscriber*, e.g. blending factor and serial number.

5 Conclusion and Final Remarks

We explained the wide agreement of all participants involved in a wireless LAN hotspot scenario concerning central security requirements. On the first view only the subscriber's wish for unobservability on the one hand and the provider's great interest in non-repudiable service usage on the other hand seem to conflict. With our prototype implementation we have demonstrated that this supposed conflict can easily be solved with the means of a multilateral secure system design. We strongly believe that our approach has the potential to put some new life into the domain of electronic cash as it does not suffer from drawbacks coming from exchanging virtual money with real goods. Instead, we use electronic coins to pay for the virtual good of using a wireless LAN hotspot. In addition, our system does not depend on AAA architectures like current systems do and thus, simplifies the roaming between different hotspot providers. For the future we plan to extend our prototype with more sophisticated features (e.g., distinct coin values and the support of electronic change) and evaluate it in a real world scenario.

References

1. Stanossek, G.: Hotspots: Nische oder UMTS-Konkurrenz? VDI Nachrichten **41** (2003)
2. Jamaluddin, J., Doherty, M., Edwards, R., Coulton, P.: A Hybrid Operating Model for Wireless Hotspot Businesses. In: Proceedings of the IEEE Consumer Communications and Networking Conference (CCNC 2004), Las Vegas, Nevada, USA (2004)
3. Anton, B., Bullock, B., Short, J.: Best Current Practices for Wireless Internet Service Provider (WISP) Roaming. Technical report, Wi-Fi Alliance (2003) Retrieved February, 14 2005 from http://www.wi-fi.org/opensection/downloads/WISPr_V1.0.pdf.
4. de Laat, C., Gross, G., Gommans, L., Vollbrecht, J., D.Spence: Generic AAA Architecture. RFC 2903, The Internet Engineering Taskforce (IETF) (2000) Retrieved February, 14 2005 from http://www.ietf.org/rfc/rfc2903.txt.
5. Buchwald, M., Greiber, K., Milosevic, F.: Hotspot Report – Der Praxistest. Industrial study, Detecon International GmbH (2003)
6. Balachandran, A., Voelker, G.M., Bahl, P.: Wireless Hotspots: Current Challenges and Future Directions. In: Proceedings of the 1st ACM International Workshop on Wireless Mobile Applications and Services on WLAN Hotspots, ACM (2003)
7. Ouyang, Y.C., Chu, C.H.: A Secure Context Transfer Scheme for Integration of UMTS and 802.11 WLANs. In: IEEE International Conference on Networking, Sensing and Control (ICNSC 2004), Taipei, Taiwan (2004)
8. Chakravorty, R., Vidales, P., Subramanian, K., Pratt, I., Crowcroft, J.: Performance Issues with Vertical Handovers: Experiences from GPRS Cellular and WLAN hot-spots Integration. In: Proceedings of the IEEE Pervasive Communications and Computing Conference (IEEE PerCom 2004). (2004)
9. Haverinen, H., Mikkonen, J., Takamki, T.: Cellular Access Control and Charging for Mobile Operator Wireless Local Area Networks. IEEE Wireless Communications (2002) 52–60
10. Matsunaga, Y., Merino, A.S., Suzuki, T., Katz, R.H.: Secure authentication system for public WLAN roaming. In: Proceedings of the 1st ACM international workshop on Wireless mobile applications and services on WLAN hotspots, ACM Press (2003) 113–121
11. Federrath, H., Jerichow, A., Pfitzmann, A.: MIXes in Mobile Communication Systems: Location Management with Privacy. In: Information Hiding. Volume 1174 of LNCS., Springer-Verlag Heidelberg (1996) 121–135
12. Beadles, M., Mitton, D.: Criteria for Evaluating Network Access Server Protocols. RFC 3169 (2001) Retrieved Feburary, 14 2005 from http://www.ietf.org/rfc/rfc3169.txt.
13. Verhoosel, J., Stap, R., Salden, A.: A Generic Business Model for WLAN Hotspots – A Roaming Business Case in the Netherlands. In: Proceedings of the 1st ACM International Workshop on Wireless Mobile Applications and Services on WLAN Hotspots, ACM (2003)
14. Chaum, D.: Blind Signatures for Untraceable Payments. In: Advances in Cryptology - Proceedings of Crypto '82, New York, Plenum Press (1983) 199–203
15. Laurie, B.: Lucre: Anonymous Electronic Tokens v1.8. Technical report (2003) Retrieved Feburary, 16 2005 from http://anoncvs.aldigital.co.uk/lucre.

Secure Group Communications over Combined Wired and Wireless Networks*

Junghyun Nam, Seungjoo Kim, and Dongho Won

Department of Computer Engineering, Sungkyunkwan University, Korea
jhnam@dosan.skku.ac.kr, skim@ece.skku.ac.kr, dhwon@dosan.skku.ac.kr

Abstract. This paper considers the fundamental problem of key agreement among a group of parties communicating over an insecure public network. Over the years, a number of solutions to this problem have been proposed with varying degrees of complexity. However, there seems to have been no previous systematic look at the growing problem of key agreement over combined wired and wireless networks, consisting of both high-performance computing machines and low-power mobile devices. In this paper we present an efficient group key agreement scheme well suited for this networking environment. Our construction is intuitively simple, and yet offers a scalable solution to the problem.

Keywords: Group key agreement, combined wired and wireless networks, mobile devices, DDH assumption.

1 Introduction

A group key agreement protocol is designed to allow a group of parties communicating over an untrusted, open network to share a secret value called a *session key*. This common session key is typically used to facilitate standard security services, such as authentication, confidentiality, and data integrity, in various applications which are likely to involve a large number of users. As these group-oriented applications proliferate in modern computing environments (e.g., video conferencing, multi-player game, and replicated database), the design of an efficient group key agreement protocol has received much attention in the literature [8,14,3,12,4,5] as an important research goal. The efficiency of group key agreement protocols is measured with respect to communication complexity, as well as computational complexity. Communication complexity is quantified as both the number of rounds of communication among users and the number of messages sent/received by users, while computational complexity is mostly concerned with the number of public-key cryptography operations that users have to perform. For a group key agreement protocol to be scalable, it is of prime importance in many real-life applications that the protocol be able to run only in a constant number of communication rounds.

* This work was supported by the University IT Research Center Project funded by the Korean Ministry of Information and Communication.

S. Katsikas, J. López, G. Pernul (Eds.): TrustBus 2005, LNCS 3592, pp. 90–99, 2005.
© Springer-Verlag Berlin Heidelberg 2005

In this paper we consider the scenario where limited-function devices, such as PDAs and handheld computers, and general-purpose computing machines like servers and desktop computers coexist participating in the same group. When one considers the broad range of wirelessly connected mobile devices used today, it is clear that integrating such network-enabled devices into secure group communication systems is timely and will be increasingly important. Although mobile devices represent an already large and growing percentage of the computing population, security is still a major gating factor for their full adoption. Despite all the work conducted over many decades, the implementation of strong protection in a mobile environment is non-trivial [2]. Security solutions targeted for more traditional networks are often not directly applicable to wireless networks due to a marked difference in computing resources between mobile devices and stationary computers.

Indeed, most of previous group key agreement protocols are not well suited for networking environments similar to our setting. Even though some constant-round protocols have been proposed [8,12,5], they are still too costly to be practical for applications involving mobile devices with limited computing resources. The reason for this is that these protocols are fully symmetric and therefore, as group size grows, the workload of every user also increases substantially, imposing an unfair, excessive burden on small mobile devices. Other constant-round protocols [4,6], while they require only a fixed amount of computation for all but one group member, do not provide perfect forward secrecy [10]; i.e., earlier session keys are compromised by loss of some underlying information at the present time. Furthermore, in these protocols one special user must perform $O(n)$ public-key cryptography operations in a group of size n, being a significant performance bottleneck in a large group setting.

In this work we focus on *contributory* key agreement protocols in which the session key is derived as a function of contributions provided by all parties. In contributory key agreement protocols, a correctly behaving party is assured that as long as his contribution is chosen at random, even a coalition of all other parties will not be able to have any means of controlling the final value of the session key. Therefore, contributory key agreement protocols are fairer and more secure than key transport protocols. Thus, it is often recommended to use contributory key agreement to prevent some parties having any kind of advantage over the others [1]. Moreover, most key transport protocols [15,13], while they focus on minimizing the cost of the rekeying operations associated with group updates, lack at least one of the important security properties: perfect forward secrecy or known key security.

Our main contribution is an efficient constant-round scheme for contributory group key agreement over combined wired and wireless networks, consisting of arbitrary numbers of mobile devices and stationary high-performance computers. While a number of problems related to group key agreement have been tackled and solved over the past years, there seems to have been no previous systematic look at the growing problem of group key agreement in this networking environment. In order to generalize the problem, we broadly divide all the users of the network into two groups, namely, users that have sufficient computational capabilities and users that have relatively low computing resources. By evenly spreading most of workload across high power users, we avoid any potential performance bottleneck of the system while keeping the computational cost of low power users at minimal. Our group key agreement scheme is also very efficient in terms of communication complexity which includes both round and message complexities. Without respect to the number of users, our scheme requires only a constant number of communication rounds and furthermore achieves optimal message complexity [3]. Communication complexity is especially relevant in today's computing environments where the rapid increase in computation power of computers exposed high network delay and congestion as a major bottleneck in group key agreement schemes.

The remainder of this paper is organized as follows. First, we review some of the most well-known protocols in the next section. Then, we set up some notation and assumptions in Section 3, and propose our group key agreement scheme in Section 4. Finally, we discuss the efficiency and the security of the proposed scheme in Section 5 and Section 6, respectively.

2   Related Work

This section describes some of previous works including all the constant-round protocols published up to date. The original idea of extending the 2-party Diffie-Hellman scheme [9] to the multi-party setting dates back to the classical paper of Ingemarsson et al. [11], and is followed by many works [8,14,3] offering various levels of complexity. But, only recently have Bresson et al. [7] proposed the first group key agreement protocol proven secure in a well-defined security model. This provably-secure protocol is based on one of the protocols of Steiner et al. [14] and requires n communication rounds to establish a session key among a group of n parties. Therefore, as group size grows large, this protocol becomes impractical particularly in wide area networks where the delays associated with communication dominate the cost of group key agreement protocols.

Fully Symmetric Protocols. Using the security model of Bresson et al. [7], Katz and Yung [12] have recently proposed the first constant-round and provably-secure protocol for group key agreement. More precisely, they provide a formal proof of security for the two-round protocol of Burmester and Desmedt [8], and introduce a one-round compiler that transforms any group key agreement protocol secure against a passive adversary into one that is secure against an active adversary. While these protocols [8,12] are very efficient in general, they are not well suited for applications deployed over a combined wired and wireless network. Due to the full symmetry of the protocols, each mobile device has to receive $O(n)$ messages, and perform 3 modular exponentiations, $O(n \log n)$ modular multiplications, $O(n)$ signature verifications, and 2 signature generations. Most recently, in [5], Bresson and Catalano have introduced another fully-symmetric protocol which requires two rounds of communication. Interestingly, unlike previous approaches, they construct the protocol by combining the properties of the ElGamal encryption scheme with standard secret sharing techniques. However, with increasing number of users, the complexity of the protocol becomes beyond the capabilities of small mobile devices.

Extremely Asymmetric Protocols. In [4], Boyd and Nieto have presented the first group key agreement protocol that can be completed in a single round of communication. But unfortunately, this protocol does not achieve perfect forward secrecy even if its round complexity is optimal; it still remains an open problem to find a one-round group key agreement protocol providing forward secrecy. In 2003, another constant-round protocol that does not achieve forward secrecy has been offered by Bresson et al. [6]. This protocol provides an efficient method to agree on a session key between a gateway and a cluster of mobile devices. However, in common with the protocol of Boyd and Nieto [4], this protocol suffers from extreme asymmetry in the sense that one distinct user performs $O(n)$ computations whereas the other users perform only $O(1)$ computations. Consequently, none of previous research addresses well the problem of group key agreement over combined wired and wireless networks.

3   Protocol Preliminaries

We fix a nonempty set $\mathcal{U}$ of n users who wish to agree on a common session key by participating in a group key agreement protocol. Let $\mathcal{U} = \mathcal{S} \cup \mathcal{R}$, where $\mathcal{S} = \{U_1, \ldots, U_{n_h}\}$ is the nonempty set of users that have sufficient computational capabilities and $\mathcal{R} = \{U_{n_h+1}, \ldots, U_n\}$ is the set of users that have relatively restricted computing resources. As depicted in Fig. 1(a), the users are arranged in a tree structure with height 2 according to their computing power. All users in $\mathcal{R}$ are at leaves in the tree while the users in $\mathcal{S}$ could be at any level in the hierarchy from 0 to 2. Let n_l denote the cardinality of $\mathcal{R}$ (i.e., $n = n_h + n_l$). Given n_h and n_l, the number of users at level 1, m, is determined as follows, aiming to minimize the maximum amount of computation that one has to perform during an execution of the protocol.

$$m = \begin{cases} 0 & \text{if } n_h = 1 \text{ or } n_h = 2 \\ n_h - 1 & \text{if } n_l \geq (n_h - 1)(n_h - 2) \\ k & \text{otherwise,} \end{cases}$$

where k is the largest positive integer such that $k^2 \leq n - 1$. Fig. 1(b) shows one extreme case where $m = 0$ (i.e., $n_h = 1$ or $n_h = 2$), and thus, the users are organized into an $(n - 1)$-ary tree with height 1.

In the next section, we first construct a two-round protocol for the extreme case $0 < n_h \leq 2$ and then show that an efficient three-round protocol for the case $n_h > 2$ can be constructed by generalizing the idea of the two-round protocol. Due to lack of space, we focus on security against passive adversaries and assume all messages are digitally signed by their source in a way that the signatures cannot be forged.

To simplify the descriptions of the protocols, we divide the set $\mathcal{U}$ into three disjoint subsets $\mathcal{L}_0$, $\mathcal{L}_1$ and $\mathcal{L}_2$ which denote the sets of users at level 0, 1 and 2,

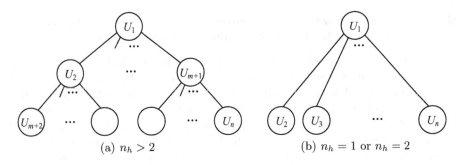

$$\text{(a) } n_h > 2 \qquad\qquad \text{(b) } n_h = 1 \text{ or } n_h = 2$$

Fig. 1. $\mathcal{U} = \mathcal{S} \cup \mathcal{R}$, $\mathcal{S} = \{U_1, \ldots, U_{n_h}\}$, $\mathcal{R} = \{U_{n_h+1}, \ldots, U_n\}$

respectively. We assume that all users know the structure of the tree and their position within the tree. Furthermore, the finite cyclic group $\mathbb{G} = \langle g \rangle$ of ℓ-bit prime order q is assumed to be known in advance. There is also a one-way hash function $H : \{0,1\}^* \to \{0,1\}^\ell$ modelled as a random oracle in the security proof.

4   The Proposed Scheme

This section introduces new constant-round protocols for group key agreement, which take advantage of the difference in computing power between users.

4.1   Basic Protocol

Consider the case $0 < n_h \leq 2$. The protocol for this case, on input three sets $\mathcal{L}_0 = \{U_1\}$, $\mathcal{L}_1 = \{U_2, \ldots, U_n\}$, and $\mathcal{L}_2 = \emptyset$, is performed in two communication rounds, the first with $n-1$ unicasts and the second with a single broadcast, as follows (see Fig. 2 for an example):

Round 1. Each user $U_i \in \mathcal{L}_1$ chooses a random $r_i \in \mathbb{Z}_q$ and computes $z_i = g^{r_i}$, and sends z_i to its parent U_1, who chooses random $s, r_1 \in \mathbb{Z}_q$ and computes $w = g^s$ and $x_1 = g^{sr_1}$.

Round 2. User U_1 computes $x_i = z_i^s$ upon receiving each z_i. After computing $X = \prod_{i \in [1,n]} x_i$ and the set $\mathcal{Y} = \{y_i \mid i \in [2,n]\}$, where $y_i = X \cdot x_i^{-1}$, user U_1 broadcasts $w \| \mathcal{Y}$ to its children.

Key computation. Upon receiving the broadcast, each user $U_i \in \mathcal{L}_1$ computes $X = y_i \cdot w^{r_i}$. All users in $\mathcal{U}$ compute their session key as $K = H(\mathcal{Y} \| X)$.

4.2   Generalized Protocol

This subsection presents our main construction which uses as a basic building block the two-round protocol described above. The idea is to distribute the users into m subgroups and to run the basic protocol for each subgroup. After having derived a shared secret value, each subgroup participates again in the basic

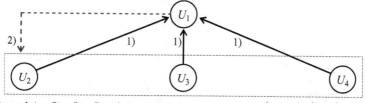

1) Round 1: $g^{r_2}, g^{r_3}, g^{r_4}$. 2) Round 2: $w = g^s$, $\mathcal{Y} = \{g^{s(r_1+r_3+r_4)}, g^{s(r_1+r_2+r_4)}, g^{s(r_1+r_2+r_3)}\}$. Session key: $K = H(\mathcal{Y} \| g^{s(r_1+r_2+r_3+r_4)})$

Fig. 2. An execution of the basic protocol with $\mathcal{U} = \{U_1, U_2, U_3, U_4\}$

protocol as a single entity to generate the final group key. Each parent $U_j \in \mathcal{L}_1$ forms a subgroup with its children (see Fig. 1(a)) and takes charge of the central control in that subgroup. We denote by $\mathcal{I}_j$ the set of indices of the children of user U_j. Now the users in three nonempty sets, $\mathcal{L}_0 = \{U_1\}$, $\mathcal{L}_1 = \{U_2, \ldots, U_{m+1}\}$ and $\mathcal{L}_2 = \{U_{m+2}, \ldots, U_n\}$, agree on a common session key as follows (see also Fig. 3):

Round 1. Each user $U_i \in \mathcal{L}_2$ chooses a random $r_i \in \mathbb{Z}_q$ and computes $z_i = g^{r_i}$, and sends z_i to its parent. The other users (i.e., the users with children) select two random values; user U_1 chooses random $s_1, k_1 \in \mathbb{Z}_q$ and computes $w_1 = g^{s_1}$ and $\hat{x}_1 = g^{s_1 k_1}$, and user $U_j \in \mathcal{L}_1$ chooses random $s_j, r_j \in \mathbb{Z}_q$ and computes $w_j = g^{s_j}$ and $x_j = g^{s_j r_j}$.

Round 2. Each user $U_j \in \mathcal{L}_1$, upon receiving each message z_i for $i \in \mathcal{I}_j$, computes $x_i = z_i^{s_j}$. After computing $X_j = \prod_{i \in \mathcal{I}_j \cup \{j\}} x_i$, the set $\mathcal{Y}_j = \{Y_i \mid i \in \mathcal{I}_j\}$, where $Y_i = X_j \cdot x_i^{-1}$, the subgroup key $k_j = H(\mathcal{Y}_j \| X_j)$, and $\hat{z}_j = g^{k_j}$, user U_j broadcasts $m_j = \hat{z}_j \| w_j \| \mathcal{Y}_j$.

Round 3. The user $U_1 \in \mathcal{L}_0$, upon receiving each message m_j for $j \in [2, m+1]$, computes $\hat{x}_j = \hat{z}_j^{s_1}$. After computing $X_1 = \prod_{j \in [1, m+1]} \hat{x}_j$, $\mathcal{Y}_1 = \{\hat{Y}_j \mid j \in [2, m+1]\}$, where $\hat{Y}_j = X_1 \cdot \hat{x}_j^{-1}$, user U_1 broadcasts $w_1 \| \mathcal{Y}_1$.

Key computation. Now for all $j \in [2, m+1]$ and all $i \in \mathcal{I}_j$, user U_i is able to generate the session key K; first U_i calculates $k_j = H(\mathcal{Y}_j \| X_j)$ with $X_j = Y_i \cdot w_j^{r_i}$ and then $K = H(\mathcal{Y}_1 \| X_1)$ with $X_1 = \hat{Y}_j \cdot w_1^{k_j}$.

5   Efficiency

To the best of our knowledge, the protocol of Burmester and Desmedt [8] (often called the BD protocol) is the most efficient one among forward-secure group key agreement protocols published up to date. Therefore, in Table 1 we compare the efficiency of our protocols with the BD protocol. As for computational costs, the table lists the amount of computation that each user has to perform.

The protocols proposed in this paper are very efficient in terms of both round and message complexities. In particular, both the two- and three-round protocols

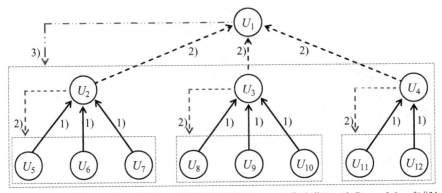

1) Round 1: $g^{r_5}, \ldots, g^{r_{12}}$. 2) Round 2: $\hat{z}_2 \| g^{s_2} \| \mathcal{Y}_2, \ldots, \hat{z}_4 \| g^{s_4} \| \mathcal{Y}_4$. 3) Round 3: $g^{s_1} \| \mathcal{Y}_1$.
Subgroup keys: $k_2 = H(\mathcal{Y}_2 \| g^{s_2(r_2+r_5+r_6+r_7)})$, $k_3 = H(\mathcal{Y}_3 \| g^{s_3(r_3+r_8+r_9+r_{10})})$,
$k_4 = H(\mathcal{Y}_4 \| g^{s_4(r_4+r_{11}+r_{12})})$. Session key: $K = H(\mathcal{Y}_1 \| g^{s_1(k_1+k_2+k_3+k_4)})$

Fig. 3. An execution of the generalized protocol with $\mathcal{U} = \{U_1, \ldots, U_{12}\}$

achieve *optimal* message complexity, requiring only n messages (see Theorem 2 of [3]). Our group key agreement protocols are also very efficient in terms of the computational cost of mobile devices. If precomputations are possible, all the exponentiations in the first round of the protocols can be performed off-line and thus, only one or two exponentiations per mobile device is required to be done on-line. Furthermore, the three-round protocol avoids any potential performance bottleneck by distributing computation among the high power users; the maximum computation rate per user is bounded by $O(\sqrt{n})$ with the reasonable assumption that the number of high power users is at least $\sqrt{n_l}$.

On the other hand, in the BD protocol, all users behave in a completely symmetric manner; each user broadcasts one message per round, and performs 3 modular exponentiations and $O(n \log n)$ modular multiplications. While this protocol takes only two communication rounds, the full symmetry negatively impacts on the overall performance of the protocol involving mobile devices. The number of messages received by each mobile device is $O(n)$ compared to $O(1)$ in our protocols. This implies that in the BD protocol, all users including mobile users have to perform $O(n)$ signature verifications. Moreover, the number of modular multiplications per user increases rapidly as group size grows.

We summarize as follows: in situations where users with equal computational capabilities communicate over a broadcast network, the fully-symmetric protocol of Burmester and Desmedt might be more favorable than our protocols which, in contrast, are well suited for more realistic settings where users with asymmetric computing powers are spread across a wide area network.

6   Security of the Protocols

The main new building block of our scheme is the two-round protocol for the case $0 < n_h \leq 2$. Hence, we restrict our discussion to proving that the security

Table 1. Complexity comparison with the protocol of Burmester and Desmedt [8]

	Communication			Computation	
	Rounds	Unicasts	Broadcasts	Restricted	Sufficient
BD	2		$2n$	$3E + O(n)V + O(n \log n)M$	
Basic	2	$n-1$	1	$2E + 1V$	$O(n)E + O(n)V$
Generalized	3	$n-m-1$	$m+1$	$3E + 2V$	$O(\sqrt{n})E + O(\sqrt{n})V$

E: Exponentiation, V: Verification, M: Multiplication

of the two-round protocol is based on the well-studied Decisional Diffie-Hellman (DDH) assumption; yet the security of the three-round protocol can be proved in a similar way by using the random self-reducibility of the DDH problem, and its proof will be given in the full version of this paper.

Before describing the details of the proof, let us first define $\mathsf{Adv}_{\mathbb{G}}^{\mathsf{ddh}}(t)$ as the maximum value, over all distinguishers $\mathcal{D}$ running in time at most t, of:

$$\left| \Pr[\mathcal{D}(g, g^x, g^y, g^{xy}) = 1 \mid x, y \leftarrow \mathbb{Z}_q] - \Pr[\mathcal{D}(g, g^x, g^y, g^z) = 1 \mid x, y, z \leftarrow \mathbb{Z}_q] \right|.$$

Now we consider the following two distributions:

$$\mathsf{Real} = \left\{ (\mathsf{T}, K) \;\middle|\; \begin{array}{l} r_1, \ldots, r_n, s \in_R \mathbb{Z}_q; \\ z_1 = g^{r_1}, \ldots, z_n = g^{r_n}, w = g^s; \\ x_1 = g^{sr_1}, \ldots, x_n = g^{sr_n}; \\ X = x_1 \cdots x_n; \\ Y_2 = X \cdot x_2^{-1}, \ldots, Y_n = X \cdot x_n^{-1} \end{array} \right\},$$

$$\mathsf{Fake} = \left\{ (\mathsf{T}, K) \;\middle|\; \begin{array}{l} r_1, \ldots, r_n, s, a_1, \ldots, a_n \in_R \mathbb{Z}_q; \\ z_1 = g^{r_1}, \ldots, z_n = g^{r_n}, w = g^s; \\ x_1 = g^{a_1}, \ldots, x_n = g^{a_n}; \\ X = x_1 \cdots x_n; \\ Y_2 = X \cdot x_2^{-1}, \ldots, Y_n = X \cdot x_n^{-1} \end{array} \right\},$$

where $\mathsf{T} = (w, z_2, \ldots, z_n, Y_2, \ldots, Y_n)$ and $K = H(Y_2 \| Y_3 \| \ldots \| Y_n \| X)$.

Lemma 1. *Let $\mathcal{D}$ be a distinguisher that, given (T, K) coming from one of the two distributions* Real *and* Fake, *runs in time t and outputs 0 or 1. Then we have:*

$$\left| \Pr[\mathcal{D}(\mathsf{T}, K) = 1 \mid (\mathsf{T}, K) \leftarrow \mathsf{Real}] - \right.$$
$$\Pr[\mathcal{D}(\mathsf{T}, K) = 1 \mid (\mathsf{T}, K) \leftarrow \mathsf{Fake}] \Big|$$
$$\leq \mathsf{Adv}_{\mathbb{G}}^{\mathsf{ddh}}(t + (4n - 6)t_{exp}),$$

where t_{exp} is the time required to compute an exponentiation in $\mathbb{G}$.

Proof. We prove the lemma by using the random self-reducibility of the DDH problem. Consider the following distribution, which is constructed from the triple $(g^s, g^{r_2}, g^{s'r_2}) \in \mathbb{G}^3$:

$$\text{Dist} = \left\{ (\mathsf{T}, K) \;\middle|\; \begin{array}{l} r_1, \alpha_3, \beta_3, \ldots, \alpha_n, \beta_n \in_R \mathbb{Z}_q; \\ z_1 = g^{r_1}, z_2 = g^{r_2}, \\ z_3 = g^{r_1\alpha_3 + r_2\beta_3}, \ldots, z_n = g^{r_1\alpha_n + r_2\beta_n}, w = g^s; \\ x_1 = g^{sr_1}, x_2 = g^{s'r_2}, \\ x_3 = g^{sr_1\alpha_3 + s'r_2\beta_3}, \ldots, x_n = g^{sr_1\alpha_n + s'r_2\beta_n}; \\ X = x_1 \cdots x_n; \\ Y_2 = X \cdot x_2^{-1}, \ldots, Y_n = X \cdot x_n^{-1} \end{array} \right\},$$

where T and K are as defined above. If $(g^s, g^{r_2}, g^{s'r_2})$ is a Diffie-Hellman triple (i.e., $s = s'$), we have $\text{Dist} \equiv \text{Real}$ since $x_i = z_i^s$ for all $i \in [1, n]$. If instead $(g^s, g^{r_2}, g^{s'r_2})$ is a random triple, it is clear that $\text{Dist} \equiv \text{Fake}$.

Lemma 2. *For any (computationally unbounded) adversary $\mathcal{A}$, we have:*

$$\Pr[\mathcal{A}(\mathsf{T}, K_b) = b \mid (\mathsf{T}, K_1) \leftarrow \text{Fake}; K_0 \leftarrow \{0,1\}^{\ell}; b \leftarrow \{0,1\}] = 1/2.$$

Proof. In experiment Fake, the transcript T constrains the values a_i by the following $n - 1$ equations:

$$\log_g y_2 = -a_2 + \sum_{i=1}^{n} a_i,$$
$$\vdots$$
$$\log_g y_n = -a_n + \sum_{i=1}^{n} a_i.$$

Since T does not constrain the values a_i any further and since the equation $\log_g X = \sum_{i=1}^{n} a_i$ is not expressible as a linear combination of the $n-1$ equations above, we have that the value of X is independent of T. This implies that

$$\Pr[\mathcal{A}(\mathsf{T}, X_b) = b \mid (\mathsf{T}, X_1) \leftarrow \text{Fake}; X_0 \leftarrow \mathbb{G}; b \leftarrow \{0,1\}] = 1/2.$$

Then, since H is a random oracle, the statement of Lemma 2 immediately follows.

Theorem 1. *Let $\mathcal{A}$ be a passive adversary attacking the protocol and running in time t. Then we have*

$$\Pr[\mathcal{A}(\mathsf{T}, K_b) = b \mid (\mathsf{T}, K_1) \leftarrow \text{Real}; K_0 \leftarrow \{0,1\}^{\ell}; b \leftarrow \{0,1\}] \leq$$
$$1/2 + \text{Adv}_{\mathbb{G}}^{\text{ddh}}(t'),$$

where $t' = t + O(nQt_{exp})$, with Q being the number of protocol transcripts obtained by $\mathcal{A}$.

Proof. This immediately follows from the lemmas 1 and 2 above, and the random self-reducibility of the DDH problem.

7   Conclusion

In this paper we have provided an efficient solution to the growing problem of contributory group key agreement over combined wired and wireless networks, which consist of both small mobile devices with limited computational resources and general-purpose computing machines with relatively high computing power. Our scheme takes only a constant number of communication rounds while achieving optimal message complexity. Furthermore, by spreading most of workload across the high power users, the scheme offers a low, fixed amount of computations to its mobile users and bounds the computational complexity of the other users by $O(\sqrt{n})$.

References

1. G. Ateniese, M. Steiner, and G. Tsudik, "New multiparty authentication services and key agreement protocols," IEEE Journal on Selected Areas in Communications, vol. 18, no. 4, pp. 628–639, April 2000.
2. N. Borisov, I. Goldberg, and D. Wagner, "Intercepting mobile communications: The insecurity of 802.11," In Proc. of ACM MobiCom'01, pp. 180–189, 2001.
3. K. Becker and U. Wille, "Communication complexity of group key distribution," In Proc. of ACM CCS'98, pp. 1–6, 1998.
4. C. Boyd and J.M.G. Nieto, "Round-optimal contributory conference key agreement," In Proc. of PKC'03, LNCS 2567, pp. 161–174, 2003.
5. E. Bresson and D. Catalano, "Constant round authenticated group key agreement via distributed computation," In Proc. of PKC'04, LNCS 2947, pp. 115–129, 2004.
6. E. Bresson, O. Chevassut, A. Essiari, and D. Pointcheval, "Mutual authentication and group key agreement for low-power mobile devices," In Proc. of the 5th IFIP-TC6/IEEE International Conference on Mobile and Wireless Communications Networks (MWCN'03), pp. 59–62, 2003.
7. E. Bresson, O. Chevassut, D. Pointcheval, and J.-J. Quisquater, "Provably authenticated group Diffie-Hellman key exchange," In Proc. of ACM CCS'01, pp. 255–264, 2001.
8. M. Burmester and Y. Desmedt, "A secure and efficient conference key distribution system," Eurocrypt'94, LNCS 950, pp. 275–286, 1994.
9. W. Diffie and M.E. Hellman, "New Directions in cryptography," IEEE Trans. on Information Theory, vol. 22, no. 6, pp. 644–654, 1976.
10. W. Diffie, P. Oorschot, and M. Wiener, "Authentication and authenticated key exchanges," Designs, Codes, and Cryptography, vol. 2, no. 2, pp. 107–125, 1992.
11. I. Ingemarsson, D. Tang, and C. Wong, "A conference key distribution system," IEEE Trans. on Information Theory, vol. 28, no. 5, pp. 714–720, 1982.
12. J. Katz and M. Yung, "Scalable protocols for authenticated group key exchange," Crypto'03, LNCS 2729, pp. 110–125, August 2003.
13. A. Perrig, D. Song, and J.D. Tygar, "ELK, a new protocol for efficient large-group key distribution," In Proc. of the IEEE Symposium on Security and Privacy, pp. 247–262, 2001.
14. M. Steiner, G. Tsudik, and M. Waidner, "Diffie-Hellman key distribution extended to group communication," In Proc. of ACM CCS'96, pp. 31–37, 1996.
15. C. Wong, M. Gouda, and S. Lam, "Secure group communications using key graphs," In Proc. of ACM SIGCOMM'98, pp. 68–79, 1998.

A Privacy Enhancement Mechanism for Location Based Service Architectures Using Transaction Pseudonyms*

Oliver Jorns, Oliver Jung, Julia Gross, and Sandford Bessler

Telecommunications Research Center Vienna (ftw.),
Donau-City-Strasse 1, 1220 Vienna, Austria
{jorns, jung, gross, bessler}@ftw.at,
http://www.ftw.at

Abstract. Third party service providers are starting to use advanced location services based on area or periodical notification in order to develop innovative applications. However, such functions can be easily misused for tracking users and building their activity profiles, if privacy enhancement mechanisms are not integrated into the service architecture. In this paper we present a protocol based on transaction pseudonyms that protects the user's address from being disclosed and associated with their location. Based on hash chains, the pseudonyms are used to authorize service and the localization requests, making possible ad hoc service usage without registration. We further analyze security aspects of the proposed protocol.

1 Introduction

Increasingly, applications for mobile users take advantage of user personalized data, such as online status (presence), location, contact address, user preferences, etc. These applications are only the beginning of a new class of context-aware services which will "know" how, where and when to contact the user without their explicit intervention. Such applications raise however serious privacy concerns, especially in cases where the trustworthiness of *Application Providers* cannot be thoroughly investigated prior the service invocation.

The scenarios that motivated this work were related to Location Based Services, although other privacy information, such as presence, user addresses for receiving messages or phone calls turned out to be equally important and privacy sensitive. In the rest of the paper we assume that location information can be provided to the application by the Network Operator. Therefore, the application provides advanced notification functions which allows automatic recurrent notifications or asynchronous callbacks when the user enters or leaves a certain area. The main contributions of this work are to develop a protocol that allows:

- a user to transfer to an application a request under a pseudonym that is passed from the application to the network and is recognized by the latter

---

* This work was supported by the Austrian K*plus* program.

S. Katsikas, J. López, G. Pernul (Eds.): TrustBus 2005, LNCS 3592, pp. 100–109, 2005.

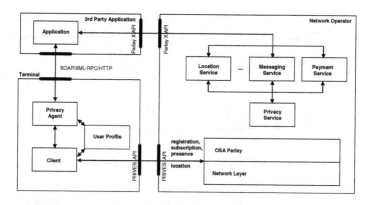

Fig. 1. System Architecture

- the application logic (workflow) to call different Network Services using its own and the user's pseudonym
- the Network Services (e.g location, messaging) to authorize requests from the application based on the contained pseudonyms
- a user to invoke a service without prior registration (and event to pay for it via the network user account)
- certain protection against security attacks

The remainder of the paper is organized as follows: in section 2 we give a general description of the system architecture, its components and the interfaces between them. We go on with a detailed description of the service protocol interactions in section 3 and analyze the security of the protocol and its underlying mechanisms in section 4. In section 5 we conclude with further research topics.

2   System Architecture

As stated in the previous section, the privacy enhancing architecture invokes three actors: the (third party) Application Provider, the Network Operator and the User (terminal), see Fig. 1. The architecture makes use of Parlay X Web Service interfaces, specified recently by the OSA/Parlay Group [1], which promise to open the Network Services for Third Party Application Providers. Among these SOAP [2] APIs, there are location, presence, payment, call control, and messaging interfaces [1]. All these interfaces use an EndUserIdentifier to identify a certain user for a location request or for sending an SMS message. Currently, the Network Operator has to check the authorization to perform each requested operation. The check could also be part of the new *Privacy Service*. Similar to the *Identity Broker* entity in [3] which translates identity attributes into pseudonyms, a *Privacy Agent* generates pseudonyms on the basis of attributes that are stored in the *User Profile* database. The Privacy Agent in the user terminal and its counterpart, the Privacy Service, exchange at the beginning secret information allowing the Privacy Service to authorize requests and

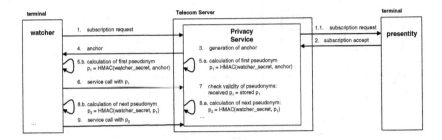

Fig. 2. Transaction Pseudonym Initialisation

translate the pseudonyms back to the public user addresses without disclosure to the application.

In the protocol analysis presented in the next section, we use the roles of *watcher* and *presentity*, which are derived from the presence terminology and which denote the user that localises and the localised user, respectively. In most applications in which a user seeks location privacy, both roles are contained in the same terminal.

3   Service Protocol Interactions

This section describes messages exchanged between services used in this architecture. First, we describe the interactions that allow a user to contact another user and in this context apply for authorisation of subsequent location requests by applications. In the same way, we describe the subscription process of applications. Then, we go into deails of services that receive location information from the Location Service at regular intervals.

3.1   User Subscription Phase

The general model is based on the subscription of a user to private information of themself or other users. The subscription interaction has a two-fold objective: first, to initialize a pseudonym exchange phase between two entities (between user's Privacy Agent and Network Operator's Privacy Service or between an application and Privacy Service) and second, to request the authorization from the presentity for subsequent private information (location) delivery.

3.2   Service Initialisation

As the presentity receives and accepts a *subscription request* from the watcher (Message 1 - 2 in Figure 2), the Privacy Service generates a random number r we subsequently call *anchor* (Step 3). Each anchor is the arithmetical basis for all *Presentity Transaction Pseudonym* (PTP) calculations regarding one particular presentity. The first PTP is calculated on the basis of this anchor and the secret

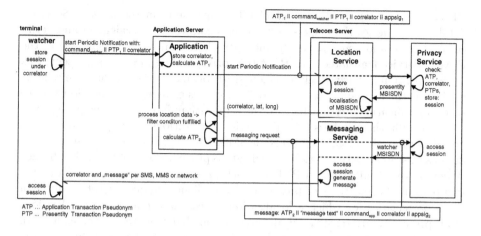

Fig. 3. Periodic Notification Service Interactions

shared with the watcher: $PTP_1 = h_{kwatcher}(r)$ (Step 5.1). Each $PTP_1...PTP_n$ is associated with just one particular presentity. Next, the user's Privacy Agent receives the anchor from the Privacy Service and thereupon also computes PTP_1 (Message 4, Step 5.b). It therefore applies the same calculation as the Privacy Service with the result that both the user's Privacy Agent and the Privacy Service share the same PTP to address one particular presentity. Since each application needs to exchange pseudonyms with the Privacy Service as well and provided that business contracts between the application Provider and the Network Operator already exist, the exchange of the anchor and the shared key can also be done offline and in advance to the first serivce invocation. However, from the cryptographic point of view the *Application Transaction Pseudonym* (ATP) is calculated in the same way as PTPs, starting with the initial $ATP_1 = h_{kapp}(r)$ with anchor r and the shared secret k_{app}.

3.3   Service Invocations

In order to initiate a service request (e.g. the periodic notification service), the client first generates a *transport message* (e.g. SOAP or XML-RPC) which contains the command (in this case `startPeriodicNotification(.)`). Further, this message includes PTPs of each presentity the periodic notification process shall be started for. Additionally, each message appends a signature we denote *correlator*. The client uses the signature as a session identifier which allows him later to controll and terminate active localisation processes. As the application receives the transport message from the watcher, it uses the appended signature correlator as session identifier and computes the next ATP. The newly generated ATP is appended to the client's transport message and again signed for data integrity reasons. This extended transport message is then forwarded to the respective Location Service. Upon receipt, the Location Service first contacts the Privacy Service which checks the validity of the ATP signature. Next, given all pseudonyms are valid, that is all PTPs are found in the Privacy Service's database, it queries the respective watcher's password to recalculate and verify the correlator and hence prove the integrity of the transport message. After the Privacy Service translated each PTP, the corresponding MSISDNs are sent back to the Location Service which may now start localisations on a continuing basis. Each time the location of one or more presentities changes, the Location Service sends a notification message back to the application. Eventually, the presentities locations fulfil the watchers predefined trigger conditions. Thereupon, the user is notified either via a SOAP message or SMS. If for whatever reason the watcher decides to stop an active periodic notification process ahead of time, the Privacy Agent computes all required PTP for each presentity. In order to stop distinctive periodic localisations of presentities, the client may also select a subset of those presentities for which a localisation process is active. Until localisations of all presenties are terminated all information that is stored in the context of a correlator i.e. starting with the Privacy Service or the Location Service, the application and the user's client delete all relevant data such as correlators.

3.4   Single Location Requests

If a watcher wants to know the actual position of one or more presentities, she sends a location request for one particular presentity. In contrast to periodic location notifications, single localisation requests do not require additional session management activities. Neither does the client need to generate a correlator, nor is any session information to be administered throughout the system. Beside single location requests which may include only one particular presentitiy, a watcher may also ask for the position of several presentities at the same time. A watcher may ask for the position of one or more presentities even if he has already started a periodic notification process for at least one presentity respectively up to all presentities involved in a periodic localisation process. Since from a watcher's point of view each PTP denotes exactly one presentity, different kinds of localisations may be performed by several watchers at the same time without interference even if they address the same presentities.

3.5   Interlinked Application Services

Each application service call requires the watcher to provide exactly one PTP for each presentity. Since PTPs can be used only once, this prevents applications from calling several services consecutively with the same PTP. However, applications that provide periodic notifications need to call different services, possibly multiple times. Hence, each subsequent application's service call provides the correlator and an ATP which is computed the same way as PTPs, that is, by applying the HMAC function. Before transmission, the application generates a message signature. For this purpose, it concatenates the command (e.g. `sendMessage(.)`), the actual ATP, the `correlator` as well as the whole user's transport message. The secret shared between the application and the Privacy Service is the key for the HMAC function. Thereupon, the Privacy Service can verify each request on the basis of the signature and associate each ATP to one particular application. The correlator is used by the Privacy Service to recover the current service session which can thereupon deduce the watcher as well as each presentities identity.

4   Security Considerations

In this section we analyse different security and privacy aspects of the proposed system. First, we discuss the cryptographic primitives used to protect the protocol functions. Next, we analyse the protocol and how potential attacks may affect the system. Finally, we discuss general aspects concerning security and privacy of each of each component of the system and its interactions.

4.1   Cryptographic Primitives

PRIVES uses hash chains based on the Keyed-Hash Message Authentication Code ($HMAC$) [4,5] as underlying security function. It is constructed from a randomly chosen anchor r by consecutively applying a hash function on r such that

$$h_k^i(r) = h_k(h_k^{i-1}(r)), \ i = 1, 2, \dots$$

where h_k denotes the keyed hash function with the key k. The requirements for a secure hash functions are [6]:

1. Pre-image Resistance: For a given hash value y it is impossible to find x, where $h(x) = y$.
2. Second Pre-image Resistance: For a given x_1 it is computationally infeasible to find x_2 such that $h(x_1) = h(x_2)$.
3. Collision Resistance: It is infeasible to find a pair (x_1, x_2) such that $h(x_1) = h(x_2)$.

The security of the hash chain depends heavily on the security of the underlying HMAC scheme which in turn is based on standard hash functions. The most popular of them to be used with HMAC are SHA-1 [7] and MD5 [8]. These hash functions are initialised with a fixed initial value (IV), while in contrast HMAC is initialised with a secret key instead. Recently attacks on hash functions have been discovered and gained significant attention in the cryptographic community [9], [10]. With these attacks it is possible to find collisions for hash functions. That means, it is possible to find a pair (x_1, x_2) such that $h(x_1) = h(x_2)$. However, this works only for a limited number of selected values of x and not for arbitrary values. To launch a successful attack against HMAC much more effort is required. Adversaries are able to attack the HMAC scheme if they are capable of finding the output $y = h_k(x)$ of the keyed hash function without knowing the key are also able to attack the underlying hash function in one of the two possible ways:

1. The attacker is able to find a collision with a randomly chosen secret key where the hash value is not known.

2. The attacker is able to find the output of the hash function with a randomly chosen secret key.

These attacks are currently considered to be impractical and thus HMAC still remains secure [11]. Finding collisions mainly has an impact on the generation of signatures, where an adversary is able to produce the same hash value for two distinct messages resulting in the same valid signature for the two messages, e.g. $SIG(h(x_1)) = SIG(h(x_2))$. The security of our scheme is build on the pre-image resistance of HMAC and the underlying hash function. Thus, the second attack described above would have serious impact on the security of PRIVES. But this would also imply that the randomness of the hash function is very poor and it would be possible to predict the output of the hash function although the input is only partially known. But so far the randomness properties of hash functions are not in question. The recent attacks neither enable an attacker to finde collisions starting from a random and secret initial value nor to generate known outputs from a random and secret initial value. Finding collisions in the unkeyed hash function with a fixed IV is much easier because an attacker needs no interactions with the legitimate user in order to produce a high number of input/output pairs for launching a brute force attack. In the key-less case, the attacker can work in finding collisions independently of any user or key because initial value is fixed and publicly known. In contrast to this keyed hash functions like HMAC replace the initial value by a randomly chosen secret key. With the result that the input to the hash function used with HMAC is only partly known to an attacker. The HMAC scheme is still considered to be secure in terms of collision resistance. Moreover, in order to attack our protocol one must be able to generate a valid HMAC pre-images without knowing the secret key k. All recent attacks are aiming at breaking the collision resistance of a hash function, whereas the security of our scheme is based on its pre-image resistance.

4.2   Protocol Security Details

Transaction Pseudonym Interception: Transaction pseudonyms are a reliable mechanism to hide the identity of a user. But the protocol needs not only to be reliable in terms of user's privacy. Another important requirement is to protect the integrity of each transport message. Analyses of our protocol turn out that the weakest communication links in our architecture are those between the Privacy Agent and the application as well as between the application and the Telecom Server. The communication link between the client and the network operator's OSA/Parlay interface is assumed to be secure since these messages do not leave the domain of the network operator. We see that the use of PTPs provides at least data confidentiality. But as the following example shows, without integrity protection mechanisms some may start malicious service invocations.

Consider the following example: An intruder intercepts a SOAP, HTTP or XML-RPC transport message while in transit from the watcher to the application. Since the transport message is sent in cleartext it is easy to find the command and all PTPs. The intruder may construct a new message by simply

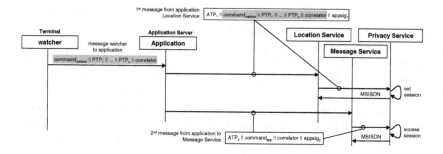

Fig. 4. Secure message exchange

changing the original command. For example, the original transport message contains the location lookup command `getLocation()` which returns the coordinates of one or more presentities (expressed by PTPs) immediately. When this command is replaced by e.g. `startPeriodicNotification()` a long term process is initiated. This causes severe harm to the watcher who intends to start a single location lookup routine. To protect watchers from this kind of Man-in-the-middle attacks, digital signatures can be used to guarantee transport message integrity.

Mobile Client Transport Message Integrity: In order to provide end-to-end integrity of transport messages that are in transit from the Privacy Agent to the Privacy Service, the watcher appends a digital signature termed correlator. It is calculated by the use of the HMAC hash function which takes the command (e.g. `startPeriodicNotification()`) and the respective PTPs as input. The secret $k_{watcher}$ shared with the Privacy Service is used as password:

$$\texttt{correlator} = h_{k_{watcher}}(\texttt{command}_{watcher}||\text{PTP}_1||\text{PTP}_2||\ldots||\text{PTP}_n)$$

As depicted in Fig. 4 the transport message has the following format:

$$\texttt{command}_{watcher}||\text{PTP}_1||\text{PTP}_2||\ldots||\text{PTP}_n||\texttt{correlator}$$

When the Privacy Service receives this message, it first recalculates the correlator to verify that the content of the transport message was not modified. Any modification like substitution of the command or any of the PTPs results in hash value irregularities whereupon the message is discarded. The application relies on the integrity of the received transport message's content as well as the appendant correlator and forwards it to the respective service without additional verification. In contrast to digital signatures, that are based on asymmetric keys, HMAC hash values also provide secure transport message integrity but without the need of long-term keys.

4.3   Service Application Authentication

In general, applications generate two types of messages. The first one contains the complete transport message of a watcher (correlator and PTPs) and is used to start a service. The second message type requires only the correlator of the original transport message and is mainly used to control active sessions or invoke additional services. $\text{command}_{watcher}$ contains the information about which service to call but no information about the presentity's identity. If required, other anonymizing techniques such as described in [12] can additionally be applied to veil any information about the requestor. Despite anonymous and unverifiable messages, economic incentives induce applications to forward these messages to the destined network service. To do so, it first generates an *Application Transaction Pseudonym* (ATP) to provide message authenticity. But, the application must also guarantee message integrity to avoid erroneous or intentional substitution of the ATP or the transport message. Therefore, it calculates an application signature appsig which inseperably concatenates the input of the hash function:

$$\text{appsig} = h_{kapp}(\text{ATP}_1||\text{command}_{watcher}||\text{PTP}_1||\text{PTP}_2||\ldots||\text{PTP}_n)||\text{correlator}).$$

The composition of the second message type is similar except that this time the application uses only the correlator of the transport message (see Fig. 3). This time, the message has the following format:

$$\text{ATP}_2||\text{command}_{app}||\text{correlator}||\text{appsig}$$

To sum up, it is essential that any message, no matter if it is conveyed by the user or the application, can be further anonymized, but nevertheless all mandatory information such as the command operation, the identities of the watcher and the presentities as well as the application cannot be forged or reused but can be recovered only by the Privacy Service.

4.4 Protocol Error Recovery

If for any reason (due to transmission error or Man-in-the-middle Attack) a pseudonym cannot be verified by the Privacy Service, it returns an exception message. Thereupon, the Privacy Agent initiates a subscription request for the relevant presentities. As the subscription status is still valid, the Privacy Service computes for each involved presentity a new anchor and the first PTP. Like the Privacy Service, the Privacy Agent computes the first PTP for the next service call on the basis of the received anchor.

5   Concluding Remarks

While in the near future proliferation of innovative services that use network operator's services are expected to enter the market, users are also increasingly concerned about their privacy. In this paper, we have presented a service architecture that allows users to invoke applications without explicit registration and thus use services offered by the network operators. The protocol we propose allows users and a trusted Privacy Service to exchange transaction-pseudonyms that are light-weight hash values and can be easily generated in mobile devices with limited computing resources. The protocol maintains message confidentiality, authenticity and integrity assurances without the need of long-term keys. At present we have implemented the basic functionality that includes the subscription phase as well as the single location lookup scenario that is based on the proposed protocol [13]. The prototype application makes use of a geographical information web service which provides digital maps on the basis of geographical coordinates that are received from the Location Service. We plan to continue our implementations and develop further services such as Messaging and Presence as well as more complex applications which implement periodic notifications.

References

1. Parlay: Parlay x. URL: http://www.parlay.org/ accessed 03/05 (2005)
2. W3C: (Soap (simple object access protocol) version 1.2) URL: http://www.w3.org/TR/soap accessed 03/05.
3. Alamaki, T., Bjorksten, M., Dornbach, P., Gripenberg, C., Gyorbiro, N., Marton, G., Nemeth, Z., Skytta, T., Tarkiainen, M.: Privacy enhancing service architectures. In: Workshop on Privacy Enhancing Technologies, PET2002. (2002) 99–109
4. Bellare, M., Canetti, R., Krawczyk, H.: Keying hash functions for message authentication. In Koblitz, N., ed.: Advances in Cryptology—CRYPTO '96. Volume 1109 of Lecture Notes in Computer Science., Springer-Verlag (1996) 1–15
5. ISO/IEC 9797-2: Information Technology — Security Techniques — Message Authentication Codes (MACs) - Part 2: Mechanisms Using a Dedicated Hash-Function. International Organization for Standardization, Geneva, Switzerland. (2002)
6. Menezes, A.J.A.J., Van Oorschot, P.C., Vanstone, S.A.: Handbook of applied cryptography. The CRC Press series on discrete mathematics and its applications. CRC Press, 2000 N.W. Corporate Blvd., Boca Raton, FL 33431-9868, USA (1997)
7. National Institute of Standards and Technology: Secure hash standard (SHS). Federal Information Processing Standards Publication 180-2 (2002)
8. Rivest, R.: RFC 1321: The MD5 message-digest algorithm (1992) Status: INFORMATIONAL.
9. Wang, X., Lai, X., Daum, M.: Collisions for hash functions MD4, MD5, HAVAL-128 and RIPEMD (2004) http://eprint.iacr.org/2004/199.pdf.
10. Wang, X., Yin, Y.L., Yu, H.: Collision search attacks on SHA1 (2005) http://www.infosec.sdu.edu.cn/paper/sha-attack-note.pdf.
11. ECRYPT Network of Excellence: Recent collision attacks on hash functions: ECRYPT position paper. URL: http://www.ecrypt.eu.org/documents/ECRYPT-hash-statement.pdf accessed 03/05 (2004)
12. Andersson, C., Lundin, R., Fischer-Huebner, S.: Enabling anonymity for the mobile internet using the mcrowds system. In: FIP WG 9.2, 9.6/11.7 Summer School on Risks and Challenges of the Network Society, Karlstad University Studies (2004)
13. Jorns, O., Bessler, S., Pailer, R.: An Efficient Mechanism to ensure Location Privacy in Telecommunication Service Applications. In: Proc. International Conference on Network Control and Engineering, Palma de Mallorca, Spain (2004)

Making Money with
Mobile Qualified Electronic Signatures

Heiko Rossnagel and Denis Royer

Chair of Mobile Commerce and Multilateral Security,
Johann Wolfgang Goethe University Frankfurt, Gräfstr. 78,
60054 Frankfurt, Germany
[heiko.rossnagel|denis.royer]@m-lehrstuhl.de
http://www.m-lehrstuhl.de

Abstract. In 1999 the directive 1999/93/EC of the European Parliament and of the Council was enacted, providing a legal framework for a common introduction of electronic signatures in Europe. So far the signature market has failed miserably. Mobile electronic signatures could be a potential and promising way to increase the market acceptance of electronic signatures. In this contribution we used an infrastructure for qualified mobile electronic signatures proposed in [Ross2004] as the basis of our assumptions. This infrastructure does not require the mobile operator to act as a certificate service provider (CSP). Instead the user can freely choose a CSP and add the signature functionality along with the required certificates later on demand. The mobile operator would act as the card issuer and would only profit from traffic caused by signature applications. However, mobile operators will only enter the signature market if they expect a profit in return. Therefore, we take a look at the economic feasibility of mobile qualified electronic signatures from the viewpoint of a mobile operator (MO) and try to predict the return on investment. Also, the CSP will only accept this infrastructure, by giving up the control over the signature card, if profits can be expected. Therefore, we examine potential revenue sources for CSPs, using new business models proposed in [LiRo2005] that have the potential to be far more successful than the current ones. Our prediction shows that mobile qualified electronic signatures can be quite profitable for both parties.

1 Introduction

With the directive 1999/93/EC of the European Parliament and of the Council [ECDir1999] legal requirements for a common introduction of electronic signatures in Europe were enacted. The directive sets a framework of requirements for security of technology used for electronic signatures. Based on certificates issued by certification authorities, which certify public keys for a person registered by a registration authority, electronic signatures can be created with a so-called "secure signature creation device" (SSCD), carrying the private keys of a person. The EC-directive distinguishes between "electronic signatures" and "advanced electronic signatures" [ECDir1999]. Certification service providers can issue certificates for advanced signatures that will be qualified if they meet the requirements of Annex I of the directive.

S. Katsikas, J. López, G. Pernul (Eds.): TrustBus 2005, LNCS 3592, pp. 110–118, 2005.
© Springer-Verlag Berlin Heidelberg 2005

Those advanced signatures with qualified certificates will be referred to in this paper as qualified signatures.

The market share of EC-directive conforming signature cards is disappointingly low, failing to meet any involved party's expectations. The lack of customers prevents companies from investing in signature products. As a result almost no commercial usage for qualified electronic signatures exists. Consequently no customers seek to obtain signature products.

Mobile signatures are expected to have a great potential to break up this deadlock of missing applications and customers. These mobile signatures are electronic signatures which are created using a mobile device and rely on signature or certification services in a location independent telecommunication environment. They allow signatory mobility beyond fixed, secure desktop workstations with trusted, personal signing equipment [FrRaRo2003]. Although using mobile devices for signature creation has several shortcomings (e.g. display size, communication costs, limited computing power), the high market penetration of cell phones [GSM2005] and the mobility gained make this effort potentially successful and promising.

Two possible signing approaches in the mobile environment have been proposed in the past: signatures created in centralised signing server environments located at service providers like mobile network carriers; and electronic signatures created inside the signatory's mobile device using a smart card. In [Ross2004] we concluded that only client signatures are capable to meet the requirements for advanced electronic signatures of the EC-directive. Also we concluded that signature capable Subscriber Identity Module (SIM) cards provide the most convenient solution for the customer.

However, mobile operators will only enter the signature market if they expect a profit in return. Given the current market situation this seems to be very unlikely if the mobile operator (MO) has to operate its own trust centre. But there is also the possibility for the mobile operator to only issue the signature capable SIM card without offering any certification services. In that case the customer has to choose a certification service provider (CSP) that issues a certificate for the public key stored on the SIM card [Ross2004]. Therefore, the mobile operator will only make profits caused by the traffic of signature applications. This would also enable CSPs to reach a lot of potential adopters of their technology and to increase their customer base. Of course the CSPs must be willing to accept the standard set by the MO, but given their current losses they should have a major interest in doing so.

However, using a single smart card for multiple purposes raises new questions and challenges. The SIM card is issued by the telecommunication provider, while the SSCD used to be issued by a certification service provider. Combining both functions in one card raises the question how the CSP can issue a certificate for a card that never was in its possession. In [Ross2004] we proposed a protocol called Certification on Demand (COD) that solves this problem:

The mobile operator sells SIM cards equipped with a key generator for one or more key pair(s) which can be used for the signing functionality. After obtaining the SIM-card from the mobile operator, the customer can then generate the keys and activate the signature component and the public key(s) can be certified by any certification service provider on demand.

Through the separation of the telephone functionality and the (possibly later) certification of the user's identity by a certification service provider, both functions can be
sold separately and can be obtained from different providers.

This will lead to increased costs for the signature capable SIM card. But

The mobile operator can also expect a traffic increase caused by signature services.
No changes to the existing distribution infrastructure of mobile operators are necessary. The customer is not forced to certify his keys and can use the SIM for telephone
functionality only [Ross2004].

As stated above a mobile operator will only invest in signature capable SIM cards
if an increase in revenue can be expected. Therefore, we are trying to forecast if
enough traffic can be generated to make the issuing of signature capable SIM cards
profitable for the mobile operator and also to provide a prediction of the potential
return on investment. In addition, we will examine the potential revenues gained by a
CSP that is accepting such mobile signatures and is using new business models as
proposed in [LiRo2004].

This paper is structured as follows: In section 2 we will present our method of fore-
casting the potential benefits as well as our initial assumptions. In section 3 the results
of our calculation will be presented and in section 4 we will conclude our findings.

2 Our Forecasting Approach

The complex nature of the mobile communication market and its key players make it
difficult to come up with a generalised approach for the prediction of future trends.
Nevertheless, using a combination of different methods, such as simulation, investment theory, or scenario techniques, one can analyse the possible direction of the
future development of such technologies and their diffusion into the market
[Pott1998].

Looking at the approach taken for this analysis, the market for mobile signatures
was modelled from the perspectives of a mobile operator and a certification service
provider. In order to display the diffusion rate of the COD technology, it is important
to anticipate the willingness of the customers to switch to the technology. Based upon
the number of users in the market for mobile signatures, one can forecast the additional data traffic, produced by the signature applications by each individual user.
Furthermore, this data traffic generates revenue for the mobile operator and certification transactions for the CSP.

For the analysis conducted here, we chose a time period of 3 years and two basic
scenarios (namely: optimistic and conservative) for the development of the market
segmentation, the market composition, and the market growth for both market players. Finally, we used the current yield of 3,85% as interest rate for our financial calculations, representing the market's interest rate for general investments and being our
comparative value for the internal rate of return (IRR).

2.1 Initial Assumptions for a Mobile Operator

Starting with the segmentation of the market for mobile signatures, we assumed that
the market can be split into three different consumer panels, representing the different

usage by the user (assumption MO1), namely pro, mid, and private users. While for example private users only generate a small amount of traffic, it is more likely that pro users will be the key players in this market, similar to the early days of mobile telecommunications [GrVe2001]. Furthermore, we assumed that the distribution of the panels is mainly composed of pro and mid users (assumption MO2). This is based upon the fact that mobile signatures will at first most likely be used for professional purposes. Though having the biggest future potential in the market growth, the private users only play a minor role in our calculations. Table 1 gives an overview of the market composition and segmentation for the chosen scenarios analysed here:

Table 1. Development of the data-traffic per quarter

Panel / Market Segmentation	Optimistic			Conservative		
	Traffic per Quarter:					
	Year 1	Year 2	Year 3	Year 1	Year 2	Year 3
Pro Users (60,00%)	1000kB	1500kB	2500kB	600kB	800kB	1200kB
Mid Users (30,00%)	500kB	750kB	1000kB	150kB	200kB	250kB
Private Users (10,00%)	100kB	200kB	250kB	50kB	75kB	125kB

For the calculation of the mobile operator's traffic we used an average size of 5kb for a certification transaction [UMTS2003]. Taking the optimistic case for a pro user in year 1 as an example, this would sum up to 200 transactions per quarter (about 63 working days), which would mean that an average "pro" user would conduct about 3 certification service transactions per working day (assumption MO3). This is still a considerably low and conservative number. Especially, when taking into consideration that a lot of the traffic will not be caused by certification services themselves, but instead by applications, that have been impossible to be offered without electronic signatures, e.g. transaction services in a mobile brokerage scenario as presented by [MuRoRa2005]. Therefore, we assumed that an average transaction will cause between 20kB and 60kB of traffic, depending on the usage scenario (assumption MO4). This would mean that a pro user in the optimistic scenario in year 1 would on average conduct one transaction every 3 days.

Moreover, the development of the market and its growth for the given period must also be taken into consideration. In order to avoid the overestimates of the PKI market in recent studies [Data1999], we used the actual growth rate of a similar technology to predict our projected market development. We chose to use the development of Secure Socket Layer (SSL) [IDC2004] as the basis of our predictions (assumption MO5). This is due to the fact that both technologies are similar in two major ways:

(1) Both are preventive innovations, because they lower the probability that some unwanted event (loss of confidentiality for SSL; loss of integrity and accountability for electronic signatures) may occur in the future [Rogers2003].

(2) Furthermore, both represent interactive innovations, meaning that they are of little use to an adopting individual unless other individuals with whom the adopter wishes to communicate also adopt [MaRo1999].

Therefore, we assumed that the more market participants are available and the more services are offered, the more people will actually enter the market for mobile qualified electronic signatures. These positive network effects [ShVa1998] [Econ1996] [KaSh1986] are represented by an increasing market growth of the customer base per quarter (see Table 2). For the optimistic scenario, these figures are based upon the current market growth rates for SSL products with a fixed annual value of 15%. For the conservative scenario we used a fixed rate of 2,50% for the growth rate. As stated before, this is used as a simplification, assuming that the market for mobile signature services will mostly be used for certain specialised applications (e.g. access to company portals), taking into consideration that the overall market for additional services will not be as successful and innovative as anticipated before. However, even in this niche market scenario, a small but steady growth of 2,50% per year can be expected, especially in the sector of applications targeted on the professional market.

Table 2. Market growth

	Optimistic			Conservative		
	Year 1	Year 2	Year 3	Year 1	Year 2	Year 3
Market Growths	15,00%	30,00%	45,00%	10,00%	12,50%	15,00%

For the initial customer base, we assumed a quantity of 10.000 (conservative) to 15.000 (optimistic) SIMs in the market (assumption MO6). These customers could for example stem from prototype projects, conducted by the mobile operator or certification service providers, which will stay in the market after an initial testing phase for this technology.

In order to calculate the actual revenue for the financial analysis, we used the current average price for GPRS data traffic of mobile operators in Germany of 0,01€ per KB (assumption MO7). Moreover, it is likely that future prices for data traffic will be significantly lower. So, a decline of the price for data traffic of 25% per year has also been taken into consideration (assumption MO8).

Looking at the investment that has to be done by the mobile operator, we identified the costs for the initial evaluation of the SIM against EAL 4+ of the Common Criteria (150.000 €) (assumption MO9) and the costs for the initial setup of the infrastructure (500.000 €), such as additional personnel costs and billing systems (assumption MO10). Furthermore, the mobile operator has to issue the crypto enabled SIM to its customers, whereby additional, variable costs will arise (assumption MO11). For our calculation we used the average price a mobile operator charges to its customers for the exchange of a SIM card (about 20,00 € per card). These costs are bound to the number of new mobile users being added to the market (assumption MO12). Moreover, a fixed sum of 200.000€, for the additional annual personnel and process costs, is added to the cash outflows (assumption MO13). By using a higher value for this parameter, the actual cash outflows would be overcompensated, due to the fact that parts of the personnel and process costs are already covered by the exchange fee for the crypto enabled SIM (assumption MO14).

2.2 Initial Assumptions for a Certification Service Provider

For the CSP, we took a similar approach: Based upon the traffic figures for a mobile operator and using the scenario laid out by [LiRo2005], we modelled the market for a CSP. Table 3 gives an overview of the pricing scheme for a certification transaction (assumption CA1) and the distribution of the market segments with regard to the mobile operator (assumption CA2). Moreover, the average size of a transaction is presented (assumption CA3), which is used to calculate the actual number of transactions per user, using the traffic data of the mobile operator (cp. Table 1):

Table 3. Pricing scheme and market composition for the CSP

User Panel / Rate / Market share		Initial Costs	Basic Rate / Year	Certification Transaction	Average KB / Transaction
Pro Users	*Public (33.3%)*	0,00 €	60,00 €	0,05€	60KB
	Business (33,3%)	0,00 €	30,00 €	0,10€	60KB
	Flatrate (33,3%)	0,00 €	85,00 €	0,00€	60KB
Mid Users	*Independence*	0,00 €	15,00 €	0,25€	35KB
Private Users	*Starter*	15,00€	0,00 €	0,40€	20KB

Looking at the investment that has to be done by an existing CSP, in order to offer such a service, we estimated 5 Mio € for the setup of the needed infrastructure and processes (assumption CA4). Furthermore, 1 Mio € of additional running costs per year are added to the cash outflows, including items such as personnel cost, etc (assumption CA5).

3 Results

Starting with our initial customer base of 15.000 SIMs for the market growth (see Table 2) we projected the customer base development. By the end of year 3 and using the optimistic scenario, about 300.000 customers have entered the market, while in the conservative scenario only 56.000 users are actively using our proposed infrastructure. Figure 1 illustrates this prediction of the market development.

In the optimistic scenario the critical mass of customers in order to induce positive network effects [MaRo1999] will be reached in quarter 9. These positive network effects lead to a very high diffusion rate of the product in the following quarters. In the conservative scenario, however, the critical mass necessary to achieve positive-network effects will not be reached within our 3 year time frame of this analysis. Therefore, the diffusion of the proposed technology will be significantly slower.

Based upon this customer base development, we calculated the potential annual cash in- and outflows for a 3 year period, using the projected traffic per user and group and the projected price per KB. Also, the temporal variances of the price and the traffic usage were taken into consideration. The results for the MO and the CSP are shown in Table 4 and 5.

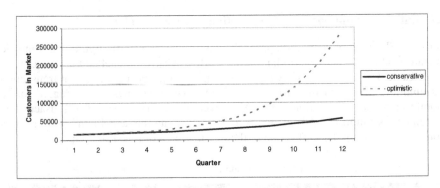

Fig. 1. Customer base development

Table 4. Projected Cash In- and Outflows for the Mobile Operator

	Year 1	Year 2	Year 3
	Optimistic Scenario		
Cash Inflows	569.233,00 €	1.575.567,00 €	7.371.262,00 €
Cash Outflows	-356.240,00 €	-1.046.760,00 €	-4.656.860,00 €
Result	212.993,00 €	528.807,00 €	2.714.402,00 €

	Conservative Scenario		
Cash Inflows	285.422,00 €	444.008,00 €	834.056,00 €
Cash Outflows	-299.300,00 €	-460.260,00 €	-678.980,00 €
Result	-13.878,00 €	3.748,00 €	138.460,00 €

The results of the preliminary stages can now be used for the assessment of the investment. As Table 6 shows, the optimistic scenario for the mobile operator will pay back within 1,91 years and for the CSP within 2,35 years. The IRR will reach a 90,52% for the MO and 42,01% for the CSP for the analysed 3 year period. The conservative scenarios on the other hand will not reach the break even point within the timeframe of our analysis, due to their slower growth of the customer base. The same effects also apply to the IRR, which is negative in both cases. The development of the net present value of both market players is illustrated in Figure 2.

In the optimistic scenario the investment into mobile signatures would be very advisable for mobile operators and CSPs, generating a considerable amount of revenue. Although not looking attractive, the conservative scenarios will break even, once they reach a critical mass of adopters. Due to further calculations we conducted, investing into mobile signatures will be profitable by year 5. Since both scenarios represent extreme cases, we expect that the actual market development will be within this range. Therefore, the investment into mobile signatures based upon the proposed infrastructure seems to be profitable for all market players.

Table 5. Projected Cash In- and Outflows for the CSP

	Year 1	Year 2	Year 3
	Optimistic Scenario		
Cash Inflows	452.903,00 €	2.550.297,00 €	14.221.343,00 €
Cash Outflows	-1.000.000,00 €	-1.000.000,00 €	-1.000.000,00 €
Result	-547.098,00 €	1.550.297,00 €	13.221.343,00 €

	Conservative Scenario		
Cash Inflows	253.803,00 €	794.524,00 €	2103.045,00 €
Cash Outflows	-1.000.000,00 €	-1.000.000,00 €	-1.000.000,00 €
Result	-746.197,00 €	-205.476,00 €	1.103.045,00 €

Table 6. Results of the investment calculation

	Opt. MO	Con. MO	Opt. CSP	Con. CSP
NPV after 3 Years	2.468.986,91 €	-521.428,01 €	7.715.396,02 €	-4.924.198,16 €
Payback Period	1,91 Years	> 3 Years	2,35 Years	> 3 Years
IRR after 3 Years	90,52%	Negative	42,01%	Negative

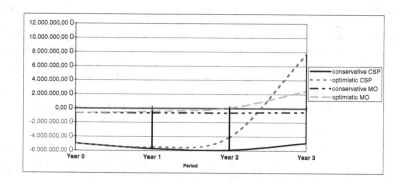

Fig. 2. Development of the investments' NPV – MO & CSP

4 Conclusion

Mobile signatures are a promising approach to break the deadlock between missing customers and missing applications. The high market penetration of mobile phones enables CSPs to target a lot of new potential customers. We used the infrastructure proposed in [Ross2004] that allows the mobile operator to only act as the card issuer while earning revenue from the transferred data, caused by signature services. The qualified certificate of the user will be issued by a CSP of choice, enabling market competition between CSPs. However, a mobile operator will only issue signature capable SIM cards if a positive return on investment can be expected. Also, a CSP will only accept this infrastructure and the ensuing loss of control over the SSCD if this would lead to a profit increase. Therefore, we presented a forecast of the potential market development, using two extreme scenarios (optimistic and conservative) and a set of initial assumptions, based upon the market mechanisms of related technologies. By means of these basic figures, we projected the potential cash in-/outflows for each scenario. As our results show, mobile qualified electronic signatures seem to be a profitable investment for mobile operators as well as certificate service providers.

References

[Data1999]   Datamonitor (1999) Global PKI Markets, 1999- 2003.

[ECDir1999]   DIRECTIVE 1999/93/EC OF THE EUROPEAN PARLIAMENT AND OF THE COUNCIL of 13 December 1999 on a Community framework for electronic signatures

[Econ1996]   Economides, N. (1996) The Economics of networks. International Journal of Industrial Organization, 673-699.

[FrRaRo2003]   L. Fritsch, J. Ranke, and H. Rossnagel: Qualified Mobile Electronic Signatures: Possible, but worth a try? In: Information Security Solutions Europe (ISSE) 2003 Conference, Vienna Austria

[GrVe2001]   H. Grüber, F. Verboven: The Diffusion of Mobile Telecommunication Innovations in the European Union, European Economic Review 45 (2001): 577-588.

[GSM2005]   GSM   Association: GSM   Statistics www.gsmworld.com/news/statistics/index.shtml

[IDC2004]   C. Kolodgy, G. Pintal: IDC - Worldwide SSL-VPN Appliance 2005-2009 Forecast and 2004 Vendor Shares: Delivering Secure Application Access.

[KaSh1986]   Katz, M.L. and Shapiro, C. (1986) Technology Adoption in the Presence of Network Externalities. The Journal of Political Economy, 94, 822-841.

[LiRo2005]   S. Lippmann, H. Rossnagel: Geschäftsmodelle für signaturgesetzkonforme Trust Center; in Ferstl, O., Sinz, E., Eckert, S., and Isselhorst, T., (eds.) Wirtschaftsinformatik 2005. Heidelberg: Physica-Verlag, 2005, pp. 1167-1187.

[MaRo1999]   Mahler, A. and Rogers, E.M. (1999) The diffusion of interactive communication innovations and the critical mass. Telecommunications Policy, 719-740.

[MuRoRa1998]   J. Muntermann, H. Rossnagel, K. Rannenberg: Mobile Brokerage Infrastructures - Capabilities and Security Requirements. Proceedings of the 13th European Conference on Information Systems (ECIS 2005), Regensburg, 2005.

[Pott1998]   I. Potthof: Kosten und Nutzen der Informationsverarbeitung: Analyse und Beurteilung von Investitionsentscheidungen, DUV/Gabler, Wiesbaden, 1998

[Rogers2003]   E. M. Rogers: The Diffusion of Innovations, Fifth Edition, Free Press, New York, London, Toronto, Sidney, 2003

[Ross2004]   H. Rossnagel: Mobile Qualified Electronic Signatures and Certification on Demand, Proceedings of the 1st European PKI-Workshop Research and Applications (EuroPKI 2004), Springer LNCS 3093, S. 274-286.

[ShVa1998]   Shapiro, C.; Varian, H.R.: Information rules: A strategic Guide to the Network Economy, Boston, 1998

[UMTS2003]   UMTS Forum (2003) 3G Offered Traffic Characteristics, UMTS Forum Spectrum Aspects Group (SAG), No. 33, Nov 2003

Efficient Certificate Revocation System Implementation: Huffman Merkle Hash Tree* (HuffMHT)

Jose L. Muñoz, Jordi Forné, Oscar Esparza, and Manel Rey

Technical University of Catalonia (Telematics Engineering Department),
1-3 Jordi Girona, C3 08034 Barcelona (Spain)
{jose.munoz, jordi.forne, oscar.esparza}@entel.upc.edu

Abstract. The public-key is usually made public by way of a digital document called Identity Certificate (IC). ICs are valid during quite long periods of time. However, there are circumstances under which the validity of an IC must be terminated sooner than assigned and thus, the IC needs to be revoked. In this paper, we present practical aspects of a certificate revocation system called Huffman Merkle Hash Tree (HuffMHT). HuffMHT provides an efficient and balanced performance with regards other proposals in the sense that the system does not save bandwidth at the expense of processing capacity and viceversa. Finally, some performance results of HuffMHT are exposed as well.

1 Introduction

A Public Key Infrastructure (PKI) is required to securely deliver public-keys to widely-distributed users or systems. The public key is usually made public by way of a digital document called Identity Certificate (IC). The PKI is responsible for the Identity Certificates (ICs) not only at the issuing time but also during the whole life-time of the certificate. An IC has a bounded life-time: it is not valid prior to the activation date and it is not valid beyond the expiration date. Typically, the validity period of an IC ranges from several months to several years. In this context, certificate revocation can be defined as *"the mechanism under which an issuer can invalidate the binding between an identity and a public-key before the expiration of the corresponding certificate"* (see also [4] for more details). Thus, the existence of a certificate is a necessary but not sufficient evidence for its validity, the PKI needs to provide its end users with the ability to check, at the time of usage, that certificates are still valid (not revoked). This feature is commonly known in the PKI as the status checking.

The Revocation Dictionary ($\mathcal{RD}$) can be defined as the cryptographic structure that contains the status data about the revoked certificates of the PKI

---

* This work has been supported by the Spanish Research Council under the project ARPA (TIC2003-08184-C02-02) and the European Research Council under the project UBISEC (IST-FP6 506926).

S. Katsikas, J. López, G. Pernul (Eds.): TrustBus 2005, LNCS 3592, pp. 119–127, 2005.
© Springer-Verlag Berlin Heidelberg 2005

domain. The master copy of the $\mathcal{RD}$ for a set of certificates is updated by a Trusted Third Party (TTP) called "issuer". The update process must reflect the revocations and expirations (if a certificate has expired it makes no sense to store revocation information about it). The $\mathcal{RD}$ issuer is also responsible for making publicly available the status data. Usually, the end entities that want to perform a status checking do not have a straight connection to the issuer, they get the status data from intermediate entities instead. In this sense, the issuer can distribute the $\mathcal{RD}$ using two kind of intermediate entities:

- **Repositories (offline status checking).** In this case repositories are not TTPs because the cryptographic evidence for the status data is previously produced by a trusted issuer. The simplest structure for offline distribution is a signed "black" list that includes all the identifiers (serial numbers) of all revoked but not expired certificates issued by the PKI domain. There are several standards based on this idea, below we mention them.

  Traditional Certificate Revocation List (CRL) is the most mature offline system. CRL is part of X.509 [12] and it has also been profiled for the Internet in [1]. A CRL is a digitally signed list of revoked certificates where for each entry within the list the following information is stored: the certificate serial number, the revocation reason and the revocation date. *Delta-CRL* (D-CRL) [3] is an attempt of reducing the size of the CRLs. A Delta-CRL is a small CRL that provides information about the certificates whose status have changed since the issuance of a complete list called Base-CRL. In *CRL-Distribution Points* (CRL-DP) [3] each list contains the status information of a certain subgroup of certificates and each subgroup is associated with a distribution point. Each certificate has a pointer to the location of its distribution point. The *Certificate Revocation Tree* (CRT) [5] and the *Authenticated Dictionary* (AD) [11] are both based on hash trees [6]. The hash tree allows content to be retrieved in a trusted fashion with only a small amount of trusted data. The content is stored in the leaves of the hash tree but only the root of the tree is trusted (this structure is further discussed in the next Section).

- **Responders (online status checking).** In this case the cryptographic evidence for the status data is produced online by the responder, that is to say, responders are TTPs. Online schemes usually use the responder's signature over the status data as cryptographic evidence. Notice that end entities are not required to be aware of the back-end infrastructure used to collect the revocation information and maintain the responder's local database[1]. The most popular online protocol used by responders is the *Online Certificate Status Protocol* (OCSP) [10] that has been proposed by the PKIX workgroup of the IETF.

Many benefits can be found in offline status checking. Since repositories are not TTPs, there is not a private key to be protected and the compromise of a reposi-

---

[1] The responder database is usually updated by means of a CRL or requesting other responders.

tory does not compromise the security of the revocation system. Furthermore, it is easy to add redundancy for status checking in the PKI domain and provides a low-cost status checking in terms of processing capacity necessary in the repository. Traditionally, the main drawback of offline systems is the communication overhead introduced in the status checking which hinders its development in bandwidth-constrained environments (such as m-commerce).

In this paper, we present Huffman Merkle Hash Tree (HuffMHT), a revocation system that provides an efficient status checking using repositories. HuffMHT presents the inherent advantages of offline distribution and also keeps a good performance in terms of processing capacity and communication overhead. Besides, HuffMHT is not constrained by large populations, being scalability one of its main advantages and becoming therefore a realistic and practical system. HuffMHT uses the statistics of the status checking, like in the Huffman algorithm for source coding, for building an unbalanced MHT that minimises the average communication overhead in the status checking process.

The rest of the paper is organised as follows: in Section 2, we describe AD-MHT and HuffMHT. In Section 3, we introduce the most relevant practical aspects that must be taken into account to implement HuffMHT and the design decisions made. In Section 4, we present performance results of HuffMHT compared to AD-MHT that show the better performance of HuffMHT. Finally, we conclude in Section 5.

2 Related Work

2.1 ADMHT

We need first to describe AD-MHT [7], an implementation of a certificate revocation system that uses the data structures proposed by Naor and Nissim in their Authenticated Dictionary (AD) [11]. AD-MHT is based in a balanced hash tree. A sample balanced hash tree is depicted in Figure 1.

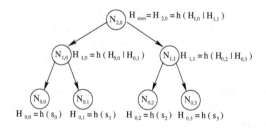

Note: h is a OWHF

Fig. 1. Sample AD-MHT

We denote by $N_{i,j}$ the nodes within the tree here i and j represent respectively the i-th level and the j-th node. We denote by $H_{i,j}$ the cryptographic value stored by node $N_{i,j}$. Nodes at level 0 are called "leaves" and they represent the data stored in the tree. In the case of revocation, leaves represent the set Φ of certificates that have been revoked: $\Phi = \{s_0, s_1, \ldots, s_j, \ldots, s_{n-1}\}$. Here s_j is the data stored by leaf $N_{0,j}$. Then, $H_{0,j}$ is computed as (1)

$$H_{0,j} = h(s_j). \tag{1}$$

Here h is a One Way Hash Function (OWHF). To build the tree, a set of k adjacent nodes at a given level i; $N_{i,j}$, $N_{i,j+1}$, $\ldots, N_{i,j+k-1}$, are combined into one node in the upper level, node that we denote by $N_{i+1,j}$. Then, $H_{i+1,j}$ is obtained by applying h to the concatenation of the k cryptographic variables (2)

$$H_{i+1,j} = h(H_{i,j}|\,H_{i,j+1}|\,\ldots|\,H_{i,j+k-1}). \tag{2}$$

At the top level there is only one node called "root". The $\mathcal{D}$igest of the tree is defined as the H_{root} value and a validity period signed by the issuer. The $\mathcal{P}ath_{s_j}$ can be defined as the set of cryptographic values necessary to compute H_{root} from the leaf s_j.

Example. Let us suppose that a certain user wants to find out if s_1 belongs to the sample tree of Figure 1. Then $\mathcal{P}ath_{s1} = \{H_{0,0}, H_{1,1}\}$ and the response verification consists in checking that the $H_{2,0}$ computed from the $\mathcal{P}ath_{s_1}$ matches $H_{2,0}$ included in the $\mathcal{D}$igest

$$H_{root} = H_{2,0} = h(h(h(s_1)|H_{0,0})|H_{1,1}). \tag{3}$$

Notice that the hash tree can be pre-computed by a TTP and distributed to a repository because a leaf cannot be added or deleted to the $\mathcal{RD}$ without modifying H_{root}^2 which is included in the $\mathcal{D}$igest.

The sample tree of Figure 1 is a binary tree because adjacent nodes are combined in pairs to form a node in the next level ($k = 2$).

2.2   HuffMHT

Despite the good behaviour of balanced hash trees compared to CRLs [7], they have higher communication costs than online systems which is still a problem in bandwidth-constrained environments. HuffMHT uses the statistics of the status checking for building an unbalanced hash tree. The idea is to provide shorter paths for the leaves that have the higher request rates. This structure minimises the average length of the membership response provided by the $\mathcal{RD}$ compared to balanced hash trees. A formal evaluation of this performance based on the average communication between a client and a server is presented in [8].

The unbalanced hash tree performs better than the balanced hash trees when the membership of certain elements of the dictionary is verified more frequently than other elements. In the case of revocation this might happen in many scenarios, for instance, in the Business-to-Consumer scenario (B2C) where status data

---

[2] To do such a thing, an attacker needs to find a pre-image of a OWHF which is by definition computationally infeasible.

of the servers' certificates is requested more often compared to clients'. Anyway, in the worst case (the request rate is equiprobable for all the data contained by the tree) our approach leads to a binary balanced tree.

Below, we outline the algorithm[3] that builds the hash tree (for further information see [8]). Let us assume that Π_i is the probability for membership of element s_i to be requested, then

1. Line up the set of elements by falling probabilities Π_i.
2. The two elements with least probabilities are combined to generate a new node as explained in the previous Section. The new node (a internal tree's node) now is considered to have a probability the sum of probabilities of the two elements.
3. Go to the first step until a single node which probability is 1 is generated. This element will be the root of the tree.

3   Key Implementation Aspects

The basic idea of the HuffMHT has already been exposed, but several implementation decisions have to be properly addressed in order to implement a practical system. In particular, the most critical problems to solve are derived from the fact that tree adjacent leaves do not contain consecutive serial numbers. In this section, we briefly describe several key aspects that we had to face during the implementation phase.

3.1   Content of the Tree Leaves

The AD-MHT implementation stores single certificates in the tree leaves which are ordered by serial number in the last level. This eases searching information within the tree and supports the dynamism of the tree. To demonstrate the validity of a certain certificate, the next evidences must be given:

– The existence of a minor adjacent to the target certificate which is revoked.
– The existence of a major adjacent to the target certificate which is revoked.
– It must be demonstrated that those previous adjacent leaves are effectively adjacent in the tree.

However, this "adjacency checking" is not practical for the HuffMHT, because the leaves in the last level of the tree, instead of being ordered by their serial number, are randomly ordered depending on their probability. To overcome this problem, HuffMHT stores serial number intervals in the tree leaves, making "adjacency checking" not necessary.

---

[3] The algorithm we use to build the unbalanced binary tree is equivalent to the one used by Huffman in the binary coding [2].

3.2   Searching Leaves in the Tree

The leaves of the AD-MHT are sorted and, therefore, is quite straightforward
to implement a searching algorithm of complexity $O(log(N))$ for a tree with N
leaves. However, due to its unpredictable topology, the HuffMHT seems to lack
of the necessary dynamism to implement an efficient searching within it. In this
section, we will show that the same codification used to build the tree can be
easily used to implement an efficient leaf-searching algorithm. This idea leads us
to implement a practical revocation system with a computational overhead in
the server comparable with the AD-MHT system.

There are two main data structures in the HuffMHT: the hash tree and the
associated list. The "associated list" (AL) is a sorted list which stores all the
necessary information to efficiently reach a target leaf within the tree. The AL
is formed by tuples of three values (4):

$$< minor\,certificate,\, major\,certificate,\, codification >\qquad (4)$$

The codification shows the path to follow from the root to reach the leaf
storing the revocation information, the cryptographic value, of that interval.
The criterion applied to get the codification of a leaf is: being in a parent node,
if codification indicates '1' redirect to the right child and redirect to the left child
if codification indicates '0'. Note that the codification of a leaf exactly matches
with its associated binary Huffman code.

With respect to the hash tree, its topology depends exclusively on the requests statistics (unbalanced). A sample HuffMHT tree is shown in Figure 2:

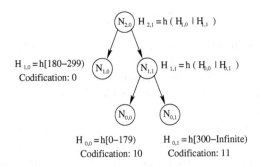

Fig. 2. A sample HuffMHT tree. The certificates with serial numbers 180 and 300 are
revoked. The interval [180-299) is checked with probability 0,5, while the others are
checked with probability 0,25 each one.

It can be seen that leaves can be found in any level and each has its codification associated. Table 1 shows the AL corresponding to this sample tree. The
table is sorted, allowing a searching algorithm of complexity $O(log(N))$. When
a certificate is found in the AL, its associated codification directly indicates its
position in the HuffMHT. The searching algorithm is as simple as starting at

Table 1. Associate list (AL) of the sample HuffMHT tree shown in Figure

Table entry	Minor certificate	Major certificate	Codification
#1	0	179	10
#2	180	299	0
#3	300	Infinite	11

the root node and, depending on the bit of the codeword; move to the right (1) or to the left (0), form the first to the last bit of the codeword.

For example, let us assume that we are requesting about the status of the certificate with a serial number of 150. From the AL we obtain that 10 is the codification associated from this range. To search the position of the leaf in the tree, we begin in the root node, then the first 1 lead us to $N_{1,1}$, and finally the last 0 lead us to node $N_{0,0}$.

3.3   Tree Set-Up and Update

Before building the initial tree, we must know the probability of each leaf of the tree. Usually, when the system starts up, these probabilities are not known. In this case, the leaves can be considered equiprobable, leading to a balanced tree. Later, adaptive algorithms can be used to learn the actual probability of each leaf through statistical monitoring (for this purpose, counters in the repositories can be used to inform the issuer).

On the other hand, when a certificate has been revoked the status data must be updated. The tree is periodically rebuilt to include updated data and the rebuilding process is performed according to the collected statistics.

4   Evaluation

HuffMHT is not only a set of theoretical mechanisms but it is also a practical revocation system that has been implemented by the authors inside the CERVANTES platform [9]. CERVANTES is a Java platform for testing implementations of real revocation systems.

In this section, we use CERVANTES to make a brief comparison between the implementation of HuffMHT and the implementation of AD-MHT. Figure 3 shows the downlink bandwidth difference in % between the two systems regarding the population size. It is assumed that the revocation % is fixed to 10% and that there is a set of certificates that are more frequently asked than others. In this case, the group of frequently asked certificates is formed by 50 certificates that take the 30% of the status checking requests.

Figure 3 shows the better performance of HuffMHT versus AD-MHT. It can be observed that the performance of HuffMHT is better with bigger population sizes. This performance is also obviously better with smaller groups of frequently asked certificates that take more status checking requests. In any case, the HuffMHT always performs better than the AD-MHT.

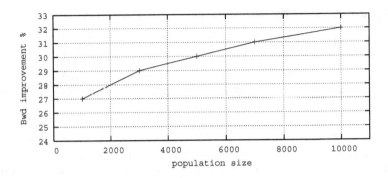

Fig. 3. Scalability performance

5 Conclusions

In this paper we have proposed an operative implementation of a system which manages to minimise the main constraint of an offline revocation system (bandwidth) maintaining a good performance in the rest of parameters (processing capacity) and all the advantages of an offline system (non-TTP distribution). System performance is what we have called balanced.

Huffman encoding allows to distribute leaves containing revocation information in a fashion which minimises the average response length. The HuffMHT provides high bandwidth savings for all kind of statistics which can be found in the status checking. The system performs better than balanced hash trees when the status of a subset of certificates is verified frequently. On the other hand, if status checking rates are similar for all certificates, our approach leads to a binary balanced tree which is the best option among the balanced trees. Besides, it has been proved that storing intervals in the leaves instead of single serial numbers leads to reduce bandwidth as well since "adjacency checking" is not necessary. HuffMHT scalability has also been proved to be high, what is essential for nowadays distributed environment.

References

1. R. Housley, W. Ford, W. Polk, and D. Solo. Internet X.509 Public Key Infrastructure Certificate and CRL Profile, 1999. RFC 2459.
2. David Huffman. A method for the construction of minimum-redundancy codes. *IRE*, 40(9):1098–1101, 1952.
3. ITU/ISO Recommendation. X.509 Information Technology Open Systems Interconnection - The Directory: Autentication Frameworks, 2000. Technical Corrigendum.
4. Iliadis J., Gritzalis S., Spinellis D., de Cock D., Preneel B., and Gritzalis D. Towards a framework for evaluating certificate status information mechanisms. *Computer Communications. Elsevier Science*, 26(16):1839–1850, 2003.

5. P.C. Kocher. On certificate revocation and validation. In *International Conference on Financial Cryptography (FC98). Lecture Notes in Computer Science*, number 1465, pages 172–177, February 1998.
6. R.C. Merkle. A certified digital signature. In *Advances in Cryptology (CRYPTO89). Lecture Notes in Computer Science*, number 435, pages 234–246. Springer-Verlag, 1989.
7. J. Muoz, J. Forné, O. Esparza, and M. Soriano. Certificate Revocation System Implementation Based on the Merkle Hash Tree. *International Journal of Information Security (IJIS)*, 2(2):110–124, 2004.
8. J. Muoz, J. Forn, O. Esparza, J. Pegueroles, and E. Pallares. Reducing the Communication Overhead of an Offline Revocation Dictionary. In *Trust and Privacy*, volume 3184 of *LNCS*, pages 269–278. Springer-Verlag, 2004.
9. J.L. Muoz, J. Forn, O. Esparza, and M. Soriano. Cervantes. a certificate validation test-bed. In *Public Key Infrastructure*, volume 3093 of *LNCS*, pages 28–42. Springer-Verlag, 2004.
10. M. Myers, R. Ankney, A. Malpani, S. Galperin, and C. Adams. X.509 Internet Public Key Infrastructure Online Certificate Status Protocol - OCSP, 1999. RFC 2560.
11. M. Naor and K. Nissim. Certificate Revocation and Certificate Update. *IEEE Journal on Selected Areas in Communications*, 18(4):561–560, 2000.
12. ITU/ISO Recommendation X.509. Information technology Open Systems Interconnection - The Directory: Public Key and Attribute Certificate Frameworks, 1997.

Secure Index Search for Groups*

Hyun-A Park, Jin Wook Byun, and Dong Hoon Lee

Center for Information Security Technologies (CIST),
Korea University, Anam Dong, Sungbuk Gu, Seoul, Korea
{kokokzi, byunstar, donghlee}@korea.ac.kr

Abstract. A secure index search protocol makes it possible to search for the index of encrypted documents using specified keywords even without decrypting them. An untrusted server storing the documents learns nothing more than the search result about the documents without revealing the keyword. Secure index search protocols in the literature only consider a search process between a single-user and a server. However, in real organizations such as government offices or enterprises with many departments, a group search occurs more often. In this paper, we study natural extension of previous results, i.e., secure index search between a server and group members, where a file may be shared by a group or a person with a server. The difficulty in designing such a group setting arises from dynamic group, where each member of the group may join to or leave from the group. To resolve this difficulty efficiently, we propose novel secure index search protocols without re-encryption of the old encrypted documents when group keys are updated.

Keywords: Index search, privacy, database, keyword, hierarchical group.

1   Introduction

When documents contain sensitive data, those are usually encrypted and then stored for secrecy. A secure index search protocol enables a legitimate querier to search encrypted documents with a keyword in a server without decrypting them and revealing any information on the documents to any other, even to the server. Up until now, there have been many works on the search protocols for encrypted documents, but they only consider the search between a single-user and a server [1,2,6,7,9,11,13].

In practical environments, however, a document may be shared by a group or a person, and a server stores documents shared by different groups and persons. For example, the departments of organizations such as companies and municipal offices store their documents at a server, search, and update them as needed. Since there may be the documents requiring security, those documents are encrypted and then stored in order to make them fetchable only by employees in a

---

* This research was supported by the MIC(Ministry of Information and Communication), Korea, under the ITRC(Information Technology Research Center) support program supervised by the IITA(Institute of Information Technology Assessment).

S. Katsikas, J. López, G. Pernul (Eds.): TrustBus 2005, LNCS 3592, pp. 128–140, 2005.

specific department, while any others including the server storing the documents can not get any information about them.

In this paper, we study secure index search, which extends the search between a server and a single-user to the search between a server and multi-user (or group). In such multi-user setting, a server contains heterogeneous documents accessible by different groups or persons. Designing secure index search in the multi-user setting is not an easy work since a group may be dynamic, i.e., a person may join to and leave from the group. First, for a leaving member from a group, all documents accessible to the group should not be accessible any more. This can be resolved by updating a group key so that the leaving member cannot compute a new group key. Second, a newly joining member to a group should be able to obtain all the group keys because all documents accessible to the group must be still available. This makes the design even harder. A naive solution will be to decrypt all documents of the group, and re-encrypt them by the new group key. But this requires a large amount of computational overheads. In this paper, we propose two schemes which can search the encrypted documents without re-encrypting them.

Related Works and Our Contributions. Very recently, Goh proposed a secure index scheme [9], which defines a secure index and formulates a security model for indexes known as semantic security (or no leakage of information) against adaptive chosen keyword attack (IND-CKA). The IND-CKA captures that the contents of a document are not revealed from its index and the indexes of other documents apart from what an adversary already knows from previous query results or other channels. The author also developed an efficient IND-CKA secure index construction called Z-IDX using pseudo-random functions and Bloom filters (BF).

Boneh et al. developed the keyword search using a public key system, where they defined the concept of a public key encryption with keyword search (PEKS) and gave two constructions [2]. Chang and Mitzenmacher proposed two index search schemes using the idea of pre-built dictionaries [7].

The above protocols only consider the search between a single-user and a server. In this paper, we investigate secure index search protocols in the multi-user setting. The contributions of this paper are as follows.

- **Extension.** We extend a single-user setting into a multi-user setting so that a member in a hierarchical group can search the encrypted documents shared among the group members securely.
- **Access Control.** There are various types of encrypted documents; documents open to all members in a group, documents shared by a subgroup and private documents owned by a person. Our protocol provides access control for these documents. That is, only those people who have the search key corresponding to the documents can inspect, read and update their encrypted documents.
- **Efficiency.** The proposed schemes handle availability. That is, the schemes enable a legitimate member of a group to search both old and new documents

that have been shared by the group without re-encrypting the old documents with a new group key.

- **Privacy.** The schemes provide users with privacy against an untrusted server.
- **Forward Secrecy.** The schemes guarantee forward secrecy for leaving members of a group, i.e., they can not search documents created after their revocation.

2   Security Definition and Primitives

In this section, we describe security requirements for our schemes. We first present the security notion of IND-CKA introduced by Goh [9]. And then, we describe two properties of a one-way hash key chain which are used as primitives of our schemes.

Definition 1. IND-CKA : Semantic Security Against Adaprive Chosen Keyword Attack [9]. This notion is defined via the following game played by an adversary. Suppose the challenger C gives the adversary $\mathcal{A}$ two equal length documents V_0 and V_1, each containing some (possibly unequal) number of words, together with an index. $\mathcal{A}$'s challenge is to determine which document is encoded in the index. If the problem of distinguishing between the index for V_0 and V_1 is hard, then deducing at least one of the words that V_0 and V_1 do not have in common from the index must also be hard. If $\mathcal{A}$ cannot determine which document is encoded in the index with probability non-negligibly different from $1/2$, then we say that the index reveals nothing about its contents.

Definition 2. One-Way Hash Key Chain. Next, we discuss a one-way hash key chain, in short, one-way key chain. It is generated by selecting the last value at random and applying a one-way hash function H repeatedly. Note that the initially chosen value is the last value of the chain used. The followings are two properties of a one-way hash chain.

- **Property 1** : Anybody can deduce that an earlier value k_i really belongs to the one-way key chain by using the later value k_j of the chain and by checking $H^{j-i}(k_j)$ which equals k_i with the later value k_j.
- **Property 2** : Given the latest released value k_i of a one-way key chain, an adversary cannot find a later value k_j such that $H^{j-i}(k_j)$ equals k_i. Even when value k_{i+1} is released, the second pre-image collision resistant property prevents an adversary from finding k'_{i+1} different from k_{i+1} such that $H(k_{i+1})$ equals k_i.

3   Constructing Secure Index Search for Groups

In this section we construct a secure index search in a hierarchical group. In Figure.1 we illustrate an example of a hierarchical group. The group includes

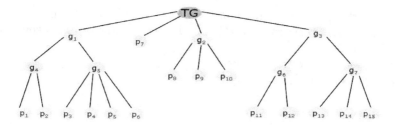

Fig. 1. An example of a group

subgroups $(g_1, g_2, ..., g_7)$ and members $(p_1, p_2, ..., p_{15})$ belonging to the corresponding groups.

Our schemes assume a group controller (GC). The GC manages group session keys for secure group communication and the search keys of all the groups for secure index search. Search keys consist of two keys; one is a document encryption key and the other is an index generation key. Due to two separated search keys, we can compress and encrypt the documents more readily, and store documents at a server more efficiently. In addition, search keys are used independently from a group session key or a member's private key for more strong security.

We construct two schemes; one is a SIS-D (secure index search in a direct way) which enables users to search directly with a server without a GC. The other is a SIS-C (secure index search via a GC) which enables users to search their encrypted documents through a GC. The GC of SIS-C takes user's place and plays rolls of a TTP (trusted third party) and a mix-net.

Each of them is again divided into two search protocols; for shared secret documents of a group and for private secret documents. In this section, four schemes are introduced; secure index search for a group user in a direct way (SIS-GD), secure index search for a private user in a direct way (SIS-PD), secure index search for a group user passing through a group controller (SIS-GC), secure index search for a private user passing through a group controller (SIS-PC).

Based on the four elementary algorithms of Z-IDX, each of our proposed protocols consist of six stages; key Generation Stage, Trapdoor Generation Stage, Index Building Stage, Data Building Stage, Uploading Stage, and Index Searching Stage.

3.1   Notation

- kg_j^i : a group session key of the subgroup g_j at i-th session.
- $KD_{g_j}^i$: a document encryption key of a subgroup g_j at i-th session.
- $KI_{g_j}^i = (gk_{j,1}^i, gk_{j,2}^i, ..., gk_{j,r}^i)$: an index generation key for a subgroup g_j at i-th session. The key consists of r keys to produce input-value for r hash functions of BF (Refer to Appendix A).
- kp_i : a private key of a user p_i.
- KDp_i : a document encryption key of a private user p_i.
- $KIp_i = (pk_{i,1}, pk_{i,2}, .., pk_{i,r})$: an index generation key of a private user p_i.

- $T_{w_j} = (x_1^i, x_2^i, .., x_r^i)$: a trapdoor for a word w_j at i-th session.
- $(y_1^i, y_2^i, ..., y_r^i) = (f(i, x_1^i), f(i, x_2^i), ..., f(i, x_r^i))$: a codeword for a keyword w_j at i-th session.
- D_i : a document with identifier i.
- I_{D_i} : an index of D_i.

3.2 SIS-D

The GC in the SIS-D only plays a roll of a key manager, and the search is processed directly between a user and a server.

SIS-GD. The search keys in SIS-GD are generated by using one-way hash key chains based on hash function. For clear understanding, all stages are described when a member p_1 of a group g_1 is in the second session. The six stages of SIS-GD are as follows.

1. **Key Generation Stage.** First, GC generates a group session key, a document encryption key and an index generation key for each group, then GC keeps the keys.

   Table 1 shows that if the first session is changed into the second session

Table 1. Key table of each group when a session is changed

Groups	Group session key	Document encryption key	Index generation key
g_1	$kg_1^1 \rightarrow kg_1^2 \rightarrow kg_1^3...$	$KD_{g_1}^1 \rightarrow KD_{g_1}^2 \rightarrow KD_{g_1}^3...$	$KI_{g_1}^1 \rightarrow KI_{g_1}^2 \rightarrow KI_{g_1}^3...$
g_2	$kg_2^1 \rightarrow kg_2^2 \rightarrow kg_2^3...$	$KD_{g_2}^1 \rightarrow KD_{g_2}^2 \rightarrow KD_{g_2}^3...$	$KI_{g_2}^1 \rightarrow KI_{g_2}^2 \rightarrow KI_{g_2}^3...$
:	:	:	:

then the first session key kg_1^1 of subgroup g_1 is changed into kg_1^2. Then a document encryption key and an index generation key are also changed as in Table 1; $KD_{g_1}^1 \rightarrow KD_{g_1}^2$, $KI_{g_1}^1 \rightarrow KI_{g_1}^2$. These search keys are generated as follows. Given a security parameter s, we choose the last key of a key chain (i.e. $KI_{g_1}^q$ and $KD_{g_1}^q$ if the length of a key chain is q.) and one-way hash function randomly. We apply the last key to a hash function repeatedly and compute all other keys : $KI_{g_1}^i = h^r(KI_{g_1}^{i+1})$, $KD_{g_1}^i = h(KD_{g_1}^{i+1})$, where $i \in [1, q-1]$ and the notation h^r means that h is applied to each of r elements independently. In this way, we can generate the search keys reversely.

$$KI_{g_1}^i = \begin{cases} KI_{g_1}^q = (gk_{1,1}^q, \ gk_{1,2}^q, ..., \ gk_{1,r}^q) \in_R \{0,1\}^{sr} \\ KI_{g_1}^{q-1} = h^r(KI_{g_1}^q) = (h(gk_{1,1}^q), \ h(gk_{1,2}^q), ..., \ h(gk_{1,r}^q)) \\ \qquad = (gk_{1,1}^{q-1}, \ gk_{1,2}^{q-1}, ..., \ gk_{1,r}^{q-1}) \\ KI_{g_1}^{q-2} = h^r(KI_{g_1}^{q-1}) = (h(gk_{1,1}^{q-1}), \ h(gk_{1,2}^{q-1}), ..., \ h(gk_{1,r}^{q-1})) \\ \qquad = (gk_{1,1}^{q-2}, \ gk_{1,2}^{q-2}, ..., \ gk_{1,r}^{q-2}) \\ ...... \\ KI_{g_1}^1 = h^r(KI_{g_1}^2) = (h(gk_{1,1}^2), \ h(gk_{1,2}^2), ..., \ h(gk_{1,r}^2)) \\ \qquad = (gk_{1,1}^1, \ gk_{1,2}^1, ..., \ gk_{1,r}^1) \end{cases}$$

$$KD_{g_1}^i = \begin{cases} KD_{g_1}^q \in_R \{0,1\}^s \\ KD_{g_1}^{q-1} = h(KD_{g_1}^q), \\ KD_{g_1}^{q-2} = h(KD_{g_1}^{q-1}) \\ \cdots\cdots \\ KD_{g_1}^1 = h(KD_{g_1}^2) \end{cases}$$

In our construction, the usage of one-way hash function h is critical. The one-wayness of h prohibits a leaving member from computing new keys after leaving. But, since it is easy to compute h, any newly joining member can obtain all the previous keys by applying the current key to h repeatedly in order to search all the documents. This eliminate decryption and re-encryption of the previous documents. For example, in the second session, a member p_1 of subgroup g_1 receives a new key kg_1^2. The key can be generated by using well-known group key protocols, such as one in [3]. Then $KD_{g_1}^2$ and $KI_{g_1}^2$, which have been computed in advance by the key chain, are encrypted with kg_1^2 and transferred to all members of subgroup g_1.

2. **Trapdoor Generation Stage.** A user p_1 chooses a pseudo-random function $f : \{0,1\}^n \times \{0,1\}^s \rightarrow \{0,1\}^s$ randomly. A document D_i consists of an unique identifier $i \in \{0,1\}^n$ and a list of words $(w_0,..,w_t) \in \{0,1\}^{nt}$. As inputs to pseudo-random function f, p_1 takes the index generation key $KI_{g_1}^2 = (gk_{1,1}^2, gk_{1,2}^2, ..., gk_{1,r}^2)$ and a word w_j, and computes the trapdoor T_{w_j} for a word w_j.
$$T_{w_j} = (f(w_j, gk_{1,1}^2), f(w_j, gk_{1,2}^2), ..., f(w_j, gk_{1,r}^2)) = (x_1, x_2, ..., x_r).$$

Namely, p_1 encrypts the keywords(a list of words) with the index generation key.

3. **Index Building Stage.** p_1 performs the followings, with the document D_i and the trapdoor T_{w_j}.

   - **Codeword**: The user computes a codeword with the trapdoor T_{w_j} for w_j in D_i where codeword $(y_1, y_2, ..., y_r)$ is $(f(i, x_1), f(i, x_2), ..., f(i, x_r))$. Namely, a user encrypts the trapdoor T_{w_j} together with an unique identifer i of the document containing a word w_j.
   - **Construction of BF for D_i**: The user inserts codeword $(y_1, y_2, ..., y_r)$ into BF. For each w_j in D_i, repeat the above process and construct BF for D_i. (Refer to [12].)
   - **Building an index**: The user produces $I_{D_i} = (i\|BF)$ as the index for D_i, i.e., this BF is the index for the document D_i with identifier i.

4. **Data Building Stage and Uploading Stage.** After encrypting the document D_i with the second session document encryption key $KD_{g_1}^2$, p_1 concatenates them with an unique identifier i and sends the results to a server together with the indexes $\{I_{D_i}\}$ generated in the 3rd stage.
$$C = [\{E_{KD_{g_1}^2}(D_i) \| i\}, \{I_{D_i} = (i \| BF)\}]$$

The server stores the received ciphertexts C.

GC	User	Server
Setup		
1. Key Generation		
$kg_1^1 \rightarrow kg_1^2$		
$KD_{g_1}^1 \rightarrow KD_{g_1}^2$		
$KI_{g_1}^1 \rightarrow KI_{g_1}^2$		
$\longrightarrow$	**2. Trapdoor Generation**	
	$T_{w_j} = (f(w_j, gk_{1,1}^2), ..., f(w_j, gk_{1,r}^2))$	
	3. Index Building	
	$I_{D_i} = (i\|BF)$	
	4. DataBuilding	
	Uploading	
	$\longrightarrow$	$C = [\{E_{KD_{g_1}^2}(D_i) \| i\}$
		$, \{I_{D_i} = (i \| BF)\}]$
Searching		
	5. Index Searching	
	5.1.Query T_{w_2}, T_{w_1}	
	$\longrightarrow$	5.2. Generate codeword,
		BF test
		5.3. Return $\{E_{KD_{g_1}^2}(D_i)\}$,
		$\{E_{KD_{g_1}^1}(D_i)\}$
5.4.Decrypt		$\longleftarrow$

Fig. 2. SIS-GD

5. **Index Searching Stage.** Since a keyword w may be included in the document at the second session or/and the first session, a user p_1 must compute the trapdoors $T_{w_2} = (x_1^2, x_2^2, .., x_r^2)$ and $T_{w_1} = (x_1^1, x_2^1, .., x_r^1)$ for the keyword w with $KI_{g_1}^2$ and $KI_{g_1}^1 = h^r(KI_{g_1}^2)$. That is, p_1 has to produce trapdoors as many as the number of the sessions, which is possible because p_1 can compute all the previous search keys by applying the current search key to hash function h. Then, p_1 sends all generated trapdoors to a server. The server computes the codewords for the keyword with trapdoors T_{w_2}, T_{w_1}, and identifiers of all documents $D_i's$.

$$(y_1^2, y_2^2, ..., y_r^2) = (f(i, x_1^2), f(i, x_2^2), ..., f(i, x_r^2))$$

$$(y_1^1, y_2^1, ..., y_r^1) = (f(i, x_1^1), f(i, x_2^1), ..., f(i, x_r^1))$$

Next, the server performs BF test. If there exists i passing BF test to the codewords $(y_1^2, y_2^2, ..., y_r^2)$ and $(y_1^1, y_2^1, ..., y_r^1)$, the server sends documents $\{E_{KD_{g_1}^2}(D_i)\}$, $\{E_{KD_{g_1}^1}(D_i)\}$ corresponding to i to p_1. Receiving $\{E_{KD_{g_1}^2}(D_i)\}$ and $\{E_{KD_{g_1}^1}(D_i)\}$, p_1 decrypts them and obtains the documents;

$$\{D_{KD_{g_1}^2}(E_{KD_{g_1}^2}(D_i))\}, \{D_{KD_{g_1}^1}(E_{KD_{g_1}^1}(D_i))\}, \text{ where } KD_{g_1}^1 = h(KD_{g_1}^2).$$

If it's the q-th session, a user must produce q trapdoors and decrypt the received documents until obtaining the plaintexts by applying the current key to a hash function repeatedly. We illustrate a SIS-GD protocol in Figure 2.

SIS-PD. In SIS-PD protocol, p_1 has three keys; a private key kp_1 which GC knows, the document encryption key KDp_1, and the index generation key KIp_1. Two keys KDp_1 and KIp_1 are generated by a user oneself and are not known even to GC. The search processes are well depicted in the full paper.

Table 2. GC's key for each group when a session is changed

group	group's key	the GC's document encryption key for each group	the GC's index generation key for each group
g_1	$kg_1^1 \rightarrow kg_1^2 \rightarrow kg_1^3 ...$	KD_{g_1}	KI_{g_1}
g_2	$kg_2^1 \rightarrow kg_2^2 \rightarrow kg_2^3 ...$	KD_{g_2}	KI_{g_2}
⋮	⋮	⋮	⋮

3.3   SIS-C (via GC)

Since SIS-D is a direct search system, a user's computational overhead is increased as the number of sessions grows. In order to keep the search keys for each group to be unchanged in spite of session changes, SIS-C scheme assumes that users must pass through the GC. Accordingly, GC in SIS-C must perform the search process instead of a user. Furthermore, we can also guarantee a user the protection of privacy by giving GC authority to play roles of a TTP and a mix-net.

SIS-GC. GC keeps key matching table as in Table 2. Although the group session key of subgroup g_1 is changed from kg_1^1 to kg_1^2, GC's document encryption key and index generation key (KD_{g_1}, KI_{g_1}) corresponding to the subgroup g_1 are not changed but fixed. When a member p_1 of subgroup g_1 intends to store and search the shared data of subgroup g_1, the search processes are shown in Figure 3.

SIS-PC. The server in SIS-GC can never know what are the keyword, the content of data, and the identity of a user, whereas GC knows everythings about the search processes. Of course, it doesn't matter because the GC plays a role of TTP. Nevertheless, p_1 with private purpose may want even GC not to know all informations abot the search as in SIS-PD. So p_1 generates the search keys and performs all the search processes by oneself. A private user only passes through the GC. Refer to the full paper for the detail search process.

4   Privacy and Secrecy

4.1   Privacy

The Privacy proposed in our schemes has the following properties.

- An untrusted server can search a secret keyword without learning the word and cannot learn anything about the plaintext when only given the ciphertext.

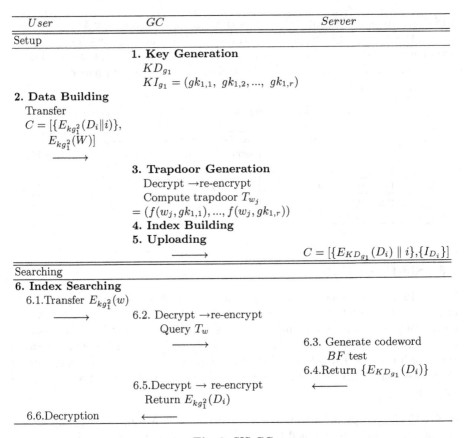

Fig. 3. SIS-GC

- An untrusted server cannot correlate a keyword with the searched documents.
- An untrusted server cannot determine whether the searched documents are the secret documents for a person or the shared documents for a group.

In SIS-GC, GC can learn all process about the search. However, except for GC, privacy can be provided almost perfectly to users against the untrusted server. The followings guarantee our schemes to hold the above properties.

- A trapdoor : An untrusted server cannot learn a keyword from a trapdoor.
- The GC as a mix-net : In this paper, the GC plays a role of a mix-net which have the following three phases.
  1. Encryption/decryption phase : Input data is encrypted or decrypted. Also, the user's information address is removed or encrypted in this step.
  2. Batch generation phase : Input data is processed by batch.
  3. Mixing phase : Input data are processed by a pseudo-random permutation function.

A mix network is a multi-party protocol that takes as input a list of cipher-text items and from this produces a new, random list of ciphertext items such that there is a one-to-one correspondence between the underlying plaintexts of input and output items. In other words, the underlying output plaintexts represent a random permutation of the underlying input plaintexts. The security of a mix network is characterized by the infeasibility for an adversary of determining which output items correspond to which input items [16]. Moreover, since the information of address is removed or encrypted in the encryption/decrypion phase, the untrusted server cannot know who queries with which keyword. And he doesn't know the contents of the retrieved documents, too [5,8].

- The encrypted documents : Returning the encrypted documents to the GC, the server cannot know the contents of returning documents and also the destination of it.

By passing through a GC, SIS-C provides anonymity of a sender/receiver and untraceability. Also the server cannot know the contents of the searched documents corresponding to the trapdoor of a keyword as well as whether the documents are a single-user's secret data or the group members' shared data.

Although SIS-D is a direct search without passing through a GC, as the same manner in SIS-G, a user of SIS-D also queries the trapdoor for a keyword and the server returns the encrypted documents. Hence the server cannot know the contents of the searched documents corresponding to the trapdoor of a keyword. Accordingly, we can say that SIS-D provides privacy in the search system, too.

4.2   Secrecy

The search process in our schemes is based on the serach algorithm of Z-IDX. The security of secure algorithm in Z-IDX is proven semantic secure against adaptively chosen keyword attack in [9], so we do not mention it.

Next, we consider the security requirements for dynamic groups. The group key secrecy depends on the security of a group key agreement protocol used in our schemes. If we use a secure group key agreement protocol, then our schemes satisfy the group key secrecy.

Forward secrecy can be provided in both SIS-D and SIS-C. For a leaving member, new group keys are generated randomly, and the user in SIS-C can not know new session keys. Hence, SIS-C guarantees forward secrecy. Not receiving a new session key from the GC, a leaving user of SIS-D can never know a new session key due to one-wayness property of the key chain. Since he cannot produce any valid trapdoor for the sessions after leaving, he cannot search the encrypted documents thereafter.

On the other hand, our schemes don't provide a joiner with backward secrecy. However, backward secrecy is useless for our schemes. New joiners of a group such as a company or a government office would rather require to search both old and new documents, because they have to refer to old documents to perform successive tasks of the group. By the Property 1 of a one-way hash key chain, this requirement can be accomplished.

5   Discussion

Since the proposed schemes are the initial schemes of the search system for groups, there is no previous schemes to be compared with.

Comparing SIS-D with SIS-C, the difference are originated from that SIS-D is a direct search scheme between a user and a server using the one-way hash key chain and SIS-C is the search passing through a GC.

In SIS-GD, a user must generate q trapdoors as the same number of the changed sessions for one keyword, and has to decrypt the received documents till obtaining the plaintexts by applying the current key to a hash function repeatedly. Although it's much more efficient than re-encrypting all of the old documents, it does not fit for the mobile system whose membership change is very dynamic.

However, our system is not for such a mobile system but for a group like a company or a government office. Such groups manage their documents in a server by certain periods of time; every three months of a year, semiannually, annually, and so on. If the length of a key chain is selected appropriately, SIS-GD becomes more efficient for these group members to search their documents by certain periods of time.

In SIS-C, GC keeps the fixed values of search keys for each group none the less for the change of sessions so that GC does nothing but generate one trapdoor for one keyword. Since a user must pass through the GC, a user's computational overhead becomes much less. However, it has disadvantages of intervention of a GC and the growing number of flows. Instead, we can enhance the protection of privacy in the search system by giving a GC authority of a TTP and a mixnet.

6   Application Scenario

As an applicable system, we can consider a general hospital. For reference of Figure.1, we presume a huge group TG as a general hospital, subgroups $(g_1, g_2, ..., g_7)$ as many departments such as a surgery ward, a psychiatry ward, the department of radiology, and so on, and many members $(p_1, p_2, ..., p_{15})$ as the employees of the general hospital.

We suppose a subgroup g_1 as a psychiatry ward. Then, note that psychiatry patients' medical records must not be read by any other people than the psychiatry staffs. Only the psychiatry doctors and nurses can record and read them. In principle, it doesn't allow the patients or other people to read such medical records. Hence, our new schemes can prevent the other group's memeber from leaking some information about the hospital. Especially, considering the increasing violation of privacy(The leaking of registered information or sensitive medical records such as a venereal disease or a plastic operation history may bring about a lot of social issues) by the internal staffs, our schemes are needed more acutely.

If a new doctor join the psychiatry ward, he must refer to old documents to learn his assigned patients' history. Hence, our schemes are fit for this system because they can search all of the old and new documents without re-encrypting the previous documents.

7   Conclusion

We have discussed the new schemes extending a user into multi-users of a group in the searching system of encrypted documents.

The schemes are searchable systems under the access control giving a user the limit of access level ; the secret data of a private user, the shared secret data of a subgroup, the shared secret data of total group. One of the most important things is the possibility of searching without re-encrypting old documents. In addition, they can provide privacy by encrypting a keyword (i.e. trapdoor) and documents. Particularly, SIS-C can guarantee almost perfect privacy by giving a GC the functions of a TTP and a mix-net.

However, SIS-C must pass through the GC and SIS-D is not appropriate for a dynamic mobile system because too many trapdoors to be generated cause computational overheads. Hence, we need to work continuously to make the scheme for groups which is fit for mobile systems without GC.

Acknowledgement

We thank Dr. Hyun Jeong Kim and Hyun Sook Rhee for helpful discussions about the useful comments on an early version of this paper. We also thank anonymous referees for their valuable comments.

References

1. S. Bellovin and W. Cheswick. Privacy-enhanced searches using encrypted bloom filters. Cryptology ePrint Archive, Report 2004/022, Feb 2004.
2. D. Boneh, G. D. Crescenzo, R. Ostrovsky, and G. Persiano. Public-key encryption with keyword search. In C. Cachin, editor, Proceedings of Eurocrypt 2004, LNCS. Springer-Verlag, May 2004.
3. M. Burrnesterand Y. Desmedt. A secure and efficient conference key distribution system. The Advances in Cryptology - EUROCRYPT, 1994
4. B. Bloom. Space/time trade-offs in hash coding with allowable errors. Communications of the ACM, 13(7):422-426, Jul 1970.
5. David Chaum. Untraceable electronic mail, return addresses, and digital pseudonyms. In Communications of the ACM 4(2), February 1981.
6. B. Chor, E. Kushilevitz, O. Goldreich, and M. Sudan. Private information retrieval. Journal of the ACM, 45(6):965-981, Nov 1998.
7. Y.-C. Chang and M. Mitzenmacher. Privacy preserving keyword searches on remote encrypted data. Cryptology ePrint Archive, Report 2004/051, Feb 2004.
8. Claudia Diaz and Andrei Serjantov. Generalising Mixes. In the Proceedings of Privacy Enhancing Technologies workshop (PET 2003), March 2003.
9. Eu-Jin Goh. Secure Indexes. An early version of this paper first appeared on the Cryptology ePrint Archive on October 7th 2003. May 5, 2004

10. A. Perrig, R. Canetti, J. Tygar, and D. X. Song. Efficient authentication and signing of multicast streams over lossy channels. In IEEE Symposium on Security and Privacy, May 2000.
11. D. Song, D. Wagner, and A. Perrig. Practical techniques for searches on encrypted data. In Proceedings of IEEE Symposium on Security and Privacy, pages 44-55. IEEE, May 2000.
12. UC Berkeley—CS 170: Ecient Algorithms and Intractable Problems Handout 10 Lecturer : David Wagner February 27, 2003
13. B.Waters, D. Balfanz, G. Durfee, and D. Smetters. Building an encrypted and searchable audit log. In Proceedings of the 11th Network and Distributed System Security (NDSS) Symposium, pages 205-214. Internet Society (ISOC), Feb 2004.
14. Yih-Chun Hu, Adrian Perrig, and David B. Johnson. Efficient security mechanisms for routing protocols. In Network and Distributed System Security Symposium, NDSS03, pages 57-73, February 2003.
15. A. Perrig, D. Song, and J.D. Tygar. ELK, a new protocol for efficient large-group key distribution. In Proceedings of IEEE Symposium on Security and Privacy, pages 247-262, 2001.
16. M.Jakobsson and A. Juels. Mix and Match: Secure Function Evaluation via Ciphertexts. ASIACRYPT2000, LNCS 1976, pages 162-177, 2000.

Provision of Secure Policy Enforcement Between Small and Medium Governmental Organizations

Nikolaos Oikonomidis, Sergiu Tcaciuc, and Christoph Ruland

Institute for Digital Communication Systems, University of Siegen
{nikolaos.oikonomidis, sergiu.tcaciuc,
christoph.ruland}@uni-siegen.de

Abstract. This paper is derived from research work conducted within eMayor project, funded by the EU committee (IST-2003-507217). Motivation of the project was the fact that small and medium sized governmental organizations (SMGOs) interact frequently with citizens and/or businesses, to offer paper-based and electronic services utilizing a limited number of resources (e.g. employees and funds). SMGOs also interact with each other, in local or cross-border transactions, to exchange information on behalf of citizens, businesses or the organization itself. Main objectives of eMayor are to build a secure, inter-operable, cost-effective and open e-government platform, addressing the needs of SMGOs. The core of the eMayor platform will be built upon state-of-the-art web-services technology which enables the interoperability with existing web-services already provided by governmental organizations. However, the problem of heterogeneity of security, access control, privacy and process flow policies among the different organization remains, both on national and international level. To provide full interoperability a framework which solves the addressed issues and provides transparent coordination of different policy enforcement mechanisms is needed. Such a framework, enforcing security and access-control policies across a decentralized network of governmental organizations is discussed in this paper. First the system architecture of eMayor platform is introduced. Thereafter, general and specific security requirements that apply to an interoperable e-government platform are discussed and the trust model together with the roles which pose different authentication and authorization attributes are depicted. Results of the requirements analysis provide input for platform design. Policy enforcement mechanisms together with an overview of security solutions on identified communication channels are presented. Deployment of chosen technologies, specifically for distributed e-Government structures, is introduced taking into account the possible extensions in order to provide higher level of security standards. The paper concludes with final objectives on policy enforcement framework and outlines the work in progress.

1 Introduction and Motivation

Citizens interact at regular intervals with municipalities or municipal organizations. Public administrations offer a variety of services like requests/processing of certificates, (local) tax payment, and promotion of city information. An effective and effi-

S. Katsikas, J. López, G. Pernul (Eds.): TrustBus 2005, LNCS 3592, pp. 141–150, 2005.

cient service provision brings benefits to both municipalities and the involved citizens/customers of the particular services. Electronic services provide a unique opportunity to enhance and expand the offered services by making them more flexible, since they may provide location and time independent access to the citizens, as well as a rapid execution of services that might otherwise require a considerable amount of time and effort. These benefits are not realizable where there is a lack of the proper infrastructure to serve citizens, such as in small municipalities with limited resources and/or large areas of responsibility.

The provision of such electronic services can be achieved with the use of multimodal access mechanisms [1]. Due to the fact that exchanged data in forms and documents may contain private or sensitive data, it is imperative to introduce security mechanisms that guarantee to citizens a trustworthy means of communication. Trust can be achieved through the use of cryptographic mechanisms that assure the security requirements of confidentiality, authentication of data and users, integrity of content, non-repudiation by the origin and non-repudiation by the receiver. Further, cross-border services involve different municipalities and other public authorities in the processes. The support of municipalities across Europe in their cooperation is one of the main objectives of the eMayor project. Legal aspects are very important to be considered to run e-Services that must be legally validated.

2   eMayor Project

eMayor addresses the specific audience of SMGOs across Europe. The project looks especially at transactions that are performed on an European level. Such services typically handle the secure exchange of documents, forms, and other information across national borders. The terms of "SMGO" and "cross-border service" has been defined by the eMayor consortium. All participating municipalities fall into the category of SMGOs. They vary greatly in size, the smallest one with 10.000 inhabitants and the biggest one with well over 500.000 inhabitants.

The target group for eMayor comprises municipalities up to half a million citizens normally located in urban or metropolitan areas. The approach is to build a generic platform (*eMayor platform*) hosting municipal services that are generically designed, adapted and implemented considering specific stakeholder needs, and then validated within several municipalities.

3   Platform Description

The realization approach of eMayor has been planed to go through three major phases: requirements analysis, system design and platform implementation. During the requirements analysis phase of the project, needs and requirements of SMGOs from four different European countries have been investigated. Existing services, data formats and infrastructures were examined and evaluated. The evaluation resulted into the construction of usage scenarios. The result of the requirements analysis served as the base for the next phase towards the realization of the platform, namely the design of its architecture [2]. The main objective of the design was to provide a well-defined easy-to-implement architecture, which reflects the operational requirements set by the analysis phase and complies with legal frameworks and policies. The approach chosen for modeling the overall architecture relies on the Reference Model of Open Distributed Processing [3][4][5] which defines the following five "viewpoints" of a system:

- Enterprise Viewpoint: Purpose, scope and policies of the system.
- Information Viewpoint: Semantics of information and information processing.
- Computational Viewpoint: Functional decomposition of the system into objects which interact at interfaces.
- Engineering Viewpoint: Mechanisms and functions required to support distributed interaction between objects in the system.
- Technology Viewpoint: Choice of technology in the system

At first, the identified requirements together with the legal frameworks formed the Enterprise Viewpoint. The information that is required and the data that should be processed have been the specified in the Information Viewpoint. The interaction between system components on the functional level and their respective interfaces have been described in the Computational Viewpoint. Engineering and Technology Viewpoints have been placed in the implementation phase.

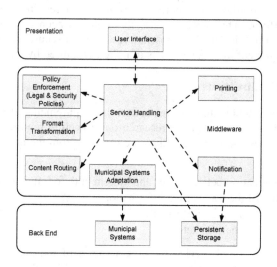

Fig. 1. Top-level view of the eMayor system

The system design resulted into the specification of an architecture, which is now described at the top-level, as a set of modules, each one comprising certain functionalities (Fig. 1):

- User Interface communicates with the Service Handling for the actual processing of the service. The Policy Enforcement encapsulates a set of functionalities such as auditing, access control, security mechanisms and the policies of the municipalities' legal frameworks.

- Service Handling represents the core of the eMayor platform and has dependencies to all other components. It communicates with the Policy Enforcement (e.g., for access control, encryption and digital signature of documents and messages, etc.).
- Format Transformation is responsible for transforming legal documents from a country-bound local format to a universal format for transport within the eMayor environment and vice versa.
- Content Routing provides the routing functionality for forwarding requests and legal documents from one municipality to another.
- Municipal Systems Adaptation is the linking point with the existing (legacy) systems of the municipalities.
- Persistent Storage modules handle storage to the file system or databases.
- Finally, Output Notification and Printing provide support for notification and printing services.

4 Security and Policy Enforcement Framework

It has already been stressed that policy enforcement and secure and trustworthy deployment of cross-border municipal services are major requirements for the realization of the platform. Therefore, specific research has been done focusing on these issues in order to provide the best possible results for a secure, reliable and trustworthy platform which enforces several sets of policies required by the municipalities.

4.1 Security Requirements

The participating municipalities have set security requirements of the agreed municipal services. The evaluation of the research on protection requirements showed that the security services and features, which are required from the municipalities, include the following:

- Mutual authentication between user and system both for citizens and civil servants
- Confidentiality of the transmitted information
- Integrity of the transmitted information
- Non-repudiation of certain actions

Each agreed municipal service requires a subset of the above security services. Considering the fact, that more municipal services will be added to the eMayor platform in the future, the implementation of the basic set of security services appears inevitable.

4.2 Trust Model

A trust model has been established within the platform context, in order to provide trust relationships between participating entities in the system. Certification Authorities (CAs) are considered the only trusted entities. All communicating partners establish session trust via authentication.

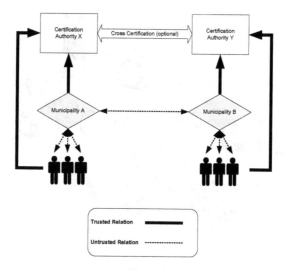

Fig. 2. Trust Model of the eMayor Platform

Fig. 2 shows that for communication between a user and a municipality authentication is needed because the relation is untrusted. Authentication is also required for communication between two municipalities. Thus, a citizen should authenticate him/herself in order to get access to the eMayor platform of a municipality and be able to submit requests for municipal services. Accordingly, a civil servant should authenticate him/herself before being able to use his/her respective eMayor services.

4.3 Security of the Communication Channels

Another point of research was to identify the physical and logical communication channels that exist in the system and between platforms. The heterogeneity of the existing municipal systems, which comes along with the heterogeneity of their existing security models, had to be taken into account. This means that a wide variety of security tokens, authentication mechanisms, signature formats and encryption technologies should be supported.

The use of security in municipal service deployment is reduced to message security, regarding the logical channels. Security of the transport layer is based on HTTP with TLS/SSL extension, if required. Thus, a secure connection is provided by redirecting to a HTTPS session provided by the web-server. The web-server should be configured accordingly.

Fig. 3 is a simplified depiction of the above assumptions. The upper scheme shows the measures for providing transport security (physical channels) and the lower scheme, the measures in order to provide application security (logical channels).

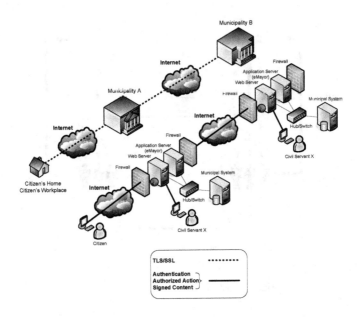

Fig. 3. Security measures on the communication channels

4.4 Policy Enforcement

At first in order to understand the term policy, a definition is given according to [3]:

"Policy: A set of rules related to a particular purpose"

In terms of predicates [3]:

"policy: predicate that states conditions valid at specific moments of time during an action occurrence."

"pre-condition: a predicate that a specification requires to be true for an action to occur."

"post-condition: a predicate that a specification requires to be true immediately after the occurrence of an action."

Within the Information Viewpoint of the system design phase a policy informational object has been specified. Thus, a policy object represents the constraints, conditions and rules that will have to be respected and enforced by the platform. Following policy types have been identified and specified (Fig. 4):

- `SecurityServicesPolicy` implements the security services that are required. A subject of research is the modeling of policies, which guide the service handling on all security-related actions within the deployment of a specific municipal service. In other terms, a `SecurityServicePolicy` will define the steps that have to be taken during the system's operation regarding the required security services.

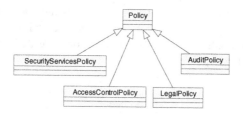

Fig. 4. Policy Types

- `AccessControlPolicy` regulates access control to the requested municipal services. The next step towards the implementation is to define the structure of these policies.
- `AuditPolicy` controls how actions are recorded in the system for auditing purposes.
- `LegalPolicy` manifests the legal rules that have to be applied during the provision of a requested service.

The Policy information object can be in one of two states. As shown in Fig. 5, it can be either an Inactive Policy or an Active Policy.

Fig. 5. Policy states and transitions

A policy is in the Inactive state, during the process of its initial making and definition. When the policy is structured and brought into force, it passes into the Active state. At the time of a policy update, it will pass from the Active state to the Inactive state in order to apply the changes. When the update of the policy definition is complete, the policy will once again pass to the Active state [2].

A policy can also be described as a "sentence" which consists of special "words". These words reflect, in most cases, obligation, authorization and permission or prohibition. Such a sentence has – as in the normal grammatical case – subjects, verbs, objects and conditional adverbs. Additionally, constraints on possible actions are also introduced by verbs. Putting these terms into the presented model, the structure depicted in Fig. 6 is obtained.

Certain policy types make use of a subset or all of the information elements that comprise the policy. The `PolicySubject` represents the entity, which will invoke one or more `PolicyAction` objects. A `PolicyAction` may take effect on a `PolicyObject`. The result of a `PolicyAction` or even one or more `PolicyOb-`

jects are related to the `PolicyTarget`, which is the end-point within a policy. One or more `PolicyPreCondition`, `PolicyCondition` and `PolicyPost-Condition` objects control the invocation of one or more `PolicyAction` objects, depending on the policy type.

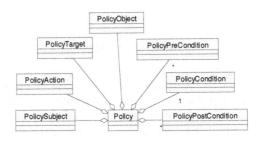

Fig. 6. Policy Elements

4.5 Development of the Policy Enforcement

Policy Enforcement will be implemented in the policy enforcement module. This module resides in the eMayor platform of each municipality. Components of the policy enforcement module comprise different sets of functionalities. Policy Enforcement Management exposes a set of "enforcer" interfaces to the Service Handling module. Policy Evaluation component contains all elements, which are responsible for taking a decision if a request or functionality complies with the appropriate policy. Policy Retrieval component queries the respective policy repositories and retrieves the appropriate policy or policy set. The model of the components and their communication within the policy enforcement module derives partially from the XACML [7] and SAML specifications [8], as part of the Web Services Security infrastructure [9][10].

Following, a general description of the classes included in the above described components is provided (Fig. 7). Policy Enforcement Management component comprises the interfaces, which are visible to the Service Handling module. These interfaces provide policy enforcement and its respective mechanisms:

- User Authentication
- User Authorization
- Verification of Digital Signatures
  Timestamping of the Documents

Policy Evaluation component consists of the `PolicyEvaluator` which is responsible for evaluating policies. After the evaluation of the specific policy or poliicy set which are relevant to the request of the Service Handling, the result (decision, in case of access control) is sent back to the Policy Enforcement Management component. Policy Mechanisms are used to realize the policy enforcement by applying them according to each policy.

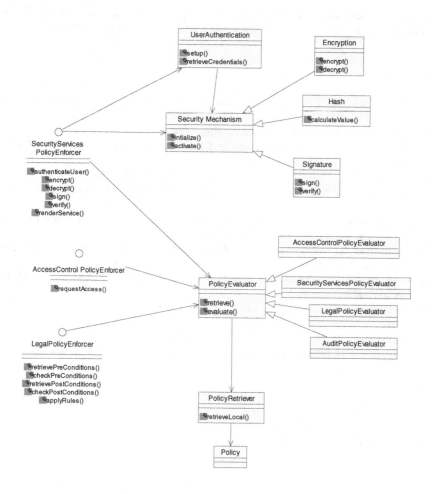

Fig. 7. Class View of the Policy Enforcement architecture

5   Conclusions and Outlook

Secure and reliable cross-border service provision on the pan-european level is an active research area and the main objective for eMayor project. The introduced framework for the policy enforcement combined with a security architecture for such platforms is also a major research topic. This topic addresses many problems, which should be solved in order to achieve the desired deployment of governmental services. Emerging technologies provide some first notion on how these problems could be solved but as in many other areas, such solutions cannot be directly applied. These solutions, require enhancements, modifications and correct combination of used technologies. The presented approach encompasses the intention to extend and continue the ongoing research, in order to provide a reliable architecture with a set of mechanisms, which can integrate secure policy enforcement into municipal electronic environments across Europe. The eMayor project aims to provide such solution.

References

1. eMayor Consortium, "Municipal Services –Analysis, Requirements and Usage scenarios", 2004
2. eMayor Consortium, "eMayor System Design", 2004
3. Information technology, Open Distributed Processing - Reference Model: Architecture, ISO, 1996
4. Mikhail Blinov, Ahmed Patel, "An application of the reference model for open distributed processing to electronic brokerage", Computer Standards and Interfaces, Elsevier Science, 2003
5. German Federal Ministry of Interior, "SAGA - Standards and Architectures for e-government Applications, version 2.0", December 2003
6. Information Technology, Open Distributed Processing - Reference Model: Enterprise Viewpoint, ISO, 2001
7. Core Specification, eXtensible Access Control Markup Language (XACML) Version 1.1, OASIS, 2003
8. Core Specification, Security Assertion Markup Language (SAML) Version 1.1, OASIS, 2004
9. Ethan Cerami, Web Services Essentials, O'Reilly, 2002
10. J. Rosenberg, D. Remy, Securing Web Services with WS-Security, SAMS, 2004

Maximizing Utility of Mobile Agent Based E-Commerce Applications with Trust Enhanced Security

Ching Lin, Vijay Varadharajan, and Yan Wang

Department of Computing,
Macquarie University, Sydney, NSW 2109, Australia
{linc, vijay, yanwang}@ics.mq.edu.au

Abstract. Utility has become an important consideration for information security. In this paper, we show that decisions by security mechanisms, such as the authorization decisions in a mobile agent based e-commerce system, have a direct impact on the utility of the underlying system. While benevolent behaviors contribute to the utility, malicious behaviors are the causes for lost of utility. Furthermore we show that a trust enhanced security framework can be deployed to maximize the utility of the mobile agent based e-commerce systems. This is due to one of the unique features of trust enhanced security solutions - the ability to use trust evaluation to "weed out" malicious entities. This paper presents a qualitative solution for utility maximization, and paves the way for future development of quantitative solutions. Finally, we study the properties of the proposed framework through simulation and present the results of the simulated studies which confirm our intuitions about utility maximization.

1 Introduction

Internet based e-commerce has been growing increasingly popular in recent years. Mobile agent is a new paradigm for distributed computing, in which mobile agents are autonomous programs and follow a route, migrate through a network of agent enabled sites to accomplish tasks on behalf of their owners. The mobile agent model, which offers unique features such as reducing the network load, executing asynchronously and autonomously, and adapting dynamically, has been considered as an attractive option to build the infrastructures of mobile e-commerce applications [7,16].

While mobile agent based e-commerce offers the above attractive features, security has been a big challenge, due to the very same reasons that have brought about the advantages. It is the mobility and autonomous nature of mobile e-commerce model that has violated many fundamental security assumptions. This presents challenges to the mobile agent security in two aspects: protection of service provider hosts is difficult, due to the fact that the identity of a requesting party can no longer be determined with certainty as in the case of an non-mobile

S. Katsikas, J. López, G. Pernul (Eds.): TrustBus 2005, LNCS 3592, pp. 151–160, 2005.

based e-commerce; clients requesting goods and services now have the difficulties in protecting its agents, because these agents are now able to roam around a series of hosts conducting itinerant mobile e-commerce transactions, such as conducting a complete travel plan for its human principal in terms of booking the airline tickets, hotel reservations and car rental etc. The hosts that the agents traverse are often competitors with each other, so collaborations between them can not always be expected. This means one host may do a numbers of malicious things to the agent in order to gain economical benefits from it. On the other hand, agents from a malicious host can also attempt to do harms to a receiving host.

Most of existing security solutions (e.g. [5,11]) for mobile agents are based on traditional security mechanisms, which can not guarantee how actually the authorized entities will behave [12]. In fact the assumptions of these traditional security models are violated by the unique nature of mobile agents [2]. The security performance is thus hindered by these violations.

While these issues are difficult to solve within the context of security mechanisms, some researchers have pointed out that trust is an important notion for mobile agent security and have developed security solutions with trust [14,17,8,9]. These trust based security models have shown the potential to overcome the drawbacks of traditional security models by ensuring a higher level of trustworthiness of authorized entities and thus raising the security levels.

In recent time, utility has been recognized as an important factor in security system development [4]. Now there is a consensus emerging that every security question is in fact an economical question concerning the utility of the underlying system [4]. It is easy to show that in a mobile agent based e-commerce system, both the protection of agents and hosts have a direct impact on the utility: attacks on a host by malicious agents will cause loss of commercial secrets such customers private information, downtime to the system, loss of customers, and eventually all these will be counted as utility loss. Attacks on agents will result in similar consequences that will also lead to the lost of utility. In this paper, for the sake of simplicity, we focus on the utility associated with the host protection - i.e. the authorization process. In the rest of the paper, we investigate the impact that security mechanisms have on system utility and show how utility can be maximized with a trust enhanced security framework.

The main contributions of this paper are:

- Discovering the direct impact on system utility by security decisions.
- Enabling utility maximization with a trust enhanced security framework.
- Presenting simulated studies of the utility maximizing properties of the proposed framework.

The paper is organized as follows. In Section 1 we identify the direct impact that security decision can have on the system utility. Section 2 describes related work. Section 3 introduces a trust enhanced security framework that maximizes utilities. In Section 4 we present the simulated studies of the proposed framework and analyze the simulation results. Finally, we provide concluding remarks and directions for future research in Section 5.

2   Related Work

2.1   Utility and Trust

The notion of utility and its application in computer science are not new. Marsh introduced the notion of utility as a member of a set of parameters used for constructing his trust model for multi-agent systems where, utility was actually used as an input for his trust calculation [10].

2.2   Traditional Authorization

Most mobile agent security systems are built on traditional security models, including two most widely used models - the *mandatory access control* (MAC) and the *discretionary access control* (DAC) models [3]. While these models aim at the enforcement of access control of system resources, they are not concerned about the system utility on which they do have a direct impact. This is because malicious behaviors can happen even after the authorization stage [12].

2.3   Payment Based Authorization

Sonntag et al. [13] has proposed a payment based scheme for mobile agent based e-commerce applications. Depending on the trustworthiness of the requesting entity, different prepaid amounts may need to be submitted to the server in order to gain the access which could not otherwise be granted. The prepaid amount should be more than the lost caused by any malicious behaviors. This proposal has introduced the notion of dynamic authorization in a sense that permissions to agents are made according to the trustworthiness of the agent and these permissions demand prepayments to insure against potential damages. Their model, while covering utility loss implicitly, does not deal with it explicitly.

3   Trust Enhanced Security Model and System Utility

In our model, we deal with utility explicitly by linking it with the operations of the underlying security models. We show that utility is, in fact, directly related to the outcomes of interactions granted by the security operations. Furthermore we demonstrate the ability of maximizing utility by the trust enhanced security operations.

3.1   The Overview of the New Framework

We now present the trust enhanced security framework that maximize the utility. Our conceptual model of the framework is depicted in Figure 1. The idea here is to use trust information, managed by the trust model, to fine tune the authorization decisions, such that malicious entities will be identified through past experiences and will be "weeded out". And it is by the removal of malicious entities (and thus the malicious behaviors) that we have the opportunity to improve authorization performance and thus the system utility. Next we describe

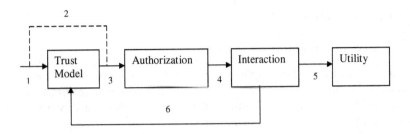

Fig. 1. Trust Enhanced Authorization for Mobile Agents

the main building blocks of our model in the following subsections. Please note that the trust model presented here is a simplistic one, and is used for the purpose of illustrating the new approach. A more detailed treatment of a practical trust model for mobile agents can be found in [9].

3.1.1   Trust Model

The trust model manages the trust information in the system. For the purpose of our study here, the trust information contains a set of pairs $\{(a, t)\}$, where a is an agent id and t ranging over $[0, 1]$ is the trust value. While $a \in A$ is a relatively static value, $t \in T$ is a dynamic one which is updated according to past experiences $e \in E$ by a trust update function:

$$\delta : T \times E \to T \qquad (1)$$

where T is a set of trust values, E is a set of experiences from previous interactions.

When requested by the incoming agent for authorization (i.e. `arrow 1` in Fig. 1, the proposed solution invokes the trust model to make a trust decision[1].

$$decision : (t > t_{th}) \to \{-1, 1\} \qquad (2)$$

Where t_{th} is the trust threshold.

When the above condition is tested true, then the agent is trusted and decision is set to 1; otherwise, the agent is regarded as malicious and decision is set to -1.

3.1.2   Authorization

This component performs the standard authorization function as per the designated base security model with only one difference - this component will only be invoked if the test in Equation 2 is true (i.e. `arrow 3` is active).

$$auth : A \times R \to P \qquad (3)$$

---

[1] Note that the dashed line 2 in Fig.1 indicates the bypassing of the trust model rendering the model to a standard authorization-only model.

Where R is a set of requests, and P a set of permissions for carrying out the requests.

3.1.3   Interaction

Once an agent has passed the test in Equation 2 and has been granted proper permissions by Equation 3, then it can proceed with its intended transactions (i.e. `arrow` 4 in Fig. 1). The interaction result will be marked as a satisfactory one if no malicious behavior has been detected, otherwise it will be marked as unsatisfactory [2]. The result will be put into the set E. This set will be fed-back (i.e. `arrow` 6 in Fig. 1) to the trust model for trust update with Equation 1, and fed-forward (i.e. `arrow` 5 in Fig. 1) to utility module for utility calculation in Equations 4 and 5.

3.1.4   Utility

Once we have obtained the set E (the interaction results), we can proceed to calculate the system utility:

$$utility : E \times F \to U \tag{4}$$

where F is a set of utility factors, and U is a set of the resultant utility values from the past interactions.

Thus the total system utility can be updated as:

$$total\_utility = \sum_{0}^{n}(U) \tag{5}$$

Where n is the number of agents $n = |A|$.

4   Simulation and Analysis

We now evaluate the proposed framework by a detailed system simulation with our new model. Let us consider a mobile agent based e-commerce system (such as an e-bookshop or a travel agency) where a service provider host is receiving agents from different owner hosts representing the customers and it needs to make the authorization decisions. We set up the following parameters for the simulation.

- Total Number of Interactions: $i = 100$
- Total Number of Agents: $n = |A| = 100$
- Trust Threshold: $t_{th} = 0.5$ [3]

---

[2] Various cryptographic checksums have been developed for checking malicious behaviors in terms of data and code tampering [15].

[3] The threshold value used here is an arbitrary one for illustrative purpose only. This is clearly an application dependent issue, e.g. different agent tasks will demand different trust values. Naturally one can infer that the agent host will use a higher trust threshold on a travel booking agent than a book enquiring agent.

- Initial Trust Value for Each Agent: $t = 0.58$ [4]
- System Utility Factor for Security Policy Compliance: $f_1 = 1$
- System Utility Factor for Security Policy Violation: $f_2 = -2$
- Trust Update Function [5]:
  - $t_{i+1} = t_i + 0.02$, when last interaction is satisfactory
  - $t_{i+1} = t_i - 0.04$, when last interaction is unsatisfactory
- Agent Behavior Probability Distribution = $\{0\%, 25\%, 50\%, 75\%, 100\%\}$
  (For simplicity, agents are evenly grouped into four behavior categories, ranging from most trustworthy to totally malicious. Their external malicious behaviors can be categorized by a set of certain probability distribution $\{0\%, 25\%, 50\%, 75\%, 100\%\}$. Here 0% means the entity is totally trustworthy, and never deviates from benevolent actions during each transaction, while 100% indicates a totally malicious entity that will attack every time when granted access).

The simulation model is implemented with MATLAB (www.mathworks.com) for the framework described in Section 3. We run the simulation for both our proposed framework and the authorization only solution (by shorting link 2 in Fig.1 to bypass the trust model).

4.1   Trust Evaluation

Many trust models have been developed for distributed systems over the years [10,1,6]. However, for our purpose, it is sufficient to use a simple trust model, with additive trust updates using previous experiences (capturing satisfactory and unsatisfactory experiences) as described in Section 3.1.1.

When the trust model is enabled (Fig.1), we had one additional layer - the trust layer to make decisions about the trust worthiness of the requesting agent. We can then decide: 1) to reject a request if the relevant trust value is less than the threshold, 2) to otherwise pass the request onto the authorization stage for a final decision.

The trust evaluation and the associated trust decisions are captured in Figs. 6,7,8,9. It is important to observe that while the mostly benevolent agents (with behavior probabilities of 0% and 25% security violations, see Figs. 6,7) are regarded as trustworthy and granted access for all the requests, the more malicious agents (with behavior probabilities of 50%, 75% and 100% security violations, see Figs. 8 and 9) are watched out closely by the trust model, and have been "weeded out" at various stages once their trust value dropped below the threshold caused by frequent malicious behaviors. It is this feature that has contributed to the vast improvement to system utility as discussed in the next section.

---

[4] The initial trust value is set arbitrarily to a value above the threshold to allow some initial interactions for all agents thus presenting a more general case for the trust model.

[5] In practice, these values are application dependent and should be set by the relevant trust policies. For more practical evaluation methods of trust update, see [9].

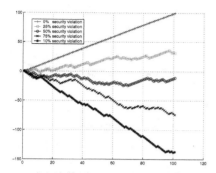

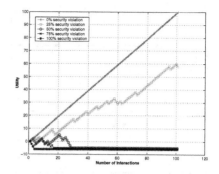

Fig. 2. Utility without Trust Management for Various Malicious Behaviors Distributions - 0% to 100% Security Violations

Fig. 3. Utility with Trust Management for Various Malicious Behaviors Distributions - 0% to 100% Security Violations

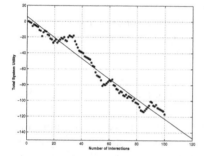

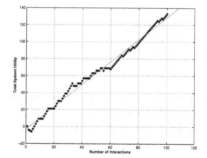

Fig. 4. Total Utility without Trust Management for Various Malicious Behaviors Distributions - 0% to 100% Security Violations

Fig. 5. Total Utility with Trust Management for Various Malicious Behaviors Distributions - 0% to 100% Security Violations

4.2   Trust Enhanced Authorization and Utility Maximization

As seen from Fig.2 and Fig.4, the authorization-only model (with `link 2` closed in Fig. 1) grants all of its permissions to recognized entities purely based on authorization policy; the trust enhanced security framework, on the other hand, uses trust to make a trust decision first, then decide if authorization needs to be invoked. While in the former case the malicious behaviors are not captured automatically to influence the security decisions, the latter framework has a trust model to evaluate the trustworthiness of each entities and to form a trust decision as an on/off switch (or a gate-keeper) for the authorization module. This effectively means that if an entity is not trusted enough (i.e. its trust value does not exceed the threshold), it won't not be evaluated by the authorization module. This would result in both the security and performance enhancements in addition to the desirable feature of utility maximization. These improvements in utility are shown in Fig.3 and Fig.5, where the new model has reversed the

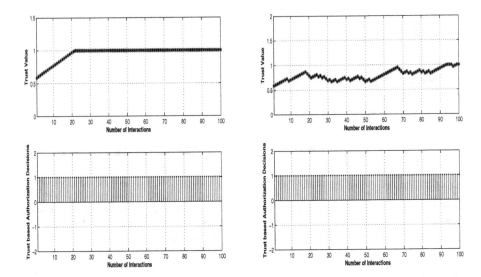

Fig. 6. Trust Evolution and Decision for Entities of 0% Security Violation

Fig. 7. Trust Evolution and Decision for Entities of 25% Security Violation

negative trends as a result of authorization-only model (see Fig.2 and Fig.4) has turned it to positive trends.

Without the trust model, the authorization-only system reacts mechanically to the agent's requests, as the authorization module grants blindly to any agent that has passed the authentication stage, either legally or illegally. It does not have the ability to make any additional decisions. Any of the malicious agents, who are granted permissions by the authorization module, will have the opportunity to attack. [6]

5 Conclusions

We have proposed a trust enhanced security approach that maximizes the underlying system utility. To our best knowledge, this paper is the first to discover direct impact on the underlying system utility by security mechanisms. Furthermore, this paper leverages trust based security model to obtain the utility maximization solution. This has, therefore, achieved the first step in linking security solutions with business objectives through utility maximization.

This paper has provided a qualitative solution to the utility maximization problem, and it has opened up a new direction for future research. Our immediate focus is to develop a quantitative model that can provide exact answers as to how much privileges/permissions should be granted for any given trust value. Such a

---

[6] While we do not consider the exact forms of attacks in this paper, a brief discussion can be found in Gong Li's book [3].

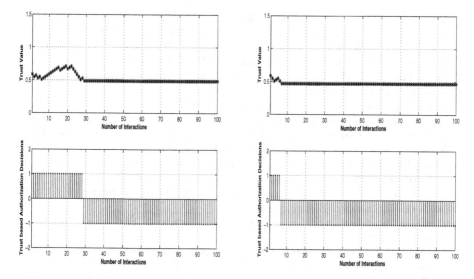

Fig. 8. Trust Evolution and Decision for Entities of 50% Security Violation

Fig. 9. Trust Evolution and Decision for Entities of 75% Security Violation

quantitative model will help achieve two objectives at the same time: fine-grained access control and precise authorization specification for utility maximization.

Furthermore, we envisage that our new approach has the potential to hold together the business analysts, developers and security experts with a common objective in developing more secure and profitable mobile e-commerce solutions.

Acknowledgements

I would like to thank the three anonymous reviewers for their valuable comments and suggestions for this paper.

References

1. T Beth, M Borcherding, and B Klein. Valuation of trust in open networks. In *Computer Security - ESORICS '94, D. Gollmann (Ed), Lecture Notes in Computer Science, Berline: Springer-Verlag*, volume 875, pages 3–18, 1994.
2. D. M. Chess. Security issues in mobile code systems. In *Mobile Agents and Security, Editor Vigna*, volume LNCS1419. Springer-Verlag, 1998.
3. Li Gong, Gary Ellison, and Mary Dageforde, editors. *Inside Java 2 Platform Security: Architecture, API Design, and Implementation, 2nd Edition*. Addison-Wesley PublishingCo., Inc., May 2003.
4. *IEEE Security and Privacy*, Volume 3, Number 1, *Economics of Information Security*. IEEE Computer Society, 2005.

5. W. Jansen. Countermeasures for mobile agent security. *Comupter Communications, Special Issue on Advances of Network Security*, November 2000.
6. Audun Josang. A logic for uncertain probabilities. *International Journal of Uncertainty, Fuzziness and Knowledge-Based Systems*, 9(3):279–311, 2001.
7. D. B. Lange and M. Oshima. *Programming and Deploying Java Mobile Agents with Aglets*. Addison-Wesley, 1998.
8. Ching Lin, Vijay Varadharajan, Yan Wang, and Yi Mu. On the design of a new trust model for mobile agent security. In *1st International Conference on Trust and Privacy in Digital Business (TrustBus04)*, volume LNCS 3184, pages 60–69, Zaragoza, Spain, September 2004. Springer Verlag, LNCS 3184.
9. Ching Lin, Vijay Varadharajan, Yan Wang, and Vineet Pruthi. Trust enhanced security for mobile agents. To appear in *7th International IEEE Conference on E-Commerce Technology 2005*, Technische Universitt Mnchen, Germany, July 19-22, 2005. IEEE Computer Society Press.
10. S. Marsh. Formalising trust as a computational concept. *PhD thesis, University of Stirling*, 1994.
11. R. Oppliger. Security issues related to mobile code and agent-based systems. *Computer Communications*, 22(12):1165–1170, July, 1999.
12. L. Rasmusson and S. Jansson. Simulated social control for secure internet commerce: Position paper at the new security paradigms workshop. 1996.
13. Michael Sonntag and Rudolf Hrmanseder. Mobile agent security based on payment. *Operating Systems Review*, 34(4):48–55, 2000.
14. Hock Kim Tan and Luc Moreau. Trust relationships in a mobile agent system. In Gian Pietro Picco, editor, *Fifth IEEE International Conference on Mobile Agents*, volume LNCS2240, Atlanta, Georgia, December, 2001. Springer-Verlag.
15. Vijay Varadharajan. Security enhanced mobile agents. *Proc. of 7th ACM Conference on Computer and Communication Security*, 2000.
16. Yan Wang, Kian-Lee Tan, and Jian Ren. Pumamart: A parallel and autonomous agents based internet marketplace. *Electronic Commerce Research and Applications (ECRA), Elsevier Science*, 3(3):294–310, 2004.
17. Uwe G. Wilhelm, Sebastian Staamann, and Levente Buttyn. On the problem of trust in mobile agent systems. *In Proceedings of 1998 Network and Distributed Security Symposium, San Diego, California, Internet Society*, March 11-13 1998.

The Fuzzy and Dynamic Nature of Trust

Elizabeth Chang[1], Patricia Thomson[1], Tharam Dillon[2], and Farookh Hussain[1]

[1] Centre for Extended Enterprise and Business Intelligence,
Curtin Business School, Curtin University of Technology, Perth, Western Australia,
elizabeth.chang, patricia.thomson,
farookh.hussain@cbs.curtin.edu.au
[2] Faculty of Information Technology,
University of Technology Sydney, Sydney, Australia
tharam@it.uts.edu.au

Abstract. Trust is one of the most fuzzy, dynamic and complex concepts in both social and business relationships. The difficulty in measuring Trust and predicting Trustworthiness in service-oriented network environments leads to many questions. These include issues such as how to measure the willingness and capability of individuals in the Trust dynamic and how to assign a concrete level of Trust to an individual or Agent. In this paper, we analyze the fuzzy, dynamic and complex nature of Trust.

The *dynamic* nature of Trust creates the biggest challenge in measuring Trust and predicting Trustworthiness. In order to develop a Trustworthiness Measure and Prediction Method, we first need to understand what we can actually measure in a Trust Relationship.

1 Introduction

Trustworthiness Measurement and prediction are complex and limited by the *fuzzy, dynamic and complex* nature of Trust. In this context, we need to consider the social aspects of fuzziness, dynamism and the complexity of Trust. Some explicit considerations are relevant to this:

- The term *fuzzy* refers to the indefinite, imprecise and sometimes unclear nature of Trust.
- The term *dynamic* refers to Trust not being stable or changing as time passes.
- The term *complex* refers to the multiple ways of measuring and the variety in views on Trust.

We note that when something cannot be explicitly defined, and is not stable and associated with a variety of views and opinions, it always difficult to manage and predict.

2 Existing Literature

Upon reviewing the existing literature on Trust, it is evident that there have not been many studies into the fuzziness, dynamism and complexity of Trust of the impact on

S. Katsikas, J. López, G. Pernul (Eds.): TrustBus 2005, LNCS 3592, pp. 161–174, 2005.
© Springer-Verlag Berlin Heidelberg 2005

Trust, Trust Measurement and Trustworthiness prediction, especially in the world of e-business and in service-oriented network environments. Some studies by Egger [4, 5, 6, & 16] consider how the usability of Websites (a Website may represent a service provider), the way content is organized and how security and privacy issues are addressed, communicate Trust to their human users. Factors considered by Egger are applicable for B2C (Business to Customer) e-commerce, where the customer (usually the client) interacts with the service providers through websites.

Kim and Moon [8] investigated how graphic design elements in a website can communicate Trust to human users. However, the studies do not investigate how the usability of a Website can assist in communicating, establishing Trust between providers and customers and Trustworthiness Measurement and prediction. Other work only provides reference to a single Trust Value and a single context for Trust Management. They do not consider other factors such as context dependence, timeslots for frames, or internal factors of interacting parties or Agents, nor have they examined all the possible fuzzy, dynamic and complex characteristics of Trust.

The psychological nature of the Trusting Agent has impact on the trust decisions to another Agent. In psychological terms, according to Myers [12] and Mallach [11] it is reasonable to assume that: People with a *'sensing preference'* will not trust any person with whom they did not have any previous interaction. Both Myers and Mallach [11] indicate that people with a 'sensing' preference have a tendency to rely on facts and experience People with an *'intuition preference'* may trust a person with whom they have not had any previous interactions. The preference of the Trusting Agent will influence its decision to trust a given Trusted Agent, with or without detailed information on the trustworthiness of the Trusted Agent. Myers [12] and Mallach [11] contend that persons with an *'intuition preference'* have a tendency to rely more on possibilities and taking risks. People with a *'thinking preference'* have a tendency to analyse things in an objective and logical fashion with little or no regard for personal values before they reach or take a decision [11]. We could also believe that if the Trusting Agent has a *thinking preference*, they will pay little or no attention to the personal values of the Trusted Agent, or to personal feelings about the Trusted Agent and make an objective and logical decision regarding whether to trust the Trusted Agent or not. People who have a *'feeling preference'* will place primary importance on personal values, before reaching a decision [11]. We could also believe that the Trusting Agents who give preference to *feeling* will place greater importance on his/her personal feelings about the Trusted Agent and values of the Trusted Agent while they decide whether or not to trust the Trusted Agent [2, 7].

3 Fuzzy and Dynamic Characteristics of Trust

The six important fuzzy and dynamic characteristics of Trust are the Implicitness in Trust, Asymmetry in Trust, Transitivity in Trust, Antonymy in Context, Asynchrony in Time Space and Gravity in Relationships. These factors create big challenges in Trustworthiness measurement and prediction. They are important to the understanding of the complexity of Trust and its measurement and prediction.

3.1 Implicitness

Trust is implicit. This means that a Trusting Agent may not be able to explicitly specify their belief, the willingness and capability of the Trusted Agent, and the *context* and the *time dependency* of Trust. These can only be *estimated*. A Trust Relationship can involve one individual only (i.e. 'I trust myself'), or involve another party or Agent (i.e. I trust my boss), or a group or an organisation (i.e. I trust the Bank).

We can most often define the context and time frame relating to a Trust Relationship, but we cannot explicitly state the *willingness* and *capability* of individuals or others involved in the Trust Relationship; nor the understanding that the context may change and as time passes, beliefs change. Trust is therefore implicit (i.e. understood by parties).

Trust is *fuzzy because* it is not obviously stated. Trust is also *dynamic* as individuals may able to define the 'context' and 'timeslot' relating to Trust but they *cannot* give explicit definitions of 'willingness' and 'capability' with regard to an individual or others about their Trust. This reinforces the view that Trust is implicit. The only thing we can do is to give *an estimate* of 'willingness' and 'capability', through behaviour monitoring, evaluation and a correlation with an individual's behaviour.

The *challenge* in Trustworthiness Measurement or Trustworthiness Prediction is the degree of the implicitness of Trust; that is the explicit measure of 'belief', ''willingness' and 'capability' in the *Trust Dynamic*. We can provide *an estimate* of this measure through a well known scientific method; namely the *correlation or regression* of behaviour or a correlation between what people say and what people do. In business we can correlate committed services with an actual delivered service to validate the Trust level.

3.2 Asymmetry

Trust is asymmetric. This means that a Trusting Agent has a certain belief in the Trusted Agent in a particular context. It *does not imply* that the Trusted Agent 'B' should have the same belief in the Trusting Agent 'A' in the same context. Hence, due to the non-mutual reciprocal nature in the Trust Relationship, Trust is asymmetric.

The characteristics of the Trust Relationship are also influenced by the Agents' internal factors (characteristics). There is no explicit understanding of the value of the Trust in the relationship between the two parties unless it is, in a human context, verbalised. In general terms, Agents do not explicitly verbalise a numeric Trust Value; they generally verbalise a level of Trust. *Fuzziness*, therefore, is evident.

Trust can change from being *symmetric to asymmetric*. Let us assume that Agent A and Agent B Trust each other to exchange or deliver high quality music to each other in 2004. With the passage of time in 2005, Agent B's capability or willingness to deliver high quality music to Agent A decreases. As a result of this, the Trust that Agent A has in Agent B in the context of procuring or delivering high quality music decreases or becomes null. Hence we see that Trust, which was initially *symmetric* (equal) between two Agents, has become *asymmetric* due to the passing of time. This is also related to the *dynamic* nature of Trust with time.

Trust is *uni-directional* (goes in one direction). This means that if we assume the Trusting Agent A to be Alice and the Trusted Agent B to be Bob, the *Trust Measure* or estimation is only from Alice to Bob or Bob to Alice, but not both. However, Bob can also be a Trusting Agent and Alice is his Trusted Agent. We consider that this is a different Trust Relationship, because it has a different *Trust Value*. The *Trust level* and the *Trust Value* are assigned by the Trusting Agent to the Trusted Agent. It needs to be clearly understood that the Trust measure or prediction is *asymmetric*, regardless as to whether it is measured in the physical world or the virtual world.

The *challenge* of a Trustworthiness Measure and prediction is conditioned on the asymmetric character of Trust. Therefore, one Trust Value does not represent both parties in a Trust Relationship. This is often implicitly assumed in a static social world which is conceptually negligent, as Trust in the social world can also imply a dynamic exchange between individuals that is sometimes multidirectional. A *Trust Measure* in a service-oriented network environment must be *uni-directional* and only from a Trusting Agent to the Trusted Agent. It is only meaningful to the Trusting Agent and for use by the Trusting Agent. The *Trust Value* can move from symmetric to asymmetric or vice versa. *Fuzziness* and *dynamism* is therefore again apparent in the situation.

3.3 Transitiveness

Trust is transitive. It is illogical to assume that *transitive Trust* is an explicit phenomenon. The *transitivity of Trust*, also known as a *derived Trust*, means that Trust is derived from an existing Trust between Agents. Note that derived Trust and the Trust from which it is derived should be considered within the same context. It is important to understand that this *derived Trust* may be explicit, but generally, it is very hard to quantify accurately. We assume then, some level of implicitness (*fuzziness*).

The *level of Trust* through a transitive introduction may be held at the same level between both parties and is dependent on the strength of the original Agent's *Trust relationship*. Transitive Trust is a very important concept in the service-oriented network environment where anonymous users or Agents often want to identify quality service through a *transitive introduction*, also known as 'a recommendation' or 'reputation'. The recommendation or reputation is *fuzzy* in the sense that a transitive introduction is context and time dependent. These dependencies are not always explicit as there is an innate inability to hold the same view or understanding about the context and the exact time frame where the Trust Value or level was assigned.

Transitive Trust is also time dependent. This means that it is dependent on when a *Trust Value* is assigned and when the *Trust Value* is recommended. Trustworthiness prediction has to take aggregated time frames or slots in order to more accurately determine a *Trust Value*. Note that this value could change when time passes. This is the dynamic characteristic of Trust. *Transitive Trust* is affected by other *opinions*.

The *challenge* of a Trustworthiness Measure and Prediction is the method of using a *transitive Trust Value*, also known as the *recommendation value*. Often we derive different *Trust Values* from different Agents about 'a particular Agent' or 'a service'. They relate to different time frames (timeslots). Additionally, we have to consider *first hand, second hand and third hand opinions*.

3.4 Antonymy

The antonymous nature of Trust is related to 'Context'; that is the Context may understood differently by two Agents, A and B, involved in a Trust relationship. Therefore, what may be clear to one Agent may not be clear to another. Fuzziness is evident in the antonymous dynamic of the Trust relationship.

The context, as seen from the perspective of Agent A, may be the opposite or different from that seen from the perspective of Agent B. We note that the 'context' may be understood in an opposite way; it is used in a different way and often implicitly recognized by either party or Agents. Each party perceives the context to be the opposite of that perceived by the other party. Agent A may see the context of the Trust relationship as one of 'buy'; Agent B may see the context of the Trust relationship as one of 'sell'.

Fuzziness is evident because of the antonymous nature of the relationship between both Agents. The challenge of the Trust measure and the Trustworthiness prediction is to define the context clearly. This is difficult to do even in the real physical world.

3.5 Asynchrony

The asynchronous nature of Trust refers to asynchrony in a 'Timeslot'. That is the timeslot of the Trustworthiness may be understood or defined differently between Trusting Agents and Trusted Agents. *Fuzziness* is inherent in any situation that becomes unclear to either party or Agents in the *Trust relationship*.

Agents may understand the *timeslot differently* for a given *same context*. The timeslots between the Agents may be the same, completely different, or partially overlapping. As a result of the asynchronous nature of timeslots, Trustworthiness prediction cannot be straight forward. The *challenge* of the Trust measure and Trustworthiness prediction is that we have to deal with different timeslots in a time space. We need both to *aggregate the timeslot* and *also average the Trust Value* over the aggregated timeslots. This is important when recommendations or Trust reputation takes place.

3.6 Gravity

The *Gravity of Trust* refers to the *gravity* of the Trust relationship; the *seriousness* of the relationship to each Agent, or the *influence* on each party to the relationship. Each Agent has their own views on whether or not the relationship means much to them, and what *influence* it could have on their business or lives. As stated in all previous examples, fuzziness and dynamism is inherent in this characteristic. Regardless of who is the Trusting Agent or the Trusted Agent, from Agent A's point of view, the Agent A to Agent B relationship within a particular context could be unimportant to Agent A. However, from Agent B's point of view, the relationship may be very important.

4 Reasoning the Fuzziness and Dynamism

In the previous section, we illustrated the six characteristics of the *fuzziness and dynamism* of Trust. We also illustrated the endogenous and exogenous factors of the Agents. Now we would like to show how these are related to each other.

4.1   Internal Factors of Trusted Agent

In order to study why Trust is *fuzzy* and *dynamic*, we now look at the Agents who are involved in the Trust Relationship and their impact on the fuzziness and dynamism of Trust. In service-oriented network environments, we have defined Trust as *the belief that the Trusting Agent has in the Trusted Agent's willingness and capability to deliver a mutually agreed service in a given context and in a given timeslot*. The key challenge is how to measure *willingness* and *capability,* so that a *Trust Value* can closely represent the truth or quality of the Trusted Agents.

Willingness symbolizes the *Trusted Agent's* will to act or be in readiness to act gladly, honestly, truthfully, reliably and sincerely in delivering on the mutually agreed behaviour. As this factor is internal to Agents, it is very hard to estimate even with scientific research methods. The willingness of a person or an Agent could change as time passes, as it may be dependent on the mood of a person. Therefore, it makes a *Trust Model* dynamic.

We have defined Capability as the talent, competence, aptitude, and ability of the Trusted Agent in delivering on the mutually agreed services. Capability signifies the Agent's intelligence. It is internal to an Agent. A person or an Agent's intelligence changes with time due to internal or external influences. Examples of external influences could be further training or study. These changes could happen in any given timeslot or over many timeslots.

These two factors are internal factors of Agents. As they are internal, we therefore cannot have direct measures because we can not obtain it on hand to qualify it. Therefore, when we derive a Trust Value, it is only an estimate or an approximate value. *Willingness* symbolizes the *Trusted Agent's* will to act or be in readiness to act gladly, honestly, truthfully, reliably and sincerely in delivering on the mutually agreed behaviour. As this factor is internal to Agents, it is very hard to estimate even with scientific research methods. The willingness of a person or an Agent could be changed as time passes, as it could be dependent on the mood of a person. Therefore, it makes the Trust Model dynamic.

4.2   Fuzzy and Dynamic Characteristics in Trust Model

The six Fuzzy and Dynamic characteristics of Trust are as follows: Implicitness in Trust, Asymmetry in Trust, Transitivity in Trust, Antonymy in Context, Asynchrony in Time, and Gravity in Relationship. In view of the six *fuzzy and dynamic* characteristics of Trust, we could distinguish that characteristics 1 to 3 are related to *Trust Value* and characteristics 4 to 6 are related to *Trust relationships*.

- 'Implicitness of Trust ', 'Asymmetry in Trust' and 'Transitivity of Trust' are related to *Trust Values* because Agents make a *decision* on Trust Values, not anything else. Therefore 'implicitness', 'asymmetry', 'transitivity' are relevant only to Trust Values;
- 'Antonym in context', 'Asynchrony in Time Space' and 'Gravity of the Relationship' are related to the *Trust Relationship*, which is context and time dependent. Agents make the perception of the context, time or gravity of the relationship. This is an Agent's own view or opinion about what they see or believe in a Trust Relationship.

4.3 Endogenous and Exogenous Characteristics

In view of the Trust Model, we see the relationship involves Agents. Each Agent has endogenous and exogenous factors that impact on Trust decision making and this in turn affects the Trust relationship. In view of the Trust Model, we see that both *endogenous* factors and *exogenous* factors are related to Agents in the Trust Model.

Endogenous factors of an Agent refer to internal factors, psychological factors and personal characteristics, knowledge or skills etc of the Agent. The endogenous factors, including psychological factors, are factors internal to the Trusting parties. These internal factors can never be captured explicitly and they change as time passes. An Agent's 'willingness' and 'capability' are part of endogenous factors. When predicting Trust in a relationship, the factors that influence the Trust decision and that cannot be explicitly managed so far, are the endogenous factors. For example, if a person's thinking is changed; no one could know or capture this immediately. *Endogenous factors* cause the changes in the Trust relationship.

However, the *endogenous factors* cannot be captured directly on hand, thus the measure and prediction of Trustworthiness of an Agent is only at an estimate or approximate level. The *challenge* of the Trustworthiness measure and prediction is that we are unable to explicitly capture the endogenous characters of Agents. Therefore, we have to develop some methods for the Trustworthiness measure and prediction that can through some external factors for which we can observe, capture and use it to give an estimate of the Trustworthiness of the Agent.

Exogenous factors are known as external factors of Trust, such as external activities, i.e. behavioural changes such as making a commitment to deliver a service or valuating an actual service delivery. These external activities can be identified and predicted. Exogenous activity influences the Trust Value and prediction; it may be caused by the environment where a business interaction is carried out or a service provider is unable to fulfil their commitments. The service-oriented environment is a heterogeneous environment and consists of anonymous, pseudo-anonymous, and non-anonymous users or machines communicating with each other for services. In P2P service-oriented networks, file sharing applications such as Gnutella and Napster enable the users to share files amongst each other. Free Net is a P2P oriented service network for anonymous storage.   SETI@HOME is an example of a pseudo anonymous P2P application for distributed computing. In non-anonymous service-oriented environments, such as Logistic networks, Agents make use of each other's resources. These resources can be either physical resources (like warehouse space or the transport capabilities) or digital resources (like each other's track-and-trace applications). However, the exogenous factors or external activity can be captured, analysed, measured and be calculated to determine a level of Trustworthiness. The challenge of the Trust measure and Trustworthiness prediction is to develop an estimation method that can handle heterogeneous environments and anonymous, pseudo-anonymous, and non-anonymous users and service providers and service interactions for predicting the Trustworthiness value.

4.4 Reason for Fuzziness and Dynamism

The six fuzzy and dynamic characteristics of Trust are triggered by Agents (Figure 1). As an Agent's endogenous factors are hard to capture and predict, and exogenous factors have a strong impact on the Agent's self development and Agent decision making. However, external factors can be captured and therefore can be used to help estimate an Agent's Trustworthiness. In view of the Trust Model (Figure 2), we see that both endogenous factors and exogenous factors are related to Peers in *Trust relationships*.

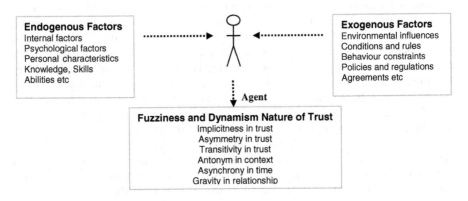

Fig. 1. Exogenous and Endogenous factors of Agents [2]

4.5   Fuzzy and Dynamic Characteristics and Trustworthiness Measure

The dynamism of Trust is influenced by the factors associated with Trust and Trust Relationships. We now analyse eight characteristics of Trust aligned with the Trust Definition and Trust Model, in order to reason factors that determine the Trust dynamics. While some changes (such as external behaviour) can be predicted, because they can be explicitly defined, others cannot be predicted (such as internal factors of Agents), because they cannot be explicitly defined. We can only give a measure or an estimate of the dynamism of Trust in the *Trust relationship*. We note that change can be caused by external factors as well as internal factors. In real life, we note that both factors could cause the change. However, the internal factors are hard to capture and predict, even with great scientific studies. This is unlike external factors, where one can feel them, predict them, and try to manage them. Therefore, the internal factors cause the dynamism or changes. These are the factors that humans or machines cannot manage. Humans or machines can manage the external factors that cause the dynamism or changes. They can be captured so they are considered to be static.

5   Managing Trust

There are several issues to be considered in the context of Managing Trust because Trust is dynamic and not always well-defined.

5.1 Measuring the Service

In most internet Trustworthiness systems, they have features on measuring service providers, merchants, or on-line shops. However, if a provider offers a very good service on books but very bad service on delivery, then the Trustworthiness value for the merchant should be distinguished. Measuring the service is the most difficult task in using the Internet, or in the service-oriented environment. It is important, that in the service-oriented network environment, we should provider service rating, or Trustworthiness of service. Each service provider may have a number of services. However, the objective here is to measure the service of the provider, rather than that of the provider.

5.2 Measuring the Product or Website

This measuring has been used in most internet Trustworthiness systems. The features include measuring service providers, merchants, or on-line shops. The measure is much simpler than measuring the service, where human intelligence behind the service and have right to give input on the quality of service. Here, for example, in measuring the product, if we say a camera is good or bad, we do not have to (and cannot) get the opinion of the 'camera' about the comments that the customer made.

5.3 Managing the Dynamism of Trust

In the existing literature the methods of managing Trust focus on assigning the Trust Value with the assumption that there is only one context and the Trust Value is assigned only for that context. This is due to the fact that many e-service providers only provide a single service (single context). However, this assumption becomes less relevant as the concept of e-services has expanded to multiple services over the last few years. Also in the literature, the methods of managing Trust only consider one Trust Value and the value does not change. These methods do not consider the dynamic nature of Trust and the change of Trust Values with time.

5.4 Time Spot, Timeslot and Time Space

We define Trustworthiness prediction as the process of determining the future Trust Value known as Trustworthiness value of the Trusted entity or Agent, given it's past repute values or historical Trust Value or direct interaction from the given time spot, slot and space. A Time Spot is a particular time at which an entity interacted with another entity and subsequently assigned a Trustworthiness value to it. The Timeslot of a Trustworthiness prediction is the breadth or duration of time over which the Trust Value from the historical Trust Value or repute value is collected. In order to analyse the dynamic behaviour of Trust Values, a *Time Space* consists of a number of non-overlapping Timeslots. An entity will have a Trust Value or *repute value* for each Timeslot. These past Trust Values or *repute values* are aggregated and used for predicting future Trust Values known as a Trustworthiness value. The Time Space of a Trustworthiness prediction is the total duration of time over which the behaviour of the Trusted entity will be analysed and the process of Trustworthiness prediction carried out. The *repute value* is a Trust Value for an entity, i.e. its reputation in a given context and in a given Timeslot as recommended by a witness entity or witness Agent.

5.5 Managing the Trust Dynamism

In order to manage Trust over the network as adequately as possible, one must consider the fuzziness and dynamism of the Trust. To give an estimate of a Trustworthiness value, we will carry out a correlation between an *expected service* and an *actual delivered service* to predict a Trustworthiness Value. For the determination of the Trustworthiness value for a Trusted entity or Agent, we choose to apply a technique used in the human world, i.e. *a correlation between an expected behaviour* and *an actual behaviour* to determine the level of Trust. We adopt this approach for the Trustworthiness prediction in e-business or e-services to overcome the dynamism of Trust. The expected behaviour of the Trusted Agent is the mutually anticipated conduct of the Trusted Agent prior to its interaction with the Trusting Agent. The correlation is the degree of similarity between the expected delivery of the Trusted Agent and actual delivery of the Trusted Agent during interaction.

5.6 Correlation of Behaviour

Correlation refers to how similar the following two factors are: (1) The impression that the Trusting Agent has of the Trusted Agent in a given context, and (2) The outcome of the interaction between the Trusting Agent and the Trusted Agent in that particular context in a given timeslot. The greater the correlation between these two factors, the higher the Trustworthiness value assigned to the Trusted Agent by the Trusting Agent and vice versa. Strong correlations between the two factors indicate that the Trusted Agent met the impression held by the Trusting Agent, in that context. Conversely, a weak correlation indicates that the Trusted Agent did not meet the impression held by a Trusting Agent.

5.7 Challenges in Trust Measure and Prediction

In the existing literature the methods of managing Trust focus on assigning the Trust Value with the assumption that there is only one context and the Trust Value is assigned only for that context. This is due to the fact that many e-service providers only provide a single service (single context). However, this assumption becomes less relevant as the concept of e-services has expanded to multiple services over the last few years. Also in the literature, the methods of managing Trust only consider one Trust Value and that the value does not change. These methods do not consider the dynamic nature of Trust and the change of Trust Values with time.

Trustworthiness is a prediction of future Trust Values that depicts the level of the Trust Relationship that the Trusting Agent has with the Trusted Agent in a given context, in a given timeslot and with a given type of initial relationship association In other words, Trustworthiness is a prediction of the Trust level against context and time with the type of initiation of the Trust relationship. The prediction can only be done by correlating the actual behaviour with the expected behaviour, in a given context and in a particular timeslot with respect to a given method of initiation. The constraint with the measurement of Trust and the prediction of Trustworthiness lies in the inability to handle the 'internal factors' of Agents, namely their 'willingness' and 'capability'.

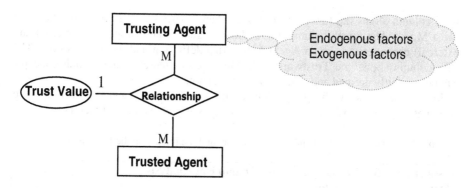

Fig. 2. Alignment of the Agent's Endogenous and Exogenous Factors in the Trust Model [2]

Table 1. The factors determining the Nature of Trust

Trust Definition Contains Concepts	Trust Model Contains concepts	Trust Characteristics	Agent Characteristics	Trustworthiness
Belief	Trust Value	Implicitness of Trust Asymmetry in Trust Transitivity of Trust		Fuzzy result
Trusting Agent and Trusted Agent	Relationship	Gravity of Relationship		Explicit result
Willingness Capability	Agents (Conceptual behaviour)		Endogenous	Fuzzy result
Delivery of the mutually agreed services	Agents (External behaviour)		Exogenous	Explicit result
A given Context	Context	Antonym in Context		Explicit result
A given Timeslot	Timeslot	Asynchrony in Time Space		Explicit result

In the Trust Model (Figure 2), we see that both *endogenous* factors and *exogenous* factors are related to Agents in the Trust Model.

Table 1 below describes the factors associated with determining the *nature of trust*.

In Table 1 below, we note that: the first column describes the concepts of Trust; the second column describes the Trust Model and all related concepts in the Trust Model (Figure 2). Column 2 is a pictorial representation of Column 1 (see Figure 2). The third column aligns the fuzzy and dynamic characteristics to the trust definition and Trust Model. The fourth column aligns the endogenous and exogenous (internal and external) characteristics of an Agent to the trust definition and the Trust Model. The fifth column shows the Trustworthiness Measure or prediction and which concepts can be explicitly defined and which concepts cannot.

In Table 2 below, we further explain what can be measured and what cannot. We note that change can be caused by *external factors* as well as internal factors

Table 2. An Agent's internal and external factors and the impact on the Dynamism of Trust

Aspects of the Trust	Relation to Agents	Dynamism Analysis
Belief Willingness Capability	Agent's internal activity	Internal factors are very hard to capture. They could be changed by both internal influence and external influence. For example, more education or an accident could change the capability of a person, or psychological advice could affect the level of willingness. However, no one can predict how much they will change with time. Therefore, *internal factors cause the dynamic* nature in the trust model.
Trusting Agent and Trusted Agent	Agent's external activity	Identifying a Trusting Agent or a Trusted Agent is an external activity. They can be explicitly defined.
Deliver the mutually agreed services	Agent's external activity	External factors can be captured though correlation of expected delivery of the service compared to the actual service that is provided.
A given Context, A given Timeslot	Agent's external activity	These are external factors and can be captured; therefore they are not the cause of the dynamism in the Trust Model.

In real life, we note that both factors could cause the change. However, the internal factors are hard to capture and predict, even after intense empirical studies of a person's psychology. This is unlike external factors, where one can directly observe them, predict them, and try to manage them. Therefore, the *internal factors* cause the dynamism or changes and they are the factors that humans or machines cannot manage. Humans or machines can manage the external factors that cause the dynamism or changes, but they can be captured so they are considered to be stable in the Trust Model.

6   Summary

The limitation with the measurement of Trust and the prediction of Trustworthiness lies in the inability to consider accurately the internal factors of Agents, namely their willingness and capability. Since capability and willingness are by and large not directly observable, we arrive at an estimation of these by utilising the external factors (expected and actual behaviours) of Agents within the context of the relationship. In addition to the endogenic factors of willingness and capability, psychological factors of Trusting Agents contribute to Trust dynamism. The preference of the Trusting Agent for 'sensing' or 'intuition' will influence their decision to Trust a given Trusted Agent, with or without detailed information on the Trustworthiness of the Trusted Agent. Whether a Trusting Agent gives preference to a 'thinking' or 'feeling' psychological disposition, will determine whether they make a decision based on facts or the personal values of the Trusted Agent.

We can conclude the following from our analysis of the dynamic nature of Trust:

- The internal factors of Agents determine the dynamic nature of the Agents
- The dynamic nature of the Agents leads to the dynamic nature of Trust, Trust relationships and Trust Values.
- 'Context', 'Time' and 'Initiation of Relationship' are not dynamic as these factors are defined by the Agents, and once defined, they do not change.

Acknowledgement

The authors would like to thank Miss Jyoti Bhattacharjya for assisting with editing, compiling and submission of the first draft paper to TrustBus.

References

1. Burton, K.A..: 'Design of the open privacy distributed reputation system', (2002), Available: [http://www.peerfear.org/papers/openprivacy-reputation.pdf] (10/11/2003)
2. Chang, E., Dillon T.S., & Hussain, F.: Trust and reputation for Service-oriented Environments-Technologies for Building Business Intelligence and Consumer Confidence, (2005), John Wiley & Sons, ISBN: 0-470- 01547-0
3. Chang, E., Talevski, A. & Dillon, T.: 'Web service integration in the extended logistics enterprise', Proceedings of the IEEE Conference on Industrial Informatics, INDIN, (2003), Banff, Canada.
4. Egger, N.F.: 'Trust me, I'm an online vendor', Towards a Model of Trust for E-Commerce System Design, (2000a), Available: [http://www.zurich.ibm.com/~mrs/chi2000/contributions/egger.html] (10/09/2003)
5. Egger, N.F.: 'Towards a model of trust for e-commerce system design', (2000b), Available: [http://www.zurich.ibm.com/~mrs/chi2000/contributions/egger.html] (29/05/2003)
6. Egger, N.F.: 'Deceptive technologies: Cash, ethics and HCI', (2003), Available: [http://www.ecommuse.com/research/publications/sigchi_bulletin.htm] (23/05/2003)
7. Hussain, F., Chang, E. & Dillon, T. S.: 'Classification of trust relationships in peer-to-peer (P2P) communications', Proceedings of the Second International Workshop on Security in Information Systems WOSIS, (2004)
8. Kim, J. & Moon, J.Y.: 'Emotional usability of customer interfaces', (1997), Available: [http://hci.yonsei.ac.kr/non/e02/97-CHI Emotional_Usability_of_Customer_Interface.pdf] (23/08/2003)
9. http://www.gnutella.com/
10. http://www.napster.com/

11. Mallach, E,G., *'Decision and data warehouse systems'*, (2000), Irwin McGraw Hill Companies
12. Myers, S.: *'Working out your Myers Briggs Type'*, (2003), Available: [http://www.teamtechnology.co.uk/tt/t-articl/mb-simpl.htm] (27/12/2003)
13. Rahman, A.A. & Hailes, S.: *'Relying on trust to find reliable information'*, (2003a), Available: http://www.cs.ucl.ac.uk/staff/F.AbdulRahman/docs/dwacos99.pdf] (7/08/2003)
14. Rahman, A.A. & Hailes, S.: *'A distributed trust model'*, (2003b), Available: http://citeseer.nj.nec.com/cache/papers/cs/ .../abdul-rahman97distributed.pdf] (5/09/2003)
15. Rahman, A.A. & Hailes, S.: *'Supporting trust in virtual communities'*, (2003c), Available: [http://citeseer.nj.nec.com/cache/papers/cs...../abdul-rahman00supporting.pdf]
16. SETI@HOME, Available: [http://pwp.netcabo.pt/knology/SETI_ENG.htm] (28/09/2003)
17. Shelat, B. & Egger, F, N., *'What makes people trust online gambling sites?'* (2002), Available: [http://www.ecommuse.com/research/publications/chi2002.pdf] (10/08/2003)
18. Smith, J. H.: *'The architectures of trust'*, (2002), University of Copenhagen
19. Wang, Y. & Vassileva, J.: *'Trust and reputation model in peer-to-peer'*, (2003), Available: [www.cs.usask ca/grads/yaw181/ publications/120_wang_y.pdf] (15/10/2003)

Towards an Ontology of Trust

Lea Viljanen

University of Helsinki, Department of Computer Science
Lea.Viljanen@cs.helsinki.fi

Abstract. Trust is a fundamental factor when people are interacting with each other, hence it is natural that trust has been researched also in relation to applications and agents. However, there is no single definition of trust that everybody would share. This, in turn, has caused a multitude of formal or computational trust models to emerge to enable trust use and dependence in applications. Since the field is so diverse, there also exists a confusion of terminology, where similar concepts have different names and, what is more disturbing, same terms are also used for different concepts. To organize the research models in a new and more structured way, this paper surveys and classifies thirteen computational trust models by the trust decision input factors. This analysis is used to create a new comprehensive ontology for trust to facilitate interaction between business systems.

1 Introduction

Trust, trust models and trust management systems have been under a lot of research in recent years. In the field of computing it is not sufficient to just define trust: for automation the concept of trust must be represented by a trust model, which can be utilized by systems enabling business interaction. Here we define a trust model to be the formal or computational realization of a trust definition, verbal or implicit. The word computational is used here loosely, meaning a model that can be utilized by computer applications. It is important to note that the models are by necessity simplifications of the complexity of trust and different models simplify differently.

Since there is no universal definition of trust, the developed models and systems relying on those models are very different in both verbal and formal trust definitions, and also in the used vocabulary. Therefore, it is beneficial to survey recent work in this area, classify the models according to their trust input factors and to develop a partial ontology. A trust ontology enables systems with different trust models to share trust relationship information and information on how this trust relationship has been formed. This is crucial in today's digital business, where different organizations with differing infrastructure must co-operate to utilize networked services.

This analysis focuses on only one aspect of trust, information to be utilized by the trust decision process. However, there are three distinct problem areas around trust. The first one is to define the facts that support trust, the second is how to find the appropriate rules to derive consequences of a set of assumptions about trust, and the third is how to use information about trust to take decisions [9]. This analysis focuses clearly on the first problem, i.e. finding a maximal set of support facts. Therefore many important trust research areas, for example reasoning logics or negotiation protocols, are not part of this analysis.

S. Katsikas, J. López, G. Pernul (Eds.): TrustBus 2005, LNCS 3592, pp. 175–184, 2005.

2   On Trust and Trust Research

Trust has been a very awkward concept in computer science since it is silently embedded in many aspects of human behaviour and it is in its very nature quite subjective. However, since trust is a part of the basic decision making framework for humans, it has also some interest from the computer systems point of view.

2.1   Trust Characteristics

There have been many definitions of trust, below are examples from Diego Gambetta and Audun Jøsang:

> trust (or, symmetrically, distrust) is a particular level of the subjective probability with which an agent assesses that another agent or group of agents will perform a particular action, both before he can monitor such action (or independently of his capacity ever to be able to monitor it) and in a context in which it affects his own action [12].

> Trust in a passionate entity is the belief that it will behave without malicious intent ... Trust in a rational entity is the belief that it will resist malicious manipulation by a passionate entity [15].

These definitions are very different and use widely different vocabulary. How can the models built on these definitions interact in any way? Before we can attempt an answer, some characteristics of trust need to be explored. Since trust is subjective, we must assume a role of some subject and evaluate the trust from that particular perspective. From this the lack of global trust is evident, i.e. there are no entities everybody trusts. From this basic property, other natural characteristics follow:

- Trust is not symmetric. If "Alice trusts Bob", it does not follow that "Bob trusts Alice".
- Trust is not distributive. If "Alice trusts (Bob and Carol)", it does not follow that "(Alice trusts Bob) and (Alice trusts Carol)".
- Trust is not associative, since the trust-operator does not map from entities to entities. Therefore "(Alice trusts Bob) trusts Carol" is not a valid trust expression. However, "Alice trusts (Bob trusts Carol)" is a possibility.
- Trust is not inherently transitive. If "Alice trusts Bob" and "Bob trusts Carol", it does not automatically follow that "Alice trusts Carol".

2.2   Trust Model Research

Early attempts to formalise trust for computer use have been in the context of authentication. Yahalom et al. developed a trust model to be used in authentication scenarios [20]. One of the earliest attempts to define trust from the general and computational point of view was Stephen Marsh's thesis [16], which drew input from the sociological trust research. After that several interesting trust models and also systems, such as PolicyMaker [4], KeyNote [3] and REFEREE [8] have emerged. Around that time also

Abdul-Rahman et al. [1], Daniel Essin [11] and Audun Jøsang [15] described their trust concepts and models.

In recent years the focus has been on more comprehensive and concrete systems having wider trust management elements, such as Poblano [7], Free Haven [10], SUL-TAN [14], TERM [2] and SECURE [5,6]. But since the applicability of trust has been widened to cover more than authentication and authorization, they do not necessarily use the same terminology or basic components. Additionally, some models do not focus on general trust management, but have tried to explore trust in various application domains, such as peer-to-peer networking or web applications.

These thirteen models span a time frame of ten years of trust model research and form a comprehensive set of research models. Thus this set is used for the actual factor analysis.

3   Taxonomy of Trust Models

One of the key differentiating elements in trust models is the list of factors required or used in the trust evaluation. Because of this factor diversity, it is impossible to give a simple taxonomy where each model sits squarely only in one classification box along this axis. Instead, a classification of factors has been developed and each model can be desribed by what set of factors it is using or, in our terminology, is aware of. A summary is shown in Figure 1.

3.1   Identity-Aware Models

All reviewed systems are identity-aware, i.e. they assume to have some identifying information on the target of the trust evaluation. This identity awareness does not require knowing the real name or other globally unique information of the communicating principal. In some models it is quite sufficient that the identity is only locally unique and temporally sufficiently stable so that it aids in recognizing the same entity in this system over time. There are models that use globally unique identities or locally unique

MODEL	Identity	Action	Business value	Capability	Competence	Confidence	Context	History	3rd party
Abdul-Rahman	X	X							X
Essin	X	X	X	X	X		X	X	X
Free Haven	X				X	X			X
Jøsang	X					X			
KeyNote	X	X							X
Marsh	X	X	X		X			X	
Poblano	X		X		X	X			
PolicyMaker	X	X					X		X
REFEREE	X	X							X
Sultan	X	X							X
TERM	X	X				X		X	X
Secure	X	X						X	X
Yahalom et al	X	X							X

Fig. 1. Trust model input factor summary

identities. For example, the Poblano system uses *peerID*, which needs to be unique across the universe of peers. An example of local identities can be found in the work of Abdul-Rahman et al.

3.2   Action-Aware Models

Most trust models have noticed that there is an action component to trust. That is, the actual trust evaluation and decision depends on what the target of our trust is trying to do in or with our system or for what purpose we are trusting the target. This is very intuitive, as we may trust one party to relay our messages but not to transfer any money. This is also reflected in the definition by Gambetta in Chapter 2 above. On the other hand, the action component is not always necessary, since there is a concept called *general trust* which is an unqualified trust towards a principal [16].

In action-aware models the set of actions can be closed or open. A closed set is a set of pre-defined actions the model supports and no others can be defined by organizations using the model. An open set of actions means that the model offers a way of defining at least some of the actions or does not restrict them to a particular set.

This concept has many names in the actual models. PolicyMaker, REFEREE and KeyNote call this *action* and Abdul-Rahman et al. have a *trust category*. Yahalom et al. use a closed set of *trust classes* for which they trust a certain principal. SULTAN uses the name *context*, but in its core the the definition is about actions and action sets. Similarly, the SECURE project uses context in the meaning of action. Essin has the concept of *activity*, although it is not used in the trust evaluation directly, but as a subcomponent in determining the capability of trust subject and subject reputation.

However, not all models use the action factor explicitly. Some specialized systems, for example Poblano and Free Haven, use the trust valuation in relation to data content received from a network peer. There the actions are implicit in the system definition, but since there is only the one basic action type and the action set is closed, Poblano or Free Haven systems are not considered action-aware.

Marsh describes a *situation*, which is a point of time relative to a specific agent, i.e. the principal evaluating trust. This definition includes the actions the other principals are attempting, therefore Marsh's model is action-aware. The TERM system has no action concept as such, but trust calculations are related to *roles* in role-based access control. There are two roles, an access role and a testifying role, so the system has two predefined actions. Hence it is action-aware, although the action set is closed.

3.3   Business Value Awareness

Between people trust implies potential loss and also potential benefit. In several models there are concepts called *risk*, *benefit* or *value*. These are all associated with a particular action and try to give impression on how the action can help us or how the misplaced trust can hurt us. Risk is the most commonly modeled business value element. However, to understand the full impact of the attempted action, risk needs to be balanced against the potential benefits or value of the action. We combine these under the common concept of *business value*, since all these concepts try to model the potential impact, positive or negative, of the attempted operation.

Marsh is using three separate business value concepts: utility, importance and risk. Utility is a measurable benefit, importance a subjective valuation of the importance of the action. These both are used in evaluating situational trust, i.e. trust in a specific situation or action. Risk is used in determining the co-operation threshold, i.e. whether to actually engage in the action in a particular situation.

The model by Essin also uses several business value factors. He uses the concept of *valuation* as the cost of the resources or assets affected by the action. He also uses *stake* which is the degree to which the entity(s) proposing to engage in the activity has a vested interest in the outcome. Stake tries to measure the level of commitment for this action and thus it is quite close to the concept of importance. He also uses the concepts of risk and benefit, although his model combines these to a single risk/benefit set.

In the Poblano P2P system, risk is a statistically computed metric of peer accessibility and performance, both viewed technically. Here the considered risk is of the type "risk of not getting the information" instead of any loss of data or money. This is however, well within the defined use of "risk", so Poblano is business value aware. Poblano also uses *importance*, which is the importance in engaging in the activity, when calculating the co-operation threshold.

The SECURE model does not have risk as part of the formal trust model, although the resulting system has an added risk and cost/benefit analysis as part of the trust evaluation. Therefore the model itself is not business-value aware.

3.4   Competence-Aware Models

One type of trust decision factor is information on the competence of the subject with regard to performing a particular action. When human clients are considered, this is an important decision factor, but with automated clients at least some degree of technical competence in following the specification should be assumed. Therefore this factor is not very common in the reviewed models.

Competence is considered by Marsh in calculating the co-operation threshold based on trust. The SULTAN model uses competence as a factor in their verbal trust definition, but surprisingly does not include it in the computational model. This concept of ability to perform a task is called *capability* by Essin. He defines capability as measurable expertise that the entity possesses about the activity, i.e. competence in this common vocabulary.

One interesting variant of this is lifting the competence evaluation from the technical to the semantic level. The Poblano model has a concept of *CodatConfidence*, which is a measure of semantic experience, i.e. the system's competence in providing us with relevant information. Similarly, the Free Haven system has a concept of *metatrust*, which signals that the data received from a node is indeed valuable information. For example, if the Free Haven system agrees with a recommendation from a third party, the third party metatrust is incremented.

3.5   Capability-Aware Models

Capability has a dual meaning in the security and trust research. On one hand, capability is considered synonymous with competence, i.e. evaluating the peer's ability to perform a certain task. On the other hand, a capability has a very specialized meaning in the field of security as a token given to a peer to access a resource. We differentiate between these two concepts and here define capability as a form of an access granting token.

This latter form is also used by Essin. In addition to the capability as competence definition, he defines capability also as demonstrable access and authority necessary to act [11]. This is capability in this second sense.

3.6 Confidence-Aware Models

As input for the trust calculation can be received from multiple sources, sometimes also as external recommendations or reputation, we may also have uncertainty associated with trust or the trust input factors. The concept of *confidence* reflects this uncertainty, although in the actual models this concept has many names.

The TERM model uses the concept of an *opinion*, meaning how much the calculating TERM server believes the trust statement. The Poblano system also uses a confidence value, *PeerConfidence*, in determining whether the trust subject is able to co-operate and thus being trustworthy.

Confidence can also relate to only one of the trust input factors. Essin uses the term *certainty* that the true identity of the trust subject is known. The Free Haven system uses the concept of *confidence rating*, which is used as a measure of how fast or slow external recommendations change our trust value in regards of that particular entity.

3.7 Context-Aware Models

The trust evaluation may depend on the evaluating system internal or external status at that particular point of time, i.e. context. If, for example, the organization firewall is experiencing heavy port scanning activity, it may be sensible to lower the trust valuation on all or some principals to limit exposure to potentially malicious activity.

Interestingly enough, this is not a very widely used factor. Essin uses it as a subfactor in determining the action valuation and subject stake in the action. In PolicyMaker, the policy is defined in an interpreted programming language and it thus can obtain some context information. The set of local policies are considered the context under which the trust is evaluated.

The SECURE model also defines trust via a policy construct. Theoretically it may be possible to include context information in the policy, but since this option is not explored in their work, SECURE is not classified here as context-aware. Neither is the SULTAN model since it uses context to mean the action to be performed (see Chapter 3.2).

3.8 History Awareness

When people interact, one of the key components in our trust evaluation is the trustee past behaviour or track record. This can be modeled using vocabulary like *experience* or *evidence* or *local reputation*.

Reputation is opinion or view of one about something [18]. There can be two types of reputation: subjective reputation is reputation calculated directly from the trustor direct experiences and external reputation is reputation received from third parties. The former type of subjective reputation is considered in this history awareness category.

Essin uses the word *reputation* but does not differentiate between subjective and external reputation. The Marsh model also includes past history data by including the trust values in all previous similar situations in the situational trust evaluation.

The TERM model includes a concept called *direct experience*. It is used by the system to evaluate trust opinions, although it is not formally defined. The SECURE model is very flexible so that it can also use history information if required by making history part of the local trust policy.

3.9   Third Party Awareness

A trust model can be open or closed. A closed model does not take into account any input from outside the actors involved in the trust evaluation. Open trust models accept information from third parties. This information can be in the form of external reputation, recommendations or even delegated decision making.

In addition to subjective reputation discussed above with regards to history-awareness, we also have external reputation. For example, we may belong to a community, which has a common reputation service with shared ontology and receive reputation information from that external source. This external type of reputation is also considered in this third party awareness category. This is not a widely used feature. In the Essin model there is reputation, either generally or bound to a specific action, as a component in the trust evaluation [11].

Recommendations are conceptually somewhat difficult. Since trust is not transitive, recommendations should not be taken directly as trust. However, third party recommendations can be an influencing factor when deciding about trust. Recommendations are considered by many models. For example the models by Yahalom et al. and Abdul-Rahman et al. use them. The SULTAN model and system also uses recommendations as a basis for new trust relationships. The Free Haven system uses the word of *referral* instead of a recommendation. The TERM model also uses recommendations, although it is said that they are used indirectly because of the transitivity issue.

Delegated decision making is not very common. The SECURE model is third party aware because it can handle *delegation* where a principal can refer to another principal's trust information.

External information can be carried in the form of a credential, which is simply a statement, purportedly made by some speaker [8]. Thus a credential is not a semantic information category, but a technical one. A credential can carry identity information, subject properties, reputation data or even capabilities. Therefore we do not categorize models as credential-aware, but the classifying factor is the semantic category such as identity or a particular property. The TERM model calls these credentials *evidence*. In some systems credentials can also be executable programs. This is true in the Keynote and PolicyMaker systems, where these programs are called *assertions*. In the REFEREE system a credential is also a program that examines the inital statements passed to it and derives additional statements.

4   Towards an Ontology of Trust

The trust model analysis above gives us a wide view on how trust has been modeled in previous research. This information makes it possible to create a domain ontology, i.e. a description of the concepts and relationships in the trust domain. Trust ontologies have been made before [13], but not based on a comprehensive analysis. This background analysis makes this new ontology widely usable and compatible with previous research models. Therefore this ontology can facilitate not only discussion across trust models, but also interoperability across different trust systems in autonomous applications.

Because different trust models emphasize different features in the concept and abstract away others, it is assumed that a union of these emphasized features across all models provides us with a maximal list of trust input factors. Based on this maximal list we formulate the following ontological structure.

First of all, trust is a relationship between two principals, the subject, trustor, and the target, trustee. The trust between trustor and trustee may depend on the the action trustor is attempting. The action may have a score of business value properties attached to it. The trustor also may use context information or history data to help in the trust

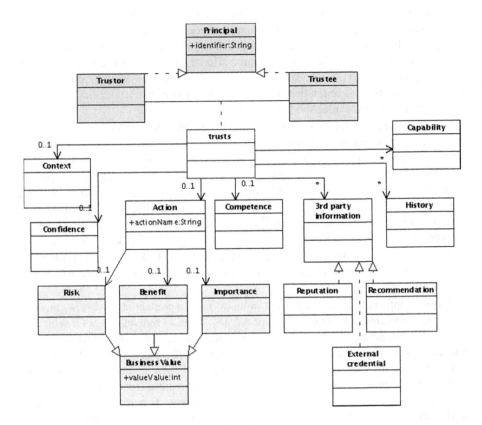

Fig. 2. Trust as a UML diagram

evaluation. The trust can also depend on the peer competence. Additionally, there can be an element of confidence attached to the trust relationship. There can also be a set of third party opinions in the form of reputation information, recommendations or credentials that influence the trust evaluation.

A UML diagram modeling these relationships in trust is presented in Figure 2. The model in the picture is a level 1 metamodel, i.e. it models a particular application domain, trust, which is represented in a UML modeling system [17]. An actual population of this model, such as defining trust relationships between concrete principals, is a level 0 metamodel and can be created utilizing this level 1 model.

The conceptualization can also be described in the OWL Web Ontology language [19]. Trust can easily be described as a trustor property used to list all trusted principals. This is a good option for describing general trust, i.e. trust not linked to a specific action. As can be seen from the general characteristics of trust discussed in Chapter 2, this property can not be a transitive or symmetric property in the OWL model. However, this is not enough for situational trust, i.e. trust which is linked to a particular action. Therefore we transform the UML model in Figure 2 to an ontology expressed in the OWL language using to ontology definition metamodel guidelines [17]. The resulting OWL file can be obtained from the URL http://tinyurl.com/4pw5p.

5   Conclusion

Thirteen very different computational trust models were analyzed on what information they require for the trust decision. This has accomplished two important goals. First, a common vocabulary for describing facts that are considered for trust calculation in the reviewed trust models was created. The models can be classified as identity-aware, action-aware, business value aware, capability-aware, competence-aware, confidence-aware, context-aware, history-aware and third-party aware in their input factors. This new vocabulary facilitates communication when models use different terminology for similar concepts.

Secondly, based on this analysis, the paper presents a new level 1 UML metamodel for the trust concept and link to the corresponding OWL ontology. This ontology can be utilized in digital business in several ways. First of all, it supports trust model sharing between organizations, although the sharing of the trust relationship data may be restricted because of privacy or security reasons. Secondly, new business applications may emerge that automatically process and integrate trust information to be usable in business scenarios. One key area could be single sign on systems or Web Services business communities, which require trust to offer services.

Acknowledgements

This article is based on work performed in the TuBE project (Trust based on evidence) at the Department of Computer Science at the University of Helsinki. The TuBE project is funded by TEKES, Nixu Oy and StoneSoft Oyj.

References

1. A. Abdul-Rahman and S. Hailes. A distributed trust model. In *Proceedings of the 1997 New Security Paradigms Workshop*, pages 48–60. ACM, 1997.
2. B. Bhargava and Y. Zhong. Authorization based on evidence and trust. In *Proceedings of the Data Warehouse and Knowledge Management Conference (DaWak), France*, 2002.
3. M. Blaze, J. Feigenbaum, and A. D. Keromytis. KeyNote: Trust management for public-key infrastructures (position paper). In *Proceedings of the 6th International Workshop on Security Protocols*, volume LNCS 1550/1998, pages 59 – 63. Springer-Verlag, Apr. 1998.
4. M. Blaze, J. Feigenbaum, and J. Lacy. Decentralized trust management. In *Proceedings of the IEEE Symposium on Security and Privacy*. IEEE, May 1996.
5. V. Cahill, E. Gray, J.-M. Seigneur, C. Jensen, Y. Chen, B. Shand, N. Dimmock, A. Twigg, J. Bacon, C. English, W. Wagealla, S. Terzis, P. Nixon, G. D. M. Serugendo, C. Bryce, M. Carbone, K. Krukow, and M. Nielsen. Using trust for secure collaboration in uncertain environments. *Pervasive Computing*, 2(3):52–61, Aug. 2003.
6. M. Carbone, M. Nielsen, and V. Sassone. A formal model for trust in dynamic networks. In *Proceedings of the First International Conference on Software Engineering and Formal Methods*, pages 54–61. IEEE Computer Society, Sept. 2003.
7. R. Chen and W. Yeager. Poblano a distributed trust model for peer-to-peer networks. Technical paper, Sun Microsystems, 2000.
8. Y.-H. Chu, J. Feigenbaum, B. LaMacchia, P. Resnick, and M. Strauss. REFEREE: Trust management for Web applications. *Computer Networks and ISDN Systems*, 29(8–13):953–964, 1997.
9. R. Demolombe. Reasoning about trust: A formal logical framework. In *Proceedings of the Second International Conference on Trust Management, iTrust 2004, LNCS 2995*, pages 291–303. Springer-Verlag, 2004.
10. R. Dingledine. The Free Haven project: Design and deployment of an anonymous secure data haven. Master's thesis, MIT, 2000.
11. D. J. Essin. Patterns of trust and policy. In *Proceedings of the 1997 New Security Paradigms Workshop*. ACM Press, 1997.
12. D. Gambetta. Can we trust trust? *Trust: Making and Breaking Cooperative Relations*, pages 213–237, 2000. Electronic edition.
13. J. Golbeck, B. Parsia, and J. Hendler. Trust networks on the semantic web. In *Proceedings of Seventh International Workshop on Cooperative Intelligent Agents CIA'03*, Helsinki, Finland, August 2003.
14. T. Grandison and M. Sloman. Specifying and analysing trust for internet applications. In *Proceedings of the 2nd IFIP Conference on e-Commerce, e-Business, e-Government I3e2002, Lisbon, Portugal*, Oct. 2002.
15. A. Jøsang. The right type of trust for computer networks. In *Proceedings of the ACM New Security Paradigms Workshop*. ACM, 1996.
16. S. Marsh. *Formalising Trust as a Computational Concept*. PhD thesis, Department of Mathematics and Computer Science, University of Stirling, 1994.
17. OMG. OWL full and UML 2.0 compared, 2004.
18. J. Sabater and C. Sierra. REGRET: A reputation model for gregarious societies. Research Report 2000-06, Institut d'Investigacio i Intelligencia Artificial, 2000.
19. W3C. OWL web ontology language overview, 2004. W3C Recommendation.
20. R. Yahalom, B. Klein, and T. Beth. Trust relationships in secure systems - a distributed authentication perspective. In *Proceedings of the 1993 IEEE Symposium on Research in Security and Privacy*, pages 150–164. IEEE Computer Society, 1993.

An Improved Group Signature Scheme

Jianhong Zhang[1], Jiancheng Zou[1], and Yumin Wang[2]

[1] College of sciences, North China University of Technology,
Shijingshan district, 100041, Beijing, China
{jhzhang, zjh}@ncut.edu.cn,
[2] State Key Lab. on ISN, Xidian University, 710071, Xi'an, Shaanxi, China
ymwang@xidian.edu.cn,

Abstract. As a special digital signature, a group signature scheme allows a group member to sign message on behalf of the group in an anonymous and unlinkability way, In case of a dispute, a designated group manager can reveal the actual identity of the signer. Anonymity and unlinkability are basic properties of group signature, which distinguish other signature schemes. Recently, based on a variant of Nyberg-Rueppel signature and knowledge proof signature, A.Miyaji et al proposed a new group signature scheme over only known-order group and claimed that the scheme is secure. Unfortunately, in this work we first show that the scheme has linkability, Namely, any one can distinguish whether two different group signatures are produced by the same signer, then give the corresponding attack on the scheme. Finally, we propose an improved scheme to overcome the above drawback:linkability and include a novel concept:individual revocation of signatures. At the same time, we give the security analysis of the improved scheme.

1 Introduction

Digital signature plays an important role to provide data integrity, authentication and undeniability for electronic transactions. Group signatures, first introduced by Chaum and van Heyst in[14]. In such a scheme each group member of a given group is allowed to sign messages on behalf of the group in an anonymous and unlinkable way. A receiver only needs the unique group public key to check the validity of a group signature. In case of a dispute, group manager can reveal the identify the identity of the signer, while other group members neither can identify the identity of the signer nor determine whether multiple signature are produced by the same group member.

With time, more security requirements were added, including unlinkability, unforgeability, collusion resistance [4], exculpability [4], and framing resistance [16]. Many practical schemes were presented, some with claims of proven security in the random oracle model [1]. However, it is often unclear what the schemes or claimed proofs in these works actually deliver in terms of security guarantees, due largely to the fact that the requirements are informal and sometimes ambiguous, not precisely specifying adversary capabilities and goals. It would be beneficial

S. Katsikas, J. López, G. Pernul (Eds.): TrustBus 2005, LNCS 3592, pp. 185–194, 2005.

in this context to have proper foundations, meaning strong formal definition and rigorously proven-secure schemes.

Anonymity and unlinkability are two important properties of group signature. Because of the anonymity and unlinkability of group signature, their properties can hide the group internal structure for a verifier, while they can assure group manager to reveal the signer's identities. Hence, group signature is widely used in electronic cash, electronic voting, electronic bid and so on. Unlinkability cannot make that the merchant (or auction center) link two transactions (or bids) of the user, thus protect the privacy of the user.

In real life, a signer often meets to mistakenly signing a message and needs himself to revoke this mistake signature. We call this revocation as **individual revocation**. While The traditional group signature revocation means that the group manager revokes signing capability of group member. To truly simulate signature revocation in real life, in the following, we construct a signature scheme to realize individual revocation.

2   Related Work

Following the first schemes constructed in [14], a number of new group signature schemes and improvements have been proposed [15, 9,10,2,3,18,8,17,14,12,7]. In [15], Chen and Pedersen constructed the first scheme, which allows new members to join the group dynamically, and suggested to use group signatures in e-bidding. Camenisch and Stadler proposed the first group signature scheme that can be used for large groups, since in their scheme the group public key and signatures have lengths independent of the group size[9]. Based on the strong RSA assumption[16], Camenisch and Michels presented an efficient group signature scheme in [10, 11]. Later, Kim et al. extended their scheme to support efficient member revocation[18]. Ateniese and Tsudik pointed out some obstacles that stand in the way of real world applications of group signatures, such as coalition attacks and member deletion [2]. At present, there have been several papers which focused on the problem of member deletion[3,8,4,18]. Ateniese et al. presented a provably secure group signature scheme in [1]. in 2003, Ateniese and de Medeiros[5] proposed another group scheme, which is not as efficient as ACJT2000 scheme. However, it aims at one big advantage over other schemes:no party is required to know any trapdoor secret. So different groups can share the same cryptographic domain without compromising security. it is new research branch of group signature.

At present, these group signature schemes available are mainly classified into two types, a public-key registration type, and a certificate-based type. In the former type, [5,6] are constructed by using only known-order groups. However, in their schemes, both a group public key and the signature size depend on the number of group members. It yields a serious problem for large groups. In the latter type,[9,8,1,4,16,7,3,2]give a membership certificate to group embers, and the group signature is based on the zero-knowledge proof of knowledge(SPK) of membership certificate. Therefore, neither a group public key nor signature size depends on the number of group members. In these previous certificate-based type group signature schemes, the membership certificate has used an RSA signature over an unknown-order group, and, thus, the size of group signature becomes huge.

Though many group signature schemes[1-5,7-15,17] were proposed and researched by many specialists. because these special properties: anonymity and unlinkability, the construction of group signature is intricate. Some schemes among group signature schemes available are *insecure*. Attack on the group signature schemes is mainly divided into unforgeability attack and unlinkability attack . the unforgeability of signature is a basic property which all secure signature schemes should satisfy. as for group signature, unlinkability problem is an important problem of group signature. Because of this property, group signature is widely used in electronic commerce such as e-bid. In the following security analysis, we mainly aim at unlinkability of the scheme to attack.

Recently, A.Miyaji[3] *et al* presents an efficient group signature scheme based on a Nyberg -Rueppel signature and knowledge proof signature. The scheme is the first scheme that is constructed on only known-order groups, and they claim that the scheme realizes the full features of unforgeability, exculpability,anonymity, traceability, unlinkability, and revocability. And the signature size and computation amount of signature generation and verification are reduced. Unfortunately, in this paper, we present security analysis of the scheme and show that the scheme is is linkable, any one can determine whether two different group signatures are produced by the same signer. Because of its linkability, it weakens the anonymity of the scheme. Finally, we give an improved scheme to overcome the linkability of the scheme.

3   Definition

A secure group signature scheme involves a group manager, a set of group members, and a set of verifiers. The group manager (for short, GM) is responsible for admitting/revoking group members, and for opening group signatures to reveal the true signers. When a potential user registers with GM, he/she becomes a group member and then can sign messages on behalf of the group. A verifier checks the validity of a group signature by using the unique group public key. The computational capability of each entity is modeled by a probabilistic polynomial-time Turing machine. We now review the definitions of forward-secure group signature schemes and their security requirements as follows. For more formal definitions on this subject, please refer to [7].

Definition 1. *A secure group signature scheme is comprised of the following procedures [9,2,3,14,16]:*

- SETUP: On input of a security parameter , this probabilistic algorithm outputs the initial group public key and the secret key for the group manager.
- JOIN: An interactive protocol between the group manager and a user that results in the user becoming a new group member. The user's output is a group-signing key.

- SIGN: A probabilistic algorithm that on input a group public key, a group signing key, and a message m outputs a group signature on m.
- VERIFY: An algorithm for establishing the validity of an alleged group signature of a message with respect to a group public key.
- OPEN: An algorithm that, given a message, a valid group signature on it, a group public key and the corresponding group manger's secret key, determines the identity of the signer.
- REVOKE: An algorithm that on input a group member's certificate, a group public key and the corresponding group manger's secret key, outputs a revocation token that revokes the group member's signing ability.

Definition 2. *A secure group signature scheme is secure if it satisfies all the following security requirements [1,2,3,14,16]:*

- Correctness: Signatures produced by a group member using SIGN procedure must be accepted by VERIFY procedure.
- Unforgeability: Only group members are able to sign messages on behalf of the group.
- Anonimity: Given a valid group signature for some message, identifying the actual signer is computationally hard for everyone but the group manager.
- Unlinkability: Deciding whether two different valid signatures were generated by the same group member is computationally hard for everyone but the group manager.
- Excupability: Even if the group manager and some of the group members collude, they cannot sign on behalf of non-involved group members.
- Traceability: The group manager can always open a valid group signature using OPEN procedure and then identify the actual signer.
- Coalition-resistance: A colluding subset of group members cannot generate a valid group signature that cannot be traced by the group manager.
- Revocability: The group manager can revoke a group member so that this group member cannot produce a valid group signature any more after being revoked.

In real life, a signer often wants himself to revoke a certain of his signature. The signature revocation means that the group manager revokes signing capability of group member in traditional group signature. To truly simulate signature revocation in real life, we include a novel conception: **individual revocation**. Individual revocation means that a signer can revoke himself a certain of his signature without affecting other signatures.

4   Review of A.Miyaji *et al* Scheme

In the following, we briefly describe A.Miyaji scheme, please interested reader refer to [3] for more detail. in the paper, the symbol "SPK" denotes knowledge proof signature.

[Setup Phase]

(1) Choose two primes p, q with $q|p-1$, and set $P = pq$.
(2) Randomly choose another a prime $\widetilde{P}$ of such that $P|(\widetilde{P}-1)$.
(3) Set two cyclic subgroups $G_P \subset Z_P^*$ with order q and $G_{\widetilde{P}} \subset Z_{\widetilde{P}}^*$ with order P.
(4) choose elements g_1, g_2, g_3 and $g_4 \in_R G_P \backslash \{1\}$ such that the discrete logarithm based on each other elements are unkonwn.
(5) Chooses an element $\widetilde{g} \in_R G_{\widetilde{P}} \backslash \{1\}$.
(6) Finally, the group manager randomly chooses a secret key $x_{GM} \in_R Z_q$ and computes $y_1 = g_1^{x_{GM}} \bmod P$ and $y_2 = g_3^{x_{GM}} \bmod P$, and publishes the group public key $Y = \{q, P, \widetilde{P}, g_1, g_2, g_3, g_4, \widetilde{g}, y_1, y_2\}$.

[Join Phase]

(1) the group member M_i chooses a membership key $x_i \in_R Z_q$, set $z_i = g_2^{x_i}$ mod P, and sends z_i with $\delta_i = SPK[\alpha : z_i = g_2^{\alpha} mod P](\'\')$ to GM.
(2) GM checks the validity of α_i, chooses a random integer $w_i \in_R Z_q$ computes $A_i = z_i g_1^{-w_i} \bmod P$ and $b_i = w_i - A_i x_{GM} \bmod q$, and sends $(A_i, b_i) \in Z_P \times Z_q$ to M_i . through a secure channel.
(3) GM adds (A_i, b_i) with M_i's identity ID_i to the member list ML.
(4) M_i verifies that $A_i y_1^{A_i} g_1^{b_i} = z_i$.
(5) GM outputs the renewed member list $ML = \{(ID_i, A_i, b_i)\}$.
(6) M_i possesses a membership key x_i and a membership certificate $(A_i, b_i) \in Z_p \times Z_q$.

[Revocation Phase]
In order to revoke a new subset of member whose revoked member list is $RML = (ID, b)$, GM computes as follows

(1) choose a new revocation base $g_4 \in_R G_P \backslash \{1\}$ and update the group public key Y .
(2) compute $V_i = g_4^{b_j} \bmod P$ for $b_j \in RML$ $(i \leq j \leq u)$.
(3) Output the renewed certificate revocation list $CRL = \{V_j | 1 \leq j \leq u\}$.

[Signing Phase]

(1) Choose a random integer $w \in_R Z_q$.
(2) Compute $T_1 = \widetilde{g}^{g_3^w} \bmod \widetilde{P}$, $T_2 = T_1^{g_4^{b_i}} \bmod \widetilde{P}$, $T_3 = g_3^{b_i} g_4^w \bmod P$, $T_4 = A_i g_3^w$ mod P, and $T_5 = y_2^w \bmod P$.
(3) $\delta_1 = SPK[(\alpha_1, \alpha_2) : T_1 = \widetilde{g}^{g_3^{\alpha_2}} mod\widetilde{P} \wedge T_2 = T_1^{g_4^{\alpha_1}} mod\widetilde{P} \wedge T_3 = g_3^{\alpha_1} g_4^{\alpha_2} mod P](m) = (c_1, s_{11}, \ldots, s_{1k}, s_{2k}, \ldots, s_{2k}) \in \{0,1\}^k \times Z_q^{2k}$
(4) Generate

$$\delta_2 = SPK[(\alpha_3, \alpha_4, \alpha_5, \alpha_6) : \alpha_3 \in Z_P \wedge T_3 = g_3^{\alpha_4} g_4^{\alpha_6} mod P \wedge T_4 = y_1^{-\alpha_3}$$
$$g_1^{-\alpha_4} g_2^{\alpha_5} g_3^{\alpha_6} mod P \wedge T_5 = y_2^{\alpha_6} mod P \wedge \widetilde{g}^{T_4} = T_1^{\alpha_3} mod\widetilde{P}](m)$$
$$= (c_2, s_3, s_4, s_5, s_6) \in \{0,1\}^k \times Z_q^3 \times Z_P$$

(5) Finally, the group signature is $\delta = \{T_1, T_2, T_3, T_4, T_5, \delta_1, \delta_2\}$

[Verification Phase]

(1) Check the validity of δ_1 and δ_2.
(2) If $T_1^{V_j} \neq T_2 \bmod \widetilde{P}$ for $\forall V_j \in CRL$, then accept the signature otherwise reject the signature.

[Tracing Phase]

(1) Recover $A_i = T_4/T_5^{1/x_{GM}} \bmod P$.
(2) Identify a signer M_i from A_i by using the member list ML.
(3) Output the signer's actual identity ID.

5   Security Analysis of A.Miyaji *et al* Scheme

After analyzing the security of the scheme[3], A.Miyaji et al have claimed that their scheme was able to realize the anonymity and unlinkability. Unfortunately, we find that this is not the fact.In the following discuss, we show that the scheme has linkability.

In the following, we show that the scheme has linkability, Namely, any one can determine whether two different group signatures are produced by the same signer, the detail attack is as follows.

Let $(T_1, T_2, T_3, T_4, T_5, \delta_1, \delta_2)$ and $(T_1', T_2', T_3', T_4', T_5', \delta_1', \delta_2')$ be two valid group signatures. To decide whether they are produced by the same group member, a verifier only need to compute the following relation.

$$\gamma = T_4^{-1} mod P \tag{1}$$

$$\mu = T_4 - T_4' mod P. \tag{2}$$

$$\theta_1 = T_1/T_1' mod \widetilde{P} \tag{3}$$

$$\theta_2 = T_1^{\gamma\mu} mod \widetilde{P} \tag{4}$$

if the equation (3) and equation (4) are equal, then it means that the two group signatures are produced by the same signer, otherwise, they are produced by the different group member.

Theorem 1. *Given a group signature* $(T_1, T_2, T_3, T_4, T_5, \delta_1, \delta_2)$, *then* T_4 *satisfies* $Gcd(T_4, P) = 1$ *in overwhelming probability* $1 - \frac{1}{2^{160}}$.

Proof. According to generation of the group signature, we know $T_4 = A_i g_3^w \bmod P$ and $P = pq$ where p, q are large primes. Thus the probability of $Gcd(T_4, P) \neq 1$ is $(p + q - 1)/pq$. Because the size of p, q is not less than 160 bits and the probability of $Gcd(T_4, P) = 1$ is $1 - \frac{(p+q-1)}{pq}$, then we have

$$Pr[Gcd(T_4, P) = 1] \geq 1 - \frac{1}{2^{160}}$$

Thus, T_4 satisfies $Gcd(T_4, P) = 1$ in overwhelming probability.

Theorem 2. *If two different group signatures* $(T_1, T_2, T_3, T_4, T_5, \delta_1, \delta_2)$ *and* $(T_1', T_2', T_3', T_4', T_5', \delta_1', \delta_2')$ *satisfy the above equation (3) and equation (4), then two group signatures must be produced by the same signer.*

Proof. According to the above signing phase, we know

$$T_1 = \tilde{g}^{g_3^w} \bmod \tilde{P}, T_4 = A_i g_3^w \bmod P$$

$$T_1' = \tilde{g}^{g_3^{w'}} \bmod \tilde{P}, T_4' = A_i g_3^{w'} \bmod P$$

hence, we have

$$\mu = T_4 - T_4' = A_i(g_3^w - g_3^{w'}) \bmod P$$

we know the order $\tilde{g}$ is P, and $Gcd(T_4, P) = 1$ in overwhelming probability by the above Theorem 1. So that we can solve the inverse γ of T_4 by the Extended Euclidean Algorithm (EEA) . it follows that

$$T_1^{T_4^{-1}} = \tilde{g}^{\gamma} = \tilde{g}^{A_i^{-1}}$$

$$\tilde{g}^{A_i^{-1}\mu} = \tilde{g}^{g_3^w - g_3^{w'}}$$

$$\tilde{g}^{g_3^w - g_3^{w'}} = T_1/T_1'$$

Finally, we can conclude that the above equation(3) and equation (4) is equal. Hence, it means that the scheme has linkability.

Unlinkability is the basic property of group signature. this property makes group signature widely be used in electronic commerce such as e-cash. The reason of producing the above attack is to use the same random number in T_1 and T_4. To overcome the attack, we can adopt two random numbers to randomize T_1 and T_4. In next section ,we will give an improved scheme.

6 The Improved Scheme

In this section, we give an improved scheme to overcome the linkability of A.Miyaji et al scheme. The improved scheme has also individual revocation beside the properties above. Individual revocation is that a group member can revoke himself a certain of his signatures. The improved scheme is as follows: Setup phase, Join phase, Revocation phase and Trace phase of our improved scheme are the similar with those of A.Miyaji scheme, only a difference is Signing phase .

Signing Phase of our improved scheme is as follows

(1) Choose two random integers $w, u \in_R Z_q$.

(2) Compute $T_1 = \tilde{g}^{g_3^w} \bmod \tilde{P}$, $T_2 = T_1^{g_4^{b_i}} \bmod \tilde{P}$, $T_3 = g_3^{b_i} g_4^w \bmod P$, $T_4 = A_i g_3^u \bmod P$, $T_5 = y_2^u \bmod P$ and $T_6 = y_1^{A_i} g_4^u \bmod P$.

(3) $\delta_1 = SPK[(\alpha_1, \alpha_2) : T_1 = \tilde{g}^{g_3^{\alpha_2}} mod\tilde{P} \wedge T_2 = T_1^{g_4^{\alpha_1}} mod\tilde{P} \wedge T_3 = g_3^{\alpha_1} g_4^{\alpha_2}$
$mod P](m) = (c_1, s_{11}, \ldots, s_{1k}, s_{2k}, \ldots, s_{2k}) \in \{0,1\}^k \times Z_q^{2k}$

(4) Generate

$$\delta_2 = SPK[(\alpha_3, \alpha_4, \alpha_5, \alpha_6, \alpha_7, \alpha_8) : \alpha_3 \in Z_P \wedge T_4 T_6 = g_1^{-\alpha_4} g_2^{\alpha_5} g_3^{\alpha_7} g_4^{\alpha_7} mod P$$
$$\wedge T_5 = y_2^{\alpha_7} mod P \wedge T_3 = g_3^{\alpha_4} g_4^{\alpha_8} \wedge T_4 = \alpha_3 g_3^{\alpha_7} \wedge T_6 = y_1^{\alpha_3} g_4^{\alpha_7} mod P](m)$$
$$= (c_2, s_3, s_4, s_5, s_6, s_7, s_8) \in \{0,1\}^k \times Z_P \times Z_q^4$$

(5) Finally, the group signature is $\delta = \{T_1, T_2, T_3, T_4, T_5, T_6, \delta_1, \delta_2\}$

In our improved scheme, we randomize $T_1, T_2, T_3, T_4, T_5, T_6$ to overcome the above attack by introducing two random number w, u. (T_4, T_5) in the signature are the ElGamal ciphertext in order to trace the identity of the signer. (T_4, T_6) is to proof the membership certificate that satisfies $A_i y_1^{A_i} g^{b_i} = z_i$ mod P. the security of our improved scheme is the same as one of A.Miyaji et al scheme[3].Namely, both schemes are based on the MDLP (the Multiple Discrete Logarithm Problem). The detail security analysis refers to [3].

The prominent property of the improved scheme is to realize individual revocation. If the group member wants himself to revoke a certain of his signatures,then he only needs to publish $g_4^{b_i}$ in revocation list and requests that the group manager renews g_4. When a user verifies a group signature, he only chooses $g_4^{b_i}$ from the revocation list, and verifies $T_1^{g_4^{s_i}} \overset{?}{=} T_2$. If it holds, then it indicates that this signature is already revoked.

7   Security Analysis of our Improved Scheme

Theorem 3. *The underlying interactive protocol of the improved group signature scheme is an honest-verifier perfect zero-knowledge proof of knowledge of a membership certificate, corresponding signing key and the corresponding random number used for encryption of ElGamal ciphertext. Furthermore, it proves that the pair(T_4, T_5) encrypts the membership certificate under the group manager's public key y_2.*

since the space is limited and the the proof can be given in a standard manner,we omit the proof here.

Theorem 4. *the improved group signature scheme is unforgeable if Nyberg-Rueppel signature scheme is existentially unforgeable under an adaptive chosen message attack in the random oracle model.*

Proof. From the above join phase of the improved group signature, we know that in fact a membership certificate (A_i, b_i) with $A_i \in Z_P$ is a Nyberg-Rueppel signature on a message z_i. Supposed that there exists an attacker A that can forge a group signature, then there exists an attacker A' that breaks the EUF-CMA of the Nyerg-Rueppel signature. the attack of A' is as follows:

1. key generation of the Nyberg-Rueppel signature scheme is the same as Setup phase of the above group signature scheme.
2. when the attacker A queries a joining oracle to join the group by giving $z_i = g_2^{x_i}$, A' asks its signing oracle to sign on z_i. Then A' sends the answer of the oracle A, which is the membership certificate.
3. Supposed that A can forge a group signature by a membership certificate that A' has never sent A. Then, A plays a role of a knowledge extractor, namely, rewinds A and chooses another random oracle to extract the member certificate (A_i', b_i') and the signing key x_i'. This is possible from Theorem 3. Then A' outputs this extracted data $(x_i', (A_i', b_i'))$ as a forged signature of Nyberg-Rueppel signature scheme.

In the following, we show that our improved scheme satisfies all features necessary of group signature.

Unforgeability: From the above Theorem 3, we can know that $\{T_1, T_2, T_3, T_4, T_5, T_6\}$ of a group signature is an commitment to membership certificate (A_i, b_i) and corresponding membership key x_i with satisfying $A_i y_i^{A_i} g_1^{b_i} = g_2^{x_i}$. it is infeasible to find a pair (A_i, b_i) corresponding a membership key x_i without the secret key of the group manager under the Multiple Discrete Logarithm assumption[3]. Therefore, the membership certificate and the group signature are unforgeable.

Exculpability: GM knows a member's membership certificate, but he can not get any information about the membership key x_i. Hence, He can sign on behalf of member M_i. It is equivalent to break the EUF-CMA of the Nyerg-Rueppel signature scheme for several members colluding to produce a membership certificate.

Anonymity: it is obvious.

Unlinkability: In the above improved scheme, we randomize $T_1, T_2, T_3, T_4, T_5, T_6$ to overcome the above attack by introducing two random number w, u. As two group signature $(T_1, T_2, T_3, T_4, T_5, T_6)$ and $(T_1', T_2', T_3', T_4', T_5', T_6')$, they are uniformly randomized by random number. So that it is hard to distinguish whether two group signatures are produced by the same signer.

Traceability: when the signature is valid, (T_4, T_5) encrypts the membership certificate A_i under the group manager's public key y_2. Therefore, the memeber certificate A_i can be uniquely traced by group manager.

8   Conclusion

In this paper, we presented security analysis of A.Miyaji *et al* group signature. By successfully attack on the scheme, we demonstrated that their scheme is insecure. More specifically, we shows that the scheme is linkable, namely any one can distinguish whether two different group signatures are produced by the same signer. At the same time, we give an improved scheme which can realize individual revocation of group signature and analyze the security of the improved scheme. It is an open problem to how design a secure and more efficient group signature scheme.

References

1. G.Ateniese, J.Camenisch, M.Joye, and G.Tsudik, A Pracical and provably secure coalition-resistant group signature. In Advances in Cryptography-CRYPTO'00, LNCS 1880, pp 255-270, Springer-Verlag .
2. G.Ateniese and G.Tsudik.Some open issues and new direction in group signatures. In Financial Cryptography(FC'99), LNCS 1648, pp 196-211.Springer-Verlag.
3. Atsuko Miyaji and Kozue Umeda, A Fully-Functional group signature scheme over only known-order group, In 2th Conference of Applied Cryptography and Network Security (ACNS2004) Springer-verlag, LNCS 3089 pp 165-179
4. G.Ateniese, D.Song, and G.Tsudik.Quasi-efficient revocation of group signatures.In Financial Cryptography (FC'02),LNCS 2357. Springer-verlag,
5. G.Ateniese and B.de medeiros. Efficient group signature without trapdoors. In Asiacrypt , Springer-verlag, 2003, http://eprint.iacr.org/2002/173
6. M.Bellare, and S.Miner.A forward-secure digital signature scheme. In Advances in Cryptography-CRYPTO'99, LNCS 1666, pp 431-448. Springer-Verlag,
7. M.Bellare, D. Micciancio, and B. Warinschi.Foundations of group signatures: formal definitions, simplified requirements, and a construction based on general assumptions. In: Advances in Cryptology - EUROCRYPT¡03, LNCS 2656, pp. 614-629. Springer-Verlag.
8. E. Bresson and J. Stern. Efficient revocation in group signatures. In: Public Key Cryptography (PKC¡01), LNCS 1992, pages 190-206. Springer-Verlag.
9. J. Camenisch and M. Stadler. Efficient group signature schemes for large groups. In: Advances in Cryptology - CRYPTO¡97, LNCS 1294, pages 410-424.
10. J. Camenisch and M. Michels. A group signature scheme with improved efficiency. In: Advances in Cryptology - ASIACRYPT¡98, LNCS 1514, pages 160-174. Springer- Verlag.
11. J. Camenisch and M. Michels. A group signature scheme based on an RSA-variant. Technical Report RS-98-27, BRICS, University of Aarhus, November .
12. J. Camenisch and A.Lysyanskaya. Dynamic accumulators and application to efficient revocation of anonymous credentials. In: Advances in Cryptology - CRYPTO 2002, LNCS 2442, pages 61-76. Springer-Verlag .
13. S. Canard and J. Traor' e.On fair e-cash systems based on group signature schemes. In: Information Security and Privacy (ACISP 2003), LNCS 2727, pp. 237-248. Berlin: Springer-Verlag.
14. D. Chaum and E. van Heyst. Group signatures. In: Advances in Cryptology - EUROCRYPT¡ 91, LNCS 950, pages 257-265. Springer-Verlag.
15. L. Chen and T. P. Pedersen.New group signature schemes. In: Advances in Cryptology - EUROCRYT¡94, LNCS 950, pages 171-181. Springer-Verlag .
16. E. Fujisaki and T. Okamoto. Statistical zero-knowledge protocols to prove modular polynomial relations. In: Advances in Cryptology - CRYPTO¡97, LNCS 1294, pages 16-30.
17. A.Kiayias and M.Yung. Extracting group signature from traitor tracing schemes. In Advances in Cryptology-EUROCRYPTO 2003, LNCS 2656, pp 630-648.
18. H.J.Kim, J.I.Lim,and D.H.Lee. Efficient and secure member deletion in group signature schemes. In information security and crytology(ICISC2000), LNCS 2015, pp 150-161, Springer-Verlag,2001.

Efficient Member Revocation in Group Signature Schemes*

Eun Young Choi[1], Hyun-Jeong Kim[1], and Dong Hoon Lee[2]

Center for Information Security Technologies(CIST),
Korea University, Anam-dong, Sungbuk-ku, Seoul, 136-701, Korea
{bluecey, khj}@cist.korea.ac.kr[1] , donghlee@korea.ac.kr[2]

Abstract. Group signature schemes allow a group member to sign messages anonymously on behalf of the group. During last decade, group signature schemes have been intensively investigated in the literature and applied to various applications. Especially, as noted in [3], the complexity of member deletion stands in the way of real world applications of group signatures. In this paper, we propose a group signature scheme with an efficient member revocation procedure. The proposed scheme is based on the scheme [18], which was turned out to be flawed [21]. We modify the scheme in [18] so as to obtain secure and efficient member revocation and unlinkability of signatures. Our revocation method is an improvement over the work of Camenisch and Lysyanskaya [9], which is known to be the most efficient scheme so far.

1 Introduction

The concept of a group signature was introduced by Chaum and van Heyst [13]. Various researches in group signature schemes have been investigated to propose an efficient one of which the length of signatures and the size of the group public key are independent of the size of the group. Group signature schemes should be also coalition resistant. With the improvement in both efficiency and security, group signature schemes have been adapted to various applications such as an electronic cash system, voting and so on. However, for group signature schemes to be adapted to real applications, a few problems need to be solved. Among them is the efficiency of member deletion. In practical applications, a group is dynamic, i.e., a membership changes frequently. In the latter case, it is necessary to prevent the deleted member from generating any valid group signature. Furthermore this revocation procedure should be performed efficiently.

Related Work. Since the work of Chaum *et al.* [13], various group signature schemes has been proposed [8,11,12,14,16], but without considering membership revocation. Kim *et al.* [18] proposed the first group signature scheme with a member deletion that is based on the Camenisch-Michels group signature scheme [10].

---

* This research was supported by the MIC(Ministry of infromation and Communication), Korea, under the ITRC(Information Technology Research Center) support program supervised by the IITA(Institute of Information Technology Assessment).

S. Katsikas, J. López, G. Pernul (Eds.): TrustBus 2005, LNCS 3592, pp. 195–205, 2005.

Whenever a member joins or leaves the group, each group member updates his secret key by doing only one modular multiplication. However, this scheme has some flaws in member deletion process, as shown in [21]. Then various group signature scheme has proposed [2,5] with considering membership revocation, which has drawback that the size of a group signature or the work of the verifier is linear in the number of revoked members. Recently, Camenisch *et al.* [9] proposed a new revocation method which is an improvement over previous works since the verification phase requires a constant work. More recently, Boneh *et al.* [4] proposed a short group signature. Whenever a member changes, each remaining member perform the modular exponentiations which is similar to the computational complexity of the scheme in [9].

Our Contributions. Among various signature schemes with a member deletion, the scheme of Camenisch *et al.* [9] is the most efficient. However, whenever a member joins or leaves a group, the scheme requires modular exponentiations. In this paper, we propose an efficient revocation method in a point of view of group members. Our scheme is the modification of Kim *et al.*'s scheme [18], which has flaws, as analyzed in [21], such that group signatures are linkable and membership revocation procedure is not secure. To remedy these flaws, we use a secure symmetric encryption algorithm to provide secure group member revocation and we modify the process of signature generation to provide unlinkability. In our scheme, whenever a member joins or leaves a group, each modification requires only one modular multiplication and one execution of symmetric encryption algorithm. Hence our model is an acceptable solution for a large group where a membership changes frequently.

2   Group Signature Model

The following parties participate in a group signature scheme.

Membership Manager : The membership manager manages each group member's membership key for group signatures and performs a join/delete algorithm for adding or deleting members.

Revocation Manager : When a dispute with a group signature occurs, the revocation manager can identify a group member who has generated the group signature with the request of the membership manager.

Users : Users join a group by the membership managers and then anonymously generate a group signature.

A group signature scheme consists of the following procedures:

• **Setup**(G_0) **:** An interactive protocol between the membership manager and the revocation manager. The outputs are the membership manager's secret key x_M and public key y_M, and the revocation manager's secret key x_R and public key y_R. i.e, the initial group G_0 is generated.

• **Join(J, G') :** An interactive protocol between the membership manager and a user that results in the user becoming a new group member. Inputs of this algorithm are set of joining member's identity denoted by $\mathbf{J}$ and the current group denoted by G'. The outputs are a group member's secret key x_I, a group member's public key y_I, a group member *secret property key* U_I, the group *public property key* U_M, the group *renewal property key* U_N and a shared symmetric key $\mathcal{K}$ with the membership manager. Then, the group renewal property key U_N is encrypted with the group members' symmetric keys and is published the group. Each valid group's member decrypts the encrypted message using own symmetric key $\mathcal{K}$, update own secret property key U_I and verify the correctness of own secret property key U_I using the group public key U_M.

- **Delete(D, G')** : Inputs of this algorithm are set of joining member's identity denoted by $\mathbf{D}$, a member's public key y_I and the current group G'. The outputs are the group's public property key U_M and the renewal property key U_N. Then each valid group member performs updating process which is similar to Join's updating processes.

- **Sign** : A signature generation algorithm that on input a message m, x_I, y_I, y_R and U_I outputs a signature σ.

- **Verify** : A verification algorithm that on input a message m, a signature σ, y_M, y_R, and U_M return 1 if and only if σ was generated by a proper group member using

- **User-Tracing** : A user tracing algorithm that on input a signature σ, a message m, x_R, and y_R outputs the identity of the group member who generated the signature σ.

- **Sign-Tracing** : A sign tracing algorithm that on input a part of a signature σ, y_I and x_R outputs 1 if and only if the signature was generated by a specific member.

A group signature scheme must satisfy the following properties:

Unforgeability of signatures : Only current group members are able to generate valid signatures. In particular, if a group member leaves a group, he should not be able to generate a valid signature any more.

Anonymity : It is infeasible to find out a member who generated a given signature except the revocation manager.

Unlinkability of signatures : Given two signatures, no one except the revocation manager can decide whether or not the signatures have been computed by a same group member.

No framing : Any coalition of group members, the membership manager, and the revocation manager can not compute a signature on behalf of non-involved honest group member. Furthermore, they should not be able to sign message on behalf of a deleted group member.

Unforgeability of user-tracing verification : Given a signature, the revocation manager should not be able to falsely blame a signer for having produced a signature.

Unforgeability of sign-tracing verification : The revocation manager should not be able to falsely insist that a signature was generated by a designated member.

3   Our Proposal

In this section we propose a modification of [18] that provides secure member revocation using secure symmetric encryption algorithm and unlinkability of signatures by modifying process of signature generation. The security of our scheme is based on RSA, modified strong RSA, DDH [10] and CDH assumption [7]. In particular, the security relies on CDH assumption. The scheme is especially described in the viewpoint of addition/deletion of a member.

3.1   System Setup

In our scheme, the system is set up by generating the group's public keys and choosing secret keys.
The membership manager executes the setup procedure as follows:

1. Choose a group $G = \langle g \rangle$ and two random elements $z, h \in G$ with the same (large) order ($\approx 2^{\ell_g}$) such that modified strong RSA and DDH assumptions hold, then publish them. Computing discrete logarithms in G to the bases g, h, or z must be infeasible. Only the membership manager can easily compute these roots, the membership manager should keep the order of G secretly.
2. Choose two large random primes p_1, q_1 ($\approx 2^{\ell_g/2}$) of the form $p_1 = 2p_2+1$, $q_1 = 2q_2+1$ where p_2, q_2 are primes such that $p_1, q_1 \neq 1 \pmod 8$ and $p_1 \neq q_1 \pmod 8$, keep p_1 and q_1 secretly, and publish $n := p_1 q_1$.
3. Select and publish a large prime p, generator α of $\mathbf{Z}_p^*$, $2 \leq \alpha \leq p-2$ such that CDH assumption holds. Choose $t \in \mathbf{Z}_p^*$ at random and keep t secretly. Compute $PK := \alpha^t \bmod p$ and publish PK.
4. Choose a public key e_N and a secret key d_N such that $e_N d_N \equiv 1 \pmod{\phi(n)}$ where n is a RSA-modulus and publish e_N.
5. Generate a signature key pair (sk_M, vk_M): sk_M is the secret signing key and vk_M is the public verification key, and publish vk_M
6. Set up hash functions $H : \{0,1\}^* \to \{0,1\}^k$, $\mathcal{H}_0 : \{0,1\}^* \to \{0,1\}^k$, $\mathcal{H}_1 : \{0,1\}^* \to \{0,1\}^k$ and security parameters $\ell, \ell_1, \ell_2, \ell_g$ and ϵ.
6. Set up a secure signature algorithm $\Sigma = (K, S, V)$.
7. Publish a counter c in order to indicate a membership exchange event and increase a counter c in the event of membership changes.

The revocation manager executes the setup procedure as follows :

1. Choose a secret key x_R randomly in $\{0, \cdots, 2^{l_g} - 1\}$.
2. Publish $y_R = g^{x_R}$ as a public key.

3.2 Join

This is an interactive protocol between the membership manager and Alice who wants to become a new group member. Through join process, Alice obtians the membership key (x_I, y_I), where $y_I \in \mathsf{G}$ holds $y_I^{x_I} = z$, and shares symmetric key with the membership manager. Also the membership manager regenerates group public property key U_M and renewal property key U_N using y_I and generates Alice's secret property key U_I. New renewal property key is encrypted with the symmetric keys of group members. Then the group's public property key and the encrypted messages is published. Before generating any signature, current members check whether the group renewal property key has been updated or not. Let $\mathcal{C} := \{I_1, I_2, \cdots, I_{m-1}\}$ be the set of current group members, and I_m be a new member, Alice. Before adding Alice to the group, the group public property key has been $U_M := y_{I_1} \cdots y_{I_{m-1}} y'$ with a random number $y' \in_R \mathsf{G}$ and a counter c. *Alice does the followings :*

1. Generate a signature key pair (sk_{I_m}, vk_{I_m}).
2. Choose random primes $\hat{x}_{I_m} \in_R \{2^{\tilde{\ell}-1}, \cdots, 2^{\tilde{\ell}} - 1\}$ and $x_{I_m} \in_R \{2^{\ell_1}, \cdots, 2^{\ell_1} + 2^{\ell_2} - 1\}$ such that $\hat{x}_{I_m} x_{I_m} \neq 1 \pmod 8$ and $\hat{x}_{I_m} \neq x_{I_m} \pmod 8$.
3. Compute $\tilde{x}_{I_m} := x_{I_m} \hat{x}_{I_m}$ and $\tilde{z} := z^{\hat{x}_{I_m}}$, and commit to $\tilde{x}_{I_m}$ and $\tilde{z}$.
4. Choose $t_m \in \mathbf{Z}_p^*$ at random, and compute $SK_m := \alpha^{t_m} \bmod p$ and the shared key $\mathcal{K}_m = (PK)^{t_m} \bmod p$ (Assume $\mathcal{K}_m$ differs from other group members' t_is , $1 \leq i \leq m-1$).
5. Generate signature $s = S_{sk_{I_m}}(SK_m)$ and compute $\mathcal{H}_0(c \parallel \mathcal{K}_m)$. Then she sends identity, SK_m, s, $\mathcal{H}_0(c \parallel \mathcal{K}_m)$, $\tilde{x}_{I_m}$, $\tilde{z}$ and their commitments to the membership manager.
6. Execute the interactive protocols corresponding to $\mathcal{W} = SPK\{ (\tau, \varrho) \mid z^{\tilde{x}_{I_m}} = \tilde{z}^\tau \wedge \tilde{z} = z^\varrho \wedge \tau \in \{2^{\ell_1} - 2^{\epsilon(\ell_2+k)+1}, \cdots, 2^{\ell_1} + 2^{\epsilon(\ell_2+k)+1} \}\}(\tilde{z})$ with the membership manager.

$\mathcal{W}$ is a statistical zero-knowledge proof of knowledge of the discrete logarithm of $\tilde{z}(= z^{\hat{x}_{I_m}})$ and an integer x_{I_m} such that $x_{I_m} \in \{2^{\ell_1} - 2^{\epsilon(\ell_2+k)+1}, \cdots, 2^{\ell_1} + 2^{\epsilon(\ell_2+k)+1} \}$ and $\tilde{z}^{x_{I_m}} = z^{\tilde{x}_{I_m}}$. Therefore the membership manager trusts Alice to have chosen $\tilde{x}_{I_m}$ and $\tilde{z}$ correctly by the proof $\mathcal{W}$.

The membership manager does the followings :

1. Check s to verify the received value SK_m and compute the shared key $\mathcal{K}_m = (SK_m)^t \bmod p$ to verify $\mathcal{H}_0(c \parallel \mathcal{K}_m)$. If successful, the membership manager accepts that $\mathcal{K}_m$ is actually shared with Alice and increases a counter c into c'. (If not, the protocol halts)
2. Generate signature $s' = S_{sk_M}(SK_m)$, and compute $\mathcal{H}_1(c' \parallel \mathcal{K}_m)$.
3. Generate Alice's public key $y_{I_m} := \tilde{z}^{1/\tilde{x}_{I_m}}$ and compute a new group's public property key $U_M := y_{I_1} \cdots y_{I_{m-1}} y_{I_m} y''$, where $y'' \in_R \mathsf{G}$.

4. Compute the new group's renewal property key $U_N := (y_{I_m} y'' / y')^{d_N}$.

5. Generate the member I_m's secret property key $U_{I_m} := (y_{I_1} y_{I_2} \cdots y_{I_{m-1}} y'')^{d_N}$.

6. Encrypt U_{I_m} and y_{I_m} with the shared symmetric key $\mathcal{K}_m$, encrypt U_N with the group members's symmetric keys, and publish $\mathcal{E}_{\mathcal{K}_i}(U_N)$, $1 \le i \le m - 1$.

7. Send $\mathcal{E}_{\mathcal{K}_m}(U_{I_m}, y_{I_m})$, s', and $\mathcal{H}_1(c' \| \mathcal{K}_m)$ to Alice and publish c', U_M.

Alice does the followings :

1. Check s', c' and $\mathcal{H}_1(c' \| \mathcal{K}_m)$ to verify the shared symmetric key. If successful, Alice accepts that $\mathcal{K}_m$ is actually shared with the membership manager(If not, the protocol halts). Then decrypt the received message $\mathcal{E}_{\mathcal{K}_m}(U_{I_m}, y_{I_m})$.

The pair (x_{I_m}, y_{I_m}) becomes the membership key of Alice. A new member I_m, Alice, verifies her public key y_{I_m} and secret property key U_{I_m} by checking $y_{I_m}^{x_{I_m}} = z$ and $(U_{I_m})^{e_N} y_{I_m} = U_M$ respectively. First, each valid group member $I_i (1 \le i \le m - 1)$ except a new member I_m decrypts the encrypted messages with the shared symmetric key $\mathcal{K}_i (1 \le i \le m-1)$ and changes his secret property key $U_{I_i} := (y_{I_1} \cdots y_{I_{i-1}} y_{I_{i+1}} \cdots y_{I_{m-1}} y')^{d_N}$ into $U'_{I_i} = U_{I_i} \cdot U_N$, where

$$U'_{I_i} = U_{I_i} \cdot U_N = (y_{I_1} \cdots y_{I_{i-1}} y_{I_{i+1}} \cdots y_{I_{m-1}} y_{I_m} y'')^{d_N}.$$

Each group member can check new value U'_{I_i} by computing $U_M = (U'_{I_i})^{e_N} y_{I_i}$.

3.3 Delete

This protocol is similar to the addition procedure of a group member. To delete the group member I_j the membership manager eliminates public key y_{I_j} from the group public property key U_M and changes a random number. The remaining group members change their secret property keys to generate a valid signature. Let the current group's public property key be $U_M := y_{I_1} \cdots y_{I_m} y'$ where $y' \in_R \mathsf{G}$ and a counter c. The membership manager performs **Delete** as follows :

1. Compute $U_M = U_M \cdot \frac{y''}{y_{I_j} y'}$ where $y'' \in_R \mathsf{G}$, i.e., $U_M = y_{I_1} \cdots y_{I_{j-1}} y_{I_{j+1}} \cdots y_{I_m} y''$.

2. Compute $U_N := (y'' / (y_{I_j} y'))^{d_N}$ and increase a counter c into c'.

3. Encrypt U_N with the group members's symmetric keys and publishes U_M, c' and $\mathcal{E}_{\mathcal{K}_i}(U_N)$, $1 \le i (i \ne j) \le m$.

Each valid group member $I_i (1 \le i \ (i \ne j) \le m)$ decrypts the encrypted messages with the shared symmetric key $\mathcal{K}_i (1 \le i \ (i \ne j) \le m)$. Then each group member I_i can change his secret property key U_{I_i} into $U'_{I_i} = U_{I_i} \cdot U_N$.

3.4 Sign

First, We define a group signature.

Definition 1. *Let ϵ, ℓ_1 and ℓ_2 be security parameters such that $\epsilon > 1$, $\ell_2 < \ell_1 < \ell_g$, and $\ell_2 < \frac{\ell_g - 2}{\epsilon} - k$ holds. A group-signature of a message $m \in \{0, 1\}^*$ is a tuple $(c, s_1, s_2, s_3, s_4, a, b, d, \alpha, \beta) \in \{0, 1\}^k \times \{-2^{\ell_2 + k}, \cdots, 2^{\epsilon(\ell_2 + k)}\} \times \{-2^{\ell_g + \ell_1 + k}, \cdots, 2^{\epsilon(\ell_g + \ell_1 + k)}\} \times \{-2^{\ell_g + k}, \cdots, 2^{\epsilon(\ell_g + k)}\} \times \{-2^{\ell_g + k}, \cdots, 2^{\epsilon(\ell_g + k)}\} \times$*

G^5 *satisfying* $c = H(g||h||y_R||z||a||b||d||\beta||z^c b^{s_1 - c2^{\ell_1}}/y_R^{s_2}||a^{s_1 - c2^{\ell_1}}/g^{s_2}||a^c g^{s_3}||$
$$d^c g^{s_1 - c2^{\ell_1}} h^{s_2}||\beta^c y_R^{s_3} h^{s_4 e_N}||m).$$

$\mathcal{R}emark$ 1. Such a group-signature would be denoted by
$$\mathcal{L} = SPK\{ \ (\theta, \lambda, \mu) \ : \ z = b^\theta/y_R^{\theta\lambda} \ \wedge \ 1 = a^\theta/g^{\theta\lambda} \ \wedge \ a = g^\lambda \ \wedge \ d = g^\theta h^{\theta\lambda}$$
$$\wedge \ \beta = y_R^\lambda h^{\mu e_N} \ \wedge \ \theta \in \Gamma') \ \}(m).$$
The non-interactive protocol corresponding to $\mathcal{L}$ is a statistical zero-knowledge proof of knowledge w_1, w_2 of the discrete logarithm of a, β and an integer x_I such that $x_I \in [2^{\ell_1} - 2^{\tilde{\ell}}, \cdots, 2^{\ell_1} + 2^{\tilde{\ell}}]$ and $y_I^{x_I} = z$.

To sign a message $m \in \{0,1\}^*$, *a group member does the followings* :

1. Choose an integer $w_1, w_2 \in_R \{0,1\}^{\ell_g}$ and compute $a := g^{w_1}$, $b := y_I y_R^{w_1}$, $d := g^{x_I} h^{x_I w_1}$, $\alpha := U_I g^{w_1} h^{w_2}$, and $\beta := y_R^{w_1} h^{w_2 e_N}$.
2. Choose $r_1 \in_R \{0,1\}^{\epsilon(\ell_2 + k)}$, $r_2 \in_R \{0,1\}^{\epsilon(\ell_g + \ell_1 + k)}$ and $r_3 \in_R \{0,1\}^{\epsilon(\ell_g + k)}$.
3. Compute $t_1 := b^{r_1}(1/y_R)^{r_2}$, $t_2 := a^{r_1}(1/g)^{r_2}$, $t_3 := g^{r_3}$, $t_4 := g^{r_1} h^{r_2}$, $t_5 := y_R^{r_3} h^{r_3 e_N}$ and compute $c := H(g||h||y_R||z||a||b||d||\beta||t_1||t_2||t_3||t_4||t_5||m)$.
4. $s_1 := r_1 - c(x_I - 2^{\ell_1})$ (in $\mathbf{Z}$), $s_2 := r_2 - cw_1 x_I$ (in $\mathbf{Z}$), $s_3 := r_3 - cw_1$ (in $\mathbf{Z}$) and $s_4 := r_3 - cw_2$ (in $\mathbf{Z}$).
The signature on the message m is $(c, s_1, s_2, s_3, s_4, a, b, d, \alpha, \beta)$.

3.5 Verifying Signatures, User-Tracing, and Sign-Tracing

Verifying Signature : Given a signature, it is verified that the signature satisfies the verification condition given in Definition 1. If it is satisfied, a verifier trusts that two random values w_1, w_2 have been chosen honestly and $\beta = y_R^{w_1} h^{w_2 e_N}$ has been formed by a signer with a valid membership key. Finally, the verifier checks if $U_M(\frac{a}{\alpha})^{e_N} \beta = b$ holds; this equality holds if and only if the signature was generated by a valid group member.

User-Tracing : To reveal the signer of a given signature $\sigma = (c, s_1, s_2, s_3, s_4, a, b, d, \alpha, \beta)$ of the message m, the revocation manager first checks its correctness and then computes $y_I' := b/a^{x_R}$. For the proof of unforgeability of user-tracing, he issues a signature $P := SPK\{ \ (\rho) : y_R = g^\rho \ \wedge \ b/y_I' = a^\rho \ \}(y_I'||\sigma||m)$ and reveals $arg := y_I'||P$. This SPK shows the equality of two discrete logarithms y_R and b/y_I', and it is a statistical zero-knowledge proof of knowledge of the discrete logarithm of $y_R (= g^{x_R})$. He looks up y_I' in the group-member list and finds the corresponding y_I.

Sign-Tracing : To find whether a signature $\sigma = (c, s_1, s_2, s_3, s_4, a, b, d, \alpha, \beta)$ was generated by a specific (illegal) member, the membership manager sends $(a, y_I^{d_N} \alpha, \beta)$ to the revocation manager where y_I is a specific member's public key. The revocation manager computes $(y_I^{d_N} \cdot \frac{\alpha}{a})^{e_N}/(\frac{\beta}{a^{x_R}})$ and checks if the result equals to U_M. If the signature was generated by the member, the revocation manager sends 1 to the membership manager. In case that the signature was not generated by the member, the revocation manager cannot acquire any information except that the member did not generate it.

3.6   Security Proof

In this section, we prove that our group signature scheme satisfies security requirements in Section 2. First, we prove the security of our scheme in point of view of *Unforgeability of signatures* in Theorem 1 and Corollary 1. Then in Theorem 2 we prove that our scheme guarantees all properties in Section 2.

In our scheme $\mathcal{P}$, the security against signature forgery attacks is related to a renewal property key U_N, since the group member must update his secret property key using a renewal property key in the event of membership change. Therefore the security of our group signature scheme is based on the security of a renewal property key. For the proof of the unforgeability, we first define security notions.

SECURITY NOTIONS. Let $\mathcal{A}$ be an adversary which tries to forge a valid signature against our group signature scheme $\mathcal{P}$. Let $Succ_{\mathcal{P},\mathcal{A}}^{gks\_cma}$ be a success probability of $\mathcal{A}$'s existential forgery under a chosen message attack against $\mathcal{P}$. Then, $\mathcal{P}$ is a CMA-secure group signature scheme if there exists a negligible function ε such that for sufficiently large k, $Succ_{\mathcal{P}}^{gks\_cma} = \max_{\mathcal{A}}\{Succ_{\mathcal{P},\mathcal{A}}^{gks\_cma}\} \leq \varepsilon(k)$.

For the security of a renewal key, we consider a renewal property key U_N as a session key in general group key distribution schemes [7]: In group key management schemes, a new session key is generated and is secretly shared between all the group members, whenever a membership changes. Therefore, we can prove the security of a renewal property key in the security model for group key management schemes. We briefly present a security model for a renewal property key based on [6] by Bresson *et al.* and [17] by Katz and Yung as follows.

We denote that $\Pi_{I_i}^j$ is an instance j of a group member I_i. An instance $\Pi_{I_i}^j$ has unique session identifier $sid_{I_i}^j$ and partner identifier $pid_{I_i}^j$. After the instance has been terminated successfully, $\Pi_{I_i}^j$ has a unique renewal property key identifier $R_{I_i}^j$ corresponding to a renewal property key U_N and $pid_{I_i}^j$ corresponds to a set of group members who obtain the same renewal property key U_N. We state the instances of the group members with the same renewal property key U_N are *partnered*. The followings queries are allowed to an adversary $\mathcal{A}$ against a renewal property key of our scheme $\mathcal{P}$.

- Send($\Pi_{I_i}^j$, M), Reveal($\Pi_{I_i}^j$), Corrupt(I_i) : These processes are similar to the queries described in [17].
- Setup(G_0), Join(J, G'), Delete(D, G') : Using these queries, $\mathcal{A}$ can start the *Setup*, *Join* or *Delete* algorithm.
- Test($\Pi_{I_i}^j$) : This query is used to define the advantage of an adversary. $\mathcal{A}$ executes this query on a *fresh* instance $\Pi_{I_i}^j$ at any time, but only once. When $\mathcal{A}$ asks this query, it receives a renewal property key U_N of the instance $\Pi_{I_i}^j$ if $b = 1$ or a random string if $b = 0$ where b is the result of a coin flip. Finally, $\mathcal{A}$ outputs a bit b'.

Based on this security model, we define the advantage of $\mathcal{A}$'s attacks against renewal property keys in our group signature scheme $\mathcal{P}$. When $\mathcal{A}$ asks a Test query to a fresh instance $\Pi_{I_i}^j$ in $\mathcal{P}$, $\mathcal{A}$ receives a coin-flip bit b and then outputs a bit b'. If the probability that $\mathcal{A}$ correctly guesses the bit b is negligible, $\mathcal{P}$ is secure in the sense that $\mathcal{A}$ cannot obtain any information about a renewal property key through the encryption messages transmitted by the membership manager's in *Join* or *Delete* algorithm.

Let $Adv_{\mathcal{A},\mathcal{P}}^{ren}$ denote the advantage for $\mathcal{A}$'s guess over the result of a coin-flip in a Test query with $\mathcal{P}$. Then we say that $\mathcal{P}$ is secure in a point of view of renewal property keys if there exists a negligible function ε such that for sufficiently large k,

$$Adv_{\mathcal{P},\mathcal{A}}^{ren} = Pr\,[b' = 1|b = 1] - Pr\,[b' = 1|b = 0] = 2Pr\,[b' = b] - 1,$$
$$Adv_{\mathcal{P}}^{ren} = \max_{\mathcal{A}}\{Adv_{\mathcal{P},\mathcal{A}}^{ren}\} \leq \varepsilon(k).$$

The security of a renewal property key of our scheme $\mathcal{P}$ is dependent on the probabilities $Succ_{\Sigma}^{cma}$ and $Succ_{G}^{cdh}$ as described in [7], since an adversary $\mathcal{A}$ against $\mathcal{P}$ can obtain information about a renewal property key only by two methods: $\mathcal{A}$ successfully performs either signature forgery attacks against the secure signature algorithm Σ or CDH attacks.

Theorem 1. *Let $\mathcal{A}$ be an active adversary against our scheme $\mathcal{P}$ in the random oracle model. Let q_s be the number of Send queries and q_H be the number of queries to the hash oracle H. Then,*

$$Adv_{\mathcal{P}}^{ren} \leq 2n \cdot Succ_{\Sigma}^{cma}(t, q_s) + 2q_H q_s \cdot Succ_{G}^{cdh}(t)$$

where n is the maximum number of group members and t is the adversary's running time.

Corollary 1. *Let $\mathcal{P}$ be our group signature scheme. Then, $\mathcal{P}$ satisfies that*
$$Succ_{\mathcal{P}}^{gks\text{-}cma} = Adv_{\mathcal{P}}^{ren}.$$

For space limited we omit the proofs. The proofs of *Theorem 1, Corollary 1* will appear in the full version. In Theorem 2, we only discuss unforgeability of signatures, sign-tracing verification and unlinkability of signatures. In Theorem 1, we have proved our scheme $\mathcal{P}$ satisfies other security properties.

Theorem 2. *Our scheme $\mathcal{P}$ guarantees unforgeability, anonymity, unlinkability, and no-framing properties.*

Proof. Since our scheme is based on the schemes [10] by Camenish *et al.*, several security properties of our scheme are satisfied as well as the schemes [10]. Hence detail proofs for some properties are omitted here.

i) **Anonymity and No-Framing**: theses properties are satisfied by our scheme $\mathcal{P}$ based on [10].

ii) **Unforgeability of Signatures** : Only the valid group members can generate valid signatures which will be able to be user-traced and sign-traced by the revocation manager. In our scheme, by the above Corollary 1 and Theorem 1, the adversary can obtain the information of a renewal property key by trying either a CDH attack or a signature forgery attack. Also a deleted member cannot easily generate an valid signature satisfying $U_M(\frac{a}{\alpha})^{e_N}\beta = b$ without the updated renewal property key.

iii) **Unforgeability of Sign-tracing Verification**: Given $(a, y_I^{d_N}\alpha, \beta)$, if the revocation manager returns 1 to the membership manager, the membership manager computes $\alpha^{e_N}b/(a^{e_N}U_M\beta)$. This value is 1 if and only if the revocation manager has executed the sign-tracing correctly.

iv) **Unlinkability of Signatures**: To link two signatures, we have to decide whether two signatures $(c, s_1, s_2, s_3, s_4, a, b, d, \alpha, \beta)$, $(c', s_1', s_2', s_3', s_4', a', b', d', \alpha', \beta')$ originate from the same group member. i.e., deciding require to decide whether $\log_g \frac{a}{\alpha} = \log_{y_R} \frac{b}{b'}$, where $c, s_1, s_2, s_3, s_4, d, \alpha, \beta$ and $c', s_1', s_2', s_3', s_4', d', \alpha', \beta'$ do not reveal useful knowledge. Under DDH assumption, this is infeasible. Hence signatures are unlinkable.

Form i, ii, iii and iv, Theorem 2 has been proved. $\square$

4 Efficiency

In the section, we compare the efficiency of our scheme with the efficiency of the scheme in [9]. A group signature scheme consists of the group manager and the group members. In practical circumstance, the computational environment of group signature schemes may be viewed as asymmetric, i.e., the group manager is a server with relatively higher computational ability and a group member is a client such as mobile elements with relatively lower computational ability. Hence whenever a member changes, the amount of group member's computation must be kept low. In case of applying dynamic accumulators to the Ateniese *et al.* scheme [1] that is based on the Camenisch *et al.* group signature scheme [10] as mentioned in [9], the group manager chooses and publishes the accumulator value. Then whenever a member joins or leaves the group, each group member has to update own membership by doing modular exponentiation.

In case of our method, whenever membership changes, each group member updates his secret property key only by decrypting the encrypted message with the shared symmetric key and doing one modular multiplication. Our scheme does not require any additional proof of knowledge. Though our scheme requires a more works of the manager, each group member does a simple operation. Therefore our scheme is more efficient than using dynamic accumulators from the viewpoint of group members. The following table shows the amount of computation of group member/manager in the case of a member join/delete event.

Table 1. Let $\mathcal{C} := \{I_1, I_2, \cdots, I_{m-1}\}$ be the set of current group members. When the group member G_m joins (leaves) the group, m $(m-1)$ is the number of members in the group. $\mathcal{C}_{Exp}$, $\mathcal{C}_{Mul}$, $\mathcal{C}_{\mathcal{E}}$ and $\mathcal{C}_{\mathcal{D}}$ are respectively the computational cost of one evaluation of the modular exponentiation, multiplication operation, one evaluation of the symmetric encryption algorithm $\mathcal{E}$, one evaluation of $\mathcal{E}$'s decryption algorithm $\mathcal{D}$.

		Computation: Join (delete)	
Scheme	Accumulator		Our scheme
Manager	$\mathcal{C}_{Exp}$ $(\mathcal{C}_{Exp})$		$\mathcal{C}_{Exp} + 3 \cdot \mathcal{C}_{Mul} + (m-1) \cdot \mathcal{C}_{\mathcal{E}}$ $(\mathcal{C}_{Exp} + 3 \cdot \mathcal{C}_{Mul} + (m-1) \cdot \mathcal{C}_{\mathcal{E}})$
Member	$\mathcal{C}_{Exp}$ $(2 \cdot \mathcal{C}_{Exp})$		$\mathcal{C}_{Mul} + \mathcal{C}_{\mathcal{D}}$ $(\mathcal{C}_{Mul} + \mathcal{C}_{\mathcal{D}})$

References

1. G. Ateniese, J. Camenisch, M. Joye and G. Tsudik. *A Practical and Provably Secure Coalition-Resistant Group Signature Scheme.* In Advances in Cryptology - CRYPTO 2000, vol.1880 of LNCS, pp.255-270, Springer-Verlag, 2000.
2. G. Atenies, D. Song and G. Tsudik. *Quasi-Efficient Revocation of Group Signatures.* In FC'02, LNCS 2357, pp.183-197, Springer-Verlag, 2002.
3. G. Ateniese and G. Tsudik. *Group Signatures a là carte.* In Tenth Annual ACM-SIAM Symposium on Discrete Algorithms (SODA'99), Baltimore, Maryland, 1999.
4. D. Boneh, X. Boyn and H. Shacham. *Short Group Signatures.* In Advances in Cryptology - CRYPTO 2004, LNCS 3152, pp. 41-55. Springer-Verlag, 2004.

5. E. Bresson and J. Stern. *Efficient Revocation in Group Signature.* In PKC2001, LNCS 1992, pp.190-206, Springer-Velag, 2001.
6. E. Bresson, O. Chevassut and D. Pointcheval. Provably Authenticated Group Diffie-Hellman Key Exchange. In *Proc. of the 8th ACM Conference on Computer and Communications Security*, pp.255-264, 2001.
7. E. Bresson, O. Chevassut, A. Fssiari and D. Pointcheval. Mutual Authentication and Group Key Agreement for Low-Power Mobile Devices. In *The Fifth IEEE International Conference on Mobile and Wireless Communications Networks*, 2003.
8. J. Camenisch. *Efficient and Generalized Group Signatures.* In Advances in Cryptology - EUROCRYPT'97, LNCS 1233, pp.465-479, Springer-Verlag, 1997.
9. J. Camenisch and A. Lysyanskaya. *Dynamic Accumulators and Application to Efficient Revocation of Anonymous Credentials.* In Advances in Cryptology - CRYPTO2002, LNCS 2442, pp.61-76, Springer-Verlag, 2002.
10. J. Camenisch and M. Michels. *A Group Signature Scheme Based on An RSA-variant.* Tech. Rep. RS-98-27, BRICS, Dept. of Comp. In Advances in Cryptology - ASIACRYPT'98, LNCS 1514, Springer-Verlag, 1998.
11. J. Camenisch and M. Michels. *Separability and Efficiency for Generic Group Signature Schemes.* In Advances in Cryptology - CRYPTO'99, LNCS 1666, pp.413-430, Springer-Verlag, 1999.
12. J. Camenisch and M. Stadler. *Efficient group signature schemes for large groups.* In Advances in Cryptology-CRYPTO'97, LNCS 1296, pp.410-424, Springer-Verlag, 1997.
13. D. Chaum and E. van Heyst, *Group Signatures.* In Advances in Cryptology - EUROCRYPT'91, LNCS 547, pp.257-265, Springer-Verlag, 1991.
14. L. Chen and T. P. Pedersen. *New Group Signature Schemes.* In Advances in Cryptology - EUROCRYPT'94, LNCS 950, pp.171-181. Springer-Verlag, 1995.
15. E. Fujisaki and T. Okamoto. *Statistical Zero Knowledge Protocols to Prove Modular Polynomial Relations.* In Advances in Cryptology - CRYPTO'97, LNCS 1294, pp.16-30, Springer-Verlag, 1997.
16. J. Furukawa and S. Yoezawa. *Group Signatures with Separate and Distributed Authorities.* In SCN 2004, LNCS 3352, pp.77-90, Springer-Verlag, 2004.
17. J. Katz and M. Yung. Scalable Protocols for Authenticated Group Key Exchange. In *Advances in Cryptology - Crypto'03* , LNCS 2729, Springer-Verlag, pp.110-125, 2003.
18. H.J. Kim, J.I. Lim and D.H. Lee. *Efficient and Secure Member Deletion in Group Signature Schemes.* In ICISC2000, LNCS 2015, pp.150-161, Springer-Verlag, 2001.
19. H. Petersen. *How to Convert Any Digital Signature Scheme into a Group Signature Scheme.* In Security Protocols Workshop, Paris, 1997.
20. D. Pointcheval and J. Sterm. Security Arguments for Digital Signatures and Blind Signatures. In *Journal of Cryptology*, 13(3) : 361-396, 2000.
21. G. Wang, F. Bao, J. Zhou, and R. H. Deng. *Security Remarks on a Group Signature Scheme with Member Deletion.* In ICICS2003, LNCS 2836, pp.72-83, Springer-Verlag, 2003.

Conditional Digital Signatures[*]

Marek Klonowski, Mirosław Kutyłowski, Anna Lauks, and Filip Zagórski

Institute of Mathematics and Computer Science,
Wrocław University of Technology
{Marek.Klonowski, Anna.Lauks, Filip.Zagorski}@im.pwr.wroc.pl
Miroslaw.Kutylowski@pwr.wroc.pl

Abstract. We consider *conditional digital signatures* (CDS for short). According to this scheme a creator of a CDS signature, say Alice, signs a message M_1 conditioned by a Bob's signature of M_2. The string created by Alice can be transformed into an Alice's digital signature of M_1, once we are given a signature of M_2 generated by Bob. Until the moment of creating a Bob's signature of M_2, Alice's signature of M_1 <u>does not exist</u> in a technical sense. This differs from the previous solutions where merely a condition about M_2 has been included into a message signed by Alice. The key feature of our scheme is that Alice prepares the CDS signature before Bob actually signs M_2.

We propose two CDS schemes – the first one prohibits checking that a signature of M_1 has been prepared by Alice until Bob signs M_2. In the second case, Alice can prove interactively that the string created hides a CDS signature of some form, but the proof is useless for a third party.

We present applications of CDS signatures in business and European legal frameworks. In particular, CDS schemes can be used to build a system in which a signature can be retrieved at a given *future* date. This feature requires only an institution signing periodically the current time. The scheme is also quite useful for wireless mobile networks, where unreliability of communication may cause many problems. CDS scheme may be used there for signing in advance even if a protocol requires a fixed sequential schedule.

1 Introduction

Digital signatures provide a reliable framework for authorization of digital documents. In certain situations digital signatures are more secure and provide more relevant practical features than handwritten signatures.

On the other hand, there are certain negative aspects of digital documents. One of them is that a party issuing a digital signature of digital data may loose control over the digital document created – it is easy to make copies and each copy is regarded to be original in the legal sense. In many situations this is an advantage, but it may happen that this is a severe disadvantage. A handwritten document after signing can be shown to parties involved and then placed in a safe deposit. In this way we can enforce some rules who can access the document and under which conditions. For classical digital signatures it is impossible - once they are presented, there are no technological

---

[*] Partially supported by KBN grant 3 T11C 011 26.

S. Katsikas, J. López, G. Pernul (Eds.): TrustBus 2005, LNCS 3592, pp. 206–215, 2005.

limitations to make a copy and distribute it. This might be a problem for instance in the case of business negotiations. The parties involved may sign protocols concerning already agreed terms as a kind of security guarantee. However, a dishonest party can show these protocols to another negotiation partner. The point is that one cannot deposit such a signed digital document in a safe.

In order to cope with this problem we investigate digital signatures such that their flow can be controlled in some way. Namely, we design signatures such that can be conditioned upon a certain event.

More precisely, we design signatures that *do not exist* after signing, but the codes created can be transformed easily into a digital signature once a particular event occurs. *Non-existence* is meant in the functional sense: European legal framework [1] demands that it is possible to perform a verification procedure, but the codes created prohibit such a verification.

Previous Results. The notion of conditional digital signatures appeared already in the literature. They reflect the possibility to include conditions and excluding clauses in legal documents. For instance, if Alice wishes to sign a contract M_1 which is valid if and only if some other document M_2 is valid (i.e. digitally signed), then she has to make a direct reference to the document M_2. So, the document M_1 will contain a statement like the following one: *"This document is valid only if M_2 has been signed by Bob."*. To avoid changes of M_2, we have to refer to the hash or the fingerprint of M_2, so our condition turns into: *"This document is valid only if document M_2, which hash value is equal to 27b4706ed908dbd6e3be3da5ad2ba85d, has been signed by Bob."*.

A variation of conditional signatures was introduced by Kim and Lee in [7]. The idea presented is straightforward and addressed for a specific, but important application - fair exchange of digital signatures. It allows secure trade (goods and money are treated as digital signatures). Later, Berta et al. [2] extended this protocol adapting it to the use on chip cards.

So far the solutions proposed provide only a basic framework. In no way they cope with the problem of uncontrolled dissemination of digital documents. They also change the contents of the signed messages, which also might be a disadvantage (a good example are messages related to stock exchange operations, where we wish to hide conditions for triggering some deal by a broker).

New Approach. In our approach, we do not require references to other documents in the message contents. We introduce *conditional digital signatures* and *conditional encryption scheme*, which have impact only on signature creation, not the message itself. The conditional encryption scheme has the following features:

- it is infeasible to recover the plaintext M, unless a specific message is signed by Bob,
- Bob need not to be aware whether M has been encrypted and what is the ciphertext in order to issue the signature mentioned.

The conditional signature scheme has the following features. Consider an Alice's signature of M_1 conditioned by Bob's signature of M_2. We have two subprocedures of the scheme:

1. issuing a pre-signature by Alice,
2. retrieving an Alice's signature from: the pre-signature and Bob's signature of M_2.

The scheme has the following features:

- signing M_1 by Alice requires an explicit decision that the signature is conditioned by Bob's signature of M_2, this decision is irrevocable – modifications in M_2 or changing the signer of M_2 prevent retrieval of Alice's signature,
- it is infeasible to recover the Alice's signature of M_1 from the pre-signature unless we are given a Bob's signature of M_2,
- one cannot prove (without involvement of Alice) that the code produced by Alice is a conditional signature of a given kind; depending on the scheme, Alice may prove it interactively, but the proof is useless for a party not involved in the interactive proof; consequently a protocol of interaction cannot be regarded as advanced digital Alice's signature of M_1 in the sense of European law systems [1],
- after Bob signs M_2 and Alice's signature of M_1 is retrieved, it is just a standard Alice's signature of M_1 with no reference to Bob and M_2.

The schemes we propose require that the first component of ElGamal signature of M_2 is published in advance. We call it a *commitment*.

2   Example Applications

Some applications of conditional signature are quite obvious (for instance they may be used to simplify protocols from [7,2]). In this section we discuss a few specific scenarios, in which using conditional digital signatures are helpful. However, the scheme presented is quite general, so they are just examples not excluding further applications.

Fair Stock Exchange. Consider a stock exchange and a person wishing to send an order depending on a future event to a broker. For example, he orders to sell shares of company ABC for at least 40 EUR when shares of DEF fall under 23 EUR. Nowadays it is impossible to keep such an order in secrecy from the broker. A dishonest broker can use knowledge on such orders for his own purpose (even if it is prohibited by law, there are thousands of ways to use such an information so that a dishonest broker cannot be accused).

Our solution to the problem mentioned is that the stock exchange publishes signatures about different share prices. The commitments for these signatures must be published in advance – one commitment for each price. If a given price level was achieved then the stock exchange signs a message " *the price of ABC is over x EUR*" and, at the same time, creates a new commitment under the message "*the price of ABC is under x EUR*".

Now, with use of conditional ciphertexts, every player can place his orders without revealing them in advance. In order to buy/sell a share of ABC if the price of DEF falls under x, he sends the ciphertexts of the order conditioned upon signature of the messages "*the price of DEF is under x EUR*".

Secure Credit Cards and Online Transactions. One of the major risks concerning the use of credit cards are frauds and use of stolen cards. Using smart cards and digital signatures improves security only if PIN-based access is not compromised (monitoring users at ATM with hidden cameras and stealing cards becomes a growing problem). It becomes even worse, since digital signatures are hard to be denied, for instance according to Polish Digital Signature Act from 2001.

Conditional digital signatures may be used for consumer protection, in particular in the case of online services. (This is a paradox, but in some legal systems in some situations there is less consumer protection if the transactions is processed online). However a payment order can be signed conditionally at time T, and the signature can be retrieved only when the financial institution issuing the card signs a message: *at time T the card number 132...27 has not been blocked*. This scenario protects the user while the seller may demand a proof that the per-signature hides a particular signature.

Time Authority. In real life we very often encounter situation when we need to reveal a particular signature at a chosen moment in the future. The reason might be business motivated or a purely technical one. To address all that issues, a Time Authority could be established that confirms periodically (e.g. every hour) the current time. More precisely, on day X immediately after hour Y it signs a message

today is X, the current time has passed Y

Time Authority keeps signing and publishing such messages for years. These time declarations can be used in the following way. Once we wish that a signature on M_1 will be revealed on day X, at time Y we construct a signature of M_1 conditioned by a signature of Time Authority of M_2 which has the form *"today is X, the current time has passed Y"*.

The presented solution is extremely simple and can be easily adapted into a PKI infrastructure or a basic public e-service. The only problem is to publish timely the signatures. As we shall see in the later sections we need also a kind of commitments to be published in advance. However, they can be generated and published in advance for a couple of years.

Let us remark that in the same way we may build a system in which a ciphertext can be opened at a chosen time. We use ciphertext which are conditioned by the signatures of Time Authority.

Protocols for Ad Hoc Systems. Due to channel faults and a limited bandwidth, in wireless mobile systems the communication between stations should be based on as simple protocols as possible. Conditional encryption and signatures offer here flexibility that can be used for simplifying interaction between stations. Let us consider the following example. Let P be a provider of some data x, U be a user and B be a billing system. A straightforward way to fetch and pay for x is the following:

(1) U requests x from P,
(2) P responds with x encrypted with a random key k, together with a ciphertext of k encrypted with the public key of B,
(3) U sends the ciphertext of k and charging request to B,

(4) B updates the billing information, deciphers k and sends it (again encrypted) to U,

(5) U retrieves k and decodes the ciphertext of x.

One can simplify step 3 and reduce transmission volume, if the following steps are executed:

(2') P responds with a ciphertext of x conditioned by the signature of the billing system stating that U is entitled to decrypt x,

(3') U sends **only** a charging request to B,

(4') B updates the billing information and sends a signature (encrypted) that U is entitled for x,

(5') U decrypts the ciphertext of x.

3   ElGamal Based Conditional Signatures

From now on we will work in cyclic group $\mathbb{Z}_p^*$ (in fact we can work in any cyclic group with hard discrete logarithm problem). In order to abbreviate notation we skip " mod p" where it is obvious from the context.

3.1   Conditional Signature Based on ElGamal Scheme

ElGamal Encryption Scheme. This algorithm was introduced in [5] and is based on difficulty of finding discrete logarithm. It works as follows:

Preliminaries: A group $\mathbb{Z}_p^*$ is chosen for prime number p. Then an generator g this group is chosen. Parameters p and g are published.

Key Setup: We chose $0 < x < p - 1$ as a private key, the corresponding public key is y such that $y = g^x$ is published.

Encryption: To encrypt message m a number $0 < k < p - 1$, is chosen uniformly at random over all elements of $\mathbb{Z}_p^*$. Then we put $\alpha := g^k$ and $\beta = m \cdot y^k$. The pair (α, β) is a ciphertext of m.

Decryption: Using private key x it is possible to compute m using the equality

$$\frac{\beta}{\alpha^x} = \frac{m \cdot y^k}{g^{kx}} = m \ .$$

ElGamal Signing Scheme.

Preliminaries and Key Setup: As before, let g be a generator of $\mathbb{Z}_p^*$. Private key $0 < x < p - 1$ is chosen at random and $y = g^x$ is published as the corresponding public key.

Signing: To sign message M Alice chooses random k which is co-prime with $p - 1$. Then she computes $a := g^k \bmod p$ and $t := k^{-1} \bmod p - 1$. Then she computes $b := t \cdot (H(M) - x \cdot a) \bmod p - 1$, where H is a secure hash function. The pair (a, b) is a signature of M.

Verification: The signature is considered valid if and only if $y^a \cdot a^b = g^{H(M)}$.

Creation of a CDS Signature. Consider Alice and Bob who use the same group $\mathbb{Z}_p^*$ with generator g. Let x_1 and x_2 be the private keys of Alice and Bob, respectively, and $y_1 = g^{x_1}$ and $y_2 = g^{x_2}$ be the corresponding public keys. Assume that Alice wants to generate a signature of document M_1 conditioned by a Bob's signature of M_2. Let Z denote the pre-signature that has to be computed by Alice.

The main feature of the pre-signature Z is that it can be easily transformed into an ElGamal signature (a_1, b_1) of M_1 when the Bob's signature (a_2, b_2) of M_2 is given. By the definition, the signature (a_1, b_1) has to satisfy the equality $y_1^{a_1} a_1^{b_1} = g^{H(M_1)}$ or equivalently $a_1^{b_1} = g^{H(M_1)} y_1^{-a_1}$ for a hash function H.

Creating a Commitment. We require that $a_2 = g^{k_2}$, for some random number k_2 co-prime with $p - 1$ is published in advance, before Bob decides to sign M_2, and before Alice creates a pre-signature. Then Bob computes and publishes $S = g^{H(M_2)} y_2^{-a_2}$. The pair (a_2, S) we called a commitment of Bob. Note that S does not depend on M_1. Also $S = a_2^{b_2}$, if (a_2, b_2) is an ElGamal signature of M_2.

Creation of a Pre-signature. Alice creates a tuple $(a_1, b_1 S^z, a_2^z)$ for a number z chosen uniformly at random. This is a pre-signature Z of M_1 conditioned by Bob's signature of M_2.

Signature Retrieval. As soon as (a_2, b_2) becomes published, we can use b_2. Notice that

$$\frac{b_1 S^z}{(a_2^z)^{b_2}} = \frac{b_1 S^z}{(a_2^{b_2})^z} = \frac{b_1 S^z}{S^z} = b_1$$

So, everybody can compute b_1. Obviously, z must be unpredictable. Otherwise anybody would remove the factor S^z from $b_1 S^z$ without Bob's signature of M_2.

Security of the Signature Scheme. The first important observation is that $a_2 = g^{k_2}$ for a generator g and a random value k_2 co-prime with $p - 1$ is also a generator of the group $\mathbb{Z}_p^*$. Thus b_1, the second element of signature of M_1, is in fact encrypted by the regular ElGamal scheme: $(b_1 S^z, a_2^z)$ is a ciphertext of b_1 for the public key $S = a_2^{b_2}$, private key b_2 and a generator a_2. So, retrieving b_1 would require breaking an ElGamal ciphertext. The second point is that revealing a_1 in advance does not help an attack on ElGamal encryption scheme. Indeed, any adversary that tries to present a valid signature has to show a pair (a, b) such that $y^a a^b = g^{H(M)}$. Since parameter a can be any value, establishing it in advance gives no information about b.

3.2   Conditional Encryption Scheme

Almost the same scheme can be used for conditional encryption. In order to encrypt x_0 Alice computes $(x_0 \cdot S^z, a_2^z)$ for a random z. Exactly as in the case of conditional signatures, one can retrieve x_0 once b_2 is published.

4   Conditional Signatures Based on Undeniable Signatures

We consider the following problem. Assume that Alice produces a pre-signature z for message M_1 and Bob's commitment c for M_2. Now, the following question arises: how a third party, say Eve, can check that z can be transformed into Alice's signature of M_1, when Bob signs M_2 according to commitment c?

A solution in which Eve could check herself validity of z would convert z into a kind of electronic signature scheme (from the point of view of legal requirements), since there would be an off-line verification process. In such a case a CDS construction would be pointless. Therefore we turn to a protocol in which Eve works in interaction with Alice and such that a transcript of a verification session does not provide a proof for a third party.

Setup. Let p, q be primes, such that $p = 2q + 1$. Let G be a subgroup of $\mathbb{Z}_p^*$ of order q. We assume that discrete logarithm problem is hard for G. Let g be a generator of G, which is used by Alice, Bob and Eve - the verifier of the pre-signature. Bob has a private key x_2 and the corresponding public key $y_2 = g^{x_2}$.

Creating a Commitment. Before creating the undeniable conditional signature by Alice, Bob chooses uniformly at random k_2. Then he computes commitment $a_2 := g^{k_2}$ and publishes it.

Creating of a Pre-signature of M_1. Let d be the private key of Alice, the corresponding public key is $e = g^d$. First, Alice chooses k uniformly at random. Then she computes

- $S := g^{H(M_2)} \cdot y_2^{-a_2}$,
- $u := S^k$,
- $v := a_2^k$,
- $U := M_1^d \cdot S^{dk}$,
- $V := a_2^{dk}$.

Then (u, v, U, V) is a pre-signature of M_1.

Interactive Signature Checking. In cooperation with Alice, Eve can verify a pre-signature of message M_1. In fact, this is a standard protocol borrowed from undeniable signatures:

- Eve chooses $i, j \in \{1, \ldots, q-1\}$ uniformly at random, computes
  $z := U^i \cdot (e \cdot V)^j \ (= M_1^{di} \cdot S^{dki} \cdot e^j \cdot a_2^{dkj})$ and presents z to Alice.
- Alice computes $w := (z)^{d^{-1} \bmod q}$ (which should be $M_1^i \cdot S^{ki} \cdot g^j \cdot a_2^{kj}$) and presents w to Eve.
- Eve computes: $w' := (M_1 \cdot u)^i \cdot (g \cdot a_2)^j$ and accepts the pre-signature, if $w = w'$.

If the pre-signature created by Alice is correct, then:

$$w = (z)^{d^{-1}} = \left(M_1^i \cdot S^{ki} \cdot g^j \cdot a_2^{kj} \right) = \left(M_1 \cdot S^k \right)^i \cdot \left(g \cdot a_2^k \right)^j = w'.$$

If $w \neq w'$ then:

- Eve chooses $\widehat{i}, \widehat{j} \in \{1, \ldots, q-1\}$ uniformly at random, computes
  $\widehat{z} := U^{\widehat{i}} \cdot (e \cdot V)^{\widehat{j}} = M_1^{d\widehat{i}} \cdot S^{dk\widehat{i}} \cdot e^{\widehat{j}} \cdot a_2^{dk\widehat{j}}$ and presents $\widehat{z}$ to Alice.

- Alice computes $\widehat{w} := (\widehat{z})^{d^{-1} \bmod q}$ which should be equal to $M_1^{\widehat{i}} \cdot S^{k\widehat{i}} \cdot g^{\widehat{j}} \cdot a_2^{k\widehat{j}} = \left(M_1 \cdot S^k\right)^{\widehat{i}} \cdot \left(g \cdot a_2^k\right)^{\widehat{j}}$ and presents $\widehat{w}$ to Eve.
- Eve computes: $\widehat{w'} = \left(M_1 \cdot S^k\right)^{\widehat{i}} \cdot \left(g \cdot a_2^k\right)^{\widehat{j}}$. If $\widehat{w} = \widehat{w'}$, she accepts the pre-signature.

If $\widehat{w'} \neq \widehat{w}$, then:

- Eve computes:

$$c := \left(w \cdot (g \cdot v)^{-j}\right)^{\widehat{i}} \text{ which should be equal to } \left(M_1 \cdot S^k\right)^{\widehat{i}\widehat{i}} \text{ and } \widehat{c} = \left(\widehat{w} \cdot (g \cdot v)^{-\widehat{j}}\right)^i$$
$$(= \left(M_1 \cdot S^k\right)^{\widehat{i}\widehat{i}}).$$

- If $c = \widehat{c}$, then she considers this pre-signature invalid. If $c \neq \widehat{c}$, then Eve knows that the pre-signature is valid, but Alice is cheating (trying to deny it).

Signature Transformation. After publishing (a_2, b_2) by Bob, we can use the component b_2 which satisfies the equality $b_2 k_2 = H(M_2) - a_2 x_2 \bmod p - 1$ according to the ElGamal scheme. So

$$\frac{U}{V^{b_2}} = \frac{M_1^d S^{dk}}{(a_2^{dk})^{b_2}} = \frac{M_1^d S^{dk}}{(a_2^{b_2})^{dk}} = \frac{M_1^d S^{dk}}{S^{dk}} = M_1^d \bmod p \,.$$

Everybody can compute M_1^d, which is the Alice's undeniable signature of message M_1. But there is still one problem: the undeniable signature, because of an interactive verification, is not a standard advanced electronic signature in the legal sense as implemented in European countries according to [1]. Nevertheless, adding few parameters to Alice's signing process and using non-interactive zero-knowledge protocol for showing the equality of discrete logarithms one can convert it to a standard (in the legal sense) advanced electronic signature.

Transformation into a Signature with Off-line Verification. To allow an off-line verification of undeniable signature of message M_1, Alice has to choose r uniformly at random. Afterwards she computes and publishes (together with the pre-signature of M_1) the following values:

- $w_1 := g^r$,
- $w_2 := M_1^r$,
- $a := H(w_1, w_2)$,
- $b := a \cdot d + r \bmod q$.

It should be stressed that these parameters do not reveal any information about d and on M_1.

Off-line Verification of M_1^d The parameters w_1, w_2, a, b together with e and M_1^d must convince the verifier that Alice has a secret value d such that $\log_g e = \log_{M_1}(M_1^d) = d$. In order to do that the verifier has to check only, if:

$$w_1 \cdot e^a = g^b \qquad \text{and} \qquad w_2 \cdot \left(M_1^d\right)^a = M_1^b$$

and of course that $a = H(w_1, w_2)$.

5   Additional Schemes

In this section we present a few extensions and modifications of the schemes presented in the previous section.

5.1   Multiple Conditions

We may change the conditional signature scheme so that multiple messages must be signed before we may derive a signature from a pre-signature. In this way we may condition emerging of a signature by signing different documents by different parties. For instance, if there are two Time Authorities we may demand that both of them sign that time t has passed, before a signature is revealed.

ElGamal based scheme can be modified slightly in order to implement a version with multiple conditions. Instead of defining a pre-signature as $(a_1, b_1 S^z, a_2^z)$ for $S = g^{M_2} y_2^{-a_2}$ we construct a pre-signature of the form

$$\left(a_1, b_1 \prod_{i+2}^{k} S_i^{z_i}, a_2^{z_2}, \ldots, a_k^{z_k}\right)$$

where $S_i = g^{M_i} y_i^{-a_i}$, y_i is the public key of the party that is supposed to sign M_i, a_i is a commitment of this party, that is, the first component of a signature (a_i, b_i) of M_i.

In order to retrieve b_1 one has to compute each $S_i^{z_i}$. This is possible once we have the numbers $b_2, \ldots, b_k$, since $S_i^{z_i} = a_i^{b_i}$.

5.2   k Out of n Conditions

In the next simple extension a signature part b_1 can be retrieved once k out of n messages $M_2 \ldots M_{n+1}$ get signed by respective parties. The scheme is based on secret Shamir's sharing scheme. Let x_0 be the secret value that has to be recovered after signatures are presented.

Creation of the Conditional Ciphertext. Let p be prime such that $p > x_0$ and $p > n$. Alice chooses uniformly at random coefficients: $w_1, \ldots, w_{k-1} < p$ and computes a polynomial $w(x)$ of degree $k - 1$:

$$w(x) = x_0 + \sum_{i=1}^{k-1} w_i \cdot x^i.$$

Then she computes $\xi_i = w(i) \bmod p$, for $i = 1, \ldots, n$. For each ξ_i Alice creates v_i which is a ciphertext of ξ_i conditioned by signature of message M_{i+1}.

Secret Recovery. Secret x_0 could be decrypted only if any k out of n messages M_2, $\ldots, M_{n+1}$ are signed. In this situation one can recover k shares of $\xi_1, \ldots, \xi_n$ and consequently the polynomial w and x_0.

6   Conclusion and Open Problems

We have presented a new cryptographic primitive that enables to get more control over the documents signed digitally. Construction of conditional signatures is quite straightforward and finally we obtain quite standard signatures.

The main practical problem of the schemes proposed is that the person signing the conditioning document has to prepare and publish some additional parameters long before signing it. The most important issue in our opinion is to construct a scheme that does not need any additional parameters during preparation of pre-signatures related to signature creation for conditioning message. Such a solution would introduce full independence between conditioned and conditioning messages. Such a construction would open perspectives for a number of new applications. However, it is not clear that such a construction is possible.

While combining the idea of conditional messages with other schemes based on discrete logarithm problem seems to be feasible, at the moment we are not aware of any scheme based on RSA.

Acknowledgment. We would like to thank Dariusz Adamski from CBKE, University of Wrocław, for discussions and some inspiration.

References

1. Directive 1999/93/EC of the European Parliament and of the Council of 13 December 1999 on a Community framework for electronic signatures. Official Journal of the European Communities L13/12-19 19. 1. 2000
2. Berta, I., Z., Buttyn, L., Vajda, I.: Migrating the Untrusted Terminal Problem Using Conditional Signatures. International Conference on Information Technology: Coding and Computing (ITCC), IEEE, 12-16, 2004.
3. Chaum, D., van Antwerpen, H.: Undeniable Signatures. CRYPTO'89, LNCS 435, Springer-Verlag, 212-216, 1990.
4. Chaum, D., Pedersen, T., P.: Wallet Databases with Observers. CRYPTO'92, LNCS 740, Springer-Verlag, 89-105, 1993.
5. ElGamal, T.: A Public Key Cryptosystem and a Signature Scheme Based on Discrete Logarithms. IEEE Transactions on Information Theory 31(4), 469-472, 1985.
6. Feige, U., Lapidot, D., Shamir, A.: Multiple Noninteractive Zero Knowledge Proofs Under General Assumptions. SIAM Journal on Computing 29(1), 1-28, 1999.
7. Lee, B., Kim, K.: Fair Exchange of Digital Signatures using Conditional Signature. Symposium on Cryptography and Information Security'2002 (SCIS), vol. 1/2, Shirahama, Japan, 179-184, 2002.
8. De Santis, A., Persiano, G.: Zero-Knowledge Proofs of Knowledge Without Interaction. 33 ACM-SIAM FOCS, 427-436, 1992.
9. Schnorr, C., P.: Efficient Signature Generation for Smart Cards. CRYPTO'89, LNCS 435, Springer-Verlag, 239-252, 1990.
10. Shamir, A.: How to Share a Secret. Communications of the ACM 22(11), 612-613, 1979.

A Mediated Proxy Signature Scheme with Fast Revocation for Electronic Transactions

Seung-Hyun Seo[1], Kyung-Ah Shim[2], and Sang-Ho Lee[1]

[1]Department of Computer Science and Engineering, Ewha Womans University
seosh@ewhain.net, shlee@ewha.ac.kr
[2]Department of Mathematics, Ewha Womans University,
11-1 Daehyun-dong, Seodaemun-ku, Seoul 120-750, Korea
kashim@ewha.ac.kr

Abstract. Proxy signature schemes allow an original signer to delegate his signing rights to a proxy signer. Most proxy signature schemes have succeeded for proxy delegations and they are considered very useful methods when one needs to delegate his signing power to other person in digital business. However, many proxy signature schemes have the defects that cannot solve proxy revocation problems. Moreover, they cannot provide the immediate revocation, even if a proxy signer colludes with any malicious attacker. In this paper, we propose a mediated proxy signature scheme with fast revocation. Our scheme solves the weaknesses of most proxy signature schemes and satisfies the security requirements for proxy signature scheme. And it also provides an effective proxy revocation whenever the original signer wants or signer's key is compromised.

1   Introduction

The growing popularity of the Internet is driving various applications for carrying out on-line transactions and message transmission. Digital signature schemes are used to provide security services such as user authentication, data integrity and non-repudiations for electronic transactions and data transmission in the Internet. Sometimes, however, a user must sign messages during a certain period of time in which he cannot do it. For example, this user may be in holidays or go on a business trip to someplace which has no computer network access. During the trip he will receive e-mail, and expect to respond to some messages quickly, and he will have to sign the important contract. Therefore, the user needs a proxy signer to sign messages on behalf of him.

The concept of a proxy signature scheme was first introduced by Mambo, Usuda, and Okamoto in 1996[8], and a number of proxy signature schemes have been proposed. The proxy signature scheme allows a designated person, called a proxy signer, to sign on behalf of an original signer. This proxy signature scheme can be used in delegation of the power to sign messages in digital business. So far, there has been four types of delegation: *full delegation*, *partial delegation*, *delegation by warrant*, and *partial delegation with warrant*[4,5,8]. In *full delegation*, the original signer gives his private key to the proxy signer. So, it has

S. Katsikas, J. López, G. Pernul (Eds.): TrustBus 2005, LNCS 3592, pp. 216–225, 2005.

the main weakness that the proxy signature cannot be distinguishable from the original signer's signature. In *partial delegation*, the original signer generates a delegation key through a trap-door permutation of his private key and gives it to the proxy signer. The proxy signer generates a proxy signature key from the proxy signer's private key and the delegation key. However, the proxy signer can abuse his delegated rights, because partial delegation does not restrict the proxy signer's signing capability. In *delegation by warrant*, the original signer uses the ordinary signature schemes without any modification and his secret key to create a warrant, which contains information regarding the particular proxy signer. The *partial delegation* does not have such a property, but it has a computational advantage over the *delegation by warrant*. The *partial delegation with warrant* combines the benefit of the *partial delegation* and the *delegation by warrant*. So this approach has fast processing speed and can eliminate the weaknesses of *full delegation* and *partial delegation* by adding an explicit warrant[4]. Most work on proxy signature schemes has focused on the type of the *partial delegation with warrant*.

The revocation of delegated rights is an essential issue of the proxy signature schemes. For instance, the employee of a company assigns his secretary to sign the contract on behalf of him. The secretary, however, may change her position in the company or leave the company. Therefore, the proxy revocation, i.e, the revocation of delegated rights is needed and it is important for the situation where proxy signer or signer's key is compromised and the delegated rights are abused. It may also happen that the original signer wants to terminate the delegated rights before the expiration of the delegation period[2,7].

However, most existing proxy signature schemes including *partial delegation with warrant* have following two weaknesses. First, the declaration of a valid delegation period in the warrant is useless because the proxy signer can still create a proxy signature and claim that his signing was done during the delegation period even if the delegation period has expired. So, a malicious proxy signer can send the proxy signature to an attacker who colludes with him. Any verifier cannot be certain of the exact time when the proxy signature was created. Second, even if the signer's key is compromised and the delegated rights are abused, or the original signer wants to revoke the delegation earlier than his plan, the original signer cannot do anything[2,7,10,11]. So, most existing proxy signature schemes cannot provide the proxy revocation, properly.

Although Sun proposed a time-stamped proxy signature scheme and claimed that the revocation problem can be solved by using a time-stamp, these schemes suffer from some security weaknesses and they cannot solve the second problem [10]. We briefly describe these weaknesses in section 3. Recently, Lu et al. and Das et al. proposed the proxy signature schemes with revocation to solve these problems[2,7]. These schemes are based on discrete logarithm problem and RSA cryptosystem, respectively. But, their schemes has many computation and it is very inefficient.

1.1   Our Contribution

In this paper, we propose a new proxy signature scheme with fast revocation, called a mediated proxy signature scheme, to solve the above weaknesses. To construct the mediated proxy signature scheme, we use a special entity, called a SEM (SEcurity Mediator), an on-line partially trusted server[1]. In the mediated proxy signature scheme, the original signer splits a delegation key, called proxy, into two parts and gives each part of proxy to the proxy signer and the SEM, respectively. To generate a proxy signature on a message, the proxy signer must first obtain a partial proxy token from the SEM. Without this token, the proxy signer cannot use his delegation key and cannot create the proxy signature. So, if the original signer immediately wants to revoke the delegation then he only instructs the SEM to stop issuing the token for the proxy signer. Therefore, our mediated proxy signature scheme can perform the immediate revocation and solve the limitations of the *partial delegation with warrant* schemes, efficiently.

The rest of this paper is organized as follows. In section 2, we describe the security requirements for the proxy signature scheme and some notations. In section 3, we describe the related works. In section 4, we propose a mediated proxy signature scheme with fast revocation. In section 5, we analyze the security and efficiency of our scheme. Finally, we draw our conclusions.

2   Preliminaries

In this section, we define the notations which are used through this paper and give the security requirements of proxy signature schemes.

2.1   Notations

- A : the original signer
- B : the proxy signer
- SEM : a security mediator, the on-line partially trusted server
- p, q : large primes with $q|p - 1$
- g : a generator of a multiplicative subgroup of $Z_p{}^*$
- $h(\cdot)$: a collision resistant one-way hash function mapping $h : \{0,1\}^* \rightarrow Z_q$
- x_A, x_B, x_S : the private key of the original signer, the proxy signer, and SEM, respectively $x_A, x_B, x_S \in_R Z_q$
- y_A, y_B, y_S : the public key of the original signer, the proxy signer, and SEM, respectively $y_A = g^{x_A} \bmod p$, $y_B = g^{x_B} \bmod p$, $y_S = g^{x_S} \bmod p$

2.2   Security Requirements

The proxy signature schemes should satisfy the following security requirements [5,8].

1. **Verifiability**: From a proxy signature, a verifier can be convinced of the original signer's agreement on the signed message.
2. **Strong unforgeability**: The original signer and third parties, who are not designated as proxy signers, cannot create a valid proxy signature. Only the proxy signer can create a valid proxy signature for the original signer.
3. **Strong identifiability**: Anyone can determine the identity of the corresponding proxy signer from a proxy signature .
4. **Strong undeniability**: Once a proxy signer creates a valid proxy signature for an original signer, the proxy signer cannot repudiate the signature creation against anyone. This is also called "non-repudiation".
5. **Prevention of misuse**: A proxy signing key cannot be used for purposes other than generating valid proxy signatures. In case of misuse, the responsibility of the proxy signer should be determined explicitly.

3   Related Works

In 1999, Sun and Chen proposed the concept of time-stamped proxy signatures [11]. The time-stamped proxy signature scheme with traceable receivers is a proxy signature scheme which can ascertain whether a proxy signature is created during the delegation period, and can trace who actually received the proxy signatures from the proxy signer. Anyone, including the original signer and the proxy signer, cannot create a valid time-stamped by oneself. The proxy signer must cooperate with the receiver to create a valid proxy signature during a predetermined delegation period. The verifier, including the original signer, can trace the receiver who actually received the proxy signature, check if the signing time was during the delegation period, and verify the validity of the proxy signature. So, the time-stamped proxy signature scheme solves the first problem of the *delegation with warrant* that anyone cannot know the exact time when the proxy signer signed a message from the warrant. However, It cannot solve the problem of immediate revocation. So, the original signer cannot immediately revoke the delegation, even if the delegated person colludes with a malicious intruder. Sun-Chen scheme has the properties of the time-stamped proxy signature, and in their scheme, the original signer can confirm the identity of receiver, who received the proxy signature from the proxy signer, to avoid the proxy signer abusing the signing power. However, Sun-Chen scheme suffers from some security weaknesses as follows: (1) Given a valid time-stamped proxy signature on a message, the original signer can forge another valid time-stamped proxy signature on the same message. (2) After signing a time-stamped proxy signature, the proxy signer can generate another valid time-stamped proxy signature on the same message without the cooperation of the receiver. (3) After obtaining a time-stamped proxy signature on a message, the receiver can forge another valid proxy signature on a same message. (4) Anyone can create a valid time-stamped proxy signature on an arbitrary message. So, malicious attacker can easy forge the proxy signature[10].

In 2000, Sun showed the weaknesses of Sun-Chen scheme. And then, Sun improved it, and proposed new time-stamped proxy signature scheme[10]. Even if

Sun claimed that his scheme provides the above properties of the time-stamped proxy signature and prevents the weaknesses of Sun-Chen scheme, Lu and Hung showed that Sun's scheme still contains weaknesses in time-stamps and suffers from malicious proxy signer attacks[6].

Recently, Lu et al. proposed a proxy signature scheme with revocation[7]. They used a trusted third party called the authentication server (AS) to provide the immediate revocation. In Lu-Hung scheme, the proxy signer must get a time-stamp from the AS to generates the proxy signature on messages. So, in case that the original signer wants to revoke the delegation before the specified delegation date, or the delegation period has expired, the authentication server does not issue the time-stamp. Therefore, Lu-Hung scheme can solve the problems of the *partial delegation with warrant*. However, the AS has to generate the signature on the time-stamp and the proxy signer verifies the AS's signature, whenever the proxy signer requests the time-stamp. Moreover, after receiving the proxy signature and time-stamp from the proxy signer, the verifier must check the AS's signature on the time-stamp, the proxy signer's signature on the message, and the original signer's signature on the warrant. So, Lu-Hung scheme is very inefficient, because the proxy signer and verifier must calculate many computation.

In 2004, Das et al. proposed a proxy signature scheme based on RSA cryptosystem with revocation[2]. They also used the AS to provide the revocation like Lu-Hung scheme. The only difference between them is that Lu-Hung scheme is based on discrete logarithm problem, on the other hand, Das et al.'s scheme is based on RSA cryptosystem. The proxy signer gets a time-stamp from the AS whenever he generates the proxy signature. So, the verifier can be assured of the exact time when a proxy signature was created, but a large computational amount of the proxy signer and verifier's computation are needed.

4   The Mediated Proxy Signature Scheme

In this section, we propose a mediated proxy signature scheme with fast revocation. Our mediated proxy signature scheme is based on the discrete logarithm problem. In our scheme, there are a verifier and three main participants: an original signer, a proxy signer, and a SEM(SEcurity Mediator)[1]. Anyone can be a verifier of the proxy signature. The SEM is a on-line partially trusted server which has responsibilities for verifying a proxy warrant and issuing a partial proxy token. Through the verification phase of the proxy warrant, the SEM confirms whether the period of delegation is valid and the identity of proxy signer exists on the revocation list or not. And then, the SEM issues the partial proxy token only if above conditions are satisfied. Without this token, the proxy signer cannot generate a proxy signature on the message. So, he cannot claim that his signing was done during the delegation period even if the delegation period has expired. Moreover, our mediated proxy signature scheme can perform the immediate revocation, unlike the time-stamped proxy signature schemes, i.e, if the original signer wants to revoke the delegation before an expiration date, he only instructs the SEM to stop issuing the token for the proxy signer. Therefore, we can solve two weaknesses of *partial delegation with warrant* schemes. Our mediated proxy signature scheme is constructed as follows:

[Proxy Key Generation Phase]

1. (Proxy generation) The original signer A generates random numbers k_B, $k_S \in_R Z_q$, and computes $k_A = k_B + k_S$, $r_A = g^{k_A}$ (mod p). He concatenates m_W and r_A, and hashes the result: $h(m_W \| r_A)$, where the warrant message, m_W, should be composed of original signer's ID, proxy signer's ID, the SEM's ID, a delegation period, and other information on the delegation. After that, he computes partial delegation keys, i.e, partial proxies, $\sigma_B = k_B + x_A h(m_W \| r_A)$ (mod q) and $\sigma_S = k_S + x_A h(m_W \| r_A)$ (mod q).
2. (Proxy delivery) The original signer A sends (m_W, r_A, σ_B) to the proxy signer B and sends (m_W, r_A, σ_S) to the SEM.
3. (Verification and alteration of the proxy) To confirm the validity of (m_W, r_A, σ_B), B computes $R_B = g^{\sigma_B}$ mod p and sends (m_W, R_B) to the *SEM*. After B receives $R_S = g^{\sigma_S}$ mod p from the *SEM*, B verifies whether or not the following equation holds: $R_B \cdot R_S = r_A \cdot y_A^{2h(m_W \| r_A)}$ mod p. Similarly, *SEM* verifies this above equation by using R_B. If the verification is successful, B and *SEM* compute alternative proxy signature keys σ_{P_B} and σ_{P_S}, respectively.

   (a) B computes $\sigma_{P_B} = \sigma_B + x_B h(m_W \| r_A)$ mod q
   (b) *SEM* computes $\sigma_{P_S} = \sigma_S + x_S h(m_W \| r_A)$ mod q

[Proxy Signature Generation Phase]

1. (Proxy validation) To generate a proxy signature on a message m, B must cooperate with the *SEM*. B chooses a random number $l_B \in_R Z_q$ and computes $L_B = g^{l_B}$ mod p for the proxy signature, and he transmits his identity and (m_W, m, r_A, R_B, L_B) to the *SEM*. *SEM* confirms (m_W, r_A, R_B) that was received in the proxy delivery and verification steps. And then, *SEM* must ascertain the following conditions, before he generates partial proxy signature on the m.

   (a) The period of proxy delegation specified in m_W should be valid.
   (b) The r_A should not be in the public revocation list maintained by the *SEM*. If the r_A is in the public revocation list, it means that the delegation had been revoked.

   If the validation step is finished correctly then *SEM* performs the proxy signature generation step.
2. (Proxy signature generation)

   (a) *SEM* generates a partial proxy signature on the m as follows:
   $l_S \in_R Z_q$, $L_S = g^{l_S}$ mod p, $L_A = g^{l_S} \cdot g^{l_B}$ mod p and $S_S = l_S + \sigma_{P_S} h(m \| L_A)$ mod q. *SEM* sends (L_A, S_S, L_S) to the B.

(b) After B receives (L_A, S_S, L_S), he verifies the token, (L_A, S_S, L_S), by computing $g^{S_S} = L_S \cdot (R_S \cdot y_S^{h(m_W||r_A)})^{h(m||L_A)}$ mod p. If the verification of the token is successful, he generates a proxy signature on the message m as follows:

$$S = S_S + l_B + \sigma_{P_B} h(m||L_A) \ mod \ q \tag{1}$$
$$= l_S + \sigma_{P_S} h(m||L_A) + l_B + \sigma_{P_B} h(m||L_A) \ mod \ q \tag{2}$$
$$= l_S + l_B + (\sigma_{P_S} + \sigma_{P_B}) h(m||L_A) \ mod \ q \tag{3}$$

The proxy signature on the message m is (m, m_W, r_A, S, L_A).

[Proxy Signature Verification Phase]

(Verification of the proxy signature) To verify the proxy signature on the m, a verifier confirms whether the following equation holds or not.

$$g^S = L_A \cdot (r_A \cdot (y_A^2 y_B y_S)^{h(m_W||r_A)})^{h(m||L_A)} \ mod \ p$$

The above congruence is computed as follows:

$$g^S = L_A \cdot (r_A \cdot (y_A^2 y_B y_S)^{h(m_W||r_A)})^{h(m||L_A)} \ mod \ p \tag{4}$$
$$= g^{l_S+l_B} \cdot (g^{k_A} \cdot (g^{2x_A} \cdot g^{x_B} \cdot g^{x_S})^{h(m_W|r_A)})^{h(m||L_A)} \ mod \ p \tag{5}$$
$$= g^{l_S+l_B+(k_A+(2x_A+x_S+x_B)h(m_W||r_A))h(m||g^{l_S+l_B})} \ mod \ p \tag{6}$$

[Revocation Phase]

If the original signer A wants to revoke the delegation before the specific delegation period or any misuse of the delegated rights is noticed, then he asks the SEM to put the r_A in a public revocation list. As soon as the proxy signer B requests a proxy token for a message m, the SEM will check the valid period of the delegation in m_W and the r_A in the public revocation list. Therefore, if the delegation period has expired or r_A exists in the revocation list, the SEM will not issue the proxy token for B. Once the delegation period has expired, the r_A of the public revocation list can be removed. So, the size of the public revocation list will not grow.

5   Analysis of the Proposed Proxy Signature Scheme

In this section, we analyze the security features of our scheme according to the security requirements. And then, we analyze the efficiency of our scheme in comparison with related works.

5.1   Security Considerations

We show that our scheme satisfies all the security requirements of proxy signature schemes stated in subsection 2.2

1. **Verifiability**: In our scheme, the proxy signature is consisted of $(m, m_W, r_A,$ $S, L_A)$. From the warrant message m_W, any verifier can know the identities of the original signer, the proxy signer and the SEM. Since the original signer's public key is needed to verify the proxy signature, the verifier can be convinced of the original signer's agreement on the proxy signed message.

2. **Strong unforgeability**: Let assume that the dishonest original signer A and the malicious attacker try to forge the proxy signer B's proxy signature. First, in the case of the dishonest original signer, he tries to send the forged proxy signature to the verifier by disguising as B. He can know partial delegation key of B, i.e, $\sigma_B = k_B + x_A h(m_W \| r_A)$ (mod q), because he generated it. And he can request SEM to generate the proxy token on message M'. But, since he cannot know the B's private key x_B due to the difficulty of DLP (Discrete Logarithm Problem), he cannot generate B's proxy signature. In the other case, if the malicious attacker eavesdrops σ_B and σ_S in the proxy delivery step, he can know partial delegation key of B. So, he chooses a random number $l'_B \in_R Z_q$ and computes $L'_B = g^{l'_B}$ mod p for forging B's proxy signature, and he transmits B's identity and $(m_W, m', r_A, R_B, L'_B)$ to the SEM. And then, he receives the proxy token on m', $(L'_S = g^{l_S}, L'_A = L'_S \cdot L'_B, S'_S = l_S + \sigma_{P_S} h(m' \| L'_A))$, from the SEM. But, since the malicious attacker cannot know B's private key x_B by the difficulty of DLP, he cannot generate the B's proxy signing key σ_{P_B}. So, he cannot forge the B's proxy signature, even if he eavesdrops the partial delegation key and obtains the proxy token from the SEM.
Therefore, the original signer and attacker cannot forge a proxy signature. Only the proxy signer can create a valid proxy signature.

3. **Strong identifiability**: In our scheme, identity information of a proxy signer is included explicitly in a valid proxy signature and m_W as a form of public key y_B. So, anyone can determine the identity of the proxy signer from the proxy signature created by him, and confirm the identity of the proxy signer from the m_W.

4. **Strong undeniability**: Anyone cannot know the B's private key due to the difficulty of DLP, only B can know his private key. Therefore, once a proxy signer creates a valid proxy signature, he cannot repudiate it, because the proxy signature is created by using his private key x_B.

5. **Prevention of misuse**: Only the proxy signer B can generate a proxy signature because only he knows his private key x_B. So, if B uses the proxy key pair for other purposes, it is his responsibility because only he can generate it. Therefore, the scenario of proxy signer's misuse is impossible. Moreover, the original signer or the malicious attacker's misuse is also prevented, because they cannot compute a valid proxy key pair.

5.2   Efficiency Considerations

We evaluate our scheme from a point of view of computational cost. We adopt a method used by Kaliski[3,8] to assess the amount of computational work. The basic rules of his method are as follows: (1) $WS(b) = 0.75WM(b)$,

(2) $WM(b_1)/b_1^2 = WM(b_2)/b_2^2$, where $WM(b)$ and $WS(b)$ are amount of computational work to perform b-bit modular multiplication and squaring, respectively. Following the well-known square and multiply approach, the amount of rasing s exponentiations, e.g. $g^s \bmod p$, is $|s|WS(|p|) + 0.5|s|WM(|p|)$. We assume that the output size of the cryptographic hash functions is 160 bits, and the size of p, q and RSA modulus n are set to 1024 bits, 160 bits and 1024 bits respectively. We compare our mediated proxy signature scheme with Sun and Chen's scheme, Sun's scheme, Lu et al.'s scheme and Das et al's scheme. Table 1 shows the efficiency comparisons with five schemes. Numbers in table 1 mean the amount of work to perform modular multiplication in p or n (= 1024) bits modulus. The computational work is divided into three stages: proxy key generation, proxy signature generation, verification of the proxy signature.

In Sun and Chen's scheme, Sun's scheme and Lu et al's scheme, all random numbers are chosen in Z_{p-1}, and generation of proxy signature key and proxy signature requires computation in Z_{p-1}. So, the amount of rasing s exponentiations(, where s is a random number in Z_{p-1}, $|s| = 1024$ bits) is $1280 \cdot WM(1024)$, and total amount of computational work in Sun and Chen's scheme, Sun's scheme and Lu et al's scheme are $19215 \cdot WM(1024)$, $23055 \cdot WM(1024)$ and $19211 \cdot WM(1024)$, respectively.

In Das et al's scheme, two large distinct primes p and q, each roughly the same size, and computes RSA modulus $n = pq$ and $\phi = (p-1)(q-1)$. And then RSA public-private key pair e or d are chosen in $[2, 3, ..., \phi]$ and the size of them is 1024 bits, and generation of proxy signature key and proxy signature requires computation in Z_n. So, the amount of rasing e or d exponentiations(, where e or d is a random number in Z_ϕ, $|e$ or $d| = 1024$ bits) is $1280 \cdot WM(1024)$, and total amount of computational work in Das et al's scheme is $14080 \cdot WM(1024)$.

In contrast with these schemes, since our scheme uses random numbers in Z_q and proxy signature key and proxy signature are generated in Z_q, the amount of rasing s exponentiations(, where s is a random number in Z_q, $|s| = 160$ bits) is $200 \cdot WM(1024)$, and total amount of computational work is $2611.12 \cdot WM(1024)$. As shown in the table 1, we can significantly reduce the total amount of computational work. Besides, Sun and Chen's scheme, Sun's scheme, Lu et al's scheme, and Das et al's scheme have much computational amount of verification stage such as $5125 \cdot WM(1024)$, $8965 \cdot WM(1024)$, $6404 \cdot WM(1024)$, and $3840 \cdot WM(1024)$ respectively, because a verifier should additionally compute to verify the validity of the time-stamp. However, our scheme does not require the

Table 1. Efficiency comparisions

	Sun-Chen	Sun	Lu	Das	Ours
Proxy key generation	3842	5124	7684	3840	1004.06
Proxy signature generation	10248	8966	5123	6400	1003.04
Proxy signature verification	5125	8965	6404	3840	604.02
Total computational amount	19215	23055	19211	14080	2611.12

verifier's additional computation. So, the computational amount of our verification stage is $604.02 \cdot WM(1024)$ and it can reduce the computational amount of verification more ten times than other schemes. This property is important because a signature may be checked by multiple users, once it is created. Therefore, our mediated proxy signature scheme provides all security requirements for proxy signature, efficiently.

6   Conclusions

Proxy signature scheme is a useful method for the electronic transactions, in case that one needs to delegate his signing power to other person. However, most proxy signature schemes cannot provide proxy revocation, properly. In this paper, we proposed the mediated proxy signature scheme to solve the proxy revocation problem. Our scheme can avoid the proxy signer abusing the signing capability by using the SEM, and provide an effective proxy revocation whenever the original signer wants or signer's key is compromised. Moreover, our scheme satisfies all security requirements for the proxy signature scheme: verifiability, strong unforgeability, strong identifiability, strong undeniability and prevention of use.

References

1. D. Boneh, X. Ding, G. Tsudik and C. M. Wong, "A method for fast revocation of public key certificates and security capabilities", *In 10th USENIX Security Symposium*, pp.297-308, 2001.
2. M.L.Das, A.Saxena and V.P.Gulati, "An efficient proxy signature scheme with revocation", *Int.Jounal Informatica*, Vol. 15, No. 4, pp.455-464, 2004.
3. B. S. Kaliski, "A response to DSS", Nov. 1991.
4. S. Kim, S. Park and D. Won, "Proxy signatures, revisited", *Proceedings of ICICS'97*, LNCS 1334, Springer-Verlag, pp.223-232, 1997.
5. B. Lee, H. Kim and K. Kim, " Strong proxy signature and its applications", *Proceedings of SCIS'2001*, pp.603-608, 2001.
6. E. J.-L. Lu and C.-J. Huang, "Cryptanalysis of a time-stamped proxy signature scheme", *Int.Jounal Informatica*, in press.
7. E.J.-L. Lu, M.-S. Hwang and C.-J. Huang, "A new proxy signature scheme with revocation", *Applied Mathematics and Computation*, Elsevier, in press, 2004.
8. M. Mambo, K. Usuda and E. Okamoo, "Proxy signatures: Delegation of the power to sign messages", *IEICE Trans. Fundamentals*, Vol.E79-A, No.9, pp.1338-1354, 1996.
9. T. Okamoto, M. Tada and E. Okamoto, "Extended proxy signatures for smart cards", *Proceedings of ISW'99*, LNCS 1729, Springer-Verlag, pp.247-258, 1999.
10. H.M. Sun, "Design of time-stamped proxy signatures with traceable receivers", *IEE Proceedings of Comput. Digit. Tech.*, Vol.147, No.6, pp.462-466, 2000.
11. H.M. Sun and B.J. Chen, "Time-stamped proxy signatures with traceable receivers", *Proceedings of the ninth national conference on Infomation security*, pp.247-253, 1999.

Privacy Enforcement for IT Governance in Enterprises: Doing It for Real

Marco Casassa Mont, Robert Thyne, and Pete Bramhall

Hewlett-Packard Labs, Trusted Systems Lab,
BS34 8QZ, Bristol, United Kingdom
{marco.casassa-mont, robert.thyne, pete.bramhall}@hp.com

Abstract. This paper describes issues and requirements related to privacy management as an aspect of improved governance in enterprises. Most of the existing related technical work is based on auditing and reporting mechanisms. The focus of this paper is on privacy enforcement for personal data: this is still a green field. To enforce the execution of privacy policies, requests to access personal data need to be checked against data requestors' rights and intents, data subjects' consent and the stated data purposes. Being able to automate and simplify the enforcement of privacy and reduce the involved costs is important for enterprises. We describe our approach and compare it against related work. In particular, we discuss our work done to add privacy-aware access control capabilities to HP Select Access - a leading-edge access control solution. A prototype has been implemented as a proof of concept. Current results, open issues and next steps are discussed.

1 Introduction

Enterprises store, manage and process large amounts of personal data about their employees, customers and partners. They need to put in place complex processes to comply with a growing list of laws and legislation often driven by local or geographical needs, including European Community data protection privacy laws, various US privacy laws (HIPPA, COPPA, SOX, GLB, etc.) and more specific national privacy initiatives [1, 2, 3]. Large enterprises that are geographically distributed across different nations might need to comply with different laws. Privacy management is an important aspect: it has implications on enterprises' IT governance [11] efforts, their compliance with regulations, customers' satisfaction, their reputation and brand.

Specifically, enterprises have to deal with *data governance processes* when handling personal and confidential data. Policies must be developed and modelled to describe how data has to be stored, accessed, manipulated, processed, managed, transferred and eventually deleted. Inventories of data must be created and subsequently kept up-to-date: gap and risk analysis tasks must be performed to check for the suitability of IT processes, frameworks and behaviours against these policies and identify risks and gaps. Eventually these policies must be deployed, enforced and audited to report anomalies and violations. All these phases are not linear and can involve vari-

S. Katsikas, J. López, G. Pernul (Eds.): TrustBus 2005, LNCS 3592, pp. 226–235, 2005.

ous refinement loops. Privacy laws, internal guidelines and data subjects' requirements have an impact on these governance processes: related privacy policies express rights, permissions and obligations on personal data.

Enterprises are already investing in identity management solutions: they want to leverage these investments and extend their functionalities to address privacy issues. In this context, the enforcement of privacy policies on personal data via systemic and verifiable manner is becoming a core requirement but it is still a green area. This paper focuses on this aspect. We introduce our R&D work done to develop a *privacy-aware access control model* and a related system, integrated with current identity management solutions, based on a common authoring, deployment and enforcement framework. A working prototype has been implemented by extending the HP Select Access product [8]. The core aspects of this prototype are presented along with a discussion of open issues and next steps.

2 Addressed Problem

The key problem addressed by this paper is the enforcement of privacy policies for personal data stored by enterprises. Closely related to this problem are the issues of modeling personal data, authoring and deploying privacy policies.

Privacy policies might impose conditions and constraints (dictated by data subjects and legislation) on which personal data can actually be accessed, given a specific context. They must keep into account aspects such as the stated *purposes* for which these data has been collected, *consent* given by data subjects and *intents* of data requestors. In addition, current privacy laws and legislation also require dealing with: *limited collection of data*; *limited use of data*; *limited disclosure of data*; *limited retention of data* [1,2,3]. As a consequence, the enforcement of related privacy policies might involve the *manipulation, transformation* and *filtering* of personal data before being accessed by a requestor.

How are all these aspects to be taken into account when accessing personal data? What does a privacy policy enforcement framework look like? How can attempts to access confidential data stored in different data repositories be intercepted and related privacy policies enforced? How transformation or filtering of requested data can be performed in an efficient way? How all these aspects can be integrated in an identity management system? Section 3 describes important related issues and requirements. Section 4 presents related work and section 5 introduces and describes our approach and solution.

3 Privacy Enforcement: Issues and Requirements

A simple example, shown in figure 1, can help to ground the concepts described so far and identify issues and requirements.

In this example an attempt to access personal data is made by an enterprise employee. The employee's intent (marketing) is consistent with the declared purposes of initially collecting the data (marketing and research). However the employee is trying to access – via an SQL query - more data than she is allowed to. The SQL query must be intercepted by the enforcement point and transformed in a way to

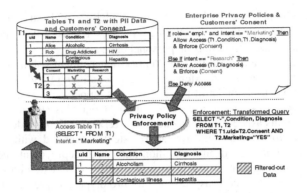

Fig. 1. Example: Privacy-aware Access Control – Consent, Purpose and Intent Management

include constraints based on data subjects' consent and the filtering of data. In this example privacy is achieved by pre-processing and transforming the query before interacting with the database. It could have involved a transformation of the query result (i.e. result post-processing) or both approaches.

In traditional approaches to privacy enforcement, these "modified" queries could have been embedded in applications and services: this would work in case of static environments that are not subject to changes. However, in the real world the situation is much more complex, especially for medium-large enterprises that need to run thousands of applications and services to underpin their businesses, have thousands/millions of customers and need to cope with ever changing business and legal needs. In real-world scenarios, data repositories storing personal data could be heterogeneous, including relational databases, LDAP directories, meta and virtual directories and legacy storage systems. Within the same data repository, personal data could be stored in different "tables", and be accessible either directly or via different "views". Privacy policies might be much more complex that the one shown in the above example. They might include data retention, notifications and authorization constraints. They might require different types of data manipulation and transformation, in addition to filtering, including data encryption, statistical modification of data, etc.

The *enforcement of privacy policies* must ensure that: the requestor's *intent* is consistent with the specified *data purposes*; data subjects' *consent* is kept into account and enforced along with preferences and constraints. All these aspects have access control implications. We argue that traditional access control systems are necessary but not sufficient to enforce privacy policies on personal data. Systems based on these traditional models do not keep into account additional contextual aspects relevant to privacy: the stated data purposes and data subjects' consents - i.e. properties associated to collected data - the intent of the requestors and any additional enterprise or customized data subjects' constraints.

Important issues are how to consider all these additional elements and build "privacy extensions" of traditional access control systems to move towards *privacy-aware access control* systems able to enforce privacy policies.

To address the above issues and make progress in building privacy enforcement solutions that can be flexibly and adaptively integrated in modern identity management solutions [12], it is important to satisfy the following core requirements [13]:

- Modeling of personal data;
- Explicit authoring and lifecycle management of privacy policies;
- Explicit deployment and enforcement of privacy policies
- Separation of privacy policies from business logics in applications and services;
- Support for auditing;
- Integration with traditional access control system;
- Simplicity and rationalization of the entire system.

4   Related Work

The common approach of enforcing privacy policies by hardcoding (embedding) privacy policies within applications and services is suitable for very simple and static environments: it shows all its limitations and maintenance costs in case of complex and dynamic organizations that need to adapt to changes. To address this problem, a comprehensive privacy-aware access control framework is required.

Relevant work in this space is described in [4]. IBM Enterprise Privacy Architecture (EPA) is introduced. The Enterprise Privacy Authorization Language (EPAL) specification [5] describes a language to represent privacy policies. This work makes advancements but it only provides general guidelines. Related solutions dealing with the management and enforcement of privacy policies usually only operate in well defined contexts and mainly by using vertical technologies.

Work on privacy enforcement for personal data has been done by IBM with their research on Hippocratic databases [6]. The drawback of their approach is that it mainly focuses at the database level (RDBMS). The enforcement of privacy policies might need to span across a broad variety of data repositories and legacy systems to include LDAP directories, meta and virtual directories, file systems and legacy data repositories. It might need to incorporate higher-level views and perspectives than just the database-level perspective.

In terms of commercially available solutions, IBM Tivoli Privacy Manager [7] provides mechanisms for defining fine-grained privacy policies and associating them to data. However it requires some duplications of administrative and enforcement frameworks, it imposes constraints on applications and databases schemas and it is vertically-based on other IBM products and solutions.

Our work specifically addresses the problem of enforcing privacy policies on personal data stored by enterprises potentially in a broad variety of data repositories. Personal data can be accessed by different types of requestors, including people, applications and services within the enterprise. Our work aims at not being invasive for applications and services: privacy policies are managed in an explicit way and not hardcoded in applications and services. We want to avoid duplications of efforts by providing a *single, integrated framework* for authoring, administering and enforcing both traditional *access control* and *privacy policies*.

5 Our Solution

This section provides details about our model to enforce privacy policies on personal data and how it can be implemented for real by extending HP Select Access [8].

Our model for a *privacy-aware access control system* explicitly deals with specified data purposes, the intent of requestors, data subjects' consent and additional access conditions and constraints on personal data. – see Figure 2.

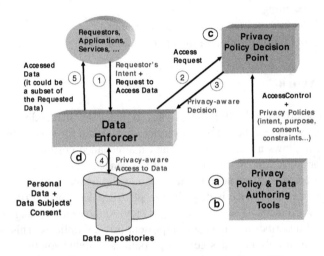

Fig. 2. Model of our Privacy-Aware Access Control System

Figure 2 shows the main aspects of this model, which consists of:

a) **Mechanisms to explicitly *model* personal data**: it describes personal data by including the types of data repositories (database, LDAP directory, etc.) where data are stored, their locations, a description of their data schemas (tables, views, classes, objects, etc.), attribute types, etc.;

b) **An integrated mechanism for authoring** *privacy policies* **along with** *traditional access control policies*. It consists of a Policy Authoring Point (PAP) that allows privacy administrators to describe and author, in an integrated way, both privacy policies and traditional access control policies;

c) **An integrated authorization framework for deploying** *access control and privacy-based policies* **and making related access decisions**: it is an integrated Policy Decision Point (PDP);

d) **A run-time mechanism –"*data enforcer*" - for** *intercepting attempts to access personal data and enforcing privacy decisions*. It is a Policy Enforcement Point (PEP). This mechanism deal with any required transformation and filtering of the requested data based on privacy decisions.

Our model leverages traditional/standard access control models (based on users/groups, their credentials and rights, access control lists and policies), and extends their Policy Authoring Points (PAPs), Policy Decision Points (PDPs) and Policy Enforcement Points (PEPs) by involving the management of purposes, consent and privacy constraints. At "run-time", attempts to access personal data are intercepted and managed in the following way (see figure 2):

1. A *data requestor*'s request to access personal data (stored in a data repository) is intercepted by the *data enforcer*. Available information about the requestor (credentials, identity, etc.) is collected, along with their intents (the intent can be explicitly declared by the requestor or could be defined by the application/service making the request);

2. The *data enforcer* interacts with the *privacy policy decision point* by passing information about the request (including the intent, requested data identifiers, etc.) and the requestor;

3. The *privacy policy decision point* makes a decision, based on available privacy policies and the context (request, requestor's information, etc.). This decision is sent back to the *data enforcer*. It can be any of the following types:

   - *No*: access to data is denied;
   - *No & conditions*: access to data is denied. Additional conditions are sent back to the requestor. To be satisfied (e.g. stronger authentication, etc);
   - *Yes*: access to data is granted;
   - *Yes & conditions*: access to (part of the) data is allowed, under the satisfaction of the attached conditions (that might require data transformations and manipulations, etc.).

4. The *data enforcer* enforces this decision. In particular, if the decision is *"Yes & conditions"* the data enforcer might have to manipulate and transform the requested personal data, before returning the result to the data requestor;

5. The *data enforcer* returns data (if any) to the data requestor, based on the enforced privacy decision.

The remaining part of this section describes a practical implementation of this model.

We believe that our model is generic enough to be adapted to and implemented in a wide variety of existing identity management solutions currently used to handle personal data. HP Select Access [8] is a significant example of "state-of-the-art" identity management solution, part of HP identity management solution suite. The HP Select Access framework can right now provide the infrastructural components needed to author, deploy and enforce privacy policies thanks to its flexible and extensible capabilities. Its core components are:

- **Policy Builder**: it is a graphical tool to author access control policies (PAP) on (web) resources managed by the system;
- **Validator**: it is a Policy Decision Point (PDP). It makes access control decisions based on the access control policies (authored with the Policy Builder) and contextual information, such as the identity of a requestor;
- **Web Enforcer plug-in**: it is a Policy Enforcement Point (PEP) for web resources;
- **Audit Server**: logs access information in a tamper evident storage.

The Policy Builder allows administrators to define access control rights (allow/deny access) on administered resources (e.g. web resources) for given enterprise users and define fine-grained access control constraints and conditions to grant/deny access to resources. This is done via a "Rule Editor": a rule (policy) can be composed by assembling an (extensible) set of rule components.

The current version of HP Select Access only deals with web resources (web services, html pages, servlets, etc.) and it only handles access control policies. The "Web Enforcer" considers these resources as "black boxes": this is not appropriate to enforce privacy constraints on personal data where fine-grained manipulation of data components might be required. Figure 3 shows the new functionalities that have been added to HP Select Access (HP SA) by our prototype:

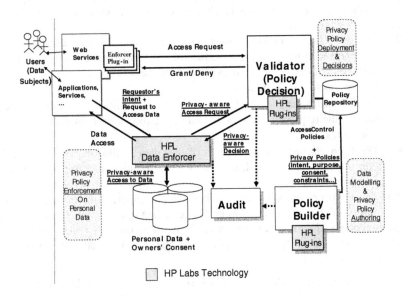

Fig. 3. Extended HP Select Access to deal with Privacy Policy Enforcement

The description of our new functionalities follows:

a. Modeling Personal data: the HP SA Policy Builder has been extended to represent "data resources" in addition to traditional IT resources (such as web resources). These data resources can be graphically accessed and authored via the Policy Builder;

b. Authoring Privacy Policies: the HP SA Policy Builder (Rule Editor) has been extended to graphically author privacy policies on "data resources" via the definition and implementation of a set of additional plug-ins based on standard APIs [13]:

- *Privacy decision plug-in*: this plug-in describes "tests" to check the intent of a requestor against allowed data purposes;
- *Data transformation plug-in*: it describes, in details, the schema/structure of the personal data to be accessed along with the types of transformations these data has to go through before being returned to the requestor. This includes: filtering out part of the data, encrypting data, doing statistical transformation of data, etc.;
- *Consent management plug-in*: it describes how to retrieve consent information (provided by the data subject) and how to link it to the correspondent data subjects' personal data;

- *Data retention plug-in*: it describes how to retrieve specific data retention information and how to link it to data subject's personal data.

As an effect of these extensions, the Policy Builder and Rule Editor can now be used to author both traditional access control and privacy policies, in an integrated way.

c. Making Privacy-aware decisions: the HP SA Validator has been extended to make privacy-aware decisions based on the above privacy policies. For each plug-in introduced in the HP Policy Builder, a correspondent plug-in has been implemented (via standard APIs) for the Validator, to convey to the system its semantic, at the decision-making time. Consistently to our model, the following types of access decisions on personal data are supported by this extended version of the Validator: *No; No & conditions; Yes; Yes & conditions*. The *Yes & conditions* decision has been explicitly added by us to provide information to the *data enforcer* on how to enforce accesses to personal data, based on privacy constraints.

d. Enforcing privacy decisions: a Data Enforcer has been built and added to the HP SA framework. This is a completely new functionality for HP Select Access. The data enforcer is in charge of enforcing privacy decisions made by the Validator. It intercepts incoming calls to data resources, interacts with the Validator, performs fine grained manipulation of data resources and deals with the interpretation and enforcement of additional constraints as defined by the privacy policies. Conceptually, the data enforcer is a *"data repository proxy"*. Applications, services and requestors believe they are still interacting with the required data repository via standard protocols or mechanisms (ODBC/JDBC, LDAP, etc.). The data enforcer sits nearby managed data repositories (e.g. databases, LDAP directories, virtual directories, etc.): a family of data enforcers - sharing a common logic but differentiated by add-ons dealing with different types of data resources (i.e. RDBMS databases, LDAP repositories, meta/virtual directories, etc.) – can be built.

At the moment, a data enforcer has been implemented for RDBMS databases as a proof of concept. Two versions of this data enforcer have currently been implemented: (1) standalone and (2) client/server. In both versions, the requestor's "intent" is transmitted to the data enforcer as an additional parameter during the database connection phase (it is passed either by the requestor or by the involved application/service). The same principles and approach can be used to implement *data enforcers* for other types of data repositories. More technical details about our approach can be found in [13]. The *auditing* capability of HP Select Access is used to log (among other things) requests to access data and related decisions and enforcements made by the system.

6   Discussion

Our privacy-based extension of HP Select Access covers the requirements described in Section 4: we explicitly model personal data, author and manage privacy policies, deploy, enforce and audit them. In our prototype the management of access control policies is integrated with privacy policies: the befit is the rationalization and simplification of the overall process.

We believe that our approach based on "data enforcers" to enforce privacy policies on personal data can minimize the impact on applications and services and make the enforcement process as much transparent as possible. In addition, current performance tests and analysis (done on databases of sizes from 100K to 500K records) are promising. No noticeable loss of performance (i.e. the time spent between sending a query to a RDBMS and retrieving the last returned record) has been registered so far, on common SQL queries. More tests and experiments are in progress on different varieties of SQL queries.

7 Next Steps

We plan to extend our prototype by adding a fine-grained management of the consent given by data subjects, deal with additional constraints on data and more complex privacy policies (via additional plug-ins). We recognize that our work on privacy enforcement has to be considered in the context of a more comprehensive set of technologies for regulatory compliance, in particular by including privacy obligation management and related enforcement capabilities [9], extended auditing capabilities [10], policy violation analytics and reporting capabilities. Our work done in related projects can be leveraged and integrated with this work.

Further research and development is also required to address aspects related to the "data enforcer" component, in terms of the flexibility of the query interception mechanism, its performance, efficiency, scalability and impacts on applications and services.

8 Conclusions

Privacy Management is important for enterprises for IT governance and regulatory compliance. The emphasis of most of the current solutions is on auditing and reporting aspects. The use of systemic technology for the explicit management and enforcement of privacy policies on personal data (stored and processed by enterprises) is an important aspect but still a green field. In currently deployed systems, this aspect is addressed with ad-hoc or very vertical solutions.

In this paper we specifically address this problem: we describe a privacy enforcement model and a technical approach to explicitly model personal data, author privacy policies and customers' consent, deploy and enforce them in an integrated framework, along with access control policies. We introduce a solution based on a privacy extension of HP Select Access - a leading edge identity management product. The management of access control policies is integrated with the management of privacy policies. This brings simplicity and rationalises management and enforcement tools. A working prototype and a related demonstrator have been built as a proof of concept, to demonstrate the feasibility of our ideas.

References

1. Rotemberg, M., Laurant, C., Privacy International: Privacy and Human Rights 2004: an International Survey of Privacy Laws and Developments, Electronic Privacy Information Center (EPIC), Privacy International. http://www.privacyinternational.org/survey/phr2004/ (2004)

2. OECD: OECD Guidelines on the Protection of Privacy and Transborder Flows of Personal Data. http://www1.oecd.org/publications/e-book/9302011E.PDF (1980)

3. Online Privacy Alliance: Guidelines for Online Privacy Policies. http://www.privacyalliance.org/, Online Privacy Alliance (2004)

4. Karjoth, G., Schunter, M.: A Privacy Policy Model for Enterprises. IBM Research, Zurich. 15th IEEE Computer Foundations Workshop (2002)

5. IBM: The Enterprise Privacy Authorization Language (EPAL), EPAL 1.1 specification. http://www.zurich.ibm.com/security/enterprise-privacy/epal/, IBM (2004)

6. Agrawal, R., Kiernan, J., Srikant, R., Xu, Y.: Hippocratic Databases, http://www.almaden.ibm.com/cs/people/srikant/papers/vldb02.pdf, IBM Almaden Research Center (2002)

7. IBM Tivoli Privacy Manager: online technical documentation - http://publib.boulder.ibm.com/tividd/td/PrivacyManagerfore-business1.1.html

8. HP: HP Openview Select Access - Overview and Features - http://www.openview.hp.com/products/select/

9. Casassa Mont, M.: Dealing with Privacy Obligations: Important Aspects and Technical Approaches, TrustBus 2004 (2004)

10. Baldwin, A.: Enhanced accountability for electronic processes, 2nd international conference on trust management. Lecture notes in computer science, vol. 2995, Springer (2004)

11. Salle, M.: IT Service Management and IT Governance: Review, Comparative Analysis and their impact on Utility Computing, HP Labs, http://www.hpl.hp.com/techreports/2004/HPL-2004-98.html, (2004)

12. Casassa Mont, M.: On Adaptive Identity Management: The Next Generation of Identity Management Solutions, HP Labs, http://www.hpl.hp.com/techreports/2003/HPL-2003-149.pdf, (2003)

13. Casassa Mont, M., Thyne, R., Bramhall, P.: Privacy Enforcement with HP Select Access for Regulatory Compliance, HP Labs, http://www.hpl.hp.com/techreports/2005/HPL-2005-10.html, (2005)

An Adaptive Privacy Management System for Data Repositories

Marco Casassa Mont and Siani Pearson

Hewlett-Packard Labs, Trusted Systems Lab,
BS34 8QZ, Bristol, United Kingdom
{marco.casassa-mont, siani.pearson}@hp.com

Abstract. This paper addresses the problem of dealing with privacy management of personal data stored by enterprises. Accesses to personal data must keep into account privacy policies based on laws, enterprise guidelines, stated purposes of data and data subjects' consent. In large organisations, people have different roles and skills: business tasks are achieved thanks to collaboration among these people. The rigid enforcement of privacy policies might create disruptions and unacceptable burdens in business practices. We introduce an innovative solution based on an adaptive privacy management system. Data are retrieved from standard data repositories: parts of these data are encrypted and associated with privacy policies. The actual access to the encrypted data is adaptive, depending on the requestor, the context and purpose. Multiple "views" on a data structure can be provided by our system. Our research and development is work in progress. We describe our current results and highlight next steps.

1 Introduction

Enterprises store large amounts of confidential data about their employees, customers and partners. Data protection and privacy laws, including [1,2], dictate increasingly strict constraints about how these data have to be protected, accessed and managed. Failure to comply with these privacy laws can have serious consequences for the reputation and brand of organizations and have negative financial impacts.

Privacy management technology can help enterprises to deal with related regulatory compliance issues and to satisfy data subjects' preferences. This paper describes our approach based on an adaptive privacy management system for data repositories. Our main objective is to enable adaptive access to confidential information based on the satisfaction of privacy policies with a minimal impact on data repositories in terms of required technological changes. The latter is important in order to aid the practical deployment of the system.

A privacy model is introduced, based on: a Privacy Virtualisation Layer used by people and applications to mediate their interactions with data repositories, as dictated by privacy policies, and one or more Privacy Management Services (i.e. trust services run by organizations or trusted third parties) dealing with the enforcement of these privacy policies. The process of disclosing confidential data is adaptive to contextual

S. Katsikas, J. López, G. Pernul (Eds.): TrustBus 2005, LNCS 3592, pp. 236–245, 2005.
© Springer-Verlag Berlin Heidelberg 2005

information i.e. not just based data requestors' rights and credentials. Our research and development is work in progress. In this paper we describe the main concepts underpinning our work and current results.

2 Addressed Problem

The key problem addressed in this paper is the management of privacy for confidential data stored by enterprises. Privacy management is not just a matter of "traditional" access control: it is necessary to capture the purpose of data, convey the consensus of the data subjects and make decisions on access requests based on the requestors' intentions. Privacy policies can dictate additional terms and conditions under which access to confidential data can be granted: this involves the satisfaction of constraints and obligations which might require the processing of credentials, trust verification and management of contextual information.

In large organisations, people have different roles and skills: business tasks are achieved thanks to collaboration among these people. The rigid enforcement of privacy policies might create disruptions in business practices and introduce unacceptable burdens. For example, confidential data can be stored in a variety of data repositories. Only technical specialists might have the right skills to retrieve these data in a way that is meaningful for business people, marketing departments or strategists. Unfortunately, privacy policy constraints might dictate that these technical people must not access confidential data: in this case they would not be able to provide a service to the business people. Similar observations apply for applications and services run by different organizations within an enterprise.

Mechanisms are required to address both privacy requirements and business needs. An entity should not be prevented from acting on behalf of other people when searching and retrieving data. Access to and disclosure of data must be adaptive: in case of non-compliance to specific privacy policies, parts of this data might be removed or simply left encrypted.

3 Related Work

A lot of work has been done on mechanisms to encrypt data in databases, such as Translucent Databases [3]. Most of these solutions focus on "confidentiality" and access control aspects rather than privacy aspects (data purposes, matching the requestors' intentions against this purpose, enforcing obligations, etc.).

Relevant work is described in [14,15] about access control policy-based encryption mechanisms for XML documents. [14] describes mechanisms for fine-grained encryption of parts of XML documents: decryption keys can either be granted to data receivers or collected from LDAP servers, based on data receivers' credentials. [15] focuses on related cryptographic mechanisms: no major details are provided on key distribution aspects. Our work is based on the similar principle of encrypting portions of data (of any type, not necessarily XML based) along with privacy policies. The main differences are: (1) the types of policies we handle. In our case policies include aspects beyond access control, such as privacy, trust, configuration of systems, etc. which might involve executions of actions (notifications, deletions, data transformations, etc.) at the access-request time; (2) we explicitly control the disclosure of decryption keys via a dedicated, active mechanism – the Privacy Management Service - rather then via passive solutions (such as LDAP servers). Our decryption keys can be generated on-the-fly (e.g. by using IBE cryptographic schema [9,10]) or can be handed by the Privacy Management Service based on the evaluation of the full context, based not only on the requestors' credentials but also on other criteria, such as trustworthiness of the platforms, contextual parameters (e.g. location, network), etc.

The work done by IBM on Hippocratic Databases [4] is based on the concept of associating privacy metadata (i.e. privacy policies) to data stored in RDBMS repositories, along with mechanisms to enforce privacy. This approach does not take into account the fact that privacy management spans across database boundaries and should encompass different types of enterprise data repositories (including LDAP repositories, virtual directories, etc.), the management of enterprise-wide privacy policies, obligations and application/service-based privacy policies.

In terms of commercial products IBM Tivoli Privacy Manager [5] provides mechanisms for defining fine-grained privacy policies and associating them to data. Privacy policies will evolve towards privacy authorization-based policies - based on the EPAL [6] specification. This approach addresses the privacy management problem purely from an access control perspective. It does not include additional aspects such as data distribution, trust management and dealing with data retention and handling privacy obligations dictated by legislation and enterprise's guidelines (which do not necessarily depend on access control aspects).

We aim at leveraging current data repository technologies and reducing to the minimum the impact on them. In our approach, interactions with data repositories can still happen as usual but with the additional guarantee that confidential data is now protected by encryption and contextually released, in a fine-grained way, based on the fulfillment of associated privacy policies.

4 Our Solution

The model underpinning our privacy management solution consists of three basic components, as shown in figure 1: (1) *A Privacy Virtualisation System*; (2) *A Privacy Management Service*; (3) *Data structures containing confidential data along with associated privacy policies*.

The *Privacy Virtualisation System* mediates the interactions between an entity (i.e. data requestor), data repositories and the Privacy Management Service. It allows users to retrieve confidential data from standard data repositories where data is stored in an encrypted way with the associated privacy policies. The storage of encrypted data and the associated policies might require some changes in the logical definition of data structures (i.e. different types of fields in tables, different LDAP classes' definitions, etc.) but no technological changes are required for data repositories. Once retrieved, confidential data is represented via *data structures* to enable their transmission. These data structures contain (potentially encrypted) data (or references to data) along with the associated privacy policies.

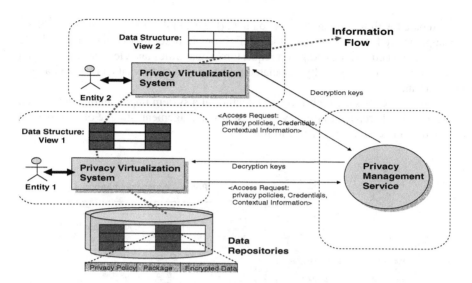

Fig. 1. Privacy Management Model

The *Privacy Management Service* is an active component that decides which confidential information can be accessed by an entity (via the Privacy Virtualization System) at a specific point in time. The process of disclosing decryption keys is adaptive, depending on the requestor's credentials, relevant privacy policies, current context and stated data purposes. When it grants access to data, the Privacy Management Service discloses decryption keys to the requestor. Decryption keys can be generated on-the-fly or be defined at the encryption time, depending on the adopted cryptographic schema. More details follow. Our approach is based on a "pull" model where data requestors, via the Privacy Virtualisation System, retrieve decryption keys by interacting with one or more Privacy Management Services.

Figure 1 shows an example where different "views" of confidential data are provided by our system to different requestors. Confidential data can be retrieved by people and applications that have no rights to access its content but are in charge of querying data repositories on behalf of other people: in this case the content cannot be decrypted but it can be sent to other entities that might have access capabilities. The Privacy Management Service can be provided by an organisation for internal consumption or by one or more external trusted third parties, to enable multi-party interactions and increase the overall trust and accountability [12].

Our solution can enforce privacy policies in a variety of scenarios, including enterprise scenarios, federated identity management scenarios and healthercare scenarios where data can be transmitted to people (or applications and services) with different roles within and/or across organisational boundaries. In all these cases the confidential information they should actually access must depend on their roles, their declared intent, stated purpose of the stored data, enterprise policies, legislation and specific customers' (opt-in and opt-out) policies. In our approach we associate fine-grained privacy policies to encrypted confidential data and force requestors to be compliant to these policies if they want to access the data.

Compared with traditional "views" on data (for example views on database tables), our approach reduces the need for their definitions in order to accommodate multiple different perspectives, depending on requestors' capabilities and clearance: access and privacy constraints are direclty associated to data and dictate what can be seen at any point in time.

Figure 2 describes the high-level architecture of a system implementing our model. Technical details related to privacy policies, key management, storage of confidential data and architectural components follow.

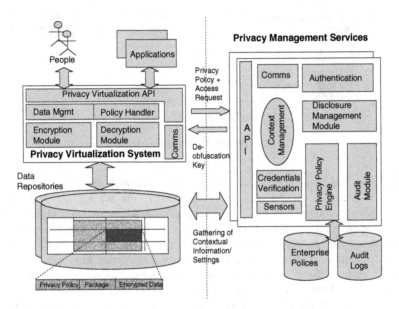

Fig. 2. High-level Architecture of our Adaptive Privacy Management System

a. Privacy Policies, Key Management and Storage of Confidential Data

Our solution enables the storage of confidential data in data repositories by using an encryption format, along with fine-grained privacy policies. Examples are described later in this section and in [12]. The content of an encrypted field (for example in a database record) can be represented as: **<privacy policy, package, encrypted data>.** It includes the encrypted data, the relevant privacy policy and additional information to check for the integrity and stickiness of this policy to the data and enable its decryption ("package"). The specific format used to represent privacy policies is not a major issue and will not be described in this paper. However it is important to stress the fact that this format must be flexible enough to express the following type of constraints [12]: privacy, authorization, obligation, preferences, trust and control.

A few examples of policies (expressed in natural language), reflecting a *user's perspective* follow: "Entities can access my data subordinated to the fact that their intent matches the e-commerce transaction purpose"; "Do not disclose my personal details to specific entities A,B,C"; "Allow the access of these data only when dealing with entity W"; "Notify me via e-mail, every time you use some of my identity information"; "Ask for my authorization every time you need to disclose this attribute to a third party"; "Interact with this trusted third party and state your intentions in order to obtain the current values of these attributes".

It is important to notice that these policies not only define access control aspects but also they might require the fulfillment of actions at the disclosure time, such as notifications or explicit requests for authorization. In our system privacy policies are written in a formal language (via logical expressions and constraints) in a way that they can be programmatically interpreted.

It is also important to ensure that a privacy policy sticks with the encrypted data and that this link cannot be broken. In our system the stickiness of policies to identity information is obtained by encrypting the identity information in a way that its decryption is a "function of" the associated policies. Any tampering with these policies prevents the decryption of data. Different cryptographic techniques are available: they can use either traditional public-key cryptography or identifier-based encryption (IBE) cryptography. They are conceptually equivalent. In both cases only the Privacy Management Service(s) can issue the correspondent decryption key(s):

- **In case public key cryptography** [7] is used, the Privacy Management Service (PMS) publishes its (certified) public key (it keeps secret the correspondent private key). When personal data associated to privacy policies must be stored in a database, a *symmetric key* is generated by the Privacy Virtualisation System (PVS) and used to encrypt these data. The symmetric key and a hash value of the associated policies are encrypted in a *package* [8] by using the PMS public key. The overall information (<policy, package, encrypted data>) is eventually stored in the data repository. The PMS is the only entity that can decrypt the above *package*, check for the integrity of the associated policies, check for their compliance and eventually disclose the symmetric key to a requestor (i.e. another PVS);

- **The alternative approach is based on IBE cryptographic technology** [9,10]. Any kind of string can be used as an IBE encryption key. Privacy policies can be used for this purpose. The correspondent IBE decryption key can only be generated by the PMS as it is the only entity that has the "secret" necessary for doing it. The PMS will check the compliance of a requestor with these policies. The generation of IBE decryption keys can be postponed in time i.e. until they are actually necessary for decryption purposes. Any tampering with the IBE encryption key will make impossible for the PMS to generate the correct decryption key.

b. Privacy Virtualisation System

The Privacy Virtualisation System mediates the storage and retrieval of confidential data. Interactions with applications and services happen via its "virtualisation APIs". These APIs consist of an extension of traditional data repositories APIs (such JDBC, LDAP, etc.) to store and retrieve data along with privacy policies and the declared

intention (i.e. the reason for making this request). This extension does not require changes to current data repositories. For example, in case of access to a relational database, two basic interactions can happen:

- **Storage and update of confidential data**: in case of SQL INSERT or UPDATE commands, the privacy API allows users to specify the association of privacy policies to the data. The Privacy Virtualisation System stores data in the database by using one of the cryptographic techniques described before;

- **Retrieval of confidential data**: the Privacy Virtualisation System intercepts SELECT queries and interacts with the Privacy Management Service to decrypt data. The actual disclosure of decryption keys depends on the current context, user's credentials and privacy policies. The answer to the query could be provided either via a traditional database result set (where part of the data could be encrypted) or via an explicit "data structure".

The representation of query results via an explicit XML-based *"data structure"* allows a "transportable" representation of the result: this can include data in clear, encrypted data (or references to data) and the associated privacy policies.

Applications and services need to be modified to be privacy-aware and to fully leverage this privacy API to handle privacy policies. This is particularly important for the storage of confidential data via the Privacy Virtualisation System, as only in this way data will be stored in an encrypted way, according to privacy criteria. In absence of this, applications can still access these data as usual (no changes are made to data repositories), except for confidential data that will be encrypted.

In addition to the "virtualisation API", the Privacy Virtualisation System contains these core components:

- **Data management module**: it formats data, depending on the underlying data repository and the requested privacy policies;
- **Policy handler module**: it interprets privacy policies. It interacts with the Privacy Management Service and provides information to obtain the decryption keys;
- **Encryption/Decryption modules**: they deal with the encryption and decryption of confidential data, as described above;
- **Communication module**: it enables secure communication with the Privacy Management Service.

c. Privacy Management Service

The Privacy Management Service is in charge of making decisions and enforcing privacy policies associated to confidential data. At the very base, the Privacy Management Service verifies that privacy policies are fulfilled before disclosing any decryption key. The Privacy Management Service consists of the following core components:

- **Communication module**: it enables secure communication with the Privacy Virtualisation System and other parties;
- **Authentication module**: it is in charge of authenticating requestors, should this be dictated by privacy policies;
- **Credential verification service**: it is in charge of verifying the integrity and validity of digital credentials;
- **Context management module**: it stores contextual information, relative both to specific interactions and the general situation;

- **Sensors**: they used by the Privacy Management Service to gather additional up-to-date contextual information, for example trust measures from Trusted Computing Group (TCG) enabled platforms [11].
- **Disclosure management module**: it (generates and) discloses decryption keys;
- **Privacy policy engine**: it is the privacy policy interpreter. It drives the interaction with the Privacy Virtualisation System, sensors and the disclosure management module;
- **Audit**: this module logs all the interactions happening with requestors, in particular related to the disclosure of decryption keys.

The disclosure process is adaptive and driven both by privacy policies and contextual information i.e. it is not purely driven by the authentication of the requestors and their access rights. Contextual information can be very rich, including system information, measures of trust of the requestors' platforms, historical information, etc. It is important to notice that the disclosure of confidential information can modify the current context and, as a consequence, enable/disable sets of privacy policies and influence future disclosures.

The Privacy Management Service can be deployed either remotely or locally to the site where the data repository is located. It could also be provided by a trusted third party to enable multi-party interactions and ensure a consistent enforcement of privacy policies. In a more advanced scenario, privacy policies can dictate to the Privacy Virtualization System to interact with multiple Privacy Management Services (each of them having specific competences) in order to access encrypted data.

5 Discussion

It is the case that our Privacy Virtualisation System can potentially be bypassed as requestors could try to access data by directly querying the data repositories or by accessing the content of files (if they have the basic access control rights). However, in this case, any encrypted data is going to be unintelligible. This forces the requestor to interact with the Privacy Management Service as dictated by the associated privacy policies.

A more problematic issue arises because once confidential data have been disclosed to a legitimate requestor (that satisifed the associated privacy policies), it may not be possible to prevent this entity from misusing these data. At this stage also the association of sticky policies to data can be broken. Unfortunately, this is a common problem for systems that must enforce privacy and at the same time must release confidential data. With our approach we ensure that sticky privacy policies are strongly associated to data at least until the first disclosure happens. Afterwards our approach can mitigate the involved risks by auditing disclosures and the context where they happened, to increase accountability. In the future, it is likely that further controls will be available: if the requestor's platform includes technologies such as security-enhanced operating systems (OS) and Trusted Computing Group (TCG) technology, these could potentially be used to control the use and propogation of decrypted data. More details on addressing the above issues can be found in [12].

An open question that needs to be addressed is the impact of our solution in terms of efficiency. We need to fully understand how applications and services will deal with the association of privacy policies to data. This is definitely work in progress.

Another important aspect that needs to be explored further is the overall lifecycle management of privacy policies and keys associated to confidential data, including their renewal and modification. The management of decryption keys is strictly related to the management of associated policies as decryption keys will be issued based on policy fulfillment. By changing a policy, our system must automatically change the associated encryption key.

Revocation of keys and one-time usage of keys have to be addressed in this context. Related to these aspects, we are currently looking at ways to change encryption keys based on successful disclosures of data. Every time data are successfully accessed (i.e. the decryption key is disclosed) the data is re-encrypted with a new key by the Privacy Virtualization System along with the associated policy. This policy could be slightly modified as well, especially in case of IBE encryption: nonces or "variable tags" can be added to policies to differentiate them without changing their semantic.

We are currently researching in this space and developing a prototype of our solution by leveraging traditional public key cryptography or IBE to provide the required encryption mechanisms. We can leverage TCG-enabled trusted platforms to provide further trust about contextual information. We have already developed policy engines able to release decryption keys based on the fulfillment of policies.

Aspects of our model might be further investigated and built in the context of the EU PRIME project [13].

6 Conclusions

This paper describes an innovative approach to allow an adaptive and incremental disclosure of confidential data depending on contextual satisfaction of privacy policies, with minimal disruption to common business interactions. Confidential information can be retrieved and transmitted between people that potentially have the right to access only parts of it: different views (in the sense of visible data) of this information are provided, depending on the requestors' credentials, the context and privacy policies. Our research and development is work in progress. Part of this research could be carried out in the EU PRIME project.

References

1. Rotemberg, M., Laurant, C.: Privacy International - Privacy and Human Rights 2004: an International Survey of Privacy Laws and Developments, Electronic Privacy Information Center (EPIC), Privacy International. http://www.privacyinternational.org/survey/phr2004/ (2004)
2. OECD: OECD Guidelines on the Protection of Privacy and Transborder Flows of Personal Data. http://www1.oecd.org/publications/e-book/9302011E.PDF (1980)
3. Wayner, P.: Translucent Databases, Flyzone Press (2002)
4. IBM: Hippocratic Databases, http://www.almaden.ibm.com/software/quest/Projects/ hippodb/ (2004)

5. IBM: IBM Tivoli Privacy Manager, online technical documentation, http://publib. boulder. ibm . com/tividd/td/PrivacyManagerfore-business1.1.html (2004)
6. IBM: The Enterprise Privacy Authorization Language (EPAL), EPAL 1.1 specification, http://www.zurich.ibm.com/security/enterprise-privacy/epal/ (2004)
7. Housley, R., Ford, W., Polk, W., Solo, D.: RFC2459: Internet X.509 Public Key Infrastructure Certificate and CRL profile, IETF (1999)
8. RSA : PKCS#7, Cryptographic Message Syntax Standard, http://www .rsasecurity. com/ rsalabs/pkcs/pkcs-7/ (1997)
9. Boneh, D., Franklin, M.: Identity-based Encryption from the Weil Pairing, Crypto 2001 (2001)
10. Cocks, C.: An Identity Based Encryption Scheme based on Quadratic Residues. Communications-Electronics Security Group (CESG), UK (2001)
11. Pearson, S. (ed.): Trusted Computing Platforms, Prentice Hall (2002)
12. Casassa Mont, M., Pearson, S., Bramhall, P.: Towards Accountable Management of Privacy and Identity Management, ESORICS 2003 (2003)
13. EU Framework VI PRIME Project: Privacy and Identity Management for Europe, http://www.prime-project.eu.org/ (2004)
14. Bertino, E., Ferrari, E.: Secure and Selective Dissemination of XML Documents, ACM TISSEC (2002) 290-331
15. Miklau, G., Suciu, D.: Controlling Access to Published Data Using Cryptography, VLDB (2003)

Privacy Preserving Data Mining Services on the Web*

Ayça Azgın Hintoğlu [1], Yücel Saygın[1], Salima Benbernou [2], Mohand Said Hacid [2]

[1] Sabancı University, Faculty of Engineering and Natural Sciences,
Tuzla,34956 Istanbul, Turkey
{aycah, ysaygin}@sabanciuniv.edu
[2] LIRIS - Lyon Research Center for Images and Intelligent Information Systems,
Lyon 1 University, Villeurbanne, France
{salima.benbernou, mohand-said.hacid}@liris.cnrs.fr

Abstract. Data mining research deals with extracting useful information from large collections of data. Since data mining is a complex process that requires expertise, it is beneficial to provide it as a service on the web. On the other hand, such use of data mining services combined with data collection efforts by private and government organizations leads to increased privacy concerns. In this work, we address the issue of preserving privacy while providing data mining services on the web and present an architecture for privacy preserving sharing of data mining models on the web. In the proposed architecture, data providers use APPEL for specifying their privacy preferences on data mining models, while data collectors use P3P policies for specifying their data-usage practices. Both parties use PMML as the standard for specifying data mining queries, constraints and models.

1 Introduction

Massive amounts of data have been collected into large data warehouses for later analysis in tabular, XML or plain text form. Such data is collected with the hope that it can be transformed into useful knowledge later on through data mining techniques. However, data mining requires a lot of expertise, and not all firms have the ability to construct and interpret data mining models. Therefore, there is a market for specialized firms on data storage and analysis. But there are challenges as well, such as security and privacy. Privacy concerns of outsourced data have been addressed recently in the literature within the context of querying and data mining [6][1][3][4][5]. We can define the data privacy of individuals as the right to have the control over the data they provided. This includes controlling (1) how the data is going to be used, (2) who is going to use it, and (3) for what purpose. In order to formally address the issue of control, some medium for privacy preference specification for the data providers and policy specification for data collectors have been recently developed by the W3C, under the P3P specification working group [8].

The idea of data mining as a service was first proposed by Sunita Sarawagi [2]. In her paper, Sarawagi et al. discusses on the usefulness of providing data mining mod-

---

* This work is funded by the PIA-BOSPHORUS programme of EGIDE (France) and TÜBİTAK (Turkey).

S. Katsikas, J. López, G. Pernul (Eds.): TrustBus 2005, LNCS 3592, pp. 246–255, 2005.
© Springer-Verlag Berlin Heidelberg 2005

els as services on the internet and enumerates the problems that needs to be addressed in order to realize these services. Privacy in such a service is the main concern when actual data contains confidential information about the data providers, such as health records of patients. In this work, we assume that the actual data, which is the medical reports of patients, is in textual form. Such data contains valuable information that could be used for research purposes. However, since it is confidential, it cannot be released to the third parties. But for research purposes, data mining queries are allowed to run on the confidential data and produce models out of it. In such a case, the data mining model itself could jeopardize the privacy of the data owners. Therefore, release of confidential portions of data mining models must be avoided using a set of constraints. In order to accomplish this, we propose an architecture where data mining queries and constraints are expressed via PMML, an XML based language for expressing data mining models developed by Data Mining Group (DMG) [7]. Moreover, we extend P3P and APPEL in order to specify data mining queries as privacy policies, and data mining constraints as privacy preferences respectively. As a case study, we considered association rules that could be used for prediction and therefore can reveal private information about the data providers. In order to block the privacy leaks induced by the association rules, we define constraints to map the original association rules to more generic ones via a taxonomy. To support our claims, let us first look at a motivating application which is used as the case study to demonstrate the proposed architecture.

Medical Research Application Suppose that an organization owns a huge medical report repository of individuals. Due to privacy concerns, the organization is not willing to share the actual reports or provide information about an individual's medical history. But, it still wishes to help the researchers investigating the associations between entities such as gender, time, location, symptom, disease and medication. In order to share these associations, the organization first extracts all such entities from each document. An example medical report with its tagged version is shown in Fig. 1.

Mr. *John Brown*, stayed in Med Hospital, *New York* from *05/05/1999* to *05/08/1999*. His tests for the *cytomegalovirus* were positive. Therefore, he was prescribed *Vitravene*. ...

Mr.<PERSON GENDER="Male"> *John Brown* </PERSON>, stayed in Med Hospital, <LOCATION> *New York* </LOCATION> from <DATE> *05/05/1999* </DATE> to <DATE> *05/08/1999* <DATE>. His tests for the <DISEASE> *cytomegalovirus* </DISEASE> were positive. Therefore, he was prescribed <MEDICATION>*Vitravene* </MEDICATION>. ...

Fig. 1. An Example Medical Record and Its Tagged Version

Thus, the researchers can now ask for the associations between different entities via a data mining query without explicitly accessing the confidential reports. However, there is still a privacy leak. Actually, apart from the actual data, some associations between entities can also be confidential and with appropriate query parameters (like support and confidence) a researcher can learn these confidential associations. In order to avoid such privacy leaks, the organization wants to restrict the association queries so that each researcher can only view the associations to which he/she is allowed to.

The rest of the paper is organized as follows. In section 2, we describe the building blocks of our framework, the Predictive Modeling Markup Language (PMML) and the Platform for Privacy Preferences (P3P), and give a brief overview on multi-level association rule mining which is used as the target data mining model in our case study. In section 3, we formally define the problem and present the architecture for privacy preserving sharing of data mining models on the web. Finally, in section 4 we give out the conclusion and state the future work.

2   Background

2.1   Predictive Modeling Markup Language (PMML)

PMML is an XML-based language that is being developed by the Data Mining Group [7]. It provides a standard way for defining and representing data mining models, by describing their inputs, outputs and parameters. This enables applications to use models obtained from multiple sources simply by reading the corresponding PMML files without having to deal with individual differences between those sources. PMML consists of the following principal components:

Mining Build Task is the natural container for any pre-processing and post-processing task specification using any content structure.
Data Dictionary defines the attributes used in the mining models.
Mining Schema lists the attributes which a user has to provide in order to apply the model together with their relative importance, outlier treatment, and usage type.
Transformation Dictionary enumerates the derived attributes defined via normalization, discretization, value mapping, or aggregation.
Taxonomies and Hierarchies organize the categorical attributes under a hierarchy which is also known as the taxonomy.
Model Parameters are the actual parameters defining the data mining models.
Model Output lists the output (e.g. association rule, decision tree) of a model.

An example association rule mining query written in PMML is shown in Fig. 2. This query defines a data mining task that will mine DOCUMENT_ENTITIES table for association rules with a minimum support of 0.6 and a minimum confidence of 0.5.

2.2   Platform for Privacy Preferences (P3P)

P3P, developed by the W3C, provides an automated way for data owners (e.g. user) to gain more control over the use of their data by the data collectors (e.g. web sites) [8]. Basically, P3P enables data collectors to encode their data-collection and data-usage practices using P3P policies [9] which are made up of statements encoded in XML describing the data practices of the data collectors. Each statement in a P3P policy is made up of the following elements:

Consequence provides further explanation about a data collector's practices and why the suggested practice may be valuable in human-readable text.
Purpose contains one or more purposes of data collection or uses of data.

Recipient contains one or more recipients of the collected data.
Retention defines the duration for which the collected information will be retained.
Data-Group describes the data to be transferred or inferred.
Extension describes the extension to the syntax.

On the other hand, the data owners can express their privacy preferences using the privacy preference language known as APPEL [10] as a set of preference-rules which can then be used by their agent to make automated decisions regarding the acceptability of machine-readable privacy policies of data collectors. The preference-rules consist of two parts:

Rule behavior specifies the action (e.g. request, block) to be taken if the rule fires.
Rule body provides the POLICY pattern that is matched against a privacy policy.

```
<PMML version="3.0" >
 <MiningBuildTask> <Extension>
  <DataMining><MiningData tableName="DOCUMENT_ENTITIES" /></DataMining>
 </Extension> </MiningBuildTask>
 <DataDictionary numberOfFields="2" >
  <DataField name="document_id" optype="categorical" />
  <DataField name="entity" optype="categorical" />
 </DataDictionary>
 <AssociationModel   minimumSupport="0.6"   minimumConfidence="0.5"
                     functionName="associationRules">
  <MiningSchema>
   <MiningField name="document_id" usageType="group" />
   <MiningField name="entity" usageType="predicted"/>
  </MiningSchema>
 </AssociationModel>
</PMML>
```

Fig. 2. An Example Association Rule Mining Query Written in PMML

2.3 Multi-level Association Rules

Association rule mining aims at finding interesting associations among large sets of data items. Let $I = \{i_1,...,i_n\}$ be a set of literals, called items. Let D be a data set of transactions where each transaction T is a set of items such that $T \subseteq I$. Then, an *association rule* derived from the data set D is an implication of the form $X \Rightarrow Y$ where $X \subset I$, $Y \subset I$ and $X \cap Y = \varnothing$. The usefulness of a rule $X \Rightarrow Y$ is measured using the *support* which is the proportion of transactions that contain both item sets X and Y. On the other hand, the interestingness of a rule is measured using the *confidence* which is the proportion of transactions containing item set Y to the ones containing item set X.

Multi-level association rule mining is to mine strong association rules among intra and inter different levels of abstraction given a transaction data set and a concept hierarchy. Privacy and sparsity of data in multidimensional space are among possible motivations behind multi-level association rule mining.

3 Privacy Preserving Data Mining Model Sharing (PPDMMS)

In this section, we present the problem of privacy preserving sharing of data mining models in order to provide privacy preserving data mining services on the web. Then, we state our assumptions and analyze the general requirements of an architecture designed for providing privacy preserving data mining services on the web. Finally, we present the proposed architecture together with a case study demonstrating the architecture.

3.1 Problem Statement

The generic problem of privacy preserving data mining model sharing can be stated as follows:

Let W be a data warehouse that consists of multiple databases and data mining models together with a set of privacy preferences P that specifies the constraints for access to data mining models. Given a data mining query Q, the problem of privacy preserving data mining model sharing is to find the set of all constraints that prevent the data mining query Q to extract any confidential information and to rewrite Q so that no confidential information is disclosed.

As an initial attempt for solving this specific problem we assume that the database schema is known to the data collectors, so that they can provide any pre-processing task specification within the data mining query. Moreover, we assume that the data collector follows the policy it has published for querying the data model, because the proposed architecture discovers the non-confidential parts of the requested model by looking at the privacy policy of the data collector.

General Requirements for PPDMMS

The general requirements of an architecture enabling privacy preserving sharing of data mining models can be enumerated as follows:

Privacy Policies. Together with their request for data, the data collectors must be able to specify their data practices via a policy. The policy must specify the intended purposes of data collection, the recipients of the collected data and the duration for which the collected data will be retained.

Privacy Preferences. In order to preserve the privacy of the data mining models, the data owner must be able to specify his preferences corresponding to the policies of data collectors. The preferences should specify the action (block/permit) to be taken as well as the constraints in order to restrict the access to the data mining models.

Data Requests. The data collectors should be able to express their data requests via the data mining queries. Therefore, the query language should either be capable of querying all types of data mining models or should be extendible.

Data Mining Models. The data owner should be able to express all types of data mining models together with its output patterns.

Constraints. The data owner should be able to express all types of constraints including data constraints (restricting the data set to be mined), level constraints (specifying the levels of data to be examined using a taxonomy), output constraints (restricting the output patterns of the data mining query) and interestingness constraints (specifying the interestingness of output patterns) in order to prevent disclosure of confidential portions of the data mining models.

3.2 PPDMMS Architecture

The proposed architecture fulfills the general requirements for PPDMMS by employing P3P, APPEL and PMML.

Privacy Policies. The privacy policies of data collectors are expressed via P3P Policies which answer the questions of "why", "for whom" and "how long" by their PURPOSE, RECIPIENT and RETENTION elements. Since, the DATA-GROUP element is incapable of expressing data collector's actual data request written as a data mining query, the EXTENSION element is used instead.

Privacy Preferences. The privacy preferences of data owners are expressed via APPEL. APPEL preferences contain both a privacy policy and an action (block, limited, request) to be taken for such a privacy policy. If the action is limited, the constraints for each policy are expressed using its EXTENSION element.

Data Requests, Constraints, Data Mining Models. The data mining queries (data requests), constraints on these queries and the data mining models which are the outputs of the constrained queries are expressed via PMML. PMML is designed to express generic data mining models. In order to express all types of data mining queries and constraints, PMML is extended using the EXTENSION element.

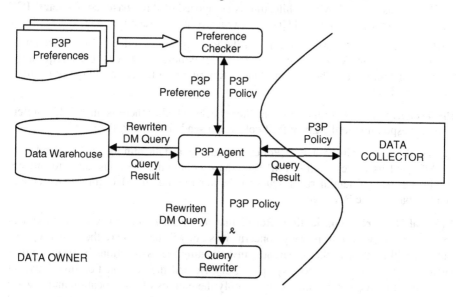

Fig. 3. Privacy Preserving Data Mining Model Sharing Architecture

```
<POLICY>
 <STATEMENT>
  <PURPOSE><develop/></PURPOSE>
  <RECIPIENT><ours/></RECIPIENT>
  <RETENTION><stated-purpose/></RETENTION>
  <DATA-GROUP>
   <DATA ref="#AssociationModel.Itemset"/>
   <DATA ref="#AssociationModel.AssociationRule"/>
  </DATA-GROUP>
  <EXTENSION>
   <PMML version="3.0" > ...
  <MiningBuildTask>  <Extension> <DataMining>
      <MiningData tableName="DOCUMENT_ENTITIES" />
  </DataMining> </Extension> </MiningBuildTask>
     ...
    <AssociationModel  minimumSupport="0.6"  minimumConfidence="0.5"
                       functionName="associationRules">
     <MiningSchema>
      <MiningField name="document_id" usageType="group" />
      <MiningField name="entity" usageType="predicted"/>
     </MiningSchema>
    </AssociationModel>
   </PMML>
  </EXTENSION>
 </STATEMENT>
</POLICY>
```

Fig. 4. An Example Privacy Policy

The proposed PPDMMS architecture is composed of three basic components, P3P Agent, Preference Checker and Query Rewriter, as can be seen in Fig. 3.

P3P Agent. The main responsibilities of the P3P Agent are to listen for the incoming query requests sent by the data collected via P3P Policies, to process these request via the help of Preference Checker and Query Rewriter and to return the query result to the Data Collector.

Preference. Checker. Preference Checker checks whether there is an APPEL preference corresponding to the given P3P Policy and sends it to the P3P Agent.

Query Rewriter. Given a P3P Policy containing a data mining query encoded in PMML, and its corresponding P3P Preference containing the constraints to prevent disclosure of confidential rules, Query Rewriter rewrites the data mining query and sends it back to the P3P Agent.

Medical Research Application. Recall that an organization owns a huge medical report repository. Due to privacy concerns it is not willing to share the actual reports, but still willing to help the researchers investigating the associations between entities such as gender, time, location, symptom, disease and medication. For simplicity, let us assume that the organization extracts only the entities of type location and disease for each document. Thus, the researchers can now query the associations between and location entities via an association rule mining query without explicitly accessing the confidential reports. An example P3P privacy policy is shown in Fig. 4. By sending this policy to the data owner, the data collector not only issues a data mining query that will mine DOCUMENT_ENTITIES table for association rules with a minimum support of 0.6 and a minimum confidence of 0.5, but also requests the resulting *Itemsets* and *AssociationRules* for research and development purposes.

Upon receiving the privacy policy, the P3P agent sends the policy to the preference checker. The preference checker checks whether there is an APPEL preference corresponding to this P3P policy. If there is such a preference, it sends this preference to the P3P agent. An example privacy preference corresponding to the example

```
<RULE behaviour="limited">
 <POLICY>
  <STATEMENT> <PURPOSE><develop/></PURPOSE>
  <DATA-GROUP>
   <DATA ref="#AssociationModel.Itemset"/>
   <DATA ref="#AssociationModel.AssociationRule"/>
  </DATA-GROUP>
  <EXTENSION> <PMML version="3.0" > ...
    <MiningBuildTask> <Extension> <DataMining>
      <MiningData tableName="DOCUMENT_ENTITIES"/>
      <Constraints>
       <RuleConstraints  maxRuleLength="2"/>
       <InterstingnessConstraint minSupport="0.8" minConfidence="0.5"/>
       <LevelConstraints>
        <Taxonomy name="City-State">
         <ChildParent childField="City" parentField="State">
           <InlineTable>
            <row><City>San Jose</City><State>CA</ State></row>
            <row><City>Long Beach</City><State>CA</ State></row>
            <row><City>New York</City><State>NY</State></row>
            <row><City>Everett</City><State>MA</State></row>
           </InlineTable>
         </ChildParent>
        </Taxonomy>
       </LevelConstraints>
      </Constraints>
    </DataMining> </Extension> </MiningBuildTask>
    ...
    <AssociationModel  functionName="associationRules">
     <MiningSchema>
      <MiningField name="document_id" usageType="group" />
      <MiningField name="entity" usageType="predicted"/>
     </MiningSchema>
    </AssociationModel>
   </PMML> </EXTENSION>
  </STATEMENT>
 </POLICY>
</RULE>
```

Fig. 5. An Example Privacy Preference

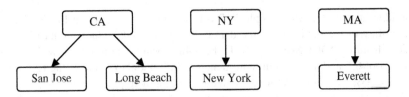

Fig. 6. An Example Taxonomy

policyis shown in Fig. 5. This preference limits the data mining queries (issued for the purpose of research and development) which will mine DOCUMENT_ENTITIES table for association rules with the following constraints:

Rule Constraint. limits the maximum allowed rule length to 2.

Interestingness Constraint. specifies the limit for minimum support and confidence as 0.8 and 0.5 respectively. Queries with lower minimum support and confidence values are restricted with these limits.

Level Constraint. forces the generalization of city entities to their corresponding state values according to the taxonomy given in Fig. 6.

Upon having the preference, the P3P agent sends this preference along with the query to the query rewriter. The query rewriter updates the data mining query and sends it back to the P3P agent. Finally, the P3P agent issues the rewritten query on the data warehouse and sends the resulting mining model to the data collector. The data mining model sent to the data collector as a result of the example policy constrained with the example privacy preference is shown in Fig. 7.

```
<PMML version="3.0" >   ...
<AssociationModel  functionName="associationRules"
    minimumConfidence="0.5"  minimumSupport="0.8"  numberOfItems="3"
    numberOfTransactions="4"  numberOfItemsets="3"   numberOfRules="2">

    ...
<Item id="1" value="NY" /> <Item id="2" value="MA" />
<Item id="3" value="cytomegalovirus" />
<Itemset id="1" support="1" numberOfItems="1">
  <ItemRef itemRef="1" />
</Itemset>
<Itemset id="2" support="1" numberOfItems="1">
  <ItemRef itemRef="3" />
</Itemset>
<Itemset id="3" support="1" numberOfItems="2">
  <ItemRef itemRef="1" /> <ItemRef itemRef="3" />
</Itemset>
<AssociationRule support="1" confidence="1"antecedent="1" consequent="2" />
<AssociationRule support="1" confidence="1"antecedent="2" consequent="1" />
</AssociationModel>
</PMML>
```

Fig. 7. Resulting Association Rule Model

4 Conclusion

In this paper, we propose an architecture in order to address the problem of privacy preserving data mining model sharing. As an initial attempt for solving this problem we analyze the general requirements of an architecture that enables sharing of privacy preserving data mining models and present the initials of the proposed system architecture together with an example case study for this specific problem. As a future work, we are going to define all possible extensions to PMML, P3P and APPEL in order to realize this architecture, express all types of constraints on data mining models, and develop algorithms for preference-policy matching and data mining query rewriting.

References

[1] R. Agrawal, R. Srikant. Privacy Preserving Data Mining. In *ACM SIGMOD Conference on Management of Data*, p 439–450, Dallas, Texas, May 2000.

[2] S. Sarawagi, S. H. Nagaralu. Data mining models as services on the Internet. *SIGKDD Explorations*, ACM Press, June 2000, pp 24-28.

[3] Verykios, V. S., Elmagarmid, A., Bertino, E., Saygin, Y., Dasseni, E. Association Rule Hiding. *IEEE TKDE*, 16(4), 2004.

[4] S. R. M. Oliviera, O. R. Zaïne. Foundations for an Access Control Model for Privacy Preservation in Multi-Relational Association Rule Mining. In *Proceedings of the IEEE International Conference on Privacy, Security and Data Mining*, p.19-26, December 01, 2002, Maebashi City, Japan.

[5] S. R. M. Oliveira, O. R. Zaiane, Y. Saygin. Secure Association Rule Sharing. In *Proceedings of the 8th Pacific-Asia Conference on Knowledge Discovery and Data Mining*. May, 2004, Sydney, Australia.

[6] H. Hacigumus, B. Iyer, C. Li, and S. Mehrotra. Executing SQL over Encrypted Data in the Database-Service-Provider Model. SIGMOD 2002.

[7] Predictive Model Markup Language (PMML). Data Mining Group. See http://www.dmg.org.

[8] The Platform for Privacy Preferences. See www.w3.org/TR/P3P/.

[9] L. Cranor, M. Langheinrich, M. Marchiori, M. Presler-Marshall, and J. Reagle. The Platform for Privacy Preferences 1.0 (P3P1.0) Specification. W3C Recommendation, April 2002.

[10] L. Cranor, M. Langheinrich, and M. Marchiori. A P3P Preference Exchange Language 1.0 (APPEL1.0). W3C Working Draft, April 2002.

Reading Your Keystroke: Whose Mail Is It?

Sylvia Mercado Kierkegaard

kierkegaard@privat.dk

Abstract. Employers want their employees to do their job and meet the company's goals. Legitimate electronic monitoring at work offers business organisations the opportunity to detect employees whose workplace behaviour indicates a serious problem. However, surveillance of employee's electronic mail is intrusion into the employee's private life. It can potentially undermine employees' respect for their employers and ruin previously good working relationships. There have been numerous litigations involving electronic mail, including several high-profile legal cases. Balancing the employer's right to monitor its workforce with the employees' right to privacy with respect to technology use is becoming an increasingly contentious issue in the workplace.

1 Introduction

The Internet has virtually changed the lifestyle of the consumer and business organizations. A vast amount of corporate communication takes place over the web, such as electronic mail (e-mail) and Instant Messaging (IM). Most companies provide employees with access to their electronic mail and the Internet. The Internet offers many opportunities for companies by reducing operating costs, enabling companies to monitor their competition, retrieve information, improve communication in the workplace and expand product lines. While advanced technology has brought significant efficiencies and opportunities to the workplace, it has also introduced new risks and liabilities for employers. Employees are using the Internet for personal use, whether for sending personal e-mail messages, playing games, downloading pornography, ordering goods online, and checking stock prices, or gambling. Some employers view Web surfing as a scourge that distracts employees and saps productivity, while others are less threatened by their employees' access to the Web.

As technology invades the workplace, concerns arise about employee privacy and to what extent employers can be connected to their employees. These problems are exacerbated as technological advances increase the employer's ability to monitor and communicate with the employee. The official definition in the (US) Privacy and Consumers Workers Act of the term "electronic monitoring" is the collection, storage, analysis, and reporting of information concerning an employee's activities by means of a computer, electronic observation and supervision, remote telephone surveillance telephone call accounting, or other form of visual, auditory, or computer-based surveillance conducted by any transfer of signals, writing, images, sounds, data, or intelligence of any nature transmitted in whole or in part by a wire, radio, electromagnetic, photo electronic, or photo-optical system. The term electronic moni-

S. Katsikas, J. López, G. Pernul (Eds.): TrustBus 2005, LNCS 3592, pp. 256–265, 2005.

toring in this paper includes the use of electronic devices to retrieve and store information, intercept and recover messages, and monitor, record and review electronic communications, etc.

Electronic mail and the Internet have transformed the relationship between employers and employees and have raised numerous issues over monitoring, privacy and data protection as well as new liabilities. Companies are looking for more efficiency, and they want to keep track of their worker's performance through electronic surveillance. However, they could face legal action from their employees because of a conflict between electronic monitoring and human rights law. What are the limits to employers' intrusions into employees' lives? This paper will look into the current laws and court decisions in Europe for a clear definition of the rights and limits of surveillance of electronic mails in the workplace.

2   Cyber Shenanigans and Monitoring Activities

Does the average employee spend an hour per day chatting online and downloading porn? According to the 2004 Workplace and Instant Messaging Survey of the of 840 U.S. companies by the American Management Association and the ePolicy Institute (Claburn , 2004), 90% of respondents spend up to 90 minutes per workday on IM and another 10% of employees spend more than half the workday (4-plus hours) on e-mail, with 86% engaged in personal correspondence. The majority (58%) of workplace users engage in personal IM chat. Survey respondents report sending and receiving the following types of inappropriate and potentially damaging IM content: attachments (19%); jokes, gossip, rumours, or disparaging remarks (16%); confidential information about the company, a co-worker, or client (9%); sexual, romantic, or pornographic content (6%). Sixty percent (60 %) of employers use software to monitor external (incoming and outgoing) e-mail.

According to a research study from Forrester Consulting (Leyden, 2004), 44 per cent of large US companies with 20,000 workers and above, pay someone to monitor the firm's outgoing mail, with 38 per cent regularly auditing email content. The omnibus study on outbound email security and content issues, co-sponsored by *Proofpoint*, found the following: more than 30% of all companies reported that they employ staff to monitor outbound email content. This technique is even more prevalent in large organizations: 43.6% of companies with more than 20,000 employees employ staff to monitor outbound email; and almost 33% of all companies reported that they conduct regular audits of outbound email content. More than 38% of large companies reported that they regularly audit the content of outbound email.

Web@Work (2004) is another comprehensive annual survey of the Internet and application usage in the workplace. Consistent with previous Web@Work studies, 51 percent of employees said they spend between one and five hours per week surfing the Internet at work for personal reasons, and those that admitted to personal surfing spend an average of 2 hours per week doing so.

Companies providing Internet access to employees do not only have the ability to make the workplace more productive, but can also provide more distraction, and increase a company's legal liability and security risk. E-mail and Internet misuse by staff has become the biggest disciplinary problem for employers. An exclusive survey by Personnel Today and KLegal (2002) shows that European employers have taken disciplinary action on more occasions in the past year against staff for misusing the Web than for dishonesty, violence and health and safety breaches combined. The survey of 212 employers finds that there were 358 disciplinary cases for Internet and e-mail use compared to a combined total of 326 cases for the other three categories. It reveals that the most common cyber crimes were excessive personal use of the Internet, sending pornographic e-mails and accessing pornographic websites (Staff Internet Abuse, 2002). With the continual blurring of the line between work and play, most employees do not feel that being able to use the Internet at work for personal tasks makes them less productive. In fact, 27 percent feel that it makes them more productive and 57 percent feel there is no change in their productivity one way or another.

3 Monitoring Devices

There are softwares available to employers that can monitor employee's e-mail use, Web sites visited, and what computer files the employee has accessed. Employers are now using these vulnerabilities in electronic mail to monitor employee electronic correspondence. According to the research firm Giga Information Group (Swanson, 2002), the market for Web-monitoring products reached $250 million in 2002, up from $180 million the previous, while the market for e-mail monitoring products hit $165 million, up from $110 million the year before. Within the past few years, employee monitoring, as measured by the sales of surveillance software, has increased at least twice as fast as the number of employees in the United States with Internet access, according to the study.

All monitoring softwares can be configured to block or quarantine messages based on keywords or phrases, which are used to detect e-mail with confidential content, e-mail with inappropriate (i.e., harassing or offensive) content, and spam messages. They all include some means of virus protection, the ability to block or delay messages based on size and number of recipients, and the ability to append a disclaimer or statement of confidentiality to an outgoing message. Some of these products also have features for monitoring message attachments and some monitor only e-mail that leaves or enters the corporate network. Other software available can record usage times, every stroke that is typed, and remotely monitor and shutdown an application! People involved in intensive word-processing and data entry jobs may be subject to keystroke monitoring. Such systems tell the manager how many keystrokes per hour each employee is performing. It also may inform employees if they are above or below the standard number of keystrokes expected. Regardless of format or software, all activities related to employee monitoring, like surveillance, is a highly complicated and controversial way to gather information for an investigation.

4 Rationales for Monitoring E-Mail

What use may be made of information that an employer gathers through its monitoring program? Companies monitor their employee's mail for the following reasons:

- Increased productivity. Net surfing and personal email waste company time and assets. Productivity will fall and take profitability with it.
- Trade secrets. There is the risk that an employee may disclose some confidential material in an email through misaddressing an email or forwarding trade secrets to a rival business or future employer.
- Legal Liability. Employees are unwittingly exposed to offensive graphic material on colleagues' computer screens.
- Support for claims. Electronic recording and storage may be considered part of a company's "due diligence" in keeping adequate records and files.
- System Overload. There are potential viruses into the company's network which needs monitoring.
- Prevent unwanted recognition of the company. Web visits can be traced back to company organization, either directly or through their Internet Service Provider (ISP).
- Performance Evaluation. Electronic monitoring can provide information on the performance of the employees in order to evaluate their courtesy and professionalism through the reviewing and monitoring of their email responses.
- Bandwidth conservation. Companies want to keep resources available for company business, identify large size e-mails, and reduce access to non -related web sites.
- Legal Compliance. The basic principle under vicarious liability is that employers are responsible for the actions of employees carried out in the course of employment.

Electronic monitoring may have real consequences for employees. Sanctions that have been imposed by companies for employees' use or abuse of electronic media at work include: dismissal, forced resignations, suspension, reprimands, wage deductions, access to Internet withdrawn and police action. However, electronic monitoring software meant to protect businesses and users against inappropriate web content could also enable unscrupulous businesses to discriminate against 'disloyal' staff. Fears have been raised that cynical organisations could use the system to detect employees who visit recruitment websites (Allen, 2001). According to the Congress's Office of Technology Assessment Report (1987), there is reason to believe that electronically monitoring the quantity or speed of work contributes to stress and stress-related illness. Monitoring often occurs in already stressful work circumstances, and the combination of surveillance with other stressors can push workers beyond reasonable tolerance levels.

The problem occurs when monitoring crosses the line from being informational to being invasive. When intrusive, personalized monitoring is taking place, working under surveillance becomes a source of worry for workers and results in an underlying sense of mistrust. Intruding into employees' private lives can potentially undermine employees' respect for their employers and ruin previously good working relationships. Keystroke monitoring has been linked with health problems including stress disabilities and physical problems like carpal tunnel syndrome (Privacy Rights Clearinghouse, 2005).The risk reduction has led to a Gestapo-like mentality that reduces trust between employers and employees and decreases productivity. Monitoring presents an "assault on personal dignity"(Rita C. Manning, 1997, p.187).

5 Legislations

Trust and Privacy are the major issues between the employers and the employees. Monitoring brings into conflict the employer's legitimate interest in protecting against the risks associated with online access for employees and the privacy interests of the employees. In the European Union, workers have adequate data protection rights although the law is still slightly unclear on the legality of electronic monitoring. The legal ambiguity of privacy laws have led to conflicting court decisions on the worker's right against their email surveillance. The issue is, of course, when do employer's legitimate business interests become an unacceptable invasion of the workers' privacy?

The rights of privacy in the workplace are guaranteed by the European Convention on Human Rights, Directive 95/46/EC on the protection of individuals with regards to the processing of personal data, Directive 2002/58/EC concerning the processing of personal data and the protection of privacy in the electronic communications sector, Article 286 EC Treaty, Regulation (EC) No. 45/2001 on the protection of individuals with regard to the processing of personal data, Charter of Fundamental Rights of the European Union, Council of Europe's Convention (108) for the Protection of Individuals with regard to Automatic Processing of Personal Data , and the European Convention for the Protection of Human Rights and Fundamental Freedoms (ECHR) .

Article 8 of the European Convention on Human Rights imposes the following duty on Member States (Right to respect for private and family life):

1. Everyone has the right to respect for his private and family life, his home and his correspondence.

2. There shall be no interference by a public authority with the exercise of this right except such as is in accordance with the law and is necessary in a democratic society in the interests of national security, public safety or the economic well-being of the country, for the prevention of disorder or crime, for the protection of health or morals, or for the protection of the rights and freedoms of others.

Article 8 provides protection against arbitrary (i.e. unjustified) interference with an individual's correspondence (expressly) and against similar surveillance of telephone conversations. The leading case concerning Article 8 was *Halford v. The United Kingdom* (73/1996/692/884) where the police intercepted the private office telephone of a senior police officer. The applicant in *Halford* alleged that her phone was being tapped in violations of Article 8 of the Convention. In the European Court of Human Rights view, telephone calls made from business premises as well as from the home may be covered by the notions of "private life" and "correspondence" within the meaning of Article 8 (1). The Applicant was not given any notice of any monitoring and therefore had a reasonable expectation that her calls would not be monitored. This was an important factor in the finding that there had been a breach of her right to privacy. The corollary of this decision is that if an employee does not have a reasonable expectation of privacy, then an employer may be free to monitor calls. This is subject to the overriding requirement that any monitoring must be for a defined purpose and must be proportionate to the objective it seeks to achieve.

In *Niemitz v. Germany* (ECHR, 23 November 1992, Series A No. 251/B, para. 29) the European Court of Human Rights pointed out, "Respect for private life must also comprise to a certain degree the right to establish and develop relationships with other human beings. There appears, furthermore, to be no reason of principle why this understanding of the notion of private life should be taken to exclude activities of a professional or business nature since it is, after all, in the course of their working lives that the majority of people have a significant, if not the greatest, opportunity of developing relationships with the outside world."

The principles of protecting written and telecommunication in Article 8 would support protection against arbitrary (i.e. unjustified) interference with an individual's correspondence including electronic mail. However, employees only have *"locus standi"* to bring the case before the European Court of Human Rights when the provisions of the Convention have not been incorporated into national law.

The Charter of Fundamental Rights of the European Union essentially repeats (in Article 7) the first paragraph of Article 8 of the Council of Europe Convention, stating that "Everyone has the right to respect for his or her private and family life, home and communications." To take account of developments in technology, the word 'correspondence' in the Convention has been replaced by 'communications'.

The European Union does not have a statutory provision that generally addresses an employer's right to monitor their employees' private electronic mail. However, there are provisions in the EU Data Protection   law that deal with privacy issues specific in employment situations. Directive 95/46/EC applies to the processing of personal data wholly or partly by automatic means, and to the processing otherwise than by automatic means of personal data which form part of a relevant filing system or are intended to form part of a filing system. "Personal data" means any information relating to an identified or identifiable natural person. Any collection, use or storage of information about workers by electronic means will almost certainly fall within the scope of the data protection legislation. The monitoring of workers' email or Internet access by the employer involves the processing of personal data. The Directive aims to protect the rights and freedoms of persons with respect to the processing of personal data by laying down guidelines determining when this processing is lawful. The guidelines relate to:

-   the quality of the data: personal data must be processed fairly and lawfully, and collected for specified, explicit and legitimate purposes. They must also be accurate and, where necessary, kept up to date. Data can only be collected for a specific purpose, and once that purpose has ended the data can no longer be held. (Article 6)
-   the legitimacy of data processing: personal data may be processed only if the data subject has unambiguously given his/her consent or processing is necessary: (Article 7) Restrictions on the processing of data require that the subject must be informed that monitoring is (or might be) taking place, and if the subject does not consent to the monitoring, they have additional rights to be informed what the purpose of the monitoring is and who is the "controller" of such monitoring for the performance of a contract to which the data subject is party .

The subject is also provided with rights of access to any data collected (Article 12). These are cases wherein the collection and distribution of data is "justified". Justifications include but are not limited to: individual consent, state security and state regulation of criminal activity (Article 13).

Article 29 sets up a Working Party on the Protection of Individuals with regard to the Processing of Personal Data, whose task is to examine any question covering the application of the national measures adopted under this Directive. In May 2002, the Working Party issued the Working Document on the Surveillance of Electronic Communications in the Workplace to complement Opinion 8/2001 in designing guidelines concerning the monitoring by the employer of e-mail and Internet use by workers. In the light of the jurisprudence of the European Courts of Human Rights, the Working Document offers guidance and concrete examples about what constitute legitimate monitoring activities and the acceptable limits of workers' surveillance by the employer. Three principles can be extracted from the case law on Article 8 of the European Convention for the Protection of Human Rights and Fundamental Freedoms:

a) Workers have a legitimate expectation of privacy at the workplace, which is not overridden by the fact that workers use communication devices or any other business facilities of the employer. However the provision of proper information by the employer to the worker may reduce the workers legitimate expectation of privacy.

b) The general principle of secrecy of correspondence covers communications at the workplace. This is likely to include electronic e-mail and related files attached thereto.

c) Respect for private life also includes to a certain degree the right to establish and develop relationships with other human beings. The fact that such relationships, to a great extent, take place at the workplace puts limits to employer's legitimate need for surveillance measures.

The Working Party is of the opinions that before employers process the personal data of employees, they should comply with the following principles:

-    **Necessity.** This principle means that the employer must check if any form of monitoring is absolutely necessary for a specified purpose before proceeding to engage in any such activity. It would only be in exceptional circumstances that the monitoring of a workers mail or Internet use would be considered necessary (e.g. criminal activity of the worker, detection of virus).

-    **Finality**. This principle means that data must be collected for a specified, explicit and legitimate purpose and not further processed in a way incompatible with those purposes. In this context the "compatibility" principle means, to use an example, that if the processing of data is justified on the basis of the security of the system, this data could not then be processed for another purpose such as for monitoring the behaviour of the worker.

-    **Transparency**. This principle means that an employer must be clear and open about his activities and that no covert e-mail monitoring is allowed except in those cases where a law in the Member State allows for that (for ex. Criminal activity).

-    **Legitimacy.** This principle means that any data processing operation can only take place if it has a legitimate purpose as pursued by the employer such as to prevent transmission of confidential information to a competitor, and it must not infringe upon the fundamental rights of the workers.

- **Proportionality**. This principle requires that personal data including those involved in monitoring must be adequate, relevant and not excessive with regard to achieving the purpose specified. The proportionality principle therefore rules out blanket monitoring of individual e-mails and Internet use of all staff other than where necessary for the purpose of ensuring the security of the system.

- **Data Accuracy** This principle requires that any data legitimately stored by an employer consisting of data from or related to a workers e-mail account or their use of the Internet must be accurate and not kept for longer than necessary.

- **Security.** This principle obliges the employer to implement appropriate technical and organizational measures to ensure that any personal data held by him is secure and safe from outside intrusion.

6 Cases and Decisions

The courts in various Member States have taken various interpretations of the Privacy Directive concerning electronic monitoring in the workplace. In *Onof v Nikon France* [Arret No. 4164 (Fr. Oct. 2, 2001)] the French Supreme Court ruled that an employee's right to private life under the Convention extended to private emails received at work, even where the employer had prohibited personal use of the facilities. In this case, Onof an employee of Nikon France was suspected of using working time for personal endeavours. Nikon France retrieved and read his email although it was marked "personal" and then dismissed him. The French Supreme Court held that the employer is not allowed to read his personal electronic mail and by doing do, is a violation of the fundamental right of secrecy in one's private correspondence even if the correspondence is conducted via an employer's email.

In Germany, the Karlsruhe Court of Appeals (Case docket number 1 WG 152/04, decision of January 10, 2005), decided a controversy between a university in Baden-Wuerttemberg and a former science employee that the purposeful filtering of emails could be punishable under German criminal law. After the employee and the university separated in 1998 in discord, the former employee maintained close contact with former science colleagues and friends by sending Emails to accounts on the university's mail server. The higher regional court affirmed in a country-wide first appellate decision on this topic that the former employee could succeed in filing criminal charges against the persons in charge at the university. In 2003, the university had arranged for Email traffic from and to former employees to become subject to technical filtering - without notification of either the sender or the recipient. According to the court ruling, someone who suppresses electronic letters as a responsible person for an enterprise or a university server renders himself punishable under German criminal law. Filtering of Email traffic is a violation of the secrecy of mail and letters. The opposite conclusion could solely be reached, according to the appellate court, with special justification, for example to defend against a virus attack (Sanctity of email, 2005).

In contrast, the Catalonian High Court (Spain) had ruled that an employer was entitled to dismiss an employee who was connected to an Internet game website during working hours for an average of 2-3 hours a day. It decided that this constituted a serious breach of his employment obligations. The court also said that measures adopted by the company to supervise the employee's PC use (software that supervised his PC use without his knowledge) did not breach his right to privacy. It was a justified measure because the employer had reasonable grounds to believe that the employee was breaching his obligations. It was also relevant because the supervision was made over a company computer and did not involve accessing the employee's private PC and password. The dismissal was therefore valid (Florez, 2001).

In *Moonsar v Fiveways Express Transport Ltd*, EAT (2004), in the office where Ms Moonsar worked as a data entry clerk, several male colleagues downloaded pornographic images from the Internet. Although they were not circulated to her, she worked in close proximity and was aware of what was happening. In addition to a successful race discrimination claim in connection with her unfair selection for redundancy, Moonsar claimed sexual harassment in respect of the pornographic material. The UK Employment Appeal Tribunal (EAT) ruled that in such cases, once a complaint had been made, the burden of proof transferred to the employer to disprove that she had suffered a detriment. The fact that she was nearby and aware of what was happening was sufficient to amount to harassment, and the employer had failed to show that Ms. Moonsar had not been affected (Personnel Today, 2004).

Judgments from the same country may appear contradictory. A woman sacked for using the office computer to book a holiday on the Internet lost her claim for unfair dismissal. An employment tribunal in Liverpool ruled that Lois Franxhi was guilty of misconduct and justifiably dismissed after using the computer at Focus Management Consultants in Cheshire, to make 150 searches on the Internet. A case of 150 searches constitutes concerted use as the employee is taking money from the employer and depriving the employer of the benefit (Herbert, 1999). An employment tribunal in Britain had also upheld a company's right to access its employees' e-mails in *Miseroy v Barclaycard*. Hilary Miseroy was sacked from the credit card firm over the content of e-mail messages on his computer. The two-day hearing in Bedford threw out Miseroy's claim of unfair dismissal, ruling the organisation had acted in a correct manner. Routine monitoring by the firm found 900 personal e-mails stored on Miseroy's computer (Personnel Today, 2003).

In a 1999 decision of the Dutch Data Protection Authority, it was decided that continuous monitoring of e-mail is not allowed, as there is no specified and legitimate purpose to such monitoring. This decision applies even where the employer's policy clearly states that the worker should have no expectation of privacy (Lee, 2000). A few common principles emerge from these and other cases. Court judgments in Denmark, Germany, the Netherlands and the UK have established the necessity for employers to have issued a clear policy or instructions on Internet/e-mail use before it is legitimate for them to dismiss or discipline employees on grounds of misuse, though one Dutch court has ruled that an employer had no obligation to give an employee prior notice that private use of Internet was not allowed. The courts in some countries - such as Germany, the Netherlands, Spain and the UK take a very dim view of employees using e-mail or the Internet for purposes of crime, harassment or distributing obscene, pornographic or offensive material (Delbert, Mormont & Schots, 2004).

7 Conclusion

Increasingly, employers are using technology to track the employee's workplace performance. Organizations would gain more benefit if they do not scrutinize their employees' every move. Basically, companies should only consider the monitoring of content if the record of traffic and the subject of e-mails achieve the business purpose and this must be communicated to the employees. Companies should not monitor the content of e-mail messages unless it is clear that the business purpose for which the monitoring is undertaken cannot be achieved by the use of a record of e-mail traffic. The best way for an employer to address the issue is to provide a clear, well-defined, written policy concerning the use of its e-mail system to every employee. It is imperative that the employer's policy advises employees of the employer's intent to monitor e-mail and Internet usage, and more importantly, to dispel any expectations of privacy in order to avoid claims of invasion of privacy. There must be discretion and objectivity, as well as an unambiguous consent from the employee. Any monitoring must be a proportionate and reasonable response to the risk faced by the employer. What is considered acceptable or normal must be defined. If electronic monitoring creates a morale problem, all of its value is diminished and the employer is better off, if he desists in his surveillance activities. A workplace policy should be in place in an open and transparent manner and must provide a balance between the legitimate rights of employers and the personal privacy rights of employees.

Do you really want to reprimand an employee for reading the day's front-page news?

References

1. Allen, P.: Staff under Threat from web Monitoring Kit. IT Week (2001)
2. Claburn, T.: Information Week.Tech Web Business Technology Network. (2004)
3. Delbert, C., Mormont, M., Schots, M.: New Technology and Respect for Privacy at the workplace. Institut des Sciences du Travail.eironline (2004)
4. Flórez, R.: More on email abuse. European Labor Law Bulletin (2001)
5. Lee, E.: Online Rights for Online Workers in Europe.UNI Europa (2000)
6. Leyden, J.: America a nation of corporate email snoops. The Registrar (2004)
7. Harris Interactive, Web@work Survey Results. Retrieved on 7 February, 2005, from, http://www.websense.com.au/company/news/research/webatwork2004.pdf
8. Herbert, I.: Court backs Dismissal of Net Surfer. Law Notes. Pearl Willis Law Site (1999)
9. Manning, R.: "Liberal and Communitarian Defenses of Workplace Privacy in Journal of Business Ethics 6, 8 (1997)
10. Privacy Rights Clearinghouse: Employee Monitoring, Is there Privacy in the Workplace? (2005) Retrieved 6 February, 2005, from, http://www.privacyrights.org/fs/fs7-work.htm
11. Sanctity of Email. Retrieved 1 March, 2005, from http://www.recht.us/
12. Staff internet abuse tops discipline. Personnel Today (2004)
13. Swanson, S.: Employers Take a Closer Look. Information Week (2002)
14. U.S. Congress, Office of Technology Assessment. The Electronic Supervisor: New Technology, New Tensions. OTA-CIT-333, September 1987.
15. Moonsar v Fiveways Express Transport Ltd, EAT. Personneltoday (2004)

A Novel Construction of Two-Party Private Bidding Protocols from Yao's Millionaires Problem

Huafei Zhu and Feng Bao

Department of Information Security, Institute for Infocomm Research, A-Star
{huafei, baofeng}@i2r.a-star.edu.sg

Abstract. In this paper, a new bidding protocol (in essence, it is Yao's millionaires problem) is implemented. We show that our implementation is provably secure in the common reference string model assuming that a static adversary corrupts one of the players.

Keywords: Bidding protocol, millionaires problem, secure two-party computation.

1 Introduction

As more business is conducted over the Internet, the security of two-party private bidding assumes increasing importance. In markets, business activities are coordinated through price, which is the value a business assigns to a resource. Since various business assign different values to resource, they need to negotiate to reach mutually acceptable agreements. Thus the technique of two-party private bidding provides a prospective realization to the business community. In essence, two-party private bidding can be stated as follows [5]: a player Alice wants to buy some good from another player Bob if the price is less than a. Bob would like to sell, but only for more than b, and neither of them wants to reveal the secret bounds a and b. Only if the result is $a \geq b$ does Alice have to reveal a and the deal takes place at this price. Thus, fundamentally, the study of two-party private bidding can be reduced to that of polynomial time evaluation of Yao's millionaires problem which is stated below [16]:

- On input a (a price offer of a player, say, Alice); and b (the fixed base price of another player, say, Bob)
- outputs a symbol λ indicating either accept if $a \geq b$ or reject if $a < b$ and at the same time there is no information leaked to any of the two players other than the result of computation.

Basically, a two-party private bidding protocol consists of two sub-protocols: a price comparison protocol – in essence, it is Yao's millionaires problem; and a fair contract signing protocol – if the agreed price a is revealed. The later topic has been extensively studied in the literature and hence we ignore the topic of fair contract signing protocol in this paper and refer to reader [1] and [2] for further reference. We thus focus our attention on the construction of efficient yet practical price comparison protocols.

S. Katsikas, J. López, G. Pernul (Eds.): TrustBus 2005, LNCS 3592, pp. 266–273, 2005.

1.1 Related Works

The development of techniques for general secure multi-party computation has shown that any two-party function can be computed securely (see [11] and [10] for further reference). Thus the technique aspects of Yao's millionaires problem is by no means new to cryptography. However, the generic secure multi-party computation does not ensure efficient implementation.

In CCS'99, Cachin proposed a novel construction of two-party private bidding protocols which combines homomorphic encryption with the Φ-hiding assumption [5]. Informally, Φ-hiding assumption states that it is computationally intractable to decide whether a given small prime divides $\phi(m)$, where m is a composite integer of unknown factorization. Since this assumption is relatively new, it is not widely accepted by cryptographic community. Thus any satisfactory implementation from different assumptions is certainly welcome.

In FC'02, Baudron and Stern [4] described a interesting auction protocol that enjoys the following properties: the biddings are submitted non-interactively and no information beyond the result is disclosed. Their solution uses a semi-trusted third party T who learns no information provided that he does not collude with any participant. The robustness against active cheating players is achieved through an extra mechanism for fair encryption of a bit.

Recent works on Yao's millionaires problem are mainly constructed from Oblivious transfers. The work of Ioannidis and Grama [13] is to find an efficient protocol for the Yao's millionaires' problem using 1-out of-2 oblivious transfers. Schoenmakers and Tuyls [15] proposed a interesting protocol of two-party computation based on the conditional gate which is based on ElGamal's encryption scheme. However, they only consider a multiplication gate for which the multiplier x is from a two-valued domain, whereas the multiplicand y is unrestricted. All the mentioned works above are provably secure in the semi-honest setting, thus any satisfactory solution to malicious probabilistic polynomial time (PPT) adversary is certainly welcome.

1.2 Our Works

In this paper, we propose the first efficient implementation of Yao's millionaires problem from Cramer-Damgård's secure linear-function evaluation protocol (LEP) for secret key zero-knowledge proof system (SKZK) [7]— a novel application of Cramer-Damgård's LEP protocol indeed. We remark that the efficiency of our implementation is due to that of the underlying Cramer-Damgård's LEP protocol. At a high level, our construction can be stated as follows.

-To securely implement the grater gate $b > a$, Alice chooses a random string $r_a \in [\lambda_1, \lambda_2]$ Bob chooses a random string $r_b \in [\lambda_3, \lambda_4]$. We assume that $\lambda_3 - \lambda_2 > \lambda$ and $\lambda_i > 0$, where λ is a security parameter related to the Baudot's protocol which will be explicitly stated in Section 3; Then two players are engaged in the LEP for secure greater gate evaluation according to the following steps:

- Step 1: On input (a, r_a) and (b, r_b), where $r_a \in [\lambda_1, \lambda_2]$ and $r_b \in [\lambda_3, \lambda_4]$ to evaluate the value $A =: (a - b)(r_a - r_b)$; Notice that A can be rewritten as follows: $A = (ar_a + s_a) - (ar_b + s_a) - (br_a + s_b) + (br_b + s_b)$, where s_a is a random string chosen by Alice from $\{0,1\}^{k_1}$ while $s_b \in \{0,1\}^{k_2}$ is chosen by Bob uniformly at random, k_1 and k_2 are secret parameters which will be explicitly stated in the Section 3 (all the computations are defined over integer domain $\mathcal{Z}$);

- Step 2: Alice and Bob run the LEP to compute $\beta_a =: (br_a + s_b)$ and $\beta_b =: (ar_b + s_a)$; At the end of execution of the protocol Alice obtains β_a while Bob obtains β_b;
- Step 3: Alice then sends $\gamma_a =: \alpha_a - \beta_a$ to Bob together with a proof that all values are correctly computed, while Bob sends $\gamma_b =: \alpha_b - \beta_b$ to Alice, together with a proof that all values are correctly computed, where $\alpha_a =: (ar_a + s_a)$ and $\alpha_b =: (br_b + s_b)$;
- Step 4: Alice and Bob computes the final value $\gamma := \gamma_a - \gamma_b$ locally;
- Step 5: $a < b$ if and only if $\gamma > 0$

Notice that, the LEP deployed in the above construction is provably secure in the common reference string model assuming that a static adversary corrupts P or V, and is our construction. Thus we have proposed efficient yet secure price negotiation protocols.

In summary, the main contribution of this paper are those — we first implement Yao's millionaires problem from Cramer-Damgård's secure linear-function evaluation protocol. Then we show that our implementation is provably secure in the common reference string model assuming that a static adversary corrupts one of the player. Finally we build a new two-party private bidding protocol as an immediately application of our implemented primitive.

2 Building Blocks

In this section, we briefly describe cryptographic primitives that are used to construct our oblivious polynomial evaluation.

2.1 Paillier's Public Key Encryption Scheme

Paillier investigated a novel computational problem, called Composite Residuosity Class Problem, and its applications to public key cryptography in [14]. Our construction will heavily rely on this probabilistic encryption scheme which is sketched below.

The public key is a k_1-bit RSA modulus $n = pq$, where p, q are two large safe primes. The plain-text space is Z_n and the cipher-text space is $Z_{n^2}^*$. To encrypt $\alpha \in Z_n$, one chooses $r \in Z_n^*$ uniformly at random and computes the cipher-text as $E_{PK}(a, r) = g^a r^n \bmod n^2$, where $g = (1 + n)$ has order n in $Z_{n^2}^*$. The private key is (p, q). It is straightforward to verify that $((1+n)^a r^n)^{\phi(n)} \bmod n^2 = 1 + an$, from which a can be computed.

The encryption function is homomorphic, i.e., $E_{PK}(a_1, r_1) \times E_{PK}(a_2, r_2) \bmod n^2 = E_{PK}(a_1 + a_2 \bmod n, r_1 \times r_2 \bmod n)$.

2.2 Fujisaki-Okamoto Commitment Scheme

Let s be a security parameter. The public key is a k_2-bit RSA modulus, where P, Q are two large safe primes. We assume that neither P nor V knows factorization N. Let g_1 be a generator of QR_N and g_2 be an element of large order of the group generated by g_1 such that both discrete logarithm of g_1 in base g_2 and the discrete logarithm of g_2 in base g_1 are unknown by P and V. We denote $C(a, r_a) = g_1^a g_2^{r_a}$ mod N a commitment to x in base (g_1, g_2), where r_a is randomly selected over $\{0, 2^s n\}$. This commitment scheme first appeared in [12] and reconsidered by Damgård and Fujisaki [9] is statistically secure commitment scheme, i.e.:

- P is unable to commit itself to two values a_1, a_2 such that $a_1 \neq a_2$ in $\mathcal{Z}$ by the same commitment unless P can factor N or solves the discrete logarithm of g_1 in base g_2 or the the discrete logarithm of g_2 in base g_1.
- $C(a, r_a)$ statistically reveals no information to V, i.e., there is a simulator which outputs simulated commitment to a which are statistically indistinguishable from true ones.

2.3 Proof of Knowledge of Encryptions

Given a cipher-text $\text{Enc}(x)$ which is computed from Paillier's encryption scheme, the prover should provide a proof that he knows x and x lies in a given interval I specified in the protocol. There is efficient protocol presented by Damgård and Jurik already [8]. The basic idea is the following: given $\text{Enc}(x)$, the prover provides a commitment $C(x, r_x)$ which is computed from Fujisaki-Okamoto commitment scheme, proves that the commitment contains the same number as the encryption, and then uses Baudot's protocol to prove that $m \in I$. More precisely,

1. Let T be the maximum bit length of x. The prover chooses at random u, an integer of length $T + 2k$, where k is a security parameter. He sends $a = \text{Enc}(u)$, $b = C(u)$ to the verifier;
2. The verifier chooses a l-bit challenge e;
3. The prover opens the encryption $a(\text{Enc}(x)^e) \bmod N^2$ and the commitment $bC(x)^e \bmod N$, to reveal in both cases the number $z = u + ex$. The verifier checks the opening were correct.

The protocol can be made non-interactive in the standard way using a hash function and the Fiat-Shamir paradigm. It is also statistically zero-knowledge in the random oracle mode.

2.4 Cramer-Damgård's Linear-Function Evaluation Protocol

In TCC'04, Cramer and Damgård [7] proposed an efficient secret-key generator for secret-key zero-knowledge proof system which is stated below and we refer reader to [7] for further reference:

1. V sends the key pk_V, the encryption $E_{pk_V}(\alpha)$ and proves in ZK that α is in the correct interval;

2. P chooses s, y as in the key generation for SKZK, makes commitments $S = Com_{pk_C}(s, rs)$, $Y = Com_{pk_C}(y, ry)$ and proves that he knows how to open these commitments to integers in the correct intervals. Similarly, he chooses $\bar{s}$, $\bar{y}$ as random numbers $2k$ bits longer than s respectively y, makes commitments $\bar{S} = Com_{pk_C}(\bar{s}, r_{\bar{s}})$, $Y = Com_{pk_C}(\bar{y}, r_{\bar{y}})$, and proves that $\bar{s}$, $\bar{y}$ were chosen in the correct intervals;

3. P uses the homomorphic property of the encryption scheme to compute encryptions $E_{pk_V}(\alpha s + y)$, $E_{pk_V}(\alpha \bar{s} + \bar{y})$, and sends these to V, who decrypts to get results β, respectively $\bar{\beta}$;

4. V sends a random k-bit challenge e. Both parties use the homomorphic properties of the commitment scheme to compute from S, Y, $\bar{S}$, $\bar{Y}$ commitments Z_s, Z_y to $z_s = \bar{s} + es$, $z_y = \bar{y} + ey$. P opens Z_s, Z_y to reveal z_s, z_y to V.

5. V checks that the openings were correct, and that $\bar{\beta} + e\beta = \alpha z_s + z_y$. If so, he accepts using α, β as keys to check proofs from P in the future. Output for P is (s, y).

The protocol described above is provably secure assuming a static adversary that corrupts P or V.

3 An Efficient Implementation of Yao's Millionaires Problem

In this section, we first present the security definition of Yao's millionaires problem; and then we make use of Cramer-Damgård's linear evaluation protocol as a subroutine to propose an efficient implementation of Yao's millionaires problem. Finally we show that our implementation is provably secure within our model.

3.1 The Definition of Security

We assume that a statistic PPT adversary corrupts either P or V (P refers to Alice while V refers to Bob in Yao's millionaires problem stated in Section 1) in our model. Thus, the security definition of Yao's millionaires problem is standard. That is,

- Security against malicious verifier – for each malicious V, there exists a simulator sim_V that plays the role of V in the ideal world such that for any polynomial time distinguisher D, the view of V in real conversation is computationally indistinguishable from that simulated by sim_V.
- Security against malicious verifier – for any malicious prover P, there exists a simulator sim_P that plays the role of P in the ideal world such that for any polynomial time distinguisher D, the view of P in real conversation is computationally indistinguishable from that simulated by sim_P.

Definition 1: A protocol securely implement Yao's millionaires problem, if it is secure against any PPT malicious verifier and any PPT malicious prover.

3.2   Our Implementation

We now describe our implement of Yao's millionaires problem in details.

- Initial phase: Alice holds a secret price offer $a \in \{0,1\}^{k_1}$, a random string $r_a \in [\lambda_1, \lambda_2]$ (an l_a-bit string) and $s_a \in \{0,1\}^{k_2}$, Alice then commits these values using Fujisaki-Okamoto commitment scheme. The commitment of a, r_a and s_a are denoted by $Com(a, u_a)$, $Com(r_a, v_a)$ and $Com(s_a, w_a)$ respectively; Similarly, Bob holds a secret base price $b \in \{0,1\}^{k_1}$, a random string $r_b \in [\lambda_3, \lambda_4]$ (an l_b-bit string) and $s_b \in \{0,1\}^{k_3}$. Bob then commits these values using the same commitment scheme. The commitment of b, r_b and s_b are denoted by $Com(b, u_b)$, $Com(r_b, v_b)$ and $Com(s_b, w_b)$ respectively; To ensure the security of our protocol, we assume that $\lambda_3 - \lambda_2 > \lambda$ and $\lambda \in \{0,1\}^l$, $k_2 \geq k_1 + l_b + k$ and $k_3 \geq k_1 + l_a + k$, where l should be sufficient long (e.g., l is length of 128-bit), and k, k_2 and k_3, l_a and l_b are all security parameters in our protocol. The following computations are defined over the integer domain $\mathcal{Z}$, thus we finally assume that the RSA moduli of the underlying Paillier's encryption [14] and that of Fujisaki-Okamoto's commitment scheme should be defined sufficient large (the public key of Fujisaki-Okamoto's commitment scheme is defined as the common reference string of our protocol).
- For fixed $C_a := Com(a, u_a)$, $C_{r_a} := Com(r_a, v_a)$ and $C_{s_a} := Com(s_a, w_a)$, Alice proves to Bob that she knows how to open the commitments of C_a, C_{r_a} and C_{s_a}. Furthermore Alice proves to Bob that $a \in \{0,1\}^{k_1}$, $r_a \in [\lambda_3, \lambda_4]$ and $s_a \in \{0,1\}^{k_2}$ using Boudot's protocol [3];
- For fixed $C_b := Com(b, u_b)$, $C_{r_b} := Com(r_b, v_b)$ and $C_{s_b} := Com(s_b, w_b)$, Bob proves to Alice that she knows how to open the commitments of C_b, C_{r_b} and C_{s_b}. Furthermore Bob proves to Alice that $b \in \{0,1\}^{k_1}$, $r_b \in [\lambda_1, \lambda_2]$ and $s_a \in \{0,1\}^{k_2}$ using Boudot's protocol [3];
- Alice and Bob then run together the Cramer-Damgård's linear-function evaluation protocol on input (C_a, C_{r_a}, C_{s_a}) and (C_b, C_{r_b}, C_{s_b}).
- At the end of execution of protocol, Alice obtains $\beta_a := (br_a + s_b)$ while Bob obtains $\beta_b = (ar_b + s_a)$;
- Alice then sends $\gamma_a =: \alpha_a - \beta_a$ to Bob, together with a proof that this value is correctly computed while Bob sends $\gamma_b =: \alpha_b - \beta_b$ to Alice, together with a proof that this value is correctly computed, where $\alpha_a =: (ar_a + s_a)$ and $\alpha_b =: (br_b + s_b)$.

  The proof of knowledge can be abstracted as the following problems: 1) given $C(i) = g^i h^{r_i}$, $c(j) = g^j h^{r_j}$, and $c(k) = g^k h^{r_k}$, Alice proves to Bob that she knows how to open the commitment $C(\delta) := C(ij + k)$ and δ is correctly computed from the above commitments; and 2) given $C(\delta)$ and $Enc(x)$, Alice proves to Bob that the value $\xi =: \delta\text{-}x$ is correctly computed from these given values. Notice that both problems in a similar way as the LEP protocol.
- Alice (Bob) computes the final value $\gamma := \gamma_a - \gamma_b$ respectively;
- $a < b$ if and only if $\gamma > 0$

3.3 The Proof of Security

Theorem: Our protocol is secure against malicious verifier and malicious prover assuming a static adversary that corrupts Alice or Bob in the common reference model. Proof: In general, if Alice is malicious, then we need to show the existence of sim_{Alice} which plays the role of Alice in the ideal world. In this time sim_{Alice} first generates system parameters as the real protocol described above except that sim_{Alice} knows the auxiliary trapdoor information of the underlying commitment scheme. We then consider two cases below:

- Case 1: Suppose Alice is a malicious verifier, i.e., Alice is one in protocol who obtains $\beta_a := (br_a + s_b)$, then there exists PPT simulator sim_{A_1} for Alice who run together with Bob in the Cramer-Damgård's linear-function evaluation protocol on input (C_a, C_{r_a}, C_{s_a}) and (C_b, C_{r_b}, C_{s_b}). Notice that the existence of sim_{A_1} has been shown in [7] and the simulation of Alice after the execution of the linear-function evaluation protocol also has already shown by Boudot [3]. By combining the two simulators together, we know that there is a simulator that simulates Alice's entire views.
- Case 2: Suppose Alice is a malicious prover, i.e., Alice is one in protocol who obtains $\beta_a := (ar_b + s_a)$, then there exists PPT simulator sim_{A_2} for Alice who run together with Bob in the Cramer-Damgård's linear-function evaluation protocol on input (C_a, C_{r_a}, C_{s_a}) and (C_b, C_{r_b}, C_{s_b}). Notice that the existence of sim_{A_2} has been shown that in [7] and the simulation of Alice after the execution of the linear-function evaluation protocol also has already shown by Boudot [3]. By combining the two simulators together, we know that there is a simulator that simulates Alice's entire views.

In each case, for a real world PPT Alice, we know that there is a simulator sim_{Alice} so that for any polynomial time distinguisher D, the view of Alice in real conversation is computationally indistinguishable from that simulated by sim_{Alice}. Similarly, we can show that our protocol is secure against any PPT malicious prover. By combining two statements, we know that our protocol is secure within our model assuming that a static adversary corrupts one of the player.

Once given a secure implementation of Yao's millionaires problem, an efficient private bidding protocol can be derived trivially according to the strategy specified in Section 1. In this way, we achieve our goal described in the abstract.

4 Conclusion

In this paper, a novel implementation of Yao's millionaires problem from Cramer-Damgård's secure linear-function evaluation protocol (LEP) [7] has been presented. And we have built a new two-party private bidding protocols from this efficiently implemented cryptographic primitive. Furthermore, we have shown that our two-party private bidding protocols is provably secure in the common reference string model assuming that a static adversary corrupts one of the player.

References

1. N. Asokan, V. Shoup, M. Waidner: Optimistic Fair Exchange of Digital Signatures (Extended Abstract). EUROCRYPT 1998: 591-606.
2. N. Asokan, Victor Shoup, Michael Waidner: Optimistic Fair Exchange of Digital Signatures. IEEE JOurnal on Selected Areas in Communications, Vol 18, No.4, 2000, 593-610.
3. Fabrice Boudot: Efficient Proofs that a Committed Number Lies in an Interval. Proc. of EUROCRYPT 2000: 431-444, Springer Verlag.
4. Olivier Baudron and Jacques Stern. Non-interactive Private Auctions. P. Syverson (Ed.): FC 2001, LNCS 2339, pp. 364-377, 2002.
5. Christian Cachin: Efficient Private Bidding and Auctions with an Oblivious Third Party. ACM Conference on Computer and Communications Security 1999: 120-127.
6. Christian Cachin, Silvio Micali, Markus Stadler: Computationally Private Information Retrieval with Polylogarithmic Communication. EUROCRYPT 1999: 402-414.
7. Ronald Cramer, Ivan Damgård: Secret-Key Zero-Knowlegde and Non-interactive Verifiable Exponentiation. TCC 2004: 223-237.
8. Ivan Damgård, Mads Jurik: Client/Server Tradeoffs for Online Elections. Proc. of Public Key Cryptography 2002: 125-140. Springer Verlag.
9. Ivan Damgård, Eiichiro Fujisaki: A Statistically-Hiding Integer Commitment Scheme Based on Groups with Hidden Order. Proc. of ASIACRYPT 2002: 125-142, Springer Verlag.
10. GOLDREICH, O. Secure multi-party computation. Manuscript, 1998.
11. GOLDREICH, O., MICALI, S., WIGDERSON, A. How to play any mental game or a completeness theorem for protocols with honest majority. In Proc. 19th Annual A CM Symposium on Theory of Computing (STOC) (1987), pp. 218-229.
12. E. Fujisaki, T. Okamoto. Statistically zero knowledge protocols to prove modular polynomial relations. Crypto'97. 16-30, 1997.
13. Ioannis Ioannidis and Ananth Grama. An efficient protocol for yao's millionaires' problem. In Proceedings of the 36th Hawaii Internatinal Conference on System Sciences 2003, 2003.
14. Pascal Paillier: Public-Key Cryptosystems Based on Composite Degree Residuosity Classes. Proc. of EUROCRYPT 1999: 223-238, Springer Verlag.
15. Berry Schoenmakers and Pim Tuyls. Pratical two-party computation based on the conditional gate. In Proceedings of Advances in Cryptology - ASIACRYPT'04, volume 3329 of LNCS, pages 119-136. Springer-Verlag, 2004.
16. A. Yao: Protocols for secure computations. Proc. 23rd IEEE Symposium on Foundations of Computer Science (FOCS'82), pages 160-164. IEEE Computer Society, 1982.

An Improved Double Auction Protocol Against False Bids

JungHoon Ha[1], Jianying Zhou[2], and SangJae Moon[1]

[1] School of Electrical Eng. & Computer Science,
Kyungpook National University, Daegu, Korea
short98@ee.knu.ac.kr, sjmoon@knu.ac.kr
[2] Institute for Infocomm Res earch (I^2R),
21 Heng Mui Keng Terrace, Singapore 119613
jyzhou@i2r.a-star.edu.sg

Abstract. M. Yokoo *et al.* analyzed some weaknesses in McAfee's double auction (MCD) protocol and proposed a robust threshold price double auction (TPD) protocol against false-name bids. Unfortunately, as their protocol strongly depends on the trust of auctioneer, the auctioneer's misbehavior may fail an auction process. In addition, their scheme is in fact not robust in terms of *comprehensive false bids*. In this paper, we further investigate weaknesses in both MCD and TPD protocols, and then propose an improved double auction protocol against false bids. We also extend it for a practical and secure double auction implementation.

1 Introduction

Currently, many auction services exist on the Internet that satisfies a variety of requirements. Auction protocols can be classified into two types, namely *one-sided auction protocols* in which a single seller (or buyer) accepts bids from multiple buyers (or seller), and two-sided or *double auction protocols* in which multiple buyers and sellers are permitted to bid/ask[1] for designated goods [2]. For one-sided auctions, such as English auction, Vickrey auction and sealed-bid auction, there have been many papers in the literature considering various security properties [4,5,9,11]. However, not much research has been done regarding the security issues in double auctions.

Recently, Wang and Leung [12] proposed a set of double auction protocols based on McAfee's [6] and Yokoo's [7] protocols. Even though their scheme possesses good security property such as full privacy protection, in fact, it is not secure due to the original weakness in McAfee's and Yokoo's protocols.

Yokoo showed that McAfee's protocol is vulnerable against false name bids which are made under a fictitious name, and then proposed a robust threshold price double auction protocol against false name bids [7,8]. As Yokoo's protocol strongly depends on the trust of auctioneer, auctioneer's misbehavior may fail

---

[1] We use the term *bid* for a buyer's declaration of value, and *ask* for a seller's declaration of value.

S. Katsikas, J. López, G. Pernul (Eds.): TrustBus 2005, LNCS 3592, pp. 274–287, 2005.

an auction process. In addition, their scheme is in fact not robust in terms of *comprehensive false bids*.

In this paper, we analyze some weaknesses in both McAfee's and Yokoo's protocols, and then propose an improved double auction protocol against false bids. Moreover, we extend it for a practical and secure double auction implementation. This is based on the improved McAfee's protocol and an anonymous signature of knowledge. In appendix, we analyze the security and efficiency of the proposed scheme.

2 MCD Protocol

In this section, we first describe McAfee's double auction protocol [6] and then analyze its weakness. We call this protocol the MCD protocol.

2.1 Protocol Description

Let declared buyers' valuations (*bids*) be $b_1, \ldots, b_m$ and declared sellers' valuations (*asks*) be $a_1, \ldots, a_n$, where

$$b_{(1)} \geq b_{(2)} \geq \ldots \geq b_{(m)} \quad \text{and} \quad a_{(1)} \leq a_{(2)} \leq \ldots \leq a_{(n)}$$

We use the notation (i) for the i-th highest valuation of buyers and the i-th lowest valuation of sellers. Choose k so that $b_{(k)} \geq a_{(k)}$ and $b_{(k+1)} < a_{(k+1)}$ hold. Since for (1) to (k), the evaluation value of the buyers is larger than that of the sellers, at most k trades are possible. The candidate of a trading price p_t is defined as

$$p_t = \tfrac{1}{2}(b_{(k+1)} + a_{(k+1)})$$

The MCD protocol works as follows,

1. If $a_{(k)} \leq p_t \leq b_{(k)}$ holds, the buyers/sellers from (1) to (k) trade at price p_t.
2. If $p_t > b_{(k)}$ or $p_t < a_{(k)}$ holds, the buyers/sellers from (1) to $(k-1)$ trade. Each buyer pays $b_{(k)}$, and each seller gets $a_{(k)}$.

If the second condition holds, since the price for buyers $b_{(k)}$ is larger than the price for sellers $a_{(k)}$, the amount $(k-1) \cdot (b_{(k)} - a_{(k)})$ is left over. It is usually assumed that the auctioneer receives this amount.

2.2 Weakness in MCD Scheme

M. Yokoo described that the MCD protocol is vulnerable against false name bids which are made under a fictitious name, such as using multiple e-mail address [7,8]. However, these malicious actions can be easily prevented by limiting multiple submission using entity authentication of registration phase and cryptographic devices. We will explain it in section 5. In addition, MCD protocol has another weakness. To explain it, we expand the meaning of the false name bids. That is, we define the word, *comprehensive false bids*, in which buyers or sellers submit even higher or lower bids than their true valuations to succeed in auction, but they in fact aren't willing to pay these valuations[2]. To have a clear understanding, we consider a simple example.

Example 1. Let us assume the true valuations of buyers and sellers are as follows.

- Buyers' valuations: $20 > 18 > 16 > 14$
- Sellers' valuations: $13 < 15 < 17 < 19$

If each participant truthfully declares his valuation, the first condition of the MCD protocol holds, and buyers and sellers from (1) and (2) trade at the price $p_t = (16 + 17)/2 = 16.5$. On the other hand, if the buyer submits a very high bid 100 instead of 14 to succeed in an auction, the declared valuations become as follows.

- Buyers' valuations: $100 > 20 > 18 > 16$
- Sellers' valuations: $13 < 15 < 17 < 19$

In this case, the number of traders[3] changes and the buyer submitting 100 instead of 14 becomes a trader, but he just pays the trading price $p_t = (16+19)/2 = 17.5$ instead of 100. We can consider his bidding as false bid in comprehensive meaning. If the buyer asserts that his bidding is true valuation, we have no idea but to trust him. As another example, consider the seller submitting 2 instead of 19. In fact, she doesn't want to sell some goods at the price 2.

- Buyers' valuations: $20 > 18 > 16 > 14$
- Sellers' valuations: $2 < 13 < 15 < 17$

In this case, the number of traders changes and the seller submitting 2 becomes a trader. People can think her bidding false because she submitted a very low valuation compared with valuations of other sellers. Unfortunately, since there is no proof to explain her false valuation, we have to believe her, so that she can trade at the price $p_t = (16 + 15)/2 = 15.5$.

From the above example 1, we know that whoever submits very high or low bid/ask can always become a trader, while he or she just pays or gets the reasonable price. Thus, any disadvantage has to be imposed for him or her submitting a false bid. We explain how to solve this problem in section 4.

3   TPD protocol

In this section, we review Yokoo's threshold price double auction protocol [8] and analyze its weakness. We call this protocol the TPD protocol.

---

[2] Hereinafter, the word *false bids* will be used including both *comprehensive false bids* and *false name bids* for the sake of convenience.

[3] Traders means the winning buyers or sellers in our scheme.

3.1   Protocol Description

First, the auctioneer determines a *threshold price* r. Auctioneer is a non-trading agent who does not desire to buy or sell the goods. He determines this threshold price without consulting the declared valuations of buyers and sellers. The declared buyers' valuations are $b_1, \ldots, b_m$ and declared sellers' valuations are $a_1, \ldots, a_n$, where

$$b_{(1)} \geq \ldots \geq b_{(i)} \geq r > b_{(i+1)} \geq \ldots \geq b_{(m)},$$
$$a_{(1)} \leq \ldots \leq a_{(j)} \leq r < a_{(j+1)} \leq \ldots \leq a_{(n)}$$

TPD protocol is defined as follows,

1. When $i = j$: the buyers and sellers from (1) to (i) trade at the price r.
2. When $i > j$: the buyers and sellers from (1) to (j) trade. Each buyer pays $b_{(j+1)}$ and each seller gets r. The auctioneer gets the amount of $j(b_{(j+1)} - r)$.
3. When $i < j$: the buyers and sellers from (1) to (i) trade. Each buyer pays r and each seller gets a_{i+1}. The auctioneer gets the amount of $i(r - a_{(i+1)})$.

3.2   Weakness in TPD Scheme

TPD protocol also has the same weakness we described in section 2.2. Here we describe another weakness in TPD protocol. TPD protocol makes two assumptions about the auctioneer, that is, the auctioneer is a non-trading agent and determines the threshold price without consulting with buyers and sellers. Even though the auctioneer cannot attend an auction process, he may desire to make more profit by choosing the relevant threshold price r. We give an example where the earnings of the auctioneer and the number of traders change with the threshold price r.

Example 2. We use the same example of TPD protocol [8]. Let us assume the true valuations of buyers and sellers are as follows.

- Buyers' valuations: $9 > 8 > 7 > 4$
- Sellers' valuations: $2 < 3 < 4 < 12$

1. When the auctioneer chooses $r = 6$, because this corresponds to case (1) of TPD protocol, the buyers and sellers from (1) to (3) trade at the price $r = 6$. At this time, the auctioneer cannot have any profit by the rules of TPD protocol.
2. When the auctioneer chooses $r = 3.5$, because this corresponds to case (2) of TPD protocol, the buyers and sellers from (1) to (2) trade. Each seller gets the threshold price $r = 3.5$ and each buyer pays 7. At this time, the auctioneers gets the profit $2 \cdot (7 - 3.5) = 7$.
3. When the auctioneer chooses $r = 8.5$, because this corresponds to case (3) of TPD protocol, only one buyer and seller can trade. The buyer pays the threshold price $r = 8.5$ and the seller gets 3. At this time, the auctioneers gets the profit $1 \cdot (8.5 - 3) = 5.5$.

In the above example 2, the auctioneer's profit depends on his selection of the threshold price r, so that the auctioneer will determine the threshold price r as 3.5 to get maximum profit[4]. In TPD protocol, since the threshold price is released after all participants have bidden, the auctioneer can choose the relevant r to make more earnings. His action can determine not only his own earnings but also the number of traders. That is, the number of traders including both winning buyers and sellers is 6, 4, 2 in cases (1), (2), (3), respectively. Even though many buyers and sellers participate in the auction process, the number of traders can be limited by the auctioneer due to his profit. In fact, this property is not desirable because the trading price doesn't depends on the demand and supply of buyers and sellers but is determined by the auctioneer's profit.

4   Improved Double Auction Protocol Against False Bids

In this section, we propose an improved double auction protocol against false bids and verify it by means of an example.

4.1   Notation

B_i, b_i : an identity and a bid of i-th buyer $(i = 1, .., m)$
S_j, a_j : an identity and an ask of j-th seller $(j = 1, .., n)$
$\mathcal{P}_{B_i}, \mathcal{I}_{S_j}$: a payment of B_i and an income of S_j, respectively
$\mathcal{U}_{B_i}, \mathcal{U}_{S_j}$: utility of B_i and S_j, respectively
$\mathcal{E}_A$: earnings of auctioneer
p_s : standard price

4.2   Protocol Description

To reflect a liberal economy and competitive pricing well, our scheme is based on demand and supply of buyers and sellers instead of threshold price. Our scheme is in fact based on MCD protocol, but we change the terms of payment and income for buyers and sellers, and add some notations for a definite analysis. That is, to explain an advantage of buyer, seller and auctioneer by an auction, we define both *utility* of participants, $\mathcal{U}$, and *earnings* of an auctioneer, $\mathcal{E}$. We call this protocol the improved MCD protocol.

Let a declared valuation of buyer B_i be b_i (*bid*) and a declared valuation of seller S_j be a_j (*ask*), where $i = 1, \ldots, m$ and $j = 1, \ldots, n$. The declared valuations are as follows[5]:

$$b_{(1)} \geq \ldots \geq b_{(f)} \geq \ldots \geq b_{(m)} \quad \text{and} \quad a_{(1)} \leq \ldots \leq a_{(f)} \leq \ldots \leq a_{(n)}$$

---

[4] In fact, the auctioneer can choose another threshold price r by considering not only above 3 cases but also other cases.

[5] The submitted b_i and a_j are rearranged in the prices. At this time, to avoid the notation confusion, we use $b_{(i)}$ and $a_{(j)}$ for rearranged bids and asks.

We use the notation (f) for the f-th highest valuation of buyers and the f-th lowest valuation of sellers. Let the buyer corresponding to $b_{(f)}$ be $B_{(f)}$ and the seller corresponding to $a_{(f)}$ be $S_{(f)}$. Choose k so that $b_{(k)} \geq a_{(k)}$ and $b_{(k+1)} < a_{(k+1)}$ hold. Since for (1) to (k), the evaluation value of the buyers is larger than that of the sellers, at most k trades are possible. To set a standard for trading price, we define standard price as follows:

$$p_s = \tfrac{1}{2}(b_{(k+1)} + a_{(k+1)})$$

The improved MCD protocol works as follows,

1. If $a_{(k)} \leq p_s \leq b_{(k)}$ holds, the trade corresponding to the buyers/sellers from (1) to (k) is possible.

   - Each buyer $B_{(f)}$ pays $\mathcal{P}_{B_{(f)}} = \tfrac{1}{2}(b_{(f)} + p_s)$ and gets an utility $\mathcal{U}_{B_{(f)}} = b_{(f)} - \mathcal{P}_{B_{(f)}} = \tfrac{1}{2}(b_{(f)} - p_s)$,
   - Each seller $S_{(f)}$ gets $\mathcal{I}_{S_{(f)}} = \tfrac{1}{2}(a_{(f)} + p_s)$ and an utility $\mathcal{U}_{S_{(f)}} = \mathcal{I}_{S_{(f)}} - a_{(f)} = \tfrac{1}{2}(p_s - a_{(f)})$,
   - The auctioneer gets $\mathcal{E}_A = \sum_{f=1}^{k} \mathcal{P}_{B_{(f)}} - \sum_{f=1}^{k} \mathcal{I}_{S_{(f)}} = \sum_{f=1}^{k} \tfrac{1}{2}(b_{(f)} - a_{(f)})$, where $f = 1, \ldots, k$.

2. If $p_s > b_{(k)}$ or $p_s < a_{(k)}$ holds, the buyers/sellers from (1) to $(k-1)$ trade.

   - Each buyer $B_{(f)}$ pays $\mathcal{P}_{B_{(f)}} = \tfrac{1}{2}(b_{(f)} + p_s)$ and gets an utility $\mathcal{U}_{B_{(f)}} = b_{(f)} - \mathcal{P}_{B_{(f)}} = \tfrac{1}{2}(b_{(f)} - p_s)$,
   - Each seller $S_{(f)}$ gets $\mathcal{I}_{S_{(f)}} = \tfrac{1}{2}(a_{(f)} + p_s)$ and an utility $\mathcal{U}_{S_{(f)}} = \mathcal{I}_{S_{(f)}} - a_{(f)} = \tfrac{1}{2}(p_s - a_{(f)})$,
   - The auctioneer gets $\mathcal{E}_A = \sum_{f=1}^{k-1} \mathcal{P}_{B_{(f)}} - \sum_{f=1}^{k-1} \mathcal{I}_{S_{(f)}} = \sum_{f=1}^{k-1} \tfrac{1}{2}(b_{(f)} - a_{(f)})$, where $f = 1, \ldots, k-1$.

4.3   Example

Example 3. Let us assume the valuations are identical to Example 1.

- Buyers' valuations: $20 > 18 > 16 > 14$
- Sellers' valuations: $13 < 15 < 17 < 19$

In this case, because the standard price is $p_s = \tfrac{1}{2}(16 + 17) = 16.5$, buyers and sellers from (1) to (2) can trade. The buyers B_1 and B_2 pay $\mathcal{P}_{B_1} = 18.25$ and $\mathcal{P}_{B_2} = 17.25$, respectively. The sellers S_1 and S_2 get $\mathcal{I}_{S_1} = 14.75$ and $\mathcal{I}_{S_2} = 15.75$, respectively. At this time, the earnings of auctioneer are $\mathcal{E}_A = 5$. Table 1 represents all auction information related to example 3. From table 1, we know that buyer submitting the higher bid has the higher utility though he makes more payment compared with another buyer. This is desirable because he has more advantage compared with his own valuation. The case of sellers is similar to it of buyers. On the other hand, if the buyer submits a very high bid 100 instead of 14 to succeed in an auction, the declared valuations become as follows. (*We will consider it as false bid.*)

Table 1. Auction results when participants submit true valuations

	$B_{(1)}$	$B_{(2)}$	$B_{(3)}$	$B_{(4)}$	$S_{(1)}$	$S_{(2)}$	$S_{(3)}$	$S_{(4)}$
Identity	B_1	B_2	B_3	B_4	S_1	S_2	S_3	S_4
$b_{(f)}/a_{(f)}$	20	18	16	14	13	15	17	19
p_s				$(16+17)/2 = 16.5$				
Trader	Y	Y	N	N	Y	Y	N	N
$\mathcal{P}_{B_{(f)}}/\mathcal{I}_{S_{(f)}}$	18.25	17.25	–	–	14.75	15.75	–	–
$\mathcal{U}_{B_{(f)}}/\mathcal{U}_{S_{(f)}}$	1.75	0.75	–	–	1.75	0.75	–	–
$\mathcal{E}_A$				5				

- Buyers' valuations: $100 > 20 > 18 > 16$
- Sellers' valuations: $13 < 15 < 17 < 19$

In this case, the number of traders changes and the buyer submitting 100 instead of 14 becomes a trader, but he has to pay much higher $P_{B_4} = 58.75$ than other traders. Even though he has very high utility compared with other buyers, it is useless for him because his bidding 100 is false. Thus, the auctioneer can make more profit. Table 2 represents auction results for the false bid of buyer B_4.

Table 2. Auction results when the buyer B_4 submit a false bid

	$B_{(1)}$	$B_{(2)}$	$B_{(3)}$	$B_{(4)}$	$S_{(1)}$	$S_{(2)}$	$S_{(3)}$	$S_{(4)}$
Identity	B_4	B_1	B_2	B_3	S_1	S_2	S_3	S_4
$b_{(f)}/a_{(f)}$	100	20	18	16	13	15	17	19
p_s				$(16+19)/2 = 17.5$				
Trader	Y	Y	Y	N	Y	Y	Y	N
$\mathcal{P}_{B_{(f)}}/\mathcal{I}_{S_{(f)}}$	58.75	18.75	17.75	–	15.25	16.25	17.25	–
$\mathcal{U}_{B_{(f)}}/\mathcal{U}_{S_{(f)}}$	41.25	1.25	0.25	–	2.25	1.25	0.25	–
$\mathcal{E}_A$				46.5				

In the above example 3, even though some participants by submitting a false bid or ask can become traders, they have to be willing to receive disadvantage. That is, buyers have to make more payment and sellers must accept much lower income. If participants are rational, they will not submit false bids receiving disadvantage, thus our proposed scheme is robust against false bids.

5   Extension of Improved MCD Protocol

In this section, we extend the improved MCD protocol to implement a secure and practical double auction protocol. To meet security requirements of double auction protocol such as anonymity, impossibility of impersonation, non-repudiation, public verifiability, and so on, we use registration phase and an anonymous signature of knowledge. The trading price and the number of traders are determined by only buyers' and sellers' valuations and our scheme has no limitation for bidding price, while the bidding price or step is limited or preset by auctioneer or auction manager in some auction researches [10,12].

5.1   Cryptographic Primitive

Signature of Knowledge. We use the signature of knowledge introduced by B. Lee *et al.* [5] as anonymous signature, in which they extended the signature of knowledge discrete logarithm introduced by Camenisch and Stadler [1].

That is, it can be used as an anonymous signature if (y^r, g^r) are challenged for a secret random number $r \in \mathbb{Z}_q$ instead of (y, g) of Camenisch and Stadler' scheme. The signer computes (c, s) satisfying $c \stackrel{?}{=} h(m\|y^r\|g^r\|(g^r)^s(y^r)^c)$ for challenged (y^r, g^r). We denote this signature as

$$V = SK[x : y^r = (g^r)^x](m),$$

where SK represents both the proof of knowledge of the private key x and a signature on message m. Readers are refereed to [5] for the technical details.

5.2   Notation

We add the following parameters to section 4.1's notation for implementing a secure and practical double auction protocol.

T_{B_i}, T_{S_j}	: an auction ticket for B_i and S_j, respectively
$Cert_A$	: certificate of A issued by CA (Certification Authority)
$Sig_A(m)$	: digital signature of message m generated by entity A
$(m_1\|\cdots\|m_n)$	: concatenation of n (binary) strings
$H(m_1\|\cdots\|m_n)$	: one-way hash function with input strings $m_1, ..., m_n$

5.3   The Proposed Double Auction Protocol

The double auction protocol consists of the following four phases: *system set-up, registration, bid/ask submission,* and *bid/ask opening.*

System Set-Up. The entities involve a manager M, m buyers B_i and n sellers S_j. The role of each entity is as follows:

Manager M

- is semi-trusted who is assumed not to release the pseudonyms of participants except because of traders identity user misbehavior[6].

---

[6] The manager may impersonate a valid participant and illegally attend an auction using an auction ticket of other participants. However, the manager's action can be monitored by participants, thus his misbehavior can be detected.

- is in charge of the registration of buyers/sellers and provides each participant with an auction ticket as pseudonym.
- publishes the signature scheme.
- releases G_q which has a group of prime order q and g is generator of G_q.
- on behalf of participants, verifies the proofs of buyers and sellers and then determines the trading price and traders according to the auction rules.

Buyer B_i

- has private key x_i and the corresponding public key $y_i = g^{x_i}$ issued by CA.
- registers with the manager and receives an auction ticket T_{B_i} from him.

Seller S_j

- has private key $\tilde{x}_j$ and the corresponding public key $\tilde{y}_j = g^{\tilde{x}_j}$ issued by CA[7].
- registers with the manager and receives an auction ticket T_{S_j} from him.

In the proposed protocol, 4 bulletin boards are used, i.e., a registration bulletin board, a submission bulletin board, an opening bulletin board, and a winner announcement bulletin board.

Registration Phase. All buyer B_i and seller S_j register with the manager M.

1. B_i chooses a random number r_i and $k_i \in \mathbb{Z}_q \backslash \{0\}$ and keeps them confidential.
2. B_i computes $c_i = H(m_i \| y_i^{r_i} \| g^{r_i} \| g^{k_i})$ and $s_i = r_i^{-1} \cdot k_i - c_i \cdot x_i$, where $m_i = (B_i \| Cert_{B_i} \| Buyer)$ and $Buyer$ indicates that he wants to buy.
3. B_i sends $(m_i, c_i, s_i, y_i^{r_i}, g^{r_i})$ to M secretely.
4. The manager checks $c_i \stackrel{?}{=} H(m_i \| y_i^{r_i} \| g^{r_i} \| (g^{r_i})^{s_i} \cdot (y_i^{r_i})^{c_i})$.
5. After verifying the correctness of (c_i, s_i) and authenticating the buyer, the manager computes $h_i = H(y_i^{r_i})$ and $v_i = Sig_M(y_i^{r_i} \| h_i)$, and generates $T_{B_i} = (y_i^{r_i} \| h_i \| v_i)$ and shuffles it on the registration bulletin board.

After the above registration, each buyer B_i can easily confirm whether his auction ticket is on that bulletin board or not. Because the auction ticket T_{B_i} can be recognized only by the buyer who knows the relevant y_i and r_i for T_{B_i}, it could be used as a pseudonym for anonymity.

Similarly, seller S_j registers with the manager M and obtains her auction ticket $T_{S_j} = (\tilde{y}_j^{\tilde{r}_j} \| \tilde{h}_j \| \tilde{v}_j)$ from the registration bulletin board.

Bid/Ask Submission Phase. Using their own auction ticket, every buyer and seller attend an auction submission phase. Each buyer B_i chooses bid valuation b_i, signs it as follows

$$V_{B_i} = SK[x_i : y_i^{r_i} = (g^{r_i})^{x_i}](b_i),$$

and then sends both valuation b_i and the signed message $V_{B_i} = (c_i, s_i, y_i^{r_i}, g^{r_i})$ to the submission bulletin board, where (c_i, s_i) are real signature pair and $(y_i^{r_i}, g^{r_i})$ are challenges for verifying signature. In a similar way, each seller S_j chooses an ask a_j and signs the message using anonymous signature of knowledge.

---

[7] To avoid the notation confusion between buyers and sellers, we just use the tilde symbol on some parameters related to sellers.

Bid/Ask Opening Phase. This phase consists of the following two step: determination of the trading price and traders, and identity announcement of traders.

Step 1: Determination of the trading price and traders

In this step, the trading price and the number of traders are determined according to the improved MCD protocol of section 4. All bids and asks released in the submission bulletin board are rearranged in the price, and then are published in the opening board. The declared valuations are as follows:

$$T_{B_{(1)}}, b_{(1)}, V_{B_{(1)}} \geq \cdots \geq T_{B_{(f)}}, b_{(f)}, V_{B_{(f)}} \geq \cdots \geq T_{B_{(m)}}, b_{(m)}, V_{B_{(m)}}$$
$$T_{S_{(1)}}, a_{(1)}, V_{S(1)} \leq \cdots \leq T_{S_{(f)}}, a_{(f)}, V_{S(f)} \leq \cdots \leq T_{S_{(n)}}, a_{(n)}, V_{S(n)}$$

Let the auction ticket corresponding to $b_{(f)}$ be $T_{B_{(f)}}$ and another auction ticket corresponding to $a_{(f)}$ be $T_{S_{(f)}}$. By auction rules, the k satisfying both $b_{(k)} \geq a_{(k)}$ and $b_{(k+1)} < a_{(k+1)}$ is chosen and the standard price is then determined as follows:

$$p_s = \tfrac{1}{2}(b_{(k+1)} + a_{(k+1)})$$

The trading price and the number of traders are determined as follows,

1. If $a_{(k)} \leq p_s \leq b_{(k)}$ holds, the buyers and sellers corresponding to auction tickets from (1) to (k) can trade.

   - Each buyer $B_{(f)}$ corresponding to auction ticket $T_{B_{(f)}}$ pays $\mathcal{P}_{B_{(f)}} = \tfrac{1}{2}(b_{(f)} + p_s)$ and gets an utility $\mathcal{U}_{B_{(f)}} = b_{(f)} - \mathcal{P}_{B_{(f)}} = \tfrac{1}{2}(b_{(f)} - p_s)$,
   - Each seller $S_{(f)}$ corresponding to auction ticket $T_{S_{(f)}}$ gets $\mathcal{I}_{S_{(f)}} = \tfrac{1}{2}(a_{(f)} + p_s)$ and an utility $\mathcal{U}_{S_{(f)}} = \mathcal{I}_{S_{(f)}} - a_{(f)} = \tfrac{1}{2}(p_s - a_{(f)})$,
   - The manager gets $\mathcal{E}_A = \sum_{f=1}^{k} \mathcal{P}_{B_{(f)}} - \sum_{f=1}^{k} \mathcal{I}_{S_{(f)}} = \sum_{f=1}^{k} \tfrac{1}{2}(b_{(f)} - a_{(f)})$, where $f = 1, \ldots, k$.

2. If $p_s > b_{(k)}$ or $p_s < a_{(k)}$ holds, the buyers and sellers corresponding to auction tickets (1) to ($k-1$) can trade.

   - Each buyer $B_{(f)}$ corresponding to auction ticket $T_{B_{(f)}}$ pays $\mathcal{P}_{B_{(f)}} = \tfrac{1}{2}(b_{(f)} + p_s)$ and gets an utility $\mathcal{U}_{B_{(f)}} = b_{(f)} - \mathcal{P}_{B_{(f)}} = \tfrac{1}{2}(b_{(f)} - p_s)$,
   - Each seller $S_{(f)}$ corresponding to auction ticket $T_{S_{(f)}}$ gets $\mathcal{I}_{S_{(f)}} = \tfrac{1}{2}(a_{(f)} + p_s)$ and an utility $\mathcal{U}_{S_{(f)}} = \mathcal{I}_{S_{(f)}} - a_{(f)} = \tfrac{1}{2}(p_s - a_{(f)})$,
   - The manager gets $\mathcal{E}_A = \sum_{f=1}^{k-1} \mathcal{P}_{B_{(f)}} - \sum_{f=1}^{k-1} \mathcal{I}_{S_{(f)}} = \sum_{f=1}^{k-1} \tfrac{1}{2}(b_{(f)} - a_{(f)})$, where $f = 1, \ldots, k-1$.

Step 2 : Identity announcement of traders

After determining the traders, the manager releases the original identities of the traders on the winner announcement bulletin board. For public verification, he publishes the registration information ($m_i = (B_i \| Cert_{B_i} \| Buyer), c_i, s_i, y_i^{r_i}, g^{r_i}, T_{B_i}$) related to winning buyers. By checking the correctness of these parameters, all entities including the lost participants or observers can identify the winning buyers. In the same way, the manager releases the registration information corresponding to the winning sellers, so that any entity can identify the traders.

6   Conclusion

We analyzed some weaknesses in MCD and TPD protocols and proposed an improved double auction protocol. Even though our scheme is based on MCD protocol, it is robust against false bids. Moreover, we extended it to meet most security requirements for a secure and practical double auction protocol.

Acknowledgment

This research was supported by University IT Research Center Project.

References

1. J. Camenisch and M. Stadler. Efficient Group Signature Scheme for Large Groups. *CRYPTO'97*, LNCS 1294, Springer Verlag, 1997.
2. D. Friedman and J. Rust. The Double Auction Market. Addison-Wesley Publishing Company, 1993.
3. W. Ham, K. Kim, and H. Imai. Yet Another Strong Sealed-Bid Auctions. *SCIS'03*, vol.1/2, pp. 11-16, 2003.
4. H. Kikuchi. $(M+1)$st-Price Auction Protocol. *Financial Cryptography'01*, LNCS 2339, Springer Verlag, 2001.
5. B. Lee, K. Kim, and J. Ma. Efficient Public Auction with One-Time Registration and Public Verifiability. *Indocrypt'01*, LNCS 2247, Springer Verlag, 2001.
6. M. Preston. A Dominant Strategy Double Auction. *Journal of Economic Theory*, (56), pp 434-450, 1992.
7. M. Yokoo, Y. Sakurai and S. Matsubara. Robust Double Auction Protocol against False-name Bids. *Proceeding of the 21st International Conference on Distributed Computing Systems*, IEEE Computer Society, pp. 147-145, 2001, pp 241-252, 2005.
8. M. Yokoo, Y. Sakurai and S. Matsubara. Robust Double Auction Protocol against False-name Bids. *Decision Support Systems*, (39), pp 241-252, 2005.
9. K. Omote and A. Miyaji. A Practical English Auctin with One-Time Registration. *ACISP'01*, LNCS 2119, pp. 221-234, Springer Verlag, 2001.
10. K. Peng, C. Boyd, E. Dawson, and K. Viswanathan. Robust, Privacy Protecting and Publicly Verifiable Sealed-Bid Auction. *ICICS'02*, LNCS 2513, pp. 147-159, 2002.
11. W. Vickrey. Counterspeculation, Auction, and Competitive Sealed Tenders. *Journal of Finance*, 16(1): 8-37, 1961.
12. C. Wang and F. Leung. Secure Double Auction Protocols with Full Privacy Protection. *ICISC'03*, LNCS 2971, pp. 215-229, Springer Verlag, 2003.

A   Analysis

A.1   Security

Anonymity. We have assumed the semi-trusted manager who doesn't open the real identity during the auction process except at the identity announcement step of traders or because of user misbehavior, while he may try to illegally attend an auction by impersonating other participants. Thus, as long as the manager does not open the real identity, the anonymity is guaranteed by the following Lemma 1.

Lemma 1. *Nobody, except the manager, can associate an auction ticket T_{B_i} or T_{S_j} with the real identity B_i or S_j of buyer or seller, respectively.*

Proof: An auction ticket is in the form of $T = (y^r\|h\|v)$, where $h = H(y^r)$, $v = Sig_M(y^r\|h)$ and $y = g^x$, and it doesn't include the identity information. That is, to recover the original ID, one has to be able to at least find the parameter y from anonymous public key y^r. Since the manager doesn't release the public key y, the only way to break anonymity is to find the private key x from $g^{x \cdot r}$ and compute $y = g^x$, then finally compare it with some certificate lists[8]. However, this is to solve discrete logarithm problem and it is also too difficult to determine a correct x because another random secret number r is used.

Impossibility of Impersonation. Since an anonymity service is provided in the proposed double auction protocol, an entity may try to illegally submit a faked bid or ask and impersonate a legal entity using the auction ticket of other participants. However, impersonation is technically impossible in our scheme, as shown in the following Theorem 1.

To induce Theorem 1, we first prove the following lemmas.

Lemma 2. *If solving the discrete logarithm problem is hard under a group for the given quintuplet (m, y^r, g^r, c, s), where x is the secret key and $y(= g^x)$ is the public key, finding random element k of the group satisfying both $c = H(m\|y^r\|g^r\|g^k)$ and $s = r^{-1} \cdot k - c \cdot x$ is equivalent to the difficulty of the discrete logarithm problem.*

Proof: It is straightforward to show the proof. Since we don't know the value of x and r from $(g^x)^r$ by the intractability of DLP under a group that solving DLP is hard in the polynomial time and k is also random elements, the only way to get k is to find the discrete logarithm of $((g^r)^s \cdot ((g^x)^r)^c)$ such that $g^k = ((g^r)^s \cdot ((g^x)^r)^c)$. It leads to solve DLP again.

Lemma 3. *An attacker who intercepts the valid signature information, (y^r, g^r), of another entity and then injects the faked bid or ask cannot generate a valid signature.*

Proof: Suppose an attacker can generate a valid signature (c', s') to inject a faked bid or ask message m' using the intercepted valid value (y^r, g^r). The attacker then releases (m', c', s', y^r, g^r), i.e., $V = SK[x : y^r = (g^r)^x](m')$, on the submission bulletin board, so that he can impersonate an entity corresponding to the parameter y^r. To pass a successful signature verification, the following equation should be satisfied:

---

[8] We also consider the case that y and the corresponding certificate have been released in another auction, so that people have some lists related to them.

$$c' \overset{?}{=} H(m'\|y^r\|g^r\|(g^r)^{s'} \cdot (y^r)^{c'}) \qquad (1)$$

That is, the attacker generates c' as follows:

$$c' = H(m'\|y^r\|g^r\|g^{k'}) \qquad (2)$$

From equations (1) and (2), the following equations are induced:

$$g^{k'} = (g^r)^{s'} \cdot (y^r)^{c'} = g^{r \cdot s' + c' \cdot x \cdot r} \qquad (3)$$

From equations (3), we know that the attacker needs to generate k' such that $k' = r \cdot s' + c' \cdot x \cdot r$. However, the only way to get both r and x is to find the discrete logarithm of g^r and then to solve another discrete logarithm problem of $y^r = (g^x)^r = (g^r)^x$, respectively. Since this is contradictory to the intractability of DLP under a group, our assumption that an attacker can generate a valid signature using the parameters (y^r, g^r) of another entity is not valid.

Lemma 4. *The manager also cannot impersonate a valid participant.*

Proof: This can be proved straightforwardly by means of Lemmas 2 and 3, so we will omit the detailed proof.

From Lemmas 2, 3 and 4, we can induce the following security theorem.

Theorem 1. *In our proposed double auction protocol, nobody, not even manager, can forge the valid signature to submit a faked bid or ask, so that he cannot impersonate other entities.*

Non-repudiation. Every participant, who has his unique key pair *i.e.*, private key x and the corresponding public key y, certified by CA, signs all messages related on bid or ask information. Thus, we can also induce the following theorem by the foregoing sentence and Theorem 1.

Theorem 2. *In the proposed scheme, every entity participating in auction process cannot deny that he has submitted ask or bid.*

Public Verifiability. In the proposed protocol, any one can check the validity of submitted signatures and offers from participants. This is achieved by the publicly verifiable secret sharing scheme, the signature of knowledge, and some zero-knowledge proofs.

A.2   Efficiency

Communication. Our protocol has very low communication overheads: one round for registration, one round for bid/ask submission, one round for determining the trading price and winners.

Computation. In terms of computation overheads, we compare the proposed protocol with Wang and Leung's protocol [12], because both schemes are based on MCD and TPD protocol. The computational cost is considered in terms of modular arithmetic, including modular exponentiation, modular multiplication and modular inversion. Table 5 represents the total computational overheads, where m and n are the number of buyers and sellers, respectively, and w indicates the possible offering prices. In Wang and Leung's protocol, note that the manager does not exist but in fact the auctioneer eves as the manager. From table 5, we can see that our protocol is more efficient than Wang and Leung's protocol regardless of the price range w.

Table 3. Total computation comparison

Computational cost		Wang and Leung	Proposed Protocol
Buyers	E	$2mw$	$3m$
	M	$3mw$	$2m$
	I	$w(2m+1)$	m
Sellers	E	$2nw$	$3n$
	M	$3nw$	$2n$
	I	$w(2n+1)$	n
Manager	E	$-$	$2(m+n)$
	M	$2\{(m-1)^w + (m-1)^w$ $+w(m+n+1)\}$	$m+n$

An Investigation of Dispute Resolution Mechanisms on Power and Trust: A Domain Study of Online Trust in e-Auctions

Glenn Bewsell[1], Rodger Jamieson[2], Adrian Gardiner[3] and Deborah Bunker[2]

[1] School of Information Technology and Computer Science, University of Wollongong,
Wollongong, NSW 2522, Australia.
gbewsell@uow.edu.au
[2] School of Information Systems, Technology and Management, The University of New South
Wales, Sydney, NSW 2052, Australia.
{r.jamieson, d.bunker}@unsw.edu.au
[3] Department of Information Systems, Georgia Southern University,
Statesboro, Georgia, USA.
a.gardine@georgiasouthern.edu

Abstract. Auctions have experienced one of the most successful transitions from a 'bricks and mortar' presence into an online environment. However, online auctions have one of the highest percentages of disputes and online fraud. This research investigates people's perceptions of dispute resolution prior to an online transaction. People's perceptions of 'power to resolve' a dispute is investigated as factor that may impact people's perceptions of online trust of e-business.

A research model is proposed that is founded in online trust theory. The research design is a quantitative study. Data collected is analysed using analysis of variance testing, and structural equation modeling (SEM). This research provides a better understanding of the dispute resolution phenomenon, and potentially opens up a new direction of research into dispute avoidance. A new 'power to resolve' construct is developed to extend theory.

1 Introduction

The research setting is consumer-to-consumer transactions at an online auction. Auctions have experienced one of the most successful transitions into an online presence. Examples of online auctions are: Amazon, eBay, Graysonline, uBid and Yahoo. These online auction sites act as intermediaries to match buyers with sellers and form transactions based on these matches for the transfer of goods and consideration. A transaction may be successful when the seller receives the consideration, the buyer receives the goods, and both the buyer and seller are satisfied. Transactions at online auctions are not always successful, sellers do not always receive their consideration, buyers do not always receive their goods, expectations are not always met and both parties are not always satisfied. Disputes arise in an online environment just as they do in more traditional business environments.

Dispute resolution mechanisms can be used to minimise the impact of a dispute and attempt to resolve a dispute over time. Empirical research is required to provide a

S. Katsikas, J. López, G. Pernul (Eds.): TrustBus 2005, LNCS 3592, pp. 288–298, 2005.
© Springer-Verlag Berlin Heidelberg 2005

greater understanding of the impact of dispute resolution mechanisms in increasing trust and reducing perceived risk. "Until such empirical research is done, any discussion regarding the relative success of on-line and off-line dispute resolution systems, and the factors underlying such success remain speculative" [1, p.346].

The potential for a dispute and availability of dispute resolution mechanisms may be salient prior to a consumer deciding to participate in an online auction. This research will investigate people's perceptions of dispute resolution mechanisms and trust prior to participation in an online auction.

2 Background and Model Development

A research model and research questions are developed from a review of trust, power, and perceived risk literature.

2.1 Trust

Trust has been defined as the "consumer's willingness to rely on the seller and take action in circumstances where such action makes the consumer vulnerable to the seller" [2]. At an online auction the seller is virtually anonymous so the buyer would look to other things as the objects of trust. The objects of trust are the online auction site, associated institutions, and system functionality. Trust is defined here as the "consumer's willingness to rely on the online auction systems and take action in circumstances where such action makes the consumer vulnerable to the online auction systems.

At an online auction the buyer may consider if the presentation of the goods is accurate, appropriate services will be included, goods sold will be made available for delivery, goods dispatched will match the auction listing, and their interests will be adequately considered if a dispute arises. The consumer is vulnerable to the online auction systems because there is a possibility of exploitation and exclusion. [3, 4].

Five major bases of trust were identified by Mc McKnight *et al.* [5] as personality, institution, cognitive, calculative and knowledge based trust.

Personality based trust is where one has a general tendency to trust others [2, 5, 6]. A potential buyer or a seller at an online auction may have a general disposition to trust online auctions.

Institution based trust "reflects the security one feels about a situation because of guarantees, safety nets, or other structures (Shapiro, 1987, Zucker, 1986)" [5, p.475]. Institutional trust or institution based trust contains three major dimensions: i) structural assurances or structures in place to support users such as third-party structures and contracts; ii) facilitating conditions such as conditions that match market expectations including, shared standards, beliefs, and values; and iii) situational normality or the situation appears normal such as web sites that appear normal [5, 7, 8]. The authors suggest that dispute resolution mechanisms provide access to: systems that support users, third-party roles, and user agreements. The authors also suggest that an online auction site that provides these mechanisms will appear more normal than one that does not.

Cognitive based trust "relies on rapid, cognitive cues or first impressions, as opposed to personal interactions (Brewer, 1981, Lewis & Weigert, 1985, Meyerson *et al.*, 1996)" [5, p.475]. Categorisation processes can provide high levels of trust in an online auction where the other person shares common values, shares common goals, have a good reputation, and possesses certain stereotypes that are appealing [5]. Furthermore illusions of control may also provide high levels of trust at an online auction such as some small action to confirm ones initial trusting belief [5].

Calculative based trust is a 'trusting stance'. This is based on someone making a calculation of the potential benefits and losses of cooperation versus non-cooperation; in line with a rational decision making approach [5]. Cooperative behaviour may be encouraged at an online auction through dispute resolution goals that encourage good behaviour and penalties that discourage bad behaviour.

Knowledge based trust "assumes that parties have firsthand knowledge of each other, based on interaction history" [5, p.475]. Buyers and sellers at an online auction interact on a transactional basis. They are unlikely to have repeat transactions with each other and are unlikely to develop firsthand knowledge of each. Buyers and sellers at an online auction may develop longer-term relationships with the online auction site itself and with associated institutions such as third-party escrow houses.

The gaps identified in the current research are, structural assurances such as contracts that provide access to recourse in case of a dispute between the parties, and situation normality in user agreements and socially constructed roles that provide a proper order. These gaps impact swift trust, the type of trust necessary to encourage the one-time consumer-to-consumer transactions you find at an online auction site, furthermore swift trust is necessary for new online auction sites to attract customers. Dispute resolution mechanisms and 'power to resolve' a dispute are believed to impact trust through access to recourse, user agreements, and socially constructed roles.

2.2 Power

Power at an online auction involves individuals, therefore power is at the social level. Social power is 'potential influence' [9] or "the ability to influence the decisions or actions of others" [10, p.38]. A range of powers could be made available in an online environment by agreement between buyers and sellers, or included in the 'Terms and Conditions' of use for that site. These powers could include coercion, reward, position, expert, referent and informational power as proposed by French & Raven [9] in their typology of power. Third-party roles such as mediators and arbitrators could provide access to these powers and these socially constructed roles could have a mastery over ambiguous circumstances.

Gaps exist in the current research of online auctions. Power between buyers and sellers has received little consideration and where power has been considered the evidence is anecdotal. There is a need for empirical research to ascertain: the types of powers required, the locus of powers made available, acceptable use of powers, and impact of powers on trust.

A relationship between power and trust is supported and power is considered antecedent to trust [10, 11]. At an online auction the buyer and the seller usually interact on a one-time transaction basis and they have no actual previous experience of the others use of power. The authors suggest that the types of power available, the balance of power, and power structures should impact trust in an online environment.

A relationship between dispute resolution and trust has also been suggested. "A website that informs potential customers that an unresolved problem can be submitted to a third party for dispute resolution has the potential to allay the customer's fears of being taken advantage of" [1, p.335]. In other words access to socially constructed roles builds trust.

This research will include power as a multidimensional construct of 'power to resolve' (PtR) a dispute. This construct is: the user's perception of the availability of power, the expected social influence, the locus of power, the potential to use power, the balance of power, and the general capability to resolve a dispute [12]. 'Power to resolve' is not the actual usage of power within a dispute as that would imply that a dispute had already occurred. This research is interested in the user's perceptions prior to a transaction so a dispute has not occurred. A higher 'power to resolve' is expected to increase the success rate of dispute resolution and this 'power to resolve' construct is believed new to this research.

2.3 Perceived Risk

Perceived risk is "the decision maker's assessment of the risk inherent in the situation" [13, pp.10-11], and is context specific. The perceived risk is riskier when the uncertainty is more uncertain; the mean expected outcome is less than the level of aspiration; and the potential consequences are extreme [13].

Many previous studies have found a relationship between trust and perceived risk [2, 7]. Perceived risk at an online auction is the user's assessment of the risk associated with the decision made and it is the perceived risk associated with participation in the online auction. Consistent with these researchers this research adopts the view that trust is antecedent to perceived risk.

2.4 Research Model

The research model (Figure 1) has a core model and an extended model. The extended model positions the core model within a wider framework of trust theory and the extended model will not be explained in this section. The core model is used in the actual research, and the constructs in the core model have solid outlines, whereas the constructs in the extended model have dotted outlines.

Four types of dispute resolution mechanisms are provided at the online auction and these types are the experimental manipulations presented in Table 1. This table acknowledges that power may reside in different places, the relationships between the parties may change and bases of power may be different. In manipulation M2 a dyadic relationship exists where the buyer and seller are expected to resolve a dispute. Manipulations M3 and M4 provides access to a triadic relationship where a mediator is included as a third party. Manipulation M4 allows a mediator to settle disputes that are unable to be resolved through consensus. A higher 'power to resolve' is expected to resolve more disputes, and a lower 'power to resolve' is expected to resolve less disputes.

In the research model 'power to resolve' is antecedent to trust. A third-party has access to power, e.g., position, expertise, systems and information. This third-party is presented as socially constructed role that may provide a proper order and access to recourse. The research model indicates that trust will increase as 'power to resolve' increases.

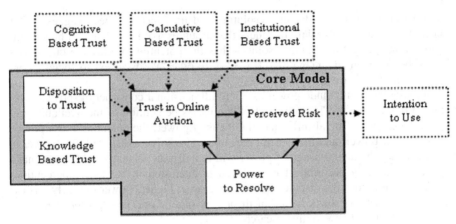

Fig. 1. Structural Research Model

Perceived risk is a dependent variable in the core model. Trust is known to negatively impact perceived risk based on other research [7]. It is also expected that those who experience a reduced complexity may have an increased tolerance to risk. It is expected that an increase in 'power to resolve' will negatively impact perceived risk. The 'power to resolve' manipulation is expected to have a direct and indirect impact on the perceived risk.

Table 1. Experimental Manipulations of Dispute Resolution Mechanisms

Treatment	Dispute Resolution Mechanisms	Power-to-Resolve
M1	Process is implied (Participants perceptions)	
M2	Buyer and seller as in a dyadic relationship	Low
M3	Mediator available for a triadic relationship (Mediator can recommend a resolution)	Medium
M4	Mediator available for a triadic relationship (Mediator can make and enforce their final decision to solve conflict)	High

3   Research Questions and Hypothesis

The research questions are: do dispute resolution mechanisms, socially constructed roles, access to recourse and power impact trust? The null hypothesis will be tested for each hypothesis.

H1: Trust will be greater for online auction sites offering dispute resolution compared with online auction sites not offering dispute resolution.

H2: Trust will be greater for online auction sites offering socially constructed roles compared with online auction sites not offering socially constructed roles.

H3: Trust will be greater for online auction sites offering arbitration compared with online auction sites not offering arbitration.

H4: There will be a positive relationship between trust and 'power to resolve' a dispute.

4 Research Methodology

One hundred and one undergraduate and postgraduate students attending information systems courses at a leading university in Sydney participated in an experimental study. Each participant was asked to assume that they wished to purchase a second-hand motor vehicle and that they had located one that matched their requirements at an online auction site. Participants should be familiar with motor vehicles and these items have been studied by a number of researchers [14]. A motor vehicle offered for online auction is expected to subject participants to information uncertainty in terms of make, model, type, colour, accessories, year, condition and the expertise of the seller. A motor vehicle is considered to have a high potential for information uncertainty compared with that of a commodity item [14]. Having looked up detailed information for this vehicle, participants understood the seller to be a private individual and that the current bid reflects a fair price. As the auction will soon be closing, participants should decide whether to place a bid for this motor vehicle. Screenshots were provided to each participant of the online auction site's home page, conditions of use, privacy, security and registration pages.

Participants were randomly allocated to one of the four manipulations of dispute resolution as identified in Table 1. Some participants did not receive any dispute resolution information (treatment M1). Other participants were provided a screenshot of a dispute resolution page that contained one of the three versions of dispute resolution (treatments M2-M4).

Once the participants were familiar with the material provided they completed a questionnaire that captured their perceptions of the online auction. The set of questions in the questionnaire contained the operational definitions of each construct in the research model presented in Figure 1. The operational definition of each construct is "necessary but rarely sufficient to capture the rich and complex ideas contained in the theoretical construct" [15, p.43]. Operational definitions previously used and tested were selected as they were better expected to capture the construct dimensions than trying to develop and test new definitions. Existing operational definitions have included multiple measures for each construct, and have scales that are valid and robust.

The 'power to resolve' (PtR) a dispute construct was necessary as a manipulation check and to test Hypothesis 4. This is a new construct that was developed based on the various dimensions of power previously identified to resolve a dispute [12, 16]. Nine questions were included for PtR and participant's ratings to these questions were averaged to provide an overall rating for PtR.

5 Data Analysis and Results

One hundred and one responses were received from postgraduate students and undergraduate students attending information systems courses. 25.9% of undergraduate students had previously used e-auctions compared with 21.3% of postgraduate students. 14.3% of undergraduate students that had used e-auctions had experienced a dispute compared with 30.0% of postgraduate students. A dispute was experienced once in every 22 online auction transactions.

5.1 Manipulation Check

The 'power to resolve' (PtR) a dispute construct was used to check that respondents understood the manipulation. Descriptive statistics of this check are presented in Table 2. Although two treatments M3 & M4 for third-party mediation were included within this study based on the findings of an earlier pre-test participants did not appear to differentiate between these two treatments, and these two treatments were combined and relabeled M_{TPM}. In other words no support was found that participants were concerned if the third-party mediator could or could not make a final decision. The mean of manipulation M2 appears different to the means of manipulations M1 and M_{TPM}. Values of skewness and kurtosis for M1 and M_{TPM} indicated that these distributions appeared normal. The M2 distribution had a larger negative value of kurtosis indicating that it clustered less and had a shorter tail.

Preconditions for parametric testing were supported. Kolmogorov-Smirnov tests support that each distribution is not significantly different to a normal distribution (sig. 0.998, 0.999, 0.981 respectively), therefore we can accept that the distributions are normal. Homogeneity of variances is supported (Levene statistic 2.441, sig. 0.093). The samples are independent.

An ANOVA test is a parametric test that tests for a difference in the means for each treatment, suitable for two or more independent samples that comprise an interval data set [17]. An ANOVA test is suitable for testing significant differences between manipulations. ANOVA testing supports that a significant difference exists between manipulations (F=5.143, & sig. = 0.008). This test supports that participants did understand differences between the manipulations.

Post-Hoc Scheffe tests support a significant difference between dispute resolution M1 (no mention of dispute resolution) and M2 (buyers and sellers) (sig. 0.025). This supports that participants prefer no mention of dispute resolution to the buyer and seller resolving their own disputes. A significant difference was found between M2 (buyers and sellers) and M_{TPM} (third-party mediation) (sig. 0.015). This supports that participants prefer dispute resolution to include access to third-party mediation to the buyer and seller resolving their own disputes. No significant difference was found between M1 (no mention of dispute resolution) and M_{TPM} (third-party mediation) (sig. 0.977). This supports that where an online auction site does not advise users' of their rights a certain expectation exists similar to that provided by a third-party mediator.

Table 2. Descriptive Statistics of 'Power to Resolve' a dispute excluding Outliers

		M1	**M2**	**M_{TPM}** (M3 & M4 Combined)
N	Valid	25	22	49
	Missing	0	0	3
Mean		3.8307	3.0641	3.7805
Std. Error of Mean		.23110	.14165	.13284
Median		3.8778	3.0389	3.8722
Std. Deviation		1.15551	.66441	.92988
Variance		1.33520	.44145	.86468

5.2 ANOVA Tests

ANOVA tests are appropriate to test hypotheses H1, H2 and H3. Preconditions for parametric tests were checked and statistical testing supported that the distributions were normal and the variances were homogeneous. The samples were independent.

ANOVA tests did not support significant differences between groups for trust (F = 1.596 & Sig. = 0.208) or for perceived risk (F = 0.020 & sig. = 0.980). It is concluded that 'power to resolve' a dispute may not impact trust and perceived risk or that the testing was inconclusive.

One possible explanation for this finding was raised by participants in a discussion that followed the main study. Participants were concerned that in a dispute sellers could choose to or not to remain anonymous and the ability for a third-party to identify a seller was no better than that of a buyer. If this explanation is correct then 'power to resolve' a dispute and dispute resolution mechanisms would need to include a capability to identify other parties.

5.3 Measurement and Structural Models

Partial Least Squares (PLS) is popular with IS researchers for structural equation modeling for it's "ability to model latent constructs under conditions of nonnormality and with small to medium sample sizes" [18, p.197]. PLS is suitable to test the measurement model (outer model), the structural model (inner model), and to determine the validity and reliability of measures developed within a theory [18]. PLS is suitable to test Hypothesis 4, to check the 'power to resolve' construct developed for this study and to test the proposed research model.

The proposed research model contains measurements that reflect the latent constructs. The measurement loading of an item to its' construct should be within the commonly accepted range of greater than 0.6 [19]. Most items in the measurement model have loadings within the acceptable range. Questions Q5, Q6, Q15, and Q18 were found to have loadings outside the acceptable range and the loading for these measures were 0.533, 0.544, 0.321 and -0.465 respectively. The measures are supported by theory so loadings outside of the acceptable range was not considered sufficient reason to delete these measures from the analysis. The analysis was completed both with and without these measures and the significant findings were not impacted.

"The reliability of a measure is defined as the extent to which it is free from random error components" [15, p.51]. The reliability for the measures was checked by construct and the results provided in Table 3. These reliabilities are within the commonly accepted range of greater than 0.7 for Cronbach's alpha [20, 21] and the latent constructs meet the accepted range for AVE of 0.5 or greater [22]. Discriminant validity was checked by comparing AVE with the correlation of a construct to other constructs. The square root of a construct's AVE should be greater than its' correlation with other construct [22]. Discriminant validity was supported. Validity and reliability has been established within this study.

The structural model was evaluated using PLS. Each construct, standardised path coefficient, t statistic, and R squared value is presented in Figure 2. The path coefficient between 'power to resolve' a dispute and trust is significant at 99% level, and between 'disposition to trust' and trust is significant at the 95% level. The other path

Table 3. Inner Model Reliability and AVE

Construct	Composite Reliability	AVE	Cronbach's Alpha	Standardised Alpha	Reliability when Items are Dropped
Disposition to Trust	0.917	0.735	0.8838	0.8838	
Power to Resolve	0.904	0.516	0.8800	0.8839	0.8862 if Q7 deleted
Trust	0.836	0.576	0.7278	0.7415	0.7913 if Q20 deleted
Perceived Risk	0.783	0.5	0.7806	0.7802	

coefficients were not found to be significant. One measurement for each participant's knowledge of online auctions was included within the questionnaire. This knowledge of online auctions measurement is not included within the tables presented here and did not improve the explanatory ability of the model.

PLS analysis supports previous studies of a relationship between 'disposition to trust' and trust. A relationship between people's perceptions of 'power to resolve' a dispute and trust is also supported. The proposed model is able to explain 43.9% (R^2) of the variation in trust. There is no critical value for the coefficient of determination (R^2), however the higher the value the better [17]. The proposed model did not explain 56.1% of the variation in trust and other factors could be included in future research to improve the model. The finding supports Hypothesis H4 that a positive relationship exists between 'power to resolve' a dispute and trust. Trust increases as the 'power to resolve' a dispute increases.

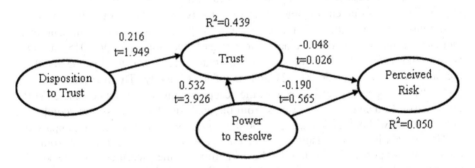

Fig. 2. Structural Equation Model

A relationship between trust and perceived risk was not supported. This research supports alternative views of the relationship between trust and perceived risk. One such view is that "the level of trust in a relationship is compared with the level of perceived risk in a situation" [6, p.719]. A motor vehicle may be considered a durable, experience, and higher-value good where financial risk may come first [23]. Participants may have considered that the level of trust was less than the level of perceived risk of bidding for or purchasing a motor vehicle and in this context a relationship is not supported between trust and perceived risk.

6 Limitations

There are no major threats or limitations to this research, because this research is focussed on perceptions prior to an online transaction, new theoretical insights in the domain of online auctions, and gaining a better understanding of dispute resolution mechanisms.

Material used in this study was prepared to resemble that of existing online auction sites. Research findings are applicable to the group studied and further research is required to generalise any findings to a wider population of online auction users. The measures are self-reported leading to a potential problem with systematic errors and random errors. These types of errors may exist because respondents may, overrate their responses, provide incorrect answers, pre-empt the desired answers, or make a mistake [15]. No evidence was found that these errors existed, care was taken in the preparation of the instruments to avoid these types of problems and participants did not appear to pre-empt desired answers, e.g., some findings did not support the research model proposed.

7 Conclusions

This study has established the salience of dispute resolution mechanisms prior to an online transaction. Significant differences were found in participants' perceptions of the types of dispute resolution provided in the manipulations. Participants were found to prefer dispute resolution that provides access to socially constructed roles rather than dispute resolution that does not. Participants do not appear to differentiate between third-party mediation that has the ability to recommend a solution to third-party mediation that has the ability to decide a final solution. Users' have an expectation of support available in a dispute even when the level of support is not articulated. Third-party roles appear to need the power to identify parties involved in online auction transactions.

A new construct 'power to resolve' a dispute has been developed and tested. This construct extends the theory of online trust.

This study has not supported trust as antecedent to perceived risk. Alternative views of the relationship between trust and perceived risk are supported by this research.

References

1. Nadler, J., Electronically-Mediated Dispute Resolution and E-Commerce. Negotiation Journal, 2001, pp. 333-347.
2. Jarvenpaa, S. L., Tractinsky, N., and Vitale, M., Consumer Trust in an Internet Store: A Cross-Cultural Validation. Journal of Computer Mediated Communication, 1999. 5(2):.
3. Lind, E. A., Social Conflict and Social Justice: Some Lessons from the Social Psychology of Justice. Leiden, The Netherlands, Leiden University Press, 1995.
4. van den Bos, K., van Schie, E.C.M., and Colenberg, S.E., Parents' Reactions to Child Day Care Organizations: The Influence of Perceptions of Procedures and the Role of Organizations' Trustworthiness. Social Justice Research, 2002. 15(1): pp. 53-62.

5. McKnight, H., Cummings, L.L. and Chervany, N.L., Initial Trust Formation in New Organizational Relationships. The Academy of Management Review, 1998. 23(3): pp. 473-490.
6. Mayer, R. C., Davis, H., and Schoorman, F.D., An Integration Model of Organizational Trust. The Academy of Management Review, 1995. 20(3): pp. 709-727.
7. Pavlou, P. A., and Gefen, D., Building Effective Online Marketplaces with Institution-Based Trust. Twenty-Third International Conference on Information Systems, 2002. pp. 1-9.
8. Pavlou, P. A., Tan, Y.-H., and Gefen, D., The Transitional Role of Institutional Trust in Online Interorganizational Relationships, in Proceedings of the 36th HICSS Conference, Hawaii, 2003.
9. French, J. R. P., Jr., and Raven, B.H., The Bases of Social power. Studies in Social Power. I. D. C. (Ed.), MI: Institute for Social Research, 1959. pp. 150-167.
10. Thorelli, H. B., Networks: Between Markets and Hierarchies. Strategic Management Journal, 1986. 7: pp. 37-51.
11. Geyskens, I., Steenkamp, J-B.E.M., and Kumar, N., Generalizations about Trust in Marketing Channel Relationships Using Meta-Analysis. International Journal of Research in Marketing, 1998. 15: pp. 223-248.
12. Beck, C. J. A., and Sales, B.D., A Critical Reappraisal of Divorce Mediation Research and Policy. Psychology, Public Policy, and Law, 2000. 6(4): pp. 989-1056.
13. Sitkin, S. B., and Pablo, A.L., Reconceptualizing the Determinants of Risk Behavior. The Academy of Management Review, 1992. 17(1): pp. 9-32.
14. Akerlof, G. A., The Market for "Lemons: Quality Uncertainty and the Market Mechanism." The Quarterly Journal of Economics, 1970. 84(3): pp. 488-500.
15. Judd, C. M., Smith, E.R., and Kidder, L.H., Research Methods in Social Relations. Orlando, Harcourt Brace, 1991.
16. Raven, B. H., The Bases of Power: Origins and Recent Developments. Journal of Social Issues, 1993. 49(4): pp. 227-253.
17. Keller, G., and Warrack, B., Statistics for Management and Economics. California, Duxbury Press, 1997.
18. Chin, W. W., Marcolin, B.L., and Newsted, P.R., A Partial Least Squares Latent Variable Modeling Approach for Measuring Interaction Effects: Results from a Monte Carlo Simulation Study and an Electronic Mail Emotion/Adoption. Information Systems Research, 2003. 14(2): pp. 189-217.
19. Chin, W. W., Issues and Opinion on Structural Equation Modelling. MIS Quarterly, 1998. 22(1): pp. vii-xvi.
20. Gefen, D., Straub, D.W., and Boudreau, M.C., Structural Equation Modeling and Regression: Guidelines for Research Practice. Communications of the Association for Information Systems, 2000. 4(7): pp. 1-70.
21. Gefen, D., Karahanna, E., and Straub, D.W., Trust and TAM in Online Shopping: An Integrated Model. MIS Quarterly, 2003. 27(1): pp. 51-90.
22. Fornell, C., and Larcker, D.F., Evaluating Structural Equation Models with Unobservable Variables and Measurement Error. Journal of Marketing Research, 1981. 18: pp. 39-50.
23. Mitchell, V-W., Consumer Perceived Risk: Conceptualisations and Models. European Journal of Marketing, 1999. 33(1/2): pp. 163-192.

A Secure Fingerprint Authentication System on an Untrusted Computing Environment

Yongwha Chung[1], Daesung Moon[2], Taehae Kim[1], SungBum Pan[3]

[1] Department of Computer and Information Science, Korea University, Korea
{Ychungy, taegar}@korea.ac.kr
[2] Biometrics Technology Research Team, ETRI, Daejeon, Korea
daesung@etri.re.kr
[3] Division of Information and Control Measurement Engineering, Chosun University, Korea
sbpan@chosun.ac.kr

Abstract. In this paper, we propose a secure and scalable solution for user authentication by using fingerprint verification on the sensor-client-server model, even with the client that is not necessarily trusted by the sensor holder or the server. In a typical implementation of fingerprint verification on the sensor-client-server model, the most time consuming step of the fingerprint verification, i.e., feature extraction, is assigned to a client because of real-time, scalability, and privacy issues. Compared to either a sensor or a server, however, the client connected to an open network and maintained by an individual user may be more vulnerable to Trojan Horse attacks. To protect Trojan Horse attacks launched at the untrusted client, our protocol has the fingerprint sensor to validate the result computed by the client for the feature extraction. However, the validation should be simple so that the resource-constrained fingerprint sensor can validate it in real-time. To solve this problem, we separate the feature extraction into binarization and minutiae extraction, and assign the time-consuming binarization to the client. After receiving the result of binarization from the client, the sensor conducts a simple validation algorithm to check the result, and then performs minutiae extraction and sends the extracted minutiae to the server. Based on the experimental results, the proposed solution for fingerprint verification can be performed on the sensor-client-server model securely, scalablely, and in real-time with the aid of an untrusted client.

Keywords: Biometrics, Fingerprint Verification, Untrusted Clients, Embedded Sensors.

1 Introduction

Traditionally, verified users have gained access to secure information systems, buildings, or equipment via multiple PINs, passwords, smart cards, and so on. However, these security methods have important weakness that can be lost, stolen, or forgotten. In recent years, there is an increasing trend of using **biometrics**, which refers the personal biological or behavioral characteristics used for user verification[1].

S. Katsikas, J. López, G. Pernul (Eds.): TrustBus 2005, LNCS 3592, pp. 299–310, 2005.
© Springer-Verlag Berlin Heidelberg 2005

The **fingerprint** is chosen as the biometrics for user verification in this paper. It is more mature in terms of the algorithm availability and feasibility[2]. At present time, the fingerprint verification system is mainly used at close range, such as for in-house room entry control, access to safes, and systems operation. In the future, it will be widely applied and diversified, particularly for a variety of approvals and settlements over networks, e-commerce via Internet, information access control, and remote personal identification.

A problem common to all **remote** biometric systems including fingerprint is that there are many ways of possible attacks in the remote biometric systems. Originally, fingerprint personal verification was put to practical use on the precondition of a close range or face-to-face interface. Therefore, protecting the fingerprint information has not been considered sufficiently. We think that this problem will have to be more considered in the near future, and the **security/privacy** as well as the **real-time** requirements should be satisfied for **large-scale**, remote user authentication services[2-5].

Furthermore, we consider the **sensor-client-server model** for remote fingerprint verification. That is, a fingerprint sensor is connected to a client and the client is connected to a server through Internet. In this model, security issues ensure that the system should be secure against possible attacks on communication channels such as **"replay" attacks**[2] or attacks on system modules such as **"Trojan Horse" attacks**[2]. There are some previous works reported to protect fingerprint information transmitted from replay attacks[6]. To the best of our knowledge, however, there has been no previous work to protect fingerprint verification systems from Trojan Horse attacks on the sensor-client-server model.

In general, fingerprint verification systems consist of Fingerprint Acquisition, Feature Extraction, and Feature Matching modules. In a typical implementation of fingerprint verification on the sensor-client-server model, the sensor acquires a fingerprint image, the client extracts some features from the image, and finally the server compares the extracted features with the stored features. Of course, the feature extraction which is the most time consuming step in fingerprint verification can be performed on either the sensor or the server. However, a typical fingerprint sensor either does not have a processor or has a low-end, embedded processor. In this paper, we assume the sensor has a low-end processor. Furthermore, the results of feature extraction determine directly the accuracy of overall fingerprint verification, and the computational workload of the feature extraction module becomes heavier to extract features accurately even with the advance of computing power. For instance, the average execution time of feature extraction submitted to the Fingerprint Verification Contest 2004 was about 1 second on a Pentium4 PC[7]. Thus, it is impossible for such low-end processors embedded in the sensor to extract features in real-time. Also, in large-scale services such as border control and Internet banking, the server may not be the right place to perform feature extraction. In [8], the collective performance of the scenario where feature extraction is performed by the server was analyzed quantitatively. Because of the heavy workload of feature extraction, such scenario is **not scalable** as the number of clients increases. In addition, this scenario requires fingerprint images to be transmitted to the server, and some people may reject this scenario due to **privacy** issues. Thus, to solve the scalable and privacy issues, it is reasonable to assign feature extraction to the client.

In this paper, we focus on the **Trojan Horse attacks on the feature extraction module of the client**. We assume that the server is possibly protected by security experts at a secure location and the fingerprint sensor[9] is integrated into a tamper-resistant hardware. Compared to the server and the sensor, the client is assumed to be maintained by an individual user who may not be a security expert. Thus, the feature extraction module of the client may be more vulnerable to Trojan Horse attacks. Suppose someone wants to perform a money-transfer transaction through Internet banking by inserting his hand-carry, fingerprint sensor into the USB port of a PC located in a hotel lobby, and a Trojan Horse program exists in the feature extraction module of the PC. Then, the Trojan Horse program in the PC can disguise itself as the feature extraction module and bypass the module. In addition, the program can submit artificially generated fingerprint features or features of a legitimate user intercepted at a previous transaction to the matching module of the server. Then, the matching module may not recognize that the features received from the client PC was generated by the Trojan Horse program, and can return a wrong matching result to the client.

To solve this security problem, the features extracted need to be transmitted from the trusted sensor to the trusted server, and the results computed by the untrusted client for feature extraction need to be validated in the sensor. In this paper, we propose a *secure* and *scalable* fingerprint verification protocol on the sensor-client-server model, and a simple algorithm for the resource-constrained sensor to validate the results computed by the untrusted client for *real-time* feature extraction. To reduce the computational workload of the sensor, we separate the feature extraction module into **binarization** and **minutiae extraction**. Binarization generates a binary fingerprint image that is one of the intermediate results produced during the feature extraction module, and minutiae extraction extracts minutiae from the binary fingerprint image. Note that, binarization requires a lot of computations, and the final minutiae can be extracted easily from the result of binarization. Thus, it is reasonable to assign binarization and minutiae extraction to the client and the sensor, respectively. However, we need an efficient way of validating the result of binarization generated by the untrusted client for the resource-constrained sensor. To validate that the binary fingerprint image was generated from the acquired fingerprint image, a validation algorithm consisting of simple operations such as calculating average gray value and variance gray value is proposed. Note that, generating a binary fingerprint image from an acquired fingerprint image requires lots of computations, whereas generating a validation image is relatively easy even on the sensor. After receiving the binary fingerprint image from the client, the sensor computes the similarity between the binary fingerprint image and the validation image. If the result of the validation is satisfied, the sensor will send minutiae to the server after extracting the minutiae from the binary image. Based on the experimental results, fingerprint verification can be performed on the sensor-client-server model securely and in real-time with the aid of a client that is not necessarily trusted by the sensor holder or the server.

The rest of the paper is structured as follows. Section 2 explains the overview of typical fingerprint verification and the attack points in remote applications, and Section 3 describes the proposed protocol and algorithm. The results of performance evaluation are described in Section 4. Finally, conclusions are given in Section 5.

2 Background

2.1 Fingerprint Verification

A fingerprint verification system shown in Fig. 1 has two phases: *enrollment* and *verification*. In the off-line enrollment phase, an enrolling fingerprint image for each user is processed, and the features called *minutiae* are extracted and stored in a server. In the on-line verification phase, the minutiae extracted from an input image are compared to the stored template, and the result of the comparison is returned. Note that the enrollment phase is performed once for each user, whereas the verification phase is performed many times after the enrollment. Thus, we will focus on the verification phase only in this paper.

In general, there are three modules involved in the verification phase[2]: Fingerprint Acquisition, Feature Extraction, and Feature Matching. **Fingerprint Acquisition** acquires an input fingerprint image for each user from a sensor. Then, **Feature Extraction** module extracts features from the acquired image. Finally, in **Feature Matching** module, the features extracted from the input image are compared with the corresponding features enrolled in the database.

Note that the feature extraction module requires a lot of integer computations for image processing, and the computational workload of this module occupies 96% of the total workload of the fingerprint verification[10]. Thus, to achieve real-time performance, it is reasonable to assign this time-consuming module to a client or a server, rather than to a resource-constrained sensor. As explained in Section 1, we assign the time-consuming module to a client as shown in Fig. 1.

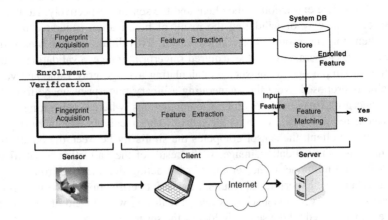

Fig. 1. Illustration of the Fingerprint Verification on the Sensor-Client-Server Model

2.2 Attack Points

As shown in Fig. 2, many of the possible attacks in fingerprint verification were iden-tified[2]: ① *attack at the sensor,* ② *attack on the channel between the sensor and the feature extractor,* ③ *attack on the feature extractor,* ④ *attack on the channel between the feature extractor and the matcher,* ⑤ *attack on the matcher,* ⑥ *attack on the sys-tem database,* ⑦ *attack on the channel between the system database and the matcher,* ⑧ *attack on the channel between the matcher and the application requesting verifica-tion.* Details of these attacks are explained in [2].

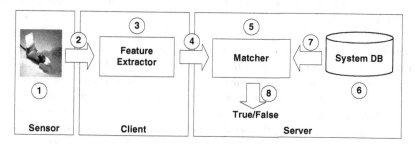

Fig. 2. Illustration of the Attack Points[6]

Note that ①,③,⑤ and ⑥ are launched against system modules; they are similar in nature and can be collectively called **"Trojan Horse" attacks**. In this paper, we focus on this Trojan Horse attack, especially attack ③. As explained in Section 1, we as-sume that the server is protected by security experts and the fingerprint sensor is inte-grated into a tamper-resistant hardware. However, the client executing the feature extraction module may not be maintained securely by an individual user and more vulnerable to Trojan Horse attacks. To avoid possible threats caused by this attack, either the sensor or the server should validate the result of the feature extraction mod-ule performed by the untrusted client. However, to validate the result in the server, the fingerprint image acquired should be transmitted to the server. For some privacy-critical applications, sending fingerprint images which are very private to each user is not acceptable. To avoid this privacy issue, checking the validity of the result from the untrusted client needs to be performed in the sensor. However, to perform the validation on the resource-constrained sensor in real-time, we need a simple and ef-fective solution.

2.3 Previous Approaches

Many researches are published to prevent possible attacks on fingerprint verification systems. However, most of them considered possible attacks on either communication channels[11-12] or feature matching module[13]. For instance, Maio and Maltoni[11] envisaged an electronic commerce system based on fingerprint verification and encryption techniques. They proposed that, in the case where both the seller and buyer cannot trust each other, the fingerprint matching be performed by a trusted third party "certifier," which also manages the fingerprint template database. When the seller is a trusted entity, it can perform the fingerprint matching and store the fingerprint template database at its site. Watermark techniques can also be applied to protect fingerprint information transmitted or stored[12].

Smartcard have received much attention from developer/integrators of fingerprint verification systems because of their internally protected storage and computational resources. Due to the limited computational power of the smart card, however, an entire fingerprint verification system can not be implemented onto a state-art-of 32-bit smartcard. Most of the solutions[13] proposed to date implement only the lightest module(i.e., feature matching) of the fingerprint verification system on a resource-constrained smart card.

To the best of our knowledge, however, there has been no previous work to protect the heaviest module – feature extraction – of the fingerprint verification systems and to achieve both scalability and real-time performance on the sensor-client-server model. As explained in Section 1, our solution effectively offloads the computational work of feature extraction from a resource-constrained sensor such as smart cards to the untrusted client and checks the validity of the results computed by the client. Although the idea of offloading time-consuming computation from a weak device to a powerful computer was employed for number theory problems such as RSA computation[14-15], offloading image processing computations in feature extraction has not been reported yet.

3   A Proposed Approach for Secure and Real-Time Fingerprint Verification

In this paper, we assume that the sensor is connected to a specific client and the client is connected to a server through the Internet. Also, each entity(i.e., sensor, client, and server) is assumed to have required public and private keys for en/decryption. Note that the key distribution problem is not the scope of this research, and there are many solutions for this problem[16].

3.1   A Proposed Protocol for Secure Fingerprint Verification

To reduce the computational workload of the sensor in feature extraction, we separate the feature extraction module into **binarization** and **minutiae extraction**. Binarization generates a binary fingerprint image that is one of the intermediate results produced during feature extraction, and minutiae extraction extracts minutiae from the binary fingerprint image. Note that, binarization requires a lot of computations, and the final minutiae can be extracted easily from the result of binarization. Thus, it is reasonable to assign binarization and minutiae extraction to the client and the sensor, respectively.

Fig. 3 shows the flow of the proposed protocol for secure fingerprint verification on the sensor-client-server model. The sensor acquires a fingerprint image and sends the image to the client in an encrypted form. After receiving the encrypted fingerprint image, the client decrypts it and generates a binary fingerprint image as an intermediate result of feature extraction. Instead of sending the binary fingerprint image to the server, the client sends it to the sensor in order to be validated that it was extracted from the fingerprint image acquired by the sensor at the current fingerprint verification request. After receiving the binary image from the untrusted client, the sensor checks the validation of the binary image by using a proposed binarization algorithm which will be explained in the following section. If the result of the validation is satisfied, the sensor extracts features(i.e., minutiae) from the binary image received from the client, and sends to the server the features. Note that, to send the features securely, a hash value is computed for the features and are digitally signed with the private key of the sensor, and the features themselves are encrypted with the shared session key between the sensor and the server. Though the sensor sends the feature to the server through the untrusted client, the client cannot read or modify the features encrypted with the session key shared between the sensor and the server. After decrypting the features and verifying the attached signature, the server compares it with the stored features to verify the user.

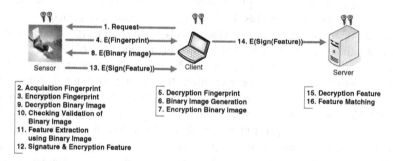

Fig. 3. The Proposed Protocol for Secure Fingerprint Verification

3.2 A Proposed Binarization Algorithm for Real-Time Execution

For the purpose of explanation, we denote the binary image for feature extraction received from a client and the simplified binary image for validation generated by a sensor as BIN_client, BIN_sensor, respectively. Note that the binary image BIN_client is generated after most time-consuming processing steps in feature extraction module such as smoothing, image enhancement, image quality estimation, direction map generation, and segmentation. Therefore, we need a simple algorithm to generate a validation image BIN_sensor which will be used to check whether BIN_client was generated correctly from the client in real-time.

In this paper, we propose a simplified algorithm to generate a validation image BIN_sensor for the sensor(shown in Fig. 4). First, to remove some noise, a smoothing operation such as median and mean filter is applied to the fingerprint

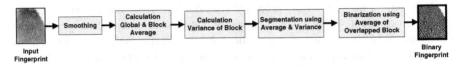

Fig. 4. The Block Diagram of the Proposed Binarization Algorithm for Validation

image acquired by the sensor. Then, to analyze the fingerprint area locally, it is divided into blocks and all the pixels within a block are assigned to the same results. Then, block average, global average, and block variance of the gray-levels are computed for the segmentation step that separates a fingerprint area(i.e., foreground) from the image. Block average and block variance are estimated for each 16×16 block. In the segmentation step, a *fingerprint area* and a *background area* are estimated as

$$Block_i = \begin{cases} F\_Block & if\ (AVG_G > \alpha AVG_B)\ \&\ (VAR_B > Threshold) \\ B\_Block & otherwise \end{cases} \quad (1)$$

where $Block_i$ is the ith block. In this equation, F_Block and B_Block represent the fingerprint area and the background area, and the gray values of F_Block and B_Block are 0 and 255, respectively. Also, the global average, the block average, the block variance, and the weight factor are denoted as AVG_G, AVG_B, VAR_B, and α, respectively.

Binarization step is to determine which pixels within a fingerprint area represent ridges. In a validation image generated by the binarization step, black and white pixels represent ridges and valleys, respectively. To analyze the fingerprint area locally, it is divided into blocks like the segmentation step. To minimize the discontinuity in block values as you cross the boundary from one block to its neighbor, a block should be smaller than its surrounding window, and windows overlap from one block to the next. In this paper, the fingerprint area is divided into 8×8 pixel blocks with each block being assigned a result from a larger surrounding 16×16 pixel window, and the areas for windows of neighboring blocks overlap by up to 1/2 as shown in Fig. 5. When the binarization step is executed for each block, a local average gray value is computed first for its window. Then, if the gray value of a pixel within the block is smaller than the local average gray value, its pixel is colored as black representing a ridge. Otherwise, it is colored as white.

Fig. 6 shows results of the simplified binarization. Fig. 6(d) shows the validation image generated by the simplified binarization algorithm, and black pixels near the edge of the image (shown in Fig. 6(c) and (d)) represent a background area generated by the segmentation step.

Finally, the binary image received from the client is compared with the validation image generated by using the simplified binarization algorithm(shown in Fig. 6(d)), and a similarity score is computed. After two images are superimposed, the number of pixels having the same gray value in the same position is counted. The similarity score is the ratio of pixels having the same pixel value to the number of pixels in the fingerprint area generated by the segmentation step.

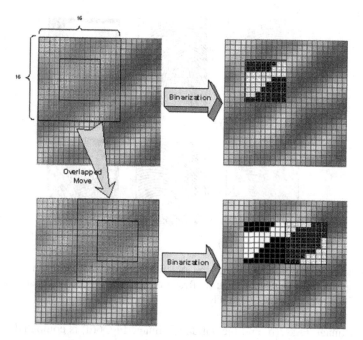

Fig. 5. Illustration of the Simplified Binarization Algorithm using Window Overlapping

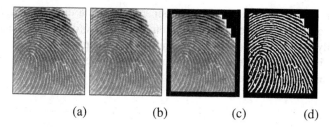

(a)　　　　　(b)　　　　　(c)　　　　　(d)

Fig. 6. Results of the Simplified Binarization. (a) Original Fingerprint Image acquired by the Sensor; (b) Result of the Smoothing Step; (c) Result of the Segmentation Step; (d) Result of the Binarization Step.

4　Performance Evaluation

For the purpose of evaluation of the proposed validation algorithm, a data set of 4,272 fingerprint images composed of four fingerprint images per one finger was collected from 1,068 individuals by using the optical fingerprint sensor[17]. The resolution of the sensor was 500dpi, and the size of captured fingerprint images was 248×292.

Fig. 7 shows results of the proposed validation algorithm. Fig. 7(a) is a fingerprint image acquired by the sensor, and Fig. 7(b) is a binary image generated by the client. To validate whether Fig. 7(b) was generated from Fig. 7(a), the similarity between

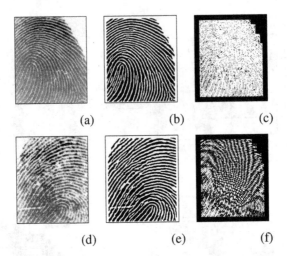

(a)   (b)   (c)

(d)   (e)   (f)

Fig. 7. Results of the Proposed Validation Algorithm. (a) and (d) Input Image; (b) and (e) Binary Image received from the Client; (c) Result of Correlation between (b) and Fig. 6(d); (f) Result of Correlation between (e) and Fig. 6(d).

the binary image Fig. 7(b) and the validation image Fig. 6(d) is computed and shown in Fig. 7(c). In Fig. 7(c), white pixels within the fingerprint area represent the same gray value in the superimposed image, and the similarity score between Fig. 7(c) and Fig. 6(d) is 91%.

However, the binary image Fig. 7(e) generated from a different finger(shown in Fig. 7(d)) looks different from the validation image Fig. 6(d), and the sensor can recognize easily that the client did not generate the binary image correctly. In this case(shown in Fig. 7(f)), the similarity score between the binary image Fig. 7(e) and the validation image Fig. 6(d) is 51%.

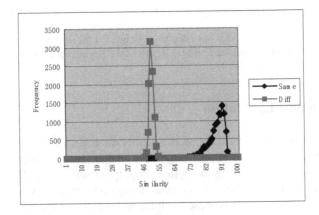

Fig. 8. The Distribution of the Similarity Scores

Figure 8 shows the distribution of the similarity scores between images from the same fingers and the similarity scores between images from different fingers. The vertical axis represents the distribution of the similarity scores, and the horizontal axis represents the scores ranging from 0 to 100. As the figure shows, the similarity scores between images from different fingers are distributed differently from the similarity scores between images from the same fingers. Thus, we can decide whether two images came from the same finger or not accurately.

Finally, we compare the execution times of the binarization by using a typical feature extraction module and the proposed validation algorithm. As shown in Table 1, the proposed algorithm can obtain a validation image in real-time even on an embedded processor ARM7.

Table 1. Summary of Execution Times of the Binarization

	Pentium 4 CPU(2GHz)	ARM7(28.56MHz)
Typical Algorithm[18]	0.74 second	6.5 second
Proposed Algorithm	0.0341 second	0.265 second

5 Conclusions

In the sensor-client-server model for remote fingerprint verification, the system should be secure against possible attacks on communication channels or attacks on system modules. In this paper, we proposed a secure and scalable fingerprint verification protocol to protect Trojan Horse attacks launched at the client, and a simple algorithm for the resource-constrained sensor to validate the results computed by the untrusted client for real-time feature extraction.

Based on the experimental results, the proposed solution for fingerprint verification can be performed on the sensor-client-server model securely, scalablely, and in real-time with the aid of an untrusted client. We believe this solution can be extended to many emerging applications such as ubiquitous computing and home network.

Acknowledgement

This research was supported by the MIC(Ministry of Information and Communication), Korea, under the Chung-Ang University HNRC-ITRC(Home Network Research Center) support program supervised by the IITA(Institute of Information Technology Assessment

References

[1] A. Jain, R. Bole, and S. Panakanti, *Biometrics: Personal Identification in Networked Society*, Kluwer Academic Publishers, 1999.
[2] D. Maltoni, et al., *Handbook of Fingerprint Recognition*, Springer, 2003.

[3] R. Bolle, J. Connell, and N. Ratha, "Biometric Perils and Patches," *Pattern Recognition*, Vol. 35, pp. 2727-2738, 2002.

[4] B. Schneier, "The Uses and Abuses of Biometrics," *Communications of the ACM*, Vol. 42, No, 8, pp. 136, 1999.

[5] S. Prabhakar, S. Pankanti, and A. Jain, "Biometric Recognition: Security and Privacy Concerns," *IEEE Security and Privacy*, pp. 33-42, 2003.

[6] X9.84, "Biometrics Information Management and Security For The Financial Services Industry," *ANSI*, 2000.

[7] D. Maio, et al., "FVC2004: Third Fingerprint Verification Competition," *Proc. International Conference on Biometric Authentication (ICBA)*, pp. 1-7, 2004.

[8] Y. Chung, et al., "Workload Dispatch Planning for Real-Time Fingerprint Authentication on a Sensor-Client-Server Model," *LNCS 3320 - PDCAT 2004*, pp. 833–838, 2004.

[9] Sony, http://www.sony.com

[10] D. Moon, et al., "Performance Analysis of the Match-on-Card System for the Fingerprint Authentication," *Proc. of International Workshop on Information Security Applications*, pp. 449-459, 2001.

[11] D. Maio and D. Maltoni, "A Secure Protocol for Electronic Commerce based on Fingerprints and Encryption," *Proc. of Conf. on Systems, Cybernetics, and Informatics*, pp. 519-525, 1999.

[12] A. Jain and U. Uludag, "Hiding Fingerprint Minutiae in Images," *Proc. of AutoID*, pp. 97-102, 2002.

[13] S. Pan, et al., "A Memory-Efficient Fingerprint Verification Algorithm using A Multi-Resolution Accumulator Array for Match-on-Card," *ETRI Journal*, Vol. 25, No. 3, pp. 179-186, 2003.

[14] J. Feigenbaum, "Encrypting Problem Instances: Or..., Can You Take Advantage of Someone Without Having to Trust Him?," *LNCS 218 - Crypto85*, pp. 477-488, 1985.

[15] C. Lim and P. Lee, "Security and Performance of Server-Aided RSA Computation Protocols," *Proc. of Crypto95*, pp. 70-83, 1995.

[16] W. Stallings, *Cryptography and Network Security*, Pearson Ed. Inc., 2003.

[17] NiGen, http://www.nitgen.com.

[18] M. Garris, et al., "User's Guide to NIST Fingerprint Image Software," *NIST*.

Security Enhancement for Password Authentication Schemes with Smart Cards

Eun-Jun Yoon[1], Woo-Hun Kim[2], and Kee-Young Yoo[1],*

[1] Department of Computer Engineering, Kyungpook National University,
Daegu 702-701, Republic of Korea
Tel.: +82-53-950-5553; Fax: +82-53-957-4846
ejyoon@infosec.knu.ac.kr, yook@knu.ac.kr
[2] Department of Information Security, Kyungpook National University,
Daegu 702-701, Republic of Korea
whkim@infosec.knu.ac.kr

Abstract. Recently, Yang-Wang-Chang proposed an improvement to Yang-Shieh's two password authentication schemes by using smart cards that can withstand a forged login attack. Yang-Wang-Chang's improved schemes, however, are still susceptible such attacks. Accordingly, the current paper demonstrates the vulnerability of Yang-Wang-Chang's schemes to these attacks and presents an improvements to resolve such a problem.

Keyword: Cryptography, Password authentication, Smart card.

1 Introduction

User authentication is an important part of security, along with confidentiality and integrity, for systems that allow remote access over untrustworthy networks, such as the Internet. As such, a remote password authentication scheme authenticates the legitimacy of users over an insecure channel, where the password is often regarded as a secret shared between the remote system and the user. Based on knowledge of the password, the user can use it to create and send a valid login message to a remote system to gain access. Meanwhile, the remote system also uses the shared password to check the validity of the login message and to authenticate the user. Therefore, it is important to protect the password in authentication schemes. There are three ways an attacker can acquire a user's password and impersonate the user in order to log in to the server [2]: (1) the attacker invades the system; (2) the attacker eavesdrops on communication messages; and (3) the legal user accidentally reveals his password. In case 3, it is very hard to prevent a user from accidentally revealing his password. The advantages of smart cards are in its storage and computation abilities. These advantages are always referred to by some scholars [3][5][6][7][8], but their schemes have to maintain a verifiable table of passwords and not to allow passwords to be changed freely.

---

* Corresponding author.

S. Katsikas, J. López, G. Pernul (Eds.): TrustBus 2005, LNCS 3592, pp. 311–320, 2005.

In 1999, Yang and Shieh [4] proposed two password authentication schemes using a smart card to achieve user authentication and to arbitrarily change a password. In addition, the remote server does not need to store the passwords or verification tables in order to authenticate the users. Subsequently, Chan and Cheng [9] pointed out that Yang and Shieh's timestamp-based scheme was vulnerable to a forged login attack, in which an intruder could impersonate legitimate users to login and access the remote server.

In 2003, Sun and Yeh [10], however, pointed out that Chan and Cheng's attack was unreasonable because Chan and Cheng forged a client's identity, and the identity did not exist in the ID table. Thus, the attacker could not be verified from the ID table. At the same time, Sun and Yeh pointed out that Yang and Shieh's two password authentication schemes were vulnerable to a forgery attack. Thereafter, in 2005, Yang-Wang-Chang [12] improved Yang and Shieh's schemes to resist Sun and Yeh's attack. Yet, Yang-Wang-Chang's improved schemes are still susceptible to a forged login attack that were developed by Sun and Yeh in [10] and Chen in [11], respectively. Accordingly, the current paper demonstrates that Yang-Wang-Chang's schemes are vulnerable to a forged login attack and it also presents improvements to the scheme in order to isolate such a problem. Our improved schemes preserve the merits of Yang-Wang-Chang's schemes, and the improved timestamp-based scheme can withstand a forged login attack. Also, the improved nonce-based scheme can withstand a message replay attack in the network without synchronization of the clocks and a forged login attack.

The remainder of this paper is organized as follows: Section 2 briefly reviews Yang-Wang-Chang's schemes and then demonstrates a forged login attack with their schemes in Section 3. The proposed schemes are presented in Section 4, while Section 5 discusses the security of the proposed schemes. The conclusion is given in Section 6.

2   Review of Yang-Wang-Chang's Schemes

This section briefly reviews Yang-Wang-Chang's timestamp-based and nonce-based password authentication schemes [12] and then, it shows how a forged login attack can penetrate their scheme.

2.1   Timestamp-Based Password Authentication Scheme

Yang-Wang-Chang's timestamp-based password authentication scheme is composed of three phases; registration, login and authentication.

Registration Phase: A new user U_i wants to register with a key information center (KIC) in order to access services. The KIC then performs the following steps:

Step 1. User U_i securely submits his identity ID_i and a password PW_i to the KIC for registration.

Step 2. Two large prime numbers p and q are generated, and let $n = p \cdot q$.

Step 3. A prime number e is chosen at random as his public key, where e is relatively prime to $(p-1)(q-1)$.

Step 4. An integer d is found as a corresponding secret key that satisfies $e \cdot d \equiv 1(\mathrm{mod}(p-1)(q-1))$.

Step 5. An integer g, which is a primitive element in both $GF(p)$ and $GF(q)$, is found, where g is KIC's public information.

Step 6. Generate a smart card's identifier CID_i for the user and compute $S_i = ID_i^{CID_i \cdot d} \bmod n$ as U_i's secret information.

Step 7. Compute h_i for U_i such that $h_i = g^{PW_i \cdot d} \bmod n$.

Step 8. Write $(n, e, g, ID_i, CID_i, S_i, h_i)$ into the smart card of U_i, and issue it through a secure channel.

Login Phase: U_i must insert his smart card into the login device when he wants to login to the remote server. The smart card will perform the following operations after U_i keys in his identity ID_i and password PW_i.

Step 1. Generate a random number r_i and compute X_i and Y_i as follows:

$$X_i = g^{r_i \cdot PW_i} \bmod n,$$
$$Y_i = S_i \cdot h_i^{r_i \cdot T_C} \bmod n. \tag{1}$$

Here, T_C is the current date and time on the login device.

Step 2. Send a message $M = \{ID_i, CID_i, X_i, Y_i, n, e, g, T_C\}$ to the remote server as a login request message.

Authentication Phase: After receiving the login request message M from U_i, the remote server will perform the following operations to identify the login user:

Step 1. The validity of ID_i is checked. The remote server will reject the login request if the ID_i is incorrect.

Step 2. Check the validity of T_C. If $(T_S - T_C) \geq \Delta T$, then the server rejects the login request. Here, T_S is the current date and time on the remote server; ΔT is the expected legitimate time interval for transmission delay.

Step 3. Check the equation $(Y_i)^e \equiv ID_i^{CID_i} \cdot X_i^{T_C} \bmod n$. If it holds, then the remote server accepts the user's login request and access.

2.2 Nonce-Based Password Authentication Scheme

Yang-Wang-Chang's nonce-based password authentication scheme is composed of three phases; registration, login and authentication.

Registration Phase: This phase is the same as the registration phase in the timestamp-based password authentication scheme.

Login Phase: U_i must insert his smart card into the login device when he wants to login to the remote server. The smart card will perform the following operations after U_i keys in his identity ID_i and password PW_i.

Step 1. The smart card sends a request login message M_1 to the remote server, where $M_1 = (ID_i, CID_i)$.

Step 2. After receiving M_1, the remote server checks whether the ID_i and the CID_i are correct. If they are correct, the remote server computes a nonce $N = f(r_j)$ and sends it back. Note that r_j is a random number and $f(r_j)$ is a one-way hash function.

Step 3. After the nonce N is received, the smart card generates a random number r_i and computes X_i and Y_i as follows:

$$X_i = g^{r_i \cdot PW_i} \bmod n,$$
$$Y_i = S_i \cdot h_i^{r_i \cdot N} \bmod n.$$
(2)

Step 4. Send a message $M_2 = \{X_i, Y_i, n, e, g\}$ to the remote server as a login request message.

Authentication Phase: After receiving the login request message M_2 from U_i, the remote server will perform the following operations to identify the login user:

Step 1. Check the equation $(Y_i)^e \equiv ID_i^{CID_i} \cdot X_i^N \bmod n$. If it holds, then the remote server accepts the user's login request and access.

3   Cryptanalysis of Yang-Wang-Chang's Schemes

In this section, we shall show that Yang-Wang-Chang's two schemes are susceptible to a forged login attack.

3.1   A Forged Login Attack on a Timestamp-Based Scheme

Unfortunately, Yang-Wang-Chang's timestamp-based password authentication scheme suffers from an authentication flaw similar to that which was developed by Sun et al. in [10] and Chen in [11], respectively. We will prove that an intruder can forge a user in an attack. In the proposed forged login attack, any intruder can pretend to be a valid user U_i and can login to the remote server successfully by using the following steps:

Step 1*. An intruder picks a valid smart card identifier CID_f, at random.

Step 2*. An intruder computes t satisfying $\gcd(e, t \cdot T_f) = CID_f$, where T_f is the current timestamp. It is easy to find such t as follows: First, an intruder chooses randomly t' such that $\gcd(e/CID_f, t') = 1$, and then computes $t = (t' \cdot CID_f)/T_f$.
Note that the information $M = \{ID_i, CID_i, X_i, Y_i, n, e, g, T_C\}$ can be easily obtained by an intruder through wiretapping the communication channel between a legal user and the remote server.

Step 3*. If $\gcd(e, t \cdot T_f) = CID_f$, let a, b be the coefficients computed by the Extended Euclidean algorithm [1], such that $a \cdot e + b \cdot (t \cdot T_f) = CID_f$.

Step 4*. Compute $X_f = (ID_i)^{-b \cdot t} \bmod n$, $Y_f = (ID_i)^a \bmod n$.

Step 5*. A forged login request message $M = \{ID_i, CID_f, X_f, Y_f, n, e, g, T_f\}$ can be sent to the remote server as a login request message.

The above forged request message can pass authentication in Yang-Wang-Chang's scheme:

$$
\begin{aligned}
(Y_f)^e &= (ID_i)^{a \cdot e} (\bmod n) \\
&= (ID_i)^{CID_f - b \cdot t \cdot T_f} (\bmod n) \\
&= ID_i^{CID_f} \cdot ((ID_i)^{-b \cdot t})^{T_f} (\bmod n) \\
&= ID_i^{CID_f} \cdot (X_f)^{T_f} (\bmod n).
\end{aligned}
\tag{3}
$$

3.2   A Forged Login Attack on a Nonce-Based Scheme

Yang-Wang-Chang's nonce-based password authentication scheme is also vulnerable to a forged login attack. The attack can be described in the following steps:

Step 1*. An intruder picks a valid smart card identifier CID_f at random.

Step 2*. An intruder computes t satisfying $\gcd(e, t \cdot N) = CID_f$, where t is a random number and N is a remote server's session nonce. It is easy to find such t as follows: First, an intruder chooses randomly t' such that $\gcd(e/CID_f, t') = 1$, and then computes $t = (t' \cdot CID_f)/N$.

Step 3*. If $\gcd(e, t \cdot N) = CID_f$, let a, b be the coefficients computed by the Extended Euclidean algorithm, such that $a \cdot e + b \cdot (t \cdot N) = CID_f$.

Step 4*. Compute $X_f = (ID_i)^{-b \cdot t} \bmod n$, $Y_f = (ID_i)^a \bmod n$.

Step 5*. A forged login request message $M_2 = \{X_f, Y_f, n, e, g\}$ is sent to the remote server as a login request message.

The above forged request message can pass authentication in Yang-Wang-Chang's scheme:

$$
\begin{aligned}
(Y_f)^e &= (ID_i)^{a \cdot e} (\bmod n) \\
&= (ID_i)^{CID_f - b \cdot t \cdot N} (\bmod n) \\
&= ID_i^{CID_f} \cdot ((ID_i)^{-b \cdot t})^N (\bmod n) \\
&= ID_i^{CID_f} \cdot (X_f)^N (\bmod n).
\end{aligned}
\tag{4}
$$

3.3   Man-in-the-Middle Forged Login Attack on a Nonce-Based Scheme

The man-in-the-middle forged login attack can be described as follows:

Step 1*. In the Login phase, the smart card sends a request login message M_1 to the remote server.

Step 2*. After receiving M_1, the remote server checks whether the ID_i and the CID_i are correct. If they are correct, the remote server computes a nonce $N = f(r_j)$ and sends it back.

Step 3*. An intruder intercepts nonce N and computes $N \cdot e$. An intruder sends $N \cdot e$ to a user's smart card.

Step 4*. After the forged nonce $N \cdot e$ is received, the smart card generate a random number r_i and computes X_i and Y_i as follows:

$$X_i = g^{r_i \cdot PW_i} \bmod n,$$
$$Y_i = S_i \cdot h_i^{r_i \cdot N \cdot e} \bmod n,$$
$$= S_i \cdot g^{PW_i \cdot d \cdot r_i \cdot N \cdot e} \bmod n, \tag{5}$$
$$= S_i \cdot g^{PW_i \cdot r_i \cdot N} \bmod n,$$
$$= S_i \cdot X_i^N \bmod n.$$

Step 5*. Message $M_2 = \{X_i, Y_i, n, e, g\}$ is sent to the remote server as a login request message.

Step 6*. An intruder intercepts M_2 and computes $(X_i^N)^{-1}$ by using the intercepting nonce N in Step 3*, and then an intruder can obtain the secret value S_i as follows:

$$S_i = Y_i \cdot (X_i^N)^{-1} \bmod n. \tag{6}$$

Step 7*. An intruder computes $X_f = X_i^e \bmod n$, $Y_f = S_i \cdot X_i^N \bmod n$.

Step 8*. A forged login request message $M_2 = \{X_f, Y_f, n, e, g\}$ is sent to the remote server as a login request message.

The above forged request message can pass authentication in Yang-Wang-Chang's scheme:

$$(Y_f)^e = (S_i \cdot X_i^N)^e (\bmod n)$$
$$= (ID_i^{CID_i \cdot d})^e \cdot (X_i^N)^e (\bmod n)$$
$$= ID_i^{CID_i} \cdot (X_i^e)^N (\bmod n) \tag{7}$$
$$= ID_i^{CID_i} \cdot (X_f)^N (\bmod n).$$

4   The Proposed Schemes

This section proposes an improved password authentication schemes to overcome the above mentioned problems with Yang-Wang-Chang's schemes. The improved schemes are also composed of three phases; registration, login and authentication.

4.1   Timestamp-Based Password Authentication Scheme

Registration Phase: A new user U_i wants to register with a key information center (KIC) in order to access services. The KIC then performs the following steps:

Step 1. User U_i securely submits his identity ID_i and a password PW_i to the KIC for registration.

Step 2. Two large prime numbers p and q are generated, and let $n = p \cdot q$.

Step 3. A prime number e is chosen at random as his public key, where e is relatively prime to $(p-1)(q-1)$.

Step 4. An integer d is found as a corresponding secret key that satisfies $e \cdot d \equiv 1 (\mathrm{mod}(p-1)(q-1))$.

Step 5. An integer g, which is a primitive element in both $GF(p)$ and $GF(q)$, is found, where g is KIC's public information.

Step 6. A secure smart card's identifier $CID_i = f(ID_i \oplus d)$ is computed for the user by the method introduced in [13][14], where $\oplus$ stands for an exclusive operation.

Step 7. Compute $S_i = ID_i^{CID_i \cdot d} \bmod n$ as U_i's secret information.

Step 8. Compute h_i for U_i such that $h_i = g^{PW_i \cdot d} \bmod n$.

Step 9. Write $(n, e, g, ID_i, CID_i, S_i, h_i, f(\cdot))$ into the smart card of U_i, and issue it through a secure channel.

Login Phase: U_i must insert his smart card into the login device when he wants to login to the remote server. The smart card will perform the following operations after U_i keys in his identity ID_i and password PW_i:

Step 1. A random number r_i is generated and CID_i^*, X_i and Y_i are computed as follows:

$$CID_i^* = CID_i^e,$$
$$X_i = g^{r_i \cdot PW_i} \bmod n, \qquad (8)$$
$$Y_i = S_i \cdot h_i^{r_i \cdot T_C} \bmod n.$$

Here, T_C is the current date and time on the login device.

Step 2. A message $M = \{ID_i, CID_i^*, X_i, Y_i, n, e, g, T_C\}$ is sent to the remote server as a login request message.

Authentication Phase: After receiving the login request message M from U_i, the remote server will perform the following operations to identify the login user:

Step 1. The validity of ID_i is checked. The remote server will reject the login request if the ID_i is incorrect.

Step 2. The validity of T_C is checked. If $(T_S - T_C) \geq \Delta T$, then the server rejects the login request. Here, T_S is the current date and time on the remote server; ΔT is the expected legitimate time interval for the transmission delay.

Step 3. Compute $(CID_i^*)^d \bmod n = CID_i$.

Step 4. The validity of CID_i is checked by verifying that $CID_i' \overset{?}{=} CID_i$, where $CID_i' = f(ID_i \oplus d)$. If it holds, then go to Step 5. Otherwise, the login request is rejected.

Step 5. Check the equation $(Y_i)^e \equiv ID_i^{CID_i} \cdot X_i^{T_C} \bmod n$. If it holds, then the remote server accepts the user's login request and allows access.

4.2   A Nonce-Based Password Authentication Scheme

Registration Phase This phase is the same as the registration phase in the timestamp-based password authentication scheme.

Login Phase: U_i must insert his smart card into the login device when he wants to login to the remote server. The smart card will perform the following operations after U_i keys in his identity ID_i and password PW_i.

Step 1. The smart card sends a request login message $M_1 = (ID_i, CID_i^*)$ to the remote server, where $CID_i^* = CID_i^e$.

Step 2. After receiving M_1, the remote server checks the validity of ID_i. If it holds, the remote server computes $CID_i = (CID_i^*)^d \mod n$ and checks the validity of CID_i by verifying $CID_i' \overset{?}{=} CID_i$, where $CID_i' = f(ID_i \oplus d)$. If the result is positive, then Step 3 proceeds. Otherwise, the login request is rejected.

Step 3. The remote server selects a random number r_j and sends it back. At the same time, the remote server computes a nonce $N = f(CID_i', r_j)$ for future use. Note that $f(x, y)$ is a one-way hash function.

Step 4. After a random number r_j is received, the smart card generates a random number r_i and computes N, X_i and Y_i, as follows:

$$
\begin{aligned}
N &= f(CID_i, r_j), \\
X_i &= g^{r_i \cdot PW_i} \mod n, \\
Y_i &= S_i \cdot h_i^{r_i \cdot N} \mod n.
\end{aligned}
\tag{9}
$$

Step 5. A message $M_2 = \{X_i, Y_i, n, e, g\}$ is sent to the remote server as a login request message.

Authentication Phase: After receiving the login request message M_2 from U_i, the remote server will perform the following operations to identify the login user:

Step 1. The equation $(Y_i)^e \equiv ID_i^{CID_i} \cdot X_i^N \mod n$ is checked. If it holds, then the remote server accepts the user's login request and allows access.

5   Security Analysis

The following analyzes the security of the proposed schemes.

Forged Login Attack: A forged login attack can succeed if the attacker can generate legitimate X_f and Y_f freely. The improved timestamp-based password authentication scheme, however, can withstand a forged login attack. An attacker can forge X_f, but he cannot forge the corresponding Y_f because he cannot get CID_i from CID_i^*, which is a difficulty of the discrete logarithm problem. For the same reason, the forged login attack cannot succeed in the nonce-based password authentication scheme.

Password Guessing Attack: In the timestamp-based and the nonce-based password authentication schemes, the attacker has two ways to guess the password PW_i. One way is to get $h_i = g^{PW_i \cdot d} \bmod n$ from the smart card; the other way is to get $X_i = g^{r_i \cdot PW_i} \bmod n$. We found that the attacker could not guess the password without d and r_i, which is a difficulty of the discrete logarithm problem. Therefore, our scheme can resist a password-guessing attack.

Smart Card Loss: When a legal user loses his smart card and it is found by an attacker, the attacker can guess the password of the legal user. We find that the attacker cannot succeed, the reason is given in the password-guessing attack section. In the timestamp-based password authentication scheme, even if the attacker uses a smart card to log in to the remote server, the attacker cannot succeed. The attacker inserts the smart card and keys a guessed password into the input device. Then the smart card computes $X_i = g^{r_i \cdot PW_{attacker}} \bmod n$ and $Y_i = S_i \cdot h_i^{r_i \cdot T_C} \bmod n$. Obviously, the attacker cannot pass the verification of the equation: $(Y_i)^e \stackrel{?}{=} ID_i^{CID_i'} \cdot X_i^{T_C} \bmod n$ because $(Y_i)^e \stackrel{?}{=} ID_i^{CID_i'} \cdot g^{r_i \cdot PW_i} \bmod n$ and $(Y_i)^e \stackrel{?}{=} ID_i^{CID_i'} \cdot g^{r_i \cdot PW_{attacker}} \bmod n$. For the same reason, the attacker cannot use the same method to login to the remote server in the nonce-based password authentication scheme.

Replay Attack: In the timestamp-based password authentication scheme, if an attacker tries to replay the verified message $M = \{ID_i, CID_i^*, X_i, Y_i, n, e, g, T_C\}$ to the remote server, the remote server would reject it because the attacker cannot pass the verification $(T_S - T_C) \geq \Delta T$ in Step 2 of the authentication phase. In the nonce-based password authentication scheme, if an attacker replays the verified message $M_1 = \{ID_i, CID_i^*\}$ to the remote server in Step 1 of the login phase, the remote server sends a new random number r_j' back. Then, the attacker replays another verified message $M_2 = \{X_i, Y_i, n, e, g\}$ to the remote server in Step 4 of the login phase. Obviously, he cannot pass the verification of the formula: $(Y_i)^e \neq ID_i^{CID_i'} \cdot X_i^{f(CID_i, r_j')} \bmod n$ in the authentication phase because the remote server records the new random number r_j' without r_j and the one-way hash function $f(x, y)$ is collision resistant.

6   Conclusion

The current paper demonstrated that Yang-Wang-Chang's two password authentication schemes are vulnerable to forged login attacks. Thus, improvements to Yang-Wang-Chang's schemes were proposed that can withstand forged login attacks. Our improved schemes preserve the merits of Yang-Wang-Chang's schemes, and the improved timestamp-based scheme can withstand the forged login attack. Also, the improved nonce-based scheme can withstand a message replay attack in the network without synchronization clocks and a forged login attack.

Acknowledgements

We would like to thank the anonymous reviewers for their helpful comments to improve our manuscript. This research was supported by the MIC (Ministry of Information and Communication), Korea, under the ITRC (Information Technology Research Center) support program supervised by the IITA (Institute of Information Technology Assessment) and partially by the Brain Korea 21 Project in 2005.

References

1. Herstein, I.N.: Topics in Algebra. Xerox Corporation. (1975)
2. Lamport, L.: Password Authentication with Insecure Communication. Communications of the ACM. Vol. 24. (November 1981). 770-772
3. Wu, T.C.: Remote Login Authentication Scheme based on a Geometric Approach. Computer Communications. Vol. 18. No. 12. (1995) 959-963
4. Yang, W.H., Shieh, S.P.: Password Authentication Scheme with Smart Cards. Computers & Security. Vol. 18. No. 8. (1999) 727-733
5. Chan, C.K., Cheng, L.M.: Cryptanalysis of a Remote User Authentication Scheme using Smart Cards. IEEE Transaction on Consumer Electronics. Vol. 46. No. 4. (2000) 992-993
6. Hwang, M.S., Li, L.H.: A New Remote User Authentication Scheme using Smart Cards. IEEE Transaction on Consumer Electronics. Vol. 46. No. 1. (2000) 28-30
7. Sun, H.M.: An Efficient Remote User Authentication Scheme using Smart Cards. IEEE Transaction on Consumer Electronics. Vol. 46. No. 4. (2000) 958-961
8. Lee, C.C., Hwang, M.S., Yang, W.P.: A Flexible Remote User Authentication Scheme using Smart Cards. ACM Operating Systems Review. Vol. 36. No. 3. (2002) 46-52
9. Chan, C.K., Cheng, L.M.: Cryptanalysis of Timestamp-based Password Authentication Scheme. Computers & Security. Vol. 21. No. 1. (2002) 74-76
10. Sun, H.M., Yeh, H.T.: Further Cryptanalysis of a Password Authentication Scheme with Smart Cards. IEICE Transactions on Communications. Vol. E86-B. No. 4. (2003) 1412-1415
11. Chen, K.F.: Attacks on the (Enhanced) Yang-Shieh Authentication. Computers & Security. Vol. 22. No. 8. (2003) 725-727
12. Yang, C.C., Wang, R.C., Chang, T.Y.: An Improvement of the Yang-Shieh Password Authentication Schemes. Applied Mathematics and Computation. Vol. 162. No. 3. (2005) 1391-1396
13. Shen, J.J., Lin, C.W., Hwang, M.S.: Security Enhancement for the Timestamp-based Password Authentication Scheme using Smart Cards. Computers & Security. Vol. 22. No. 7. (2003) 591-595
14. E.J., Yoon, E.K., Ryu, K.Y., Yoo.: Security of Shen et al.'s Timestamp-based Password Authentication Scheme. In ICCSA 2004. Springer-Verlag LNCS Vol. 3046. (2004) 665-671

Securing Operating System Services Based on Smart Cards

Luigi Catuogno, Roberto Gassirà, Michele Masullo, and Ivan Visconti

Dipartimento di Informatica ed Applicazioni,
Università degli Studi di Salerno - Italy
{luicat, robgas, micmas, visconti}@dia.unisa.it

Abstract. The executions of operating system services based on smart cards allow one to personalize some functionalities of the operating system by using the secret information stored in a smart card and the basic computations that a smart card can perform. However, current solutions for integrating smart card features in operating system services require at least a partial execution of the operating system functionalities at "user level". Such executions decrease the security and the performance of the system as they are less robust compared to the kernel-level ones.

In this paper we present the design and implementation of SmartK, a kernel module that integrates directly in the Linux kernel the support of smart cards. The use of SmartK allows one to securely personalize an operating system service still maintaining its execution at kernel level.

1 Introduction

Cryptographic protocols allow the execution of many real world economic transactions (e.g., auctions, voting) in the digital world. Nevertheless, an important role in the digital world is played by the hardware and software architectures that run cryptographic protocols. Among the different hardware and software components, a central role is played by smart cards.

Smart card is one of the most interesting technologies that have been proposed in the past and are nowadays crucially used in many digital transactions (e.g., inside satellite decoders, ATM machines). Originally, development of card-*aware* applications was a non-trivial task since there was a lack of high-level card programming languages, standard devices and development tools. Currently, several smart-card manufacturers have joined into consortia in order to define common standards for each aspect of the interaction with smart cards (e.g., physical and electrical specification for cards and readers, specifications of the provided services, communication protocols among cards, readers and host computers, data representation). Moreover, many high-level tools that satisfy many requirements of software designers and developers have been recently introduced. Such tools are *application-oriented*, that is, their use is reasonable for user-level applications but it is not practical for kernel-level executions.

We focus on the use of smart cards in operating system services. Here, the smart card allows one to personalize some functionalities of the operating system.

S. Katsikas, J. López, G. Pernul (Eds.): TrustBus 2005, LNCS 3592, pp. 321–330, 2005.

Indeed, a smart card is a tamper-resistant miniature computer that performs some basic computations on input a secret information.

However, current solutions for supporting smart card features in operating system services require at least a partial execution of the operating system functionalities at "user level". Unfortunately the execution of system functionalities at user level decreases the security of the system as user-level executions are less robust compared to the kernel-level ones. Indeed, attacks to the kernel are generally harder compared to attacks to user level applications since kernel code is specifically protected to avoid tracking and replacing attacks. Furthermore, kernel-level applications offer a better performance since they are in general not affected by context switches or frequent copies of large memory buffers among user and kernel space. Erez Zadok, in [28,17] gives accurate and strong motivations in flavor of kernel-level implementations of system-relevant applications.

In this paper we present the design and implementation of SmartK, a kernel module that integrates directly in the Linux kernel the support of smart cards. The use of SmartK allows one to securely personalize an operating system service still maintaining the execution at kernel level. More generally, SmartK is a compact and easy-to-use tool for software development of kernel applications (e.g., device drivers, filesystems, kernel modules). Our design of SmartK focuses on modularity, therefore it is possible to plug in (transparently to the applications) different modules that allow the applications to work with different cards and different readers connected to different ports. Moreover, the size of SmartK is very tiny and does not significantly affects the performance of the kernel.

We stress that the aim of SmartK is not necessarily to replace the existing smart-card frameworks. Indeed, some of them are quite suitable for many user applications. Instead, the use of SmartK is crucial when card-based services must be supported by the kernel itself. In such cases, SmartK outperforms the existing available tools. We stress also that a kernel module that runs a large high-level framework has a large (and negative) impact on the performance of the system.

2   Background

Specifications. Informally, a smart card is a plastic card (with the same size of a credit card) with either a magnetic strip or a micro chip. The physical properties of a smart card (e.g., the size, the position of contacts, their number), the electrical specifications (e.g., power, signals) and the communication protocols have been standardized, in order to allow cards, readers and applications (*off-card* applications) produced by different factories to be used together. The standard ISO-7816[9] provides a definition of these characteristics for a smart card. The card and the reader communicate by means of a master/slave half-duplex protocol. Once the card is inserted in the slot, the reader powers on it and sends to it the *reset* signal. The card sends back an important message called *Answer To Reset* (ATR). The ATR message contains all information needed to establish the connection between card and reader. The ISO-7816/3 document defines the format of the ATR message and two communication protocol: $T = 0$ and $T = 1$.

The $T = 0$ protocol is byte-oriented, and allows one to send just one command per time, the $T = 1$ is a block-oriented protocol and allows one to send sequences of commands.

ISO-7816/4 commands are sent to the card as a record called APDU (Application Protocol Data Unit) that contains the description of the invoked command and its arguments. The card also replies to the commands by means of another type of record: the Response APDU.

Development Frameworks. The known smart card frameworks are user-oriented, therefore they can be used by operating system services in the following two ways: 1) The frameworks are executed at user level. This is precisely what we want to avoid since for security reasons, operating system services should be run at kernel level. 2) The frameworks are compiled directly in the kernel. This *brute-force* approach hurts the performance of the kernel.

The "Application Independent Card Terminal Application Programming Interface for ICC applications" (CT-API)[7], is a simple package for the development of card-*aware* applications. CT-API is a library that manages the specific reader's device driver and provides a raw programming interface.

The "Interoperability Specification for ICCs and Personal Computer Systems" (PC/SC, for short)[18,19] is a standard definition of a complete framework for smart card deployment. PC/SC specifies the architecture and the components of a distributed "card environment", the services provided by each component and the protocols that components use to communicate. Moreover, PC/SC also defines a standard API for the development of off-card applications. PC/SC was initially used only on MS Windows platforms, but recently, it is also used in UNIX-like systems, with the support of the "Movement for the Use of Smart Cards in a Linux Environment (MUSCLE)"[15]. Actually, both CT-API and PC/SC implement a raw programming interface for the interaction with the smart card.

The Open Card Framework (OCF)[16] offers a powerful tool for developers of smart card-enabled software, based on the Java technology. OFC provides a high-level programming interface (composed of several Java classes) that implements the ISO-7816 protocol.

The RSA Laboratories produces and maintains the PKCS standard documents. This documents introduce a widely accepted set of specifications for cryptographic data structures, operations and procedures. Documents PKCS11 and PKCS15[21,22] concern interface and information format of Cryptographic Tokens (a set of cryptographic capable devices that includes smart cards). Moreover, they define an architecture and an API for the development of cryptographic applications based on these tokens.

The Smart Card File System (SCFS)[11] is a tool that allows the host machine to mount a smart card as a disk, and therefore to access the stored data by means of the standard UNIX system calls.

Webcard[20] implements a tiny web server on a Java card. Card-*ware* applications access to data stored on the card by using the HTTP protocol.

Trusted Computing Architectures. The Trusted Computing Group [26] consortium has been formed by some important hardware and software corporations (*e.g.* Microsoft, IBM and Intel), in order to define a standard technology for enhancing the security of computing environments that span over different platforms and devices.

According to the TCG specifications, a *Trusted Platform*, should feature a safe storage for sensitive data, the capacity of verifying the integrity of a platform component and the capability to prove to a challenger the integrity of the platform through an attestation.

The Trusted Platform Module (TPM) is a hardware device available for different platforms like PCs, PDAs and cellular phones that implement the features listed above. Applications, firmware and the other components that use the TPM features, are developed on top of a software layer defined by the Software Stack Specification (TSS). Moreover, the TPM provides cryptographic functions such as hashing, random number generation, asymmetric key generation and encryption/decryption.

Microsoft Next Generation Secure Computing Base (NGSCB)[14], is one of earliest technology based on the TCG specifications and will be integrated in the upcoming version of the Windows operating system. Microsoft stresses that NGSCB provides a lot of benefits to costumers (e.g., protection against viruses and unauthorized accesses, platform and data integrities, enhanced authentications) but many known researchers[1,25,24] are afraid by these benefits.

The trusted computing architectures could be used to achieve the secure and efficient execution of operating system services. However, these architectures are not flexible since the cryptographic tasks are only based on the secret information encoded in a secure chip plugged in the motherboard. Moreover, the cost of such technologies and the trust and ethical issues that they generate slowdown their effective use.

3   Design and Implementation of SmartK

SmartK provides a simple framework for the management of smart cards at kernel level. Specifically, the end user of the SmartK API is a generic kernel module that features a service based on smart cards. This is crucial for our main contribution, i.e., securing operating system services based on smart cards. In the design of SmartK we therefore focus on achieving an efficient kernel module that serves both other kernel modules and user applications.

SmartK exposes a very simple interface that we describe below.

– `smartk_init_card` starts the connection to the card. This procedure supplies power to the card, receives the ATR message from the card, parses it and finally, collects and stores all communication parameters like the response time (and the timeout) of the card, the communication protocol and the data representation adopted.

- smartk_data sends commands and receives the corresponding responses. This function transparently wraps all steps needed by data transfer, according with the information collected during the initialization.
- smark_cleanup_card closes the communication, cleans all memory buffers, and turns off the power to the card.

This kind of interface implements any off-card application. A similar approach (at user level) can be found in the CT-API. The applications communicate by means of the I/O port, with the reader and the card. More precisely, the application organizes the data as specified by the protocol provided by the card (for example the $T = 0$ protocol). Then the application sends the data to the reader through the port. This is achieved by sending the proper signals and, if necessary, re-encoding the data with the communication parameters that have been negotiated during the startup. Therefore our framework has been designed following an object oriented style. For each part of the communication, SmartK features a specific class and each module of SmartK implements an object of a class.

SmartK is designed to be modular, it can support different readers, each one potentially connected to the host machine by means of a different port (e.g., serial, USB). Specifically, SmartK is composed by the following four modules[1].

- smartk.o is the core of the framework and provides the interfaces to the kernel-level applications and to the the other modules of SmartK;
- pt_t0_smartk.o implements the API of SmartK according to the $T = 0$ protocol;
- ifd_towitoko_smartk.o is the Towitoko reader's driver;
- io_serial_smartk.o is a simple interface for the communication with a serial port.

The module smartk.o is the skeleton of the whole framework. It provides an object-oriented infrastructure on top of which the other modules are plugged in. Moreover, it handles the object *core* of the class *smartk* that reports the status of the card (e.g., ATR, communication parameters) and provides a general interface to the objects implemented by the other modules.

In order to achieve the modularity of the architecture, all methods of the different objects are referenced by a pointer of the core object. Thus, each object can invoke the methods of each other object by reaching them only through this object. This approach maintains each module independent of each other module and limits the number of symbols exported by each module.

Implementation details. We call "registration" the assignment of pointers of the object *core*. The module *smartk.o* provides the methods register_protocol _smartk, register_ifd_smartk and register_io_smartk that are executed to plug in the components in the framework. These methods link the related objects to the object *core*. Once the smartk.o module has been loaded, it instances the

---

[1] We now discuss the specific case of using a towitoko micro reader that is connected to a serial port, since this is the solution that we have effectively implemented. The discussion however can be generalized to any reader and any port.

smartk object `core`. Then, during their initialization phase, the other modules instance their own objects and register them by means of the corresponding registration procedure.

A *pt_smartk* object implements the communication protocol with the smart card (in our prototype, only protocol $T = 0$ is provided). It features a very simple interface composed by the following three methods: `activate_card`, `data` and `disactivate_card`.

An *ifd_smartk* object implements the functions required for the communication with the reader. Its methods allow one to enable and disable the reader and the card, transmit/receive data and power on/off the card.

A *io_smartk* object takes care of maintaining the status of the communication with the I/O port. This object summarizes the status of the port (the serial port in our prototype) and provides a set of methods to init/free the port, set/get communication parameters (baud rate, parity etc.), send/receive data to/from the port.

The communication protocol is implemented by the object *t0* of the class *pt_smartk* (module `pt_t0_smartk.o`). This object implements the $T = 0$ protocol as defined by the ISO-7816/3 document. Once the module `pt_t0_smartk.o` has been loaded, it registers the object t0. The interactions with the reader are performed by means of the methods of the `ifd` object (through their pointers in the core object).

The object *towitoko* of the class *ifd_smartk* (module `ifd_towitoko_smartk.o`) implements the driver of the reader. The module startup procedure initializes the reader through the method `init_reader` and registers the object by means of the `register_ifd_smartk` function. This function verifies that the serial port control module has been loaded and subsequently configures the port according to the reader properties. The object `towitoko` interacts with the serial port through methods of the object `serial`.

The object *serial* of the class *io_smartk* (module `io_serial_smartk.o`) performs the communication with the serial port. This module implements new *line discipline*[23]: the mechanism through with the linux kernel manages the data flow through the serial port. Once the line discipline has been enabled, the module instantiates the object `serial`, initializes and registers it by means of `register_io_smartk`.

As discussed above, all aspects of the interaction with the card are modular, thus, for example, in order to use a different reader one has to implement a different module `ifd-`*something*`.o` that has to be loaded instead of our IFD handler. Obviously, the new module has to provide a new implementation of the `ifd` object.

The test module. The module `test_mod` is a practical example of a SmartK end-user module. It was initially developed for debugging purposes, but it is an useful tool for the development of simple user-level card-*aware* applications. More precisely, this module is an example of how to write a kernel service that uses SmartK. Specifically, the services given by this module allow user applications the use of any reader, card and port by means of SmartK.

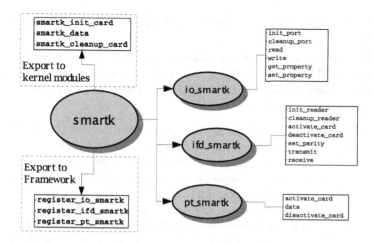

Fig. 1. SmartK data structures

Technically, `test_mod` allows user applications to communicate with smart cards by means of the usual I/O system calls on a character device (i.e., `/dev/smartk`). When the user application (*user*, for short) opens the device, the module executes the `activate_card` method of SmartK that initializes the communication and locks the device. When *user* closes the device, the module closes the communication, unlocks the device and cleans all buffers (`disactivate_card`). The `write()` operation uses the SmartK's `smartk_data` method to send APDUs to the card and to get the responses. The module keeps a private buffer where the responses returned by the `smartk_data` call are stored.

4   Securing Operating System Services

Here we discuss as a proof of concept two cases in which SmartK can be reliably used for securing operating system services based on smart cards.

Kerberos. The setting in which Kerberos [12,13] works is the following. There exists an open distributed computing environment (DCE) where the users of the workstations cannot be trusted. The setting is hostile since an intruder could pretend to be someone else. Therefore, an authentication system must be used.

Kerberos is an authentication system based on the existence of a trusted third-party that authenticate users of a DCE. More specifically, in case a user needs a service, he asks for a credential from the Kerberos authentication server (AS). The credential can be later sent to the ticket granting server (TGS) to obtain a service ticket. Finally, the service ticket allows the user to get the service from the corresponding server. The security problem of Kerberos is that an attacker can use a password guessing approach (by means of an off-line attack) to obtain the credential of another user. This problem was considered by [8] where they proposed the use of smart cards for performing user authentication in Kerberos.

Consider now the case of an operating system that needs services from another system. In this case SmartK has a crucial role for securely run this transaction. Indeed, the functionality offered by the smart card for system authentication is run completely at kernel level.

Run-time verification of executables. Run-time verification of executables constitutes a typical field of application for SmartK. Indeed, this is a service that is implemented at kernel level, since the kernel parses and runs executables. We stress that the integration of a kernel-level architecture and a user-level smart card interface is unsafe and impractical. The WLF project[4] provides kernel modules for this verification process. It is build on top of AEGIS[2,10] that provides an architecture for the secure loading of the operating system during the bootstrap. We now briefly introduce WLF and describe the implementation of a smart card-based key management scheme that has been built on top of SmartK.

WLF Overview. The WLF project [4] proposes a prototypal implementation of an architecture for integrity checking of executables (both ELF binaries and script files) at run time for the Linux operating system. In a system equipped with WLF, all executables have been signed before their installation. The kernel (that is assumed to be safe) is provided with the public keys of the trusted software providers. Each time an execution is invoked, the kernel verifiers the corresponding files. If the verification succeeds, the execution is performed as usual, otherwise, the execution fails. In the Linux kernel, each executable is interpreted and executed by its proper handler. In a WLF system each handler includes a `verify()` function that executes the signature verification task. Public keys are managed by a distinct module (that we refer to as *key agent*), that takes care of loading keys from a given repository and providing them to a WLF handler.

The SmartK Key Management Scheme for WLF. The key agent in WLF is a kernel module that takes care of loading in memory the public keys from the storage device and provides them (on demand) to the WLF handlers. Currently, WLF is equipped with two key management schemes that were developed as proofs of concept: the *basic* and the *floppy* key management scheme (respectively BKM and FKM). The BKM simply satisfies testing requirements and loads public keys from a character device (`/dev/wlf`). Users push keys (contained in a file) into the kernel by means of an `ioctl` call on the device. The FKM loads keys from a read-only floppy disk. It comes out trivially that both systems are not suitable to be used in a real-world context.

The SmartK Key Management scheme (SKM) is a kernel module that implements a key agent for WLF. Since it is loaded, the SKM loads in memory all public keys that are stored on a a given smart card, that we refer to as *WLFCard*, by means of the APIs of SmartK, and then, it provides to the WLF handlers all required public keys.

5 Concluding Remarks

In this paper, we have discussed security issues for operating system services based on smart cards. First we have introduced the importance of using of smart cards for digital transactions. Then we have given the rationale for the need of a kernel-level framework for integrating smart-card features in the kernel of the operating system. Then we discussed the design and implementation of SmartK: a kernel-level framework for development of smart card-based services and applications for the Linux operating system. The integration in the kernel of such a tool, achieves a more compact and robust implementation of any intrinsically kernel-level security service based on smart card features. We have finally discussed the use of SmartK for operating system authentications (Kerberos) and we presented the implementation of a Key Agent for WLF, an operating system service for the verification of the integrity of Linux executables at run time. As we have discussed, such applications represent a typical example of off-card applications that should be run at kernel level and hence, are suitable "end-user" for SmartK. SmartK does not significantly affect the performance of the kernel and does not significantly increase the size of the kernel memory image as the total size of the modules is less than 20 kbytes. SmartK has been developed on a Linux operating system with kernel 2.4.20[5,23], the only reader currently supported is the Towitoko micro (serial port). Only the card communication protocol $T = 0$ has been partially implemented. We also implemented a simple management application that provides the usual administrative functionalities (e.g., format card, create and store keys) built on top of the PC/SC lite framework version 1.1.1[6]. Sources are available on the SmartK Home Page at the URL http://smartk.dia.unisa.it.

Acknowledgements. We would like to thank Pino Persiano and the anonymous reviewers for many useful suggestions and comments. The work presented in this paper has been supported in part by the European Commission through the IST Programme under contract IST-2002-507932 ECRYPT.

References

1. Ross   Anderson   (2003)   TCPA   Frequently   Asked   Questions. http://www.cl.cam.ac.uk/users/rja14/tcpa-faq.html.
2. W. Arbaugh, D. Farber, J. Smith (1997) A Secure and Reliable Bootstrap Architecture. Proc. of IEEE Symposium on Security and Privacy '97, pp. 65–71.
3. S. M. Beattie, A. P. Black, C. Cowan, C. Pu, L. P. Yang (2000) CryptoMark: Locking the Stable door ahead of the Trojan Horse. White Paper, WireX Communications Inc.
4. L. Catuogno, I. Visconti (2004) An Architecture for Kernel-Level Verification of Executables at Run Time. The Computer Journal, Vol. 47, Num. 5, Pages 511-526.
5. D. P. Bovet, M. Cesati (2002) Understanding the Linux Kernel (second edition). O'Reilly Associates, Inc.
6. David Corcoran (1999) PC/SC lite API version 1.1.1. http://www.linuxnet.com.

7. Detusche Telekom *et al.* (1998) Application Independent Card Terminal Application Programming Interface for ICC Applications.
8. G. Gaskell, M. Looi (1995) Integrating Smart Cards Into Authentication Systems. Cryptography: Policy and Algorithms, pp. 270-281.
9. The International Organization for Standardization and The International Electrotechnical Commission (1995) ISO/IEC 7816 parts 1-4: Information technology - Identification cards - Integrated circuit(s) cards with contacts.
10. N. Itoi, W. A. Arbaugh, S. J. Pollak, D. M. Reeves (2001), Personal Secure Booting. LNCS vol. 2119, pp. 130–144.
11. N. Itoi, P. Honeyman, J. Rees (1999) SCFS: A UNIX Filesystem for Smartcards. *Proc. of the First USENIX Workshop on Smartcard Technology*, pp. 107-118.
12. B. Clifford Neuman and Theodore Ts'o (1994) Kerberos: An Authentication Service for Computer Networks, IEEE Communications, 32(9):33-38.
13. John T. Kohl, B. Clifford Neuman, and Theodore Y. T'so (1994) The Evolution of the Kerberos Authentication System. In Distributed Open Systems, pages 78-94. IEEE Computer Society Press.
14. Microsoft Corporation (2003), Security Model for the Next-Generation Secure Computing Base. http://www.microsoft.com.
15. MUSCLE (Movement for the use of smart cards in a Linux Environment). http://www.linuxnet.com.
16. Opencard Consortium (1998) OpenCard Framework, General Information Web Document. http://www.opencard.org.
17. S. Patil, A. Kashyap, G. Sivathanu, E. Zadok (2004) I3FS an In-Kernel Integrity Checker and Intrusion Detection File System Proceedings of the 18th USENIX Large Installation System Administration Conference (LISA '04).
18. PC/SC workgroup, (1997) Presentation of the Interoperability specification for ICCs and Personal Computer System (PC/SC) Revision 1.0, parts 1-8. http://www.pcscworkgroup.com/.
19. PC/SC workgroup, (1999) Presentation of the Interoperability specification for ICCs and Personal Computer System (PC/SC), Revision 2.0. White Paper, http://www.pcscworkgroup.com/.
20. J. Rees, P. Honeyman (2000) Webcard: a Java Card Web Server, Proc. of CARDIS 2000, pp. 197-208.
21. RSA Security Inc. (2004) PKCS11: Cryptographic Token Interface Standard v.2.20 http://www.rsasecurity.com/.
22. RSA Security Inc. (2000) PKCS15: Cryptographic Token Information Format Standard v.1.1 http://www.rsasecurity.com/.
23. A. Rubini, J. Corbet, (2001) Linux Device Drivers, second edition. O'Reilly Associates, Inc.
24. Seth Schoen (2003) Trusted Computing: Promise and Risk, Report of Electronic Frontier Foundation. http://www.eff.org.
25. Richard Stallman (2002) Can you trust your computer. http://www.gnu.org/philosophy/can-you-trust.html.
26. Trusted Computing Group (2004), TCG Specification Architecture Overview.
27. L. van Doorn, G. Ballintijn, W. A. Arbaugh (2001) Signed Executables for Linux. University of Maryland Technical Report CS-TR-4259.
28. Erez Zadok (1999) Stackable File System as a Security Tool. CS dept. Columbia University Technical Report CUCS-036-99.

Author Index

Lecture Notes in Computer Science

For information about Vols. 1–3517

please contact your bookseller or Springer